Vanderbilt Law School

Aspirations and Realities

Vanderbilt Law School
Aspirations and Realities

D. Don Welch

VANDERBILT UNIVERSITY PRESS

NASHVILLE

© 2008 Vanderbilt University Press
All rights reserved
First Edition 2008

12 11 10 09 08   1 2 3 4 5

Chapter 1 © 2003 Vanderbilt Law School

This book is printed on 100% recycled acid-free paper
made from 50% post consumer recycled paper.
Manufactured in the United States of America.

Library of Congress Cataloging-in-Publication Data

Welch, Don, 1947–
Vanderbilt law school : aspirations and realities /

D. Don Welch. — 1st ed.
p. cm.
Includes bibliographical references and index.
ISBN 978-0-8265-1582-7 (cloth : alk. paper)
1. Vanderbilt University. School of Law—History. I. Title.
KF292.V36W45 2008
340.071'176855—dc22

2007024174

For Anne, Pam, Sue Ann,
Kelly, Kay, and Elizabeth

Contents

Illustrations

Preface

The origins of this book can be traced to the afternoon that Mary Moody Wade brought a box to my office. Her husband, former Law School Dean John Wade, had recently died and she was bringing me a box of his personal papers in the hope that they would be of interest to someone at the Law School. That box sat in the corner of my office for years, as I resisted the temptation to open it. I say "temptation" because I suspected that I would be drawn into the history they represented. I feared that I would not be able to stop with looking at just one or two items, and thus I did not want to look at any of them until I could do justice to all of them.

I took the plunge into the Law School's history when Jon Bruce and I began work on an article on the School's creation and early years. That happy collaboration with Professor Bruce resulted in "Vanderbilt Law School in the Nineteenth Century: Its Creation and Formative Years." The article was published in the *Vanderbilt Law Review* in March 2003, and is reprinted here in its entirety as Chapter 1 of this book. Jon and I kept the prospect of a book-length history of the School in the backs of our minds during the project. Upon completion of the article, he decided to focus his energies elsewhere. But my suspicion about that box of Dean Wade's materials was confirmed. I had to continue.

Many people helped me along the way. I have been on the Vanderbilt campus—as a student, administrator, or faculty member—since 1969, at the Law School since 1984. Over the years I have had conversations with many Law School students, alumni, staff, and faculty members. I would like to express a particular thanks to those who consented to an interview for this project, including: John Beasley, Dent Bostick, Jeff Carr, Jim Cheek, Connie Clark, Cissy Daughtrey, James Gooch, Janie Greenwood Harris, Wayne Hyatt, Ken Jordan, Bob Knauss, Gil Merritt, Melvin Porter, Ken Roberts, Woody Sims, Charlie Warfield, and Fred Work. I owe a special debt of gratitude to Paul Kurtz, who not only regaled me with his tales of years past but who read and commented on earlier drafts of this manuscript.

The staff at the Alyne Queener Massey Law Library, and at the Special Collections & University Archives of the Jean and Alexander Heard Library at Vanderbilt were unfailingly responsive in the assistance they provided. Dean Kent Syverud granted me a research leave, without which this project would never have been possible. He and a number of other administrators at the Law School willingly and graciously picked up my administrative duties in the fall of 2004, as I made my way through a mountain of correspondence, minutes, reports, catalogues, and other archived material. I drew on the wisdom of Jim Ely, our faculty's legal history scholar. I was ably assisted by several student research assistants. In addition to those mentioned in the first note of the article reprinted in Chapter 1, I want to acknowledge the contributions of research assistants Adam Simpson, Deanna Swits, Michelle Bedoya, Lisi Madden, Drew Warth, Laverne Hill, and Kevin Bonin. Suzanne Wilson, my administrative assistant, has provided support for my work in ways too numerable to list.

Although I have received all this help, the mistakes in the text are mine. I have tried to maintain an analytical eye throughout, and not default to writing a "celebratory history" as I came to the later years. I understand that this approach inevitably yields errors of judgment and perspective, but I have been willing to run the risk of these in order to attempt a constructive contribution to understanding the School in the last quarter of the twentieth century. While I've done my best to work from an historical perspective, I realize the difficulty of achieving this goal for recent years and thus apologize now for the inevitable lapses this effort has produced.

This book is dedicated to Anne Brandt, Pam Malone, Sue Ann Scott, Kelly Sharber, Kay Simmons, and Elizabeth Workman. They are representative of the hundreds of administrators and staff members whose dedicated service has been the backbone of Vanderbilt Law School. I recognize the danger in picking just a few names out of so many colleagues I have worked with who should be recognized. I trust that those who are here unnamed, and they know who they are, will accept this symbolic honoring of their contributions to the School, for they all truly deserve to be honored.

Finally, I express my gratitude for the steadfast love and support of Celeste Reed, my wife and best friend. She is the anchor that makes the rest of this possible.

—D. Don Welch
Nashville, Tennessee

Vanderbilt Law School

Aspirations and Realities

Introduction
Aiming for the Stars

P aul Sanders is speaking off-camera, but the sparkle in his eyes is almost audible to the viewer as he relives treasured moments from his past: "The idea was you aimed to be the best and do the right thing. You aimed for the stars."[1] The 89-year-old Emeritus Professor sums up the uncommon ambition that has guided Vanderbilt University Law School since its founding. This moment, captured on a 1998 video designed to raise funds for a building expansion and renovation, echoes the refrain that has been voiced from the beginning to the present.

The Law Department was one of two departments, along with Medicine, that enrolled Vanderbilt's first students in the fall of 1874. The prevailing sentiment of the founders at that time was "to attempt nothing unless something great could be accomplished."[2] Such lofty aspirations carried forward to Dean Edward Rubin's espoused goal in 2005 for Vanderbilt to lead the way in re-inventing legal education in the twenty-first century. John Wade, the dean who remade the School in his own image, gave voice to this recurring theme in 1971, announcing that "we are expecting to make very substantial steps toward becoming the best law school in the United States."[3]

This is the story of the men and women who dedicated their careers, and in some cases their lives, to this aiming for the stars. Of course, aiming for the stars is not the same as reaching the stars. Vanderbilt Law School had certainly not fulfilled its aspirations in 1900, when the proprietary arrangement that had ruled the School was scrapped for a new, University-based model. Or in 1926 when the School was expelled from the Association of American Law Schools. Or in 1929, when the University's Chancellor proclaimed, "The School of Law must be endowed or it must die." Or in 1944, when the School's operations were suspended. Or in 1960, when Dean Wade acknowledged that even though progress had been made toward becoming one of the leading law schools in the nation, "the short-comings are still serious."[4]

Thus, this is the story of the failures and successes that those men and women experienced along the way: the limitations of the eventually-terminated proprietary arrangement that directed the operation of the first quarter century, the struggle just to keep the School in operation during the first half of the twentieth century, and the conflicts and tensions that arose later as significant progress toward the lofty goals was actually achieved.

This is also a wider story, as the history of Vanderbilt Law School is a piece of the historical context of its time. Vanderbilt's history reflects the major developments in legal education: the ascendancy of the academic model over the apprenticeship model, the triumph of the case method and then the reaction against the hegemony of that pedagogical approach, the rise of accreditation and the increasing standards for admission to law schools and to the practice of law, and the heightened competition in the legal education marketplace at the end of the twentieth century.

The School's story is intertwined with national trends and developments encompassing responses to such realities as the economic challenges of the Great Depression, the dramatic impact of two world wars, and the social upheaval of the 1950s and 1960s. More particularly, Vanderbilt's history has exemplified the contextual facts of life facing legal education in the South: the paucity of economic resources in the Reconstruction South; the stunted educational infrastructure in the region; the peculiar difficulties faced by southern schools in accreditation bodies; the abundance of inferior, non-accredited competitors; segregation; and the challenge of convincing students to cross the Mason-Dixon line. Vanderbilt's story also includes the adoption by the Ford Foundation of a mission that paralleled the goal of Commodore Cornelius Vanderbilt when he made his founding gift to the University: to advance the cause of education in the South beyond what could be achieved by the resources that were available in that region.

Many questions have been answered along the way. The questions that have been put to rest include: Will the School cease to exist? Will it join the mainstream of legal education? Will it achieve academic respectability? Will it extend its reach beyond the South? As is true of the history of any living institution, this history is only a partial telling of the story, a backward look taken at a more or less arbitrary point in time. Thus, this book is an installment in the recounting of the continuing story of Vanderbilt University Law School, and the many unanswered questions will undoubtedly be addressed by other observers in the years to come. In the final analysis, a judgment about how true Vanderbilt's aim has been will not rest on the School's placement on a published list of rankings. The answer, rather, will lie with the students and alumni, the faculty and staff, as they assess how well they have fulfilled the ambition of those who preceded them.

Vanderbilt Law School in the Nineteenth Century
Its Creation and Formative Years

Jon W. Bruce*

D. Don Welch**

INTRODUCTION

Vanderbilt University Law School is recognized today as offering one of the nation's preeminent programs in legal education.[1] Its opening in Nashville in 1874, however, was inauspicious at best, and its operation during the remainder of the nineteenth century was marked principally by modest, incremental advances. Yet an examination of the Law School's creation and formative years reveals a rich tale of administrators, faculty, students, alumni, and supporters striving to fashion an enduring, high-quality institution. This Article recounts the story of Vanderbilt Law School in the nineteenth century.[2]

*Professor of Law, Vanderbilt Law School. B.A., Hanover College; J.D., College of William and Mary.
**Associate Dean and Professor of Law, Vanderbilt Law School. B.A., Baylor University; M.A., Ph.D., Vanderbilt University.

We extend our gratitude to those individuals who helped us on this project in any respect. We wish to note in particular the contributions of the following persons: law school colleague James W. Ely, Jr.; law librarians David W. Bachman, Martin Cerjan, Janet R. Hirt, and Stephen R. Jordan; law school administrator Richelle Acker; university archivist Kathleen I. Smith; and law student research assistants Kathryn V. Eberle, Scott A. Larmer, James L. Lasser, Shawn A. Malleus, and Kenneth J. Sanney. We also wish to express our appreciation for editorial assistance provided by members of the Vanderbilt Law Review.

EXTERNAL INFLUENCES

Circumstances existing in the economy, the legal profession, and the world of legal education influenced Vanderbilt Law School's formation and evolvement.

The Economy. At the time of Vanderbilt University's founding, the country, particularly the South, was still recovering from the Civil War.[3] The region was in such a precarious economic state that University founders struggled to secure the funds necessary to create the institution.[4] But for the substantial contributions of Cornelius Vanderbilt, the University might have never come into being.[5] Vanderbilt Law School, however, benefited little from Vanderbilt family funding.[6] During the nineteenth century, the Law School was essentially a quasi-proprietary operation functioning under a lease arrangement with the University.[7]

Given these economic circumstances, pricing the Vanderbilt Law School educational product was a tricky matter.[8] Administrators needed to set Law School tuition at an amount students could afford, but at a level sufficient to sustain the School's operations. At the time of its creation in 1874, the Law School pegged annual tuition at $120.[9] This rate was the same amount charged at that time by established and thriving rival, Cumberland University School of Law in neighboring Lebanon, Tennessee.[10] It soon became evident that $120 was unduly pricey, so in 1877 the annual Law School tuition at Vanderbilt was decreased to $80.[11] Apparently, this amount was determined by administrators to be excessively low. The following year (1878) annual tuition at Vanderbilt Law School was raised to $100,[12] a level maintained throughout the remainder of the nineteenth century.[13] Interestingly, Cumberland School of Law lowered annual tuition to $100 at about this time (1879) and held it at that amount well into the twentieth century.[14] Thus, these rival institutions offered competitive tuition for most of the last quarter of the nineteenth century.[15] Viewed from a wider perspective, when Vanderbilt Law School set its annual tuition at $100 in 1878, it became one of the higher-priced law schools in the country.[16] Although its tuition remained at $100 through the end of the century, maintaining that rate placed the Law School even higher on the nationwide law school tuition scale as new law schools with lower tuition rates were established.[17]

The economy also had a broader influence on the operation of Vanderbilt Law School during its formative years. The latter part of the nineteenth century saw developments in industry, transportation, business, and banking that created a new economic order, of which a robust legal profession and an increasingly influential system of legal education centered on law school training were integral parts.[18]

The Legal Profession. Vanderbilt Law School was founded at a time when the legal profession was undergoing extensive change.[19] Transformation of the profession did not occur suddenly or smoothly; crosscurrents existed. On one hand, the profession was becoming more accessible to aspirants of various backgrounds and less clubby in nature.[20] Simultaneously, many members of the profession issued a call for higher professional standards and more rigorous examination for admission to practice.[21] Interested lawyers established local and state bar associations, as well as a national organization—the American Bar Association ("ABA") (1878).[22] This "professionalization" movement ostensibly was designed to ensure the delivery of competent legal services, but it also had the anticompetitive effect of limiting the flow of new attorneys into the profession, a development that would directly benefit existing practitioners.[23] Academic training of prospective lawyers was a significant component of the move toward professionalism in the legal world, fueling the emergence of university-related law schools such as Vanderbilt.[24]

The legal profession of the late 1800s was also experiencing a shift in the way law was practiced. Individual practitioners with a local practice were supplemented by the organization of law firms that handled legal business on a grander scale. The law firm became a staple of the legal profession due in large measure to the expanding expectations of business enterprises seeking legal services. As railroads, financial institutions, and commercial ventures of various types experienced a need for more expansive legal representation, lawyers responded with the creation of firms designed to provide the required services. By the end of the nineteenth century, law firms had become an entrenched part of the legal culture. Law schools were a relatively efficient and effective way of supplying these firms with academically trained lawyers capable of engaging in the sophisticated, business-oriented practice that was the law firm's standard fare.[25]

Vanderbilt Law School's immediate legal environment was shaped by these developments in the legal profession. Both the Nashville Bar Association and the Tennessee Bar Association were organized and became active in the last quarter of the 1800s.[26] The work of the Tennessee Bar Association's Committee on Legal Education and Admission to the Bar was directly relevant to the operation of Vanderbilt Law School.[27] For example, the Committee endorsed law school education over apprenticeship arrangements,[28] and beginning in 1883, proposed to the state legislature that a formal bar examination supervised by a Board of Examiners replace the existing slipshod scheme of examination by judges.[29] Throughout the next two decades, the Committee periodically renewed its basic recommendation for a general system of examination[30] until the state legislature finally adopted a 1903 statute providing for a state bar examination administered by a Board of Examiners.[31] Vanderbilt Law School faculty members were active on the Bar Association Committee during these years,[32] and Dean Thomas Malone was a noted supporter of the bar examination statute.[33] This Tennessee measure was part of a nationwide shift with respect to the requirements for admission to the bar; by the early twentieth century such a formal system of bar examination had become standard procedure among the states.[34]

Mirroring national trends, corporate law practice thrived in Nashville during the latter part of the nineteenth century. The city became a hub of railroad and business activities, and lawyers developed the legal expertise necessary to service these clients.[35] Indeed, longtime Vanderbilt Law School faculty member Edmund Baxter achieved distinction as legal counsel for the railroad industry,[36] as did J. M. Dickinson, who served on the law faculty for a brief period at the end of the nineteenth century.[37]

Legal Education. Vanderbilt Law School was a cog in legal education's shift from an apprenticeship approach to an academic model. A boom in the number of university-based law schools occurred during the latter stage of the nineteenth century. Concurrently, bar preparation in the form of reading law in a practicing lawyer's office declined markedly. By century's end, the systematic study of law in a university setting became the standard form of legal training.[38] As United States Supreme Court Chief Justice Morrison Waite commented in 1881: "The time has gone by . . . when an eminent lawyer in full practice could take a class of students into his office and become their teacher. . . . The consequence is that law-schools are now a necessity."[39]

The rise of the university-based law school was spurred in certain states, including Tennessee, by statutory measures that, in essence, bestowed admission to the bar on graduates of in-state law schools without examination. Known as "the diploma privilege," such statutes strongly favored law school graduates over candidates for the bar who had served an apprenticeship with a practicing attorney.[40] In Tennessee, the diploma privilege was on the books from 1860[41] until 1903.[42] The proliferation of in-state law schools of varying quality and program length, as well as the potential for abuse or outright fraud, precipitated repeal of the Tennessee diploma privilege statute.[43] Vanderbilt Law School Dean Thomas Malone was a leading advocate for this legislative reform.[44]

As law schools began to dominate legal education, they formed a national organization in 1900, the Association of American Law Schools ("AALS"), to promote and shape legal education provided at law schools.[45] Vanderbilt Law School dispatched new faculty member J. C. Bradford to serve as its representative at the AALS organizational meeting.[46] The Law School, however, did not join the Association at its inception, instead taking until 1910 to satisfy the requirements for membership.[47] This was not unusual; law schools in the South typically experienced difficulty during that period in complying with AALS standards.[48] Vanderbilt Law School's delayed entry into the AALS is consistent with the School's status at the turn of the twentieth century—an established, effectual operation with a primarily local, state, and regional outlook, but not an institution competitive with elite law programs nor heavily involved in legal education at the national level.[49]

Vanderbilt Law School faced stiff competition during the nineteenth century even in its limited sphere of operation. Neighboring Cumberland School of Law was nationally recognized and the premier law school in Tennessee, if not the area, during the bulk of the mid- to late-nineteenth century.[50] Although Cumberland's star was beginning to dim toward the end of the century,[51] Vanderbilt's law program was still not as high-profile as Cumberland's at that time.[52] Moreover, numerous other law schools, including one at the University of Tennessee, were founded in the state and region during the last quarter of the nineteenth century, adding numerous competitors to the law school marketplace.[53] Thus, at the beginning of the twentieth century, Vanderbilt Law School was both a stride behind Cumberland in name recognition[54] and facing challenge from newer law schools.[55]

PART OF "A GREAT UNIVERSITY"

The founders of Vanderbilt University saw their self-appointed task as creating "a great university."[56] Their expansive rhetoric addressed both the scope and excellence of the new institution. At the 1874 Laying of the Cornerstone of the Vanderbilt University, Methodist Bishop William Wightman sounded the theme on the founders' minds: "It will be a University—not in title only, but in fact and reality," he said, describing an educational institution that would offer "the highest and amplest culture of the time."[57] Chancellor Landon Garland, in his 1876 Founder's Day speech, captured the vision of those who created the University:

> What the opinion of the Church demanded was not a mere college, but a university in the true sense of that word—an institution in which

every subject of valuable research might be prosecuted to an extent to meet the largest demands of our youth—in which, besides the literary and scientific studies that make up the curriculum of most institutions, every useful calling and profession should have a school: such as theology, law, medicine, engineering, mining, mechanism, commerce, agriculture, and the fine arts. . . . It was the prevailing sentiment of the body to attempt nothing unless something great could be accomplished.[58]

Legal education was a significant part of the Vanderbilt vision from the University's inception. The University can be traced to 1858, when Tennessee's legislature granted a charter for Central University of the General Conference of the Methodist Episcopal Church South,[59] which included a law department with its own board of trust.[60] The Civil War, however, delayed any effort to act on the approved charter and establish a university.[61]

Following the war, Methodist efforts to create an independent theological school foundered, and the supporters of a new educational institution agreed to promote a plan for a university that would comprise a theological school, as well as a law school.[62] In early 1872, representatives from several Methodist conferences in the region adopted resolutions to establish an academic institution "where the youth of the church and country may prosecute theological, literary, scientific, and professional studies. . . ."[63] It was further specified that the university would consist of a theological school, a literary and scientific school, a normal school, a law school, and a medical school.[64] These resolutions were incorporated in the charter for The Central University of the Methodist Episcopal Church South that was issued by court decree on August 6, 1872.[65] Within a year, on June 16, 1873, the institution's name was changed to The Vanderbilt University in recognition of the crucial financial contributions of Cornelius Vanderbilt.[66]

While one might hope to find evidence of a compelling vision that would explain why legal education was included within the University's mission from the outset, that does not appear to be the Law School's story. It is not clear if University founders had any special interest in legal education,[67] or if they simply followed a typical pattern of university organization. For a variety of reasons, law schools had become an increasingly familiar feature of American universities in the second half of the nineteenth century.[68]

The original organizational structure of the Law School suggests that it was a significant component of the overall scheme for Vanderbilt University. In 1874, the Board of Trust approved an original law school organization that included the appointment of a faculty of eight, specified generous yearly compensation for the dean ($2,500) and a junior professor ($1,500), and directed that the program be "selfsustaining."[69] Chancellor James Kirkland later described this arrangement as being "on a rather pretentious scale."[70] The optimistic initial organization of the Law School was unsuccessful in its only year of operation.[71] Consequently, in 1875 the Board executed a twenty-five year "lease" agreement for the operation of the School, placing its management in the hands of three local attorneys.[72]

Although the University's founders may have underestimated the financial resources necessary to develop a top-flight law school, the Law School's operation under a quasi-proprietary lease arrangement should not be taken as evidence that it was made part of the University ex post,[73] on a second-class basis,[74] or solely for cosmetic purposes.[75] The general understanding in academe at the time was that law schools would be financially self-sufficient,[76] and Vanderbilt's founders were well aware of this convention.[77] University-based law schools with a proprietary bent frequently were linked to their central universities by relatively tenuous academic alliances and generally had a free hand operationally.[78] Vanderbilt's approach to law school/university affiliation, hence, was fairly common.[79]

It is unsurprising that founders who envisioned "a great university" included a law department among the institution's original departments. Indeed, the absence of a law school would have been notable for a university in which professional education was a central feature of its creators' aspirations. However, the quasi-proprietary nature of the Law School and its rather ambiguous administrative relationship to the University[80] were sources of tension during the term of the twenty-five year operating lease.[81]

"A FALSE START"

Vanderbilt Law School offered classes in fall 1874,[82] a full year before the main University enrolled its first crop of students.[83] But the law department's head start turned out to be "a false start."[84] What happened?

In January 1874, the Vanderbilt Board of Trust authorized a seven-person law school faculty, which included a departmental dean.[85] A few months later, in April, the Board created a junior professor slot to increase the law faculty to eight, selected individuals to fill these positions, and addressed the question of faculty compensation.[86]

The Board designated Judge William F. Cooper as the Law School's initial dean. It also named three other sitting or former judges to the School's first faculty: Edward H. East, a Board of Trust member; A. O. P. Nicholson, Chief Justice of the Tennessee Supreme Court; and H. M. Spofford, former

Louisiana Supreme Court member.[87] The remaining law faculty members selected by the Board were: Edmund D. Baxter; Thomas H. Malone; Jordan Stokes, an incorporator of the University; and William B. Reese, who filled the junior professorship.[88] Of this group of eight, only three—Baxter, Malone, and Reese—would play important faculty roles in the Law School's formative years.

The Board's selection of Cooper as dean was a logical one. He was a well-known chancery court judge who later became the Nashville Bar Association's first president, a Tennessee Supreme Court member, and the initial president of the Tennessee Bar Association.[89] He had a demonstrated interest in and some experience with law school education, having served as a professor in a short-lived law department operated by the University of Nashville for some months in the mid-1850s.[90] Coincidentally, Cooper had been involved with Vanderbilt University before being named dean of its law school; he presided at the 1873 legal proceeding in which the University's name was changed from The Central University of the Methodist Episcopal Church South to The Vanderbilt University.[91] He would also be reconnected to the Law School long after his brief stint as dean had ended. One day, Cooper's extensive personal collection of legal volumes would become a significant component of the Vanderbilt law library.[92]

With a faculty of eight headed by a capable dean, the law department at Vanderbilt needed only students and a place to hold classes. Neither would materialize as planned.

Because the principal building on campus, which was to house the classrooms, was incomplete,[93] the Law School was left to find space elsewhere. Arrangements were made with the Methodist Publishing House for quarters in which the law faculty could conduct classes and carry on the general operations of a law school.[94] Meanwhile, Reese, who had been named law faculty secretary, placed an advertisement in a local newspaper to attract students. The law department's advertisement, which appeared in the *Republican Banner* in August and September 1874, identified the faculty, described the nature of the two-year program, stated its cost—$120 per academic year, and proclaimed: "THE LAW COURSE will commence on the First Monday in October next."[95]

October arrived, but for various reasons, few law students did. First, the $120 annual tuition may have been too expensive for many prospective Southern law students; the region was still suffering economically from the impact of the Civil War.[96] Second, Vanderbilt was a start-up law school located in the same vicinity as Cumberland School of Law, a well-established provider of legal education.[97] Third, because Vanderbilt University was not yet operational, the Law School lacked the publicity, credibility, and organization that association with a functioning university can provide. Last, and perhaps most significantly, the space reserved in the Methodist Publishing House was unavailable for Law School use, a development that reportedly deterred some students from appearing and drove others away.[98] Just four prospective law students were on hand at the time classes were to begin.[99]

Faced with the embarrassment of having no suitable place to operate a law school and only a handful of students, Dean Cooper consulted with law faculty secretary Reese, Bishop Holland McTyeire (the President of the Board of Trust), and the four prospective law students. It was ultimately arranged that, rather than postpone the opening of the Law School, Reese would teach classes on his own.[100] He did so in a "very neatly fitted up" classroom in an office building, just above an insurance business.[101] Over the course of the academic year, three more students arrived, bringing the total to seven, but one stayed only briefly before taking a leave of absence.[102]

Reese, whose father was a Tennessee Supreme Court judge,[103] reportedly had received some legal training at Cumberland School of Law.[104] He was reputed to be a kind and understanding individual,[105] well liked by his students.[106] He successfully taught law to the seven young men who attended Vanderbilt Law School in its initial year of operation—1874–75.[107] Essentially, Reese was Vanderbilt Law School in its first year of existence. He received all tuition, with a guaranteed minimum of $700, for his efforts.[108]

At the end of the academic year, five students had progressed far enough in their studies to be promoted from the junior to the senior class, and one individual, William Van Amberg Sullivan, had finished all courses required for graduation.[109] It was then common for advanced law students to cover the two-year program in considerably less time;[110] in fact, Vanderbilt Law School's initial newspaper advertisement specifically mentioned this possibility,[111] as did most University announcements during the Law School's first decade.[112]

Dean Cooper administered a "very thorough" examination to Sullivan.[113] This was apparently the only academic, as distinguished from administrative, activity Cooper ever undertook on behalf of Vanderbilt Law School.[114] The examination was identical to the one given to law school graduates at Washington University in Saint Louis; Sullivan passed with flying colors and stood ready to graduate.[115] At a ceremony held on May 27, 1875, William Van Amberg Sullivan received a diploma and thus became the first individual to graduate from Vanderbilt Law School.[116]

Upon graduation, Sullivan returned to his home state of Mississippi to practice law, eventually becoming a United States Senator.[117] He had demonstrated leadership ability, as well as academic acumen, at the Law School, where he served as the founding president of the "Cornelian Debating Society," reportedly the initial student organization at Vanderbilt.[118] Years later, in 1900, Sullivan, then a Senator, returned to the Vanderbilt campus to display his oratorical skills, serving on that occasion as a principal speaker at the University's twenty-fifth anniversary celebration.[119]

One graduate, one United States Senator alumnus—a remarkable success rate for Vanderbilt Law School. But the low number of students and the overall organization of the School needed to be addressed. After just a single year in operation, a major change was due. It occurred soon after the 1875 spring term ended.

THE "LEASE"

Based on its unsatisfactory experience with the Law School's initial academic year, the Board of Trust resolved in May 1875 to reconfigure the department.[120] The Board started by receiving the resignation of Dean Cooper and several of the other law professors.[121] With the deck thus cleared, the Board executed a twenty-five year "Lease," commencing May 27, 1875, with three members of the original law faculty—Edmund D. Baxter, Thomas H. Malone, and William B. Reese ("Lessees").[122] This new organizational framework allowed the University to claim the Law School as its own, but at the same time to delegate responsibility for the School's management to three semi-independent contractors.[123] In essence, the lease agreement established a quasi-proprietary law school operating under the Vanderbilt name.[124]

Since the lease dictated the basic structure of the Law School for a quarter century, it bears scrutiny. But first, a brief look at the possible motivation of the parties to the agreement is instructive. On the University side, Board President McTyeire and Chancellor Garland had not given a great deal of attention to the formation of a law school and apparently were inclined to devote as few resources to the venture as feasible.[125] Yet, it was important from their perspective to include both a law school and a medical school in the institution to further the founders' vision of providing professional education[126] and to create a "university," rather than just another college.[127] From this viewpoint, the lease made sense. Obviously, the arrangement also appealed to the lessees—Baxter, Malone, and Reese. They could continue their local law practices and supplement their incomes by running the Law School on a part-time basis.[128] Such an arrangement was unexceptional;

law professors of that era customarily were part-time legal educators who conducted a law practice or served as a member of the judiciary.[129] The lessees also would have the opportunity to improve the quality of education available to aspiring lawyers and to engage in the process of law teaching. In this latter respect, Reese apparently found his year as an active law professor rewarding, as he seemed to discover a professional niche.[130] In any event, the three lessees were sufficiently drawn to legal education and confident in their personal/professional relationship to commit themselves to this long-term undertaking.

The "lease" itself was much more than what that term ordinarily connotes today—authorization to possess and use property for a certain period.[131] True, part of the lease dealt with the utilization of University-owned space in which to operate the law program. But the relationship was like a franchise or license agreement in that it permitted the three lawyers to use the Vanderbilt name in conducting a legal education business. Such proprietary-based arrangements were commonplace in the law school world of the late 1800s; an uneasy alliance often existed between universities that focused on scholarly pursuits and their law schools which had a decidedly practical, revenue-producing bent.[132]

Several provisions of the lease are noteworthy.[133] The University promised to provide a "suitable and commodious" classroom and a similar library for the Law School and to publish the Law School's catalogue. The Board of Trust also empowered Baxter, Malone, and Reese to retain tuition receipts,[134] guaranteeing that each lessee would earn $1,000 annually over a three-year span. Further, the Board gave the lessees "exclusive control" over the Law School, except that the University could discharge law professors for cause, discipline law students, and select the dean from the group of lessees. Malone was named dean and professor; Baxter and Reese were appointed professors. Each had a qualified right to name their own successor,[135] and as a group they could add law professors at their discretion. For the lessees' part, they promised to operate a law school "in a manner equal in every respect to the manner in which similar schools are conducted in the Universities of the United States."[136] And so Vanderbilt Law School's course was set for the remainder of the nineteenth century.

Locking the Law School into an organizational arrangement of this kind for such a long period may seem foolhardy to modern eyes. But law schools were being absorbed into the university system unevenly and uneasily throughout the latter part of 1800s.[137] Vanderbilt University was fortunate that, notwithstanding the quasi-proprietary nature of the law department's program, the three lessees would provide stable and highly competent leadership over the lease term, thereby helping the Law School and legal education in general edge toward the mainstream of academia.[138]

THE "LESSEES"

Who were these three practicing attorneys—Edmund D. Baxter, Thomas H. Malone, and William B. Reese—entrusted with the long-term management of Vanderbilt Law School on a part-time basis? Reese turned to a career in law after attending the University of Tennessee and preparing for the ministry.[139] He was apparently the only one of the three lessees who had gone to law school, reportedly having studied at Cumberland at some point.[140]

Reese shared a military background with Baxter and Malone; all had been members of the Confederate Army during the Civil War.[141] Students called Reese and Malone "Colonel" but apparently did not use that honorific title when referring to Baxter.[142] The Civil War bulked particularly large in Malone's life. In his memoirs, Malone recounts at some length his service as a Confederate officer throughout the entire war,[143] including his capture by Union forces and subsequent lengthy stint "In Prison" on Lake Erie's Johnson Island.[144]

Malone, who had a master's degree from the University of Virginia, prepared for the practice of law by serving a law office apprenticeship.[145] He entered practice in Nashville shortly before the Civil War[146] and after the war returned to the city to reestablish his legal career.[147] In time, he became a leading figure in the area of equity practice and was appointed to a chancery court judgeship.[148] Malone also achieved prominence as a business executive, being named Nashville Gas Company's president in the latter portion of the 1890s, a post he held for the remainder of his life.[149]

Malone occupied the deanship at Vanderbilt Law School from the execution of the lease in May of 1875 until he stepped down in 1904.[150] His role at the Law School during a seven-year stretch from 1882 to 1889, however, is unclear. For health reasons, Malone apparently was only titular law dean during this time.[151] Although on several occasions in the later half of the 1880s, Reese used the designation "Acting Dean" in reporting to the Board of Trust on behalf of the Law School,[152] the University Register/Announcement listed Malone as "Dean of the Faculty, and Emeritus Professor" throughout the seven-year period.[153] Malone, who had submitted his resignation and proposed his successor as professor to the Board in 1882,[154] did not teach during the years under discussion. The Board approved a professorship for W. A. Milliken as a replacement for Malone.[155] Milliken took over Malone's equity and commercial law classes[156] and served as secretary of the law faculty for a number of years.[157] When Milliken left the faculty in 1886,[158] the Law School secured the services of Andrew Allison, a Harvard Law School graduate, to cover the commercial, corporate, and equity areas until Malone resumed teaching in the 1889–90 school year.[159]

In addition to his long tenure as dean, Malone had strong familial ties to Vanderbilt Law School. His son, Thomas Jr., graduated from the Law School in 1896 and taught equity at the School for many years.[160] Moreover, Malone's daughter, Julia, married Vanderbilt Law School graduate Charles Trabue,[161] the law department's 1894 Founder's Medalist.[162]

The third lessee, Edmund Baxter, was a judge's son.[163] Baxter, who finished his schooling at age fourteen,[164] served an apprenticeship with a law firm before establishing an exceptionally successful career representing railroads.[165] His vast influence as a practitioner in this field has been assessed in the following terms: "At the national level, Ed Baxter, in his position as special counsel for nearly all southern railroads, did more than any railroad attorney to dismantle the ICC's power in cases before the Supreme Court."[166] Baxter was also considered an exceedingly capable law professor; he impressed law students with his attention to detail and demand for precision on all counts.[167]

Baxter was associated with Vanderbilt Law School from 1874 until apparently 1904, but over the last few years of this period, he served solely as a Lecturer on the Law of Interstate Commerce.[168] Moreover, in the late 1890s, he took a leave of absence from the Law School to attend to the demands of his law practice.[169]

The three lessees apportioned the curriculum among themselves.[170] Reese, after having taught all the classes in his initial year of teaching,[171] centered his attention on constitutional law, statutory, and real property courses. Naturally, Malone focused on equity; he presented classes on commercial and corporate matters as well. Baxter, for his part, offered instruction in evidence, pleading and practice, and, in his latter years on the faculty, interstate commerce. He was also heavily involved in the Law School's moot court program for a time.[172]

The nature of the lease arrangement, which placed the Law School in the hands of practitioners and distanced it from the University administratively, financially, and academically, may have stifled creativity and innovation in legal education.[173] Nevertheless, Baxter, Malone, and Reese provided steady and capable leadership for Vanderbilt Law School during its formative years.[174] Collectively they supplied the bulk of legal instruction offered

Vanderbilt law students in the nineteenth century.[175] Although Reese passed away in 1891,[176] Malone and Baxter were still associated with the Law School when the lease expired in 1900.[177]

An examination of the obituaries of the three lessees is revealing with respect to the stature accorded a faculty position at Vanderbilt Law School during the late nineteenth century and with regard to the role teaching at the School played in each individual's legal career. Reese's obituary indicates that he found "his life work" as a Vanderbilt Law School professor and includes resolutions from the "Vanderbilt law class" and the faculty of the University.[178] The newspaper articles reporting on the death of Baxter or Malone, however, generally only mention their work at Vanderbilt Law School.[179] Other professional achievements overshadowed their efforts as part-time legal educators. Seemingly, the Baxter and Malone obituary writers by and large did not consider an extended law professorship, or a deanship for that matter, at Vanderbilt Law School to be of great importance or interest.

The three lessees' accomplishments in legal education, however, were more significant than generally recognized by newspaper accounts at the time of their deaths. These individuals—Baxter, Malone, and Reese—were highly respected practitioners who gave Vanderbilt Law School credibility in the city and the state.[180] As part-time teachers and administrators, the lessees, particularly Malone,[181] provided continuity and direction for a fledgling law school, offered a sturdy educational product in the School's formative years,[182] and became involved in broader issues facing legal education,[183] all for scant financial reward.[184] In the words of Chancellor James Kirkland: "The three professors who had this department in charge for twenty-five years, and whose salaries during this time were dependent on the receipts of this department, established in the beginning rigid requirements and enforced the same with sublime indifference to their own personal advantage."[185]

CHANGES IN COMPOSITION OF FACULTY

Although the three lessees—Baxter, Malone, and Reese—provided most of the instruction at Vanderbilt Law School during the nineteenth century,[186] the Law School also employed other faculty members. As noted earlier, W. A. Milliken and Andrew Allison were appointed to take over the ailing Malone's classes during a substantial portion of the 1880s.[187]

In 1891, Reese died abruptly at the age of sixty-one, creating the need for another faculty appointment.[188] Pursuant to the lease that governed the

management of Vanderbilt Law School, Reese's widow had the right to select Reese's successor on the faculty, conditioned upon approval by Baxter,
Malone, and the Board of Trust.[189] This highly unusual method of selecting a new faculty member proved predictably problematic in practice. Mrs.
Reese chose Robert McPhail Smith to join the Law School faculty as Reese's
replacement; Baxter and Malone readily concurred.[190] An obstacle, however,
emerged at the Board of Trust level regarding Smith's religious views.[191]
Certain trustees objected to approving Smith, alleging that he had "denied
the Divine origin of the Christian religion and also the inspiration of the
Bible."[192] The Board and Smith engaged in a rapid exchange of correspondence on the subject. For his part, Smith disavowed taking such a stance
and further observed that one's "private opinions" on "these matters" were
irrelevant, but he also acknowledged the University's affiliation with the
Methodist Church and pledged to "sedulously avoid" expressing opinions in
or outside class that "might not pass in the Theological Department."[193] A
mollified Board endorsed the selection of Smith to succeed Reese.[194] Smith
taught at the Law School for several years, offering constitutional and statutory law courses previously offered by Reese.[195]

Following Smith's death during the 1897–98 school year, Vanderbilt
chose Jacob M. Dickinson, a judge and former United States Assistant Attorney General, to occupy the open professorial slot.[196] Dickinson, who was
active in the Tennessee Bar Association,[197] focused his teaching in the areas
of real property and constitutional law.[198]

In 1898, the Law School made two other faculty appointments, substantially expanding the size of the faculty. Horace H. Lurton was appointed
constitutional law professor, and Charles N. Burch was named criminal law
lecturer and law faculty secretary.[199]

Appointing Lurton was particularly important for Vanderbilt Law
School.[200] He played a leading role in the development of the Law School
after the operating lease ended[201] and brought national attention to the
School through his work as a prominent jurist.[202] Lurton, who was a judge
on the federal Sixth Circuit Court of Appeals at the time he was added to
the Vanderbilt Law School faculty,[203] had an enormously successful legal
career, culminating in his appointment as a Justice on the United States
Supreme Court.[204] He continued to sit on the Sixth Circuit throughout his
teaching career at the Law School, even during his term as Vanderbilt Law
School dean in the years 1904–10.[205] Lurton departed in 1910 upon joining
the Supreme Court.[206]

The Burch appointment was noteworthy in its own right. A member
of the class of 1889, Burch was the first in a series of Vanderbilt Law School

graduates to return to teach at the Law School.[207] Although Burch was on the Law School faculty for only two years,[208] he led the way for Vanderbilt Law School graduates to receive faculty appointments at their home institution.[209]

The appointments of Burch and Lurton represented a key component of a plan to bolster the Law School's program. Increasing the number of law faculty members was part of a concerted effort to strengthen the Law School before its operating lease ended in 1900 and the University took "direct control" of the School.[210] With these hires and Baxter's return to the podium on a limited basis after a leave of absence, the Law School was operating with five faculty members, an unprecedented position of faculty strength.[211]

Circumstances dictated that Vanderbilt Law School make a final adjustment to its faculty roster before the end of the lease term. During the 1899–1900 school year, Dickinson was named the Illinois Central Railroad's general counsel, a post based in Chicago, and left the faculty to devote his attention to this new endeavor.[212] Replacements were needed. Judges Claude Waller, the Founder's Medalist of the Vanderbilt Law School class of 1890,[213] and J. Willis Bonner, immediate past President of the Tennessee Bar Association,[214] were called upon to take over Dickinson's courses.[215] Although Waller taught at the Law School only in the 1899–1900 academic year,[216] he remained associated with the University as a Vanderbilt Board of Trust member.[217] Bonner served as a Law School faculty member intermittently for most of the following decade.[218]

When the Law School lease lapsed in 1900, the Board of Trust reconstituted the faculty, expanding it to eight members, and established a faculty salary scale.[219] Only Malone and Lurton remained as professors, with Malone continuing as dean.[220] The Board added four professors, one adjunct professor, and one instructor. The six fresh faces were: (1) James C. Bradford, who was to run the moot court program;[221] (2) John Bell Keeble, an 1888 Vanderbilt Law School graduate and future long-term dean of the Law School,[222] who was given the responsibility of serving as secretary of the faculty as well as filling a professorial slot; (3) Percy D. Maddin, an 1882 Law School graduate and prominent bank attorney;[223] (4) James C. McReynolds, a future United States Supreme Court Justice;[224] (5) Thomas A. Street, who served as adjunct professor; and (6) Thomas H. Malone, Jr., the dean's son and an 1896 Law School graduate,[225] who was employed as an instructor.[226] This post-lease faculty is remarkable in that two of its eight members, Lurton and McReynolds, would become United States Supreme Court Justices.[227]

The attorneys who were appointed to the Vanderbilt law faculty in 1900, although an accomplished group of professionals, were part-time legal educators.[228] Thus, Vanderbilt Law School entered the twentieth century still burdened with being only an ancillary endeavor for those who ran the institution; the faculty's primary professional interests lay elsewhere. Vanderbilt was in the mainstream in this regard; at that time law school faculties typically were composed of practicing attorneys and sitting judges.[229]

LAW STUDENTS

Vanderbilt law students were immersed in campus life, playing an energetic role in cultural, social, athletic, and academic affairs from the initial days of the University.[230] Law students reportedly formed the first student organization on campus, founding the Cornelian Debating Society, named after Cornelius Vanderbilt, on March 27, 1875.[231] They also created the University's initial student publication, the short-lived *Vanderbilt Austral*.[232] This section examines the composition of this lively and engaged body of law students and then explores areas in which their involvement in campus activities presented problems for University administrators.

The Student Body. Law students in the last quarter of the nineteenth century more nearly resembled undergraduate students than the post-baccalaureate students of today's law schools.[233] Indeed, law students pursued a *bachelor* of laws degree.[234] Of the nation's law schools that had admission requirements in the period from 1874 to 1900, few required more than an academic background that would meet college entrance standards.[235] Vanderbilt Law School was one of the many law schools that had not established any standard for admission of entry-level students.[236] Nonetheless, Vanderbilt law students of the era were not a group of mere teenagers fresh from high school; in fact, some had graduated from college.[237] The average age of Vanderbilt law students was approximately twenty-one in the School's earliest years, gradually increasing to twenty-two later in the lease term.[238]

By modern standards, the law classes at Vanderbilt during this quarter century were homogenous, with apparently no women or African-American students enrolled.[239] Such homogeneity was common for the time; relatively few women were admitted to law school programs,[240] and separate law schools for African-American students were maintained.[241]

Vanderbilt Law School, however, did attract several Native American students to its program during the latter part of the nineteenth century.[242] For example, William Wirt Hastings and William P. Thompson, 1889 graduates of the Law School, grew up in Indian Territory as members of the

Cherokee Nation. They had been childhood friends and following graduation became law partners in Tahlequah, Indian Territory, the Cherokee Nation's capital.[243] Hastings was named Cherokee Nation Attorney General and later was elected to represent Oklahoma in Congress, holding office for nearly two decades.[244] Thompson eventually became a Commissioner of the Supreme Court of Oklahoma.[245]

In addition, a few members of the Chickasaw Nation received their legal education at Vanderbilt Law School in the mid-to-late 1890s. Under a Chickasaw Nation legislative measure,[246] a group of young Chickasaw men were chosen to attend Vanderbilt University to prepare for tribal leadership roles in government and education.[247] Three of those students entered the Law School;[248] two completed the program. Joseph H. Goforth graduated in 1897,[249] and Jacob L. Thompson received his law degree in 1898.[250] Both returned to Indian Territory where they practiced law.[251] Goforth became a county judge,[252] and Thompson occupied a number of administrative posts in the Chickasaw Nation.[253]

Vanderbilt Law School occasionally attracted an international student in the nineteenth century. During this period, the Law School enrolled at least four students from foreign countries, three from Japan and one from Brazil.[254] The admission of a few international students created a more diverse student body but presented challenges if a particular student was not fluent in English. For example, in 1889, the law faculty reported to the Chancellor that it had been unable to evaluate satisfactorily the academic progress of a "manifestly studious" international student because of "his limited knowledge of the English language."[255] The Board of Trust responded by authorizing "a certificate of attendance for his two years in the Law School,"[256] which was awarded the student at graduation.[257] A similar issue arose again in 1890, when the Board approved, upon the law faculty's recommendation, an LL.B. degree for another international student "although he has not studied with us the law of procedure . . . , speaks English but little, and does not propose ever to practise law."[258] The Board approved this degree with the understanding that "this precedent [would be limited] strictly to the case of foreigners who do not intend to practise law."[259]

During the nineteenth century, Vanderbilt law students were also somewhat diverse with respect to their home states.[260] Each academic year law students came from a number of states, frequently ten or more, and as many as fifteen (1889–90).[261] Neighboring jurisdictions, particularly Kentucky and Mississippi, were strong feeder states.[262] Texas also supplied numerous law students, and California was well represented, particularly in the 1890s. Nonetheless, Tennessee predictably was the substantial leader in providing students to Vanderbilt Law School in the nineteenth century.[263] The percentage of Tennesseans in the student body exceeded fifty percent in the 1870s. That percentage dropped to an all-time low of twenty-two percent by the 1887–88 academic year, only to rise again in the mid-1890s.[264] Tennesseans once again constituted a majority of the Vanderbilt Law School student body, and the number of other home states represented declined along with the percentage of out-of-state students. This loss of geographic reach in the 1890s may have motivated Chancellor Kirkland to urge a post-lease arrangement designed to boost the Law School's "popularity."[265]

Nineteenth-century Vanderbilt law graduates often pursued professional opportunities outside the area.[266] Among what could be called the inaugural graduating "class" of 1876 was a graduate who practiced law in British Columbia and another who served as a United States Attorney in Alaska.[267] Graduates in subsequent classes occupied a variety of practice, corporate, government, academic, and judicial positions in numerous states across the country.[268]

"Usurping . . . Authority." The University administration did not always appreciate law students' enthusiastic involvement in campus life, as their actions sometimes conflicted with established expectations of student conduct.[269] Two such problems arose surrounding the introduction of a moot court exercise into graduation ceremonies and the creation of a student publication, the *Vanderbilt Austral.*[270]

A moot court performance presented by law students during graduation festivities developed into a popular part of the occasion each year.[271] But the initiation of this moot court event caused Chancellor Garland to draft a letter to Dean Malone just before the University's initial general commencement in 1876, objecting to the law students' plans.[272] "Surely," Garland wrote, "they do not intend to do this of their own accord, thereby usurping the authority which resides only in the Faculty of the University."[273] A pencil notation on the surviving copy of this letter indicates that it was not posted.[274] Instead, Garland forwarded a more temperate message to Malone, offering "no objection" as long as the performance was "a private arrangement," conducted in a Law School classroom (not the University chapel), and scheduled so as to avoid interfering with "duly authorized" commencement activities.[275] Notwithstanding Garland's concerns, the moot court performance was held in the chapel and turned out to be a major University event at the 1876 graduation and subsequent graduations.[276] Soon Garland began to attend.[277]

Law students found other ways to push the limits of authorized behavior. During the spring term of 1879, the *Vanderbilt Austral,* the self-proclaimed first "University paper," was published, initially "under the auspices of the Law Department."[278] In light of University faculty rejection of every student proposal to publish a periodical, law student entrepreneurs obtained funding for the *Austral* through a campus sale of stock at five dollars a share.[279] The *Austral* covered a variety of subjects of interest to the University community,[280] criticized a Board of Trust policy that restricted the area in which academic department students could live,[281] and lambasted University faculty opposition to student publications.[282] On this last topic the student editors pointedly observed: "The paper was ridiculed; the minds of the students presumptuous enough to write for the paper were disparaged; and it was publicly told us that there was not ability enough here, nor would be for many decades, to run a paper, which is saying but little for the training of the professors or the work of the University since its inauguration."[283]

In his report to the Board of Trust that spring, Chancellor Garland referred to the publication of the *Austral* as a "flagrant violation of law," noting that the law students who created the paper were "under the impression that they were not bound by any prohibition laid upon the other students of the University."[284] He asserted that the "clandestinely published" paper was "demoralizing" to the student body in that it signaled that "violations of the law may be committed with impunity if done in secrecy."[285] Garland concluded that it was important for the students to be cognizant of the Trustees' authority "to purge out any disorganizing element."[286]

The *Vanderbilt Austral* never opened for business in its second academic year. Apparently the names of the students involved in its publication became public by virtue of an imprudent bulletin board posting. The administration reportedly required those students, as a condition of enrollment for the 1879 fall semester, to agree to shut down the *Austral*.[287]

The controversies aroused by the actions of law students were attributable, in part, to a lack of clarity about the reach of University disciplinary regulations.[288] The Law School's operating lease specified: "The Law Students shall be subject to the University discipline in like manner with the students of the other departments."[289] In practice, however, differences appeared because of perceptions that the rules governing the general student body did not unequivocally apply to law students.[290] Thus, relying on "a special contract," Dean Malone asserted exemptions for law students from University rules governing where students could live and requiring them to attend chapel services. Chancellor Garland disavowed knowledge of such an arrangement, but agreed not to enforce the rules at issue and sought direction from the Board of Trust with respect to enforcing general University regulations against law students.[291] The Board responded by delegating decisions about where students could live to the faculties of the individual schools and by directing a council of deans headed by Garland, known as the University Senate, to convene each month to foster consistency and compatibility among the schools.[292]

Perhaps in response to the University administration's unease, all matriculating law students began signing a pledge in 1890: "I promise to obey the laws of the University."[293] In 1897, the pledge was expanded: "I promise to obey the laws of the University and the Library."[294] It is unknown what law student activities or legalistic defenses might have prompted this more comprehensive formulation. It appears likely, however, that Chancellor Kirkland's desire to dissolve the quasi-proprietary law school arrangement at the end of the operating lease in 1900 reflected, in part, a determination to bring the regulation of law students more firmly under central University authority.[295]

ACADEMIC PROGRAM

In one sense, an academic program begins with admission standards. On this score, Vanderbilt Law School was wholly lacking in its early days. During the nineteenth century, Vanderbilt maintained no academic standards for the admission of entry-level law students.[296] This practice was common then.[297] Even those law schools that had admission standards generally did not establish criteria any more demanding than the prevailing academic requirements for entering college.[298] In any case, Vanderbilt Law School found competitive and financial reasons for maintaining a policy of standardless admission throughout the nineteenth century; the institution was required to recruit a sufficient number of law students to remain an economically viable academic entity.[299]

Near the end of the century, Vanderbilt law faculty members evinced concern about the insufficient academic preparation of law students.[300] Ultimately, Dean Malone proposed to the Board of Trust that he and Chancellor Kirkland explore the possibility of adopting some educational requirement—for example, a college degree—for admission to the Law School.[301] Kirkland agreed to consider the matter, but, ever concerned about increasing the size of the Law School's student body,[302] he viewed the notion of requiring a college degree for law school admission as probably premature for a Southern institution.[303] The issue was shelved; admission requirements were not imposed at Vanderbilt Law School during the period under consideration (1874–1900).[304]

Once admitted, law students at Vanderbilt faced a program of legal study that ostensibly extended over a two-year period, bifurcated into a junior and a senior year.[305] After successful completion of this endeavor, a student received a bachelor of laws degree.[306] The two-year duration of the program, however, was not firm.[307] Indeed, the law faculty signaled from the Law School's opening that the required coursework could be completed in less time.[308] A substantial number of students, including the Law School's first graduate,[309] seized the opportunity to compress their legal education and were awarded degrees after just one year at the Law School.[310] For many years, the law faculty tolerated, even facilitated, this academic shortcut on the articulated grounds that numerous Vanderbilt law students had studied law before enrolling or had difficulty devoting the time and money demanded by a two-year program.[311] Moreover, a reality of the marketplace could not be ignored; rival forms of legal study existed—the still viable apprenticeship method and one-year law school programs,[312] such as that offered at neighboring Cumberland.[313]

Over time the law faculty apparently came to the conclusion that the intellectual quality of the law school experience suffered for those students who finished in one year. Thus, at the start of the 1890s, the law faculty created three full-tuition scholarships for the senior year to be given to the top students in the junior class in order to entice them to stay in school for the entire two-year program.[314] Then in 1892, the law faculty required law students to secure the dean's endorsement in order to pursue the one-year degree track.[315] Finally, in 1893, Vanderbilt Law School established two years as the unalterable duration of its program.[316] This decision to mandate a two-year program was made at the risk of declining enrollments.[317] Fortunately for the Law School, the size of its student body decreased only slightly the following year and then rebounded completely in subsequent years.[318] Indeed, near the end of the century, Chancellor Kirkland expressed the hope that at some point the Law School could extend its academic program to three years.[319]

The fluidity of the length of the Law School's academic program during the period from 1874 to 1900 must be viewed in light of the standard in legal education at the time. At Vanderbilt Law School's creation, law schools nationwide were divided between one-year and two-year programs, with two-year programs predominating.[320] Over the last quarter of the nineteenth century, law schools moved toward longer academic programs—of two or three years duration, with three-year programs in the ascendancy at century's end.[321] Hence, Vanderbilt was within the legal education mainstream of the time with its loose, then firm, two-year academic program in law[322] and its aspiration to develop a three-year course of study.[323]

The Vanderbilt Law School faculty articulated from the start an approach to legal education that guided their work:[324]

> It will be the aim of the Professors to pursue such a plan of instruction as will lay a broad foundation of principle upon which the student may build his own superstructure according to the laws of the place where he may locate, and the branch of the profession he may adopt; and for this purpose special attention will be paid to the mental discipline and training of the student, and to the teaching of those general principles of reason which underlie all positive systems of Law.[325]

Thus did the University and law faculty express their desire to prepare students broadly for legal practice.[326] The law school classroom experience was intended "to expand the intellect rather than to teach points of local practice or rules of local law."[327] Similarly, "daily examinations" were to be conducted to promote independent thinking over pure memorization.[328]

Course offerings remained relatively constant at Vanderbilt Law School over the last quarter of the nineteenth century. Subjects presented at both the beginning and end of this period included pleading, contracts, domestic relations, criminal law, real property, corporations, partnership, torts, evidence, constitutional law, moot court, equity, and wills.[329]

Published expectations of law students in the classroom, however, were uneven. Academic standards were established for a bachelor of laws degree—law students were required to achieve a seventy-five percent score on a "searching examination in writing" every semester,[330] as well as to have satisfactorily performed "daily recitations."[331] The Law School's earliest announcements, however, cast doubt on the seriousness with which classroom work was sometimes taken:[332] "Students will find it much to their advantage to enter promptly at the beginning of the Session, but they may do so at any time."[333] Perhaps in response to students taking advantage of this laxness, the faculty stiffened its stance in 1884: "Students should present themselves punctually at the opening of the Session. The loss of a few lectures at the beginning may prove to be a serious embarrassment to subsequent progress."[334]

The Law School's public description of "the diploma privilege" also reflects tightened standards.[335] Initially, the law faculty called attention to its willingness to exercise its authority to grant licenses to practice law to students who did not earn a law degree.[336] Beginning in 1884, the statement on the diploma privilege in the Law School's announcement no longer highlighted this possibility.[337]

Early announcements described classroom methodology at Vanderbilt Law School as follows: "Instruction is given by Lectures, daily Examinations and by Moot-courts."[338] Law School announcements also included a list of the textbooks that students were to use in the course of their legal studies.[339] The School's lecture/quiz/textbook approach to law teaching was unremarkable; it was the norm in legal education at that time.[340]

Moot court, however, was emphasized at Vanderbilt Law School[341] and was detailed in early Law School announcements: "Students are required to prepare pleadings on statements of cases made for the purpose, argue the cases, draw the proper judgments and decrees, prepare bills of exceptions, and prosecute appeals or writs of error to the Appellate Court."[342] This description of moot court exercises hardly does justice to this component of the curriculum; moot court occupied a central place in the instructional program offered at the Law School during its formative years.[343] Indeed, later Law School announcements expanded the explanation of moot court, pointing out that law students would handle more than one hundred moot court cases during each academic year, that moot court occupied a position of "prominence" in the institution's overall academic program, and that Professor Baxter devoted his teaching efforts to "[t]his feature of the school."[344]

The emphasis on moot court is consistent with the nature of the Vanderbilt Law School faculty—active attorneys who taught law as a collateral activity.[345] Indeed, the Law School endeavored to accentuate the way in which its faculty's practitioner background enhanced the classroom experience.[346] The School's inaugural catalogue professed the "hope . . . that, coming daily to their Lectures fresh and heated from the contests of the bar, they may be able to impart to the study of the law a measure of the enthusiasm inseparably connected with the practice; and, at all events, they will continually keep prominent before the student the live law and practical questions of the day."[347]

The Vanderbilt law faculty apparently made no dramatic adjustment in instructional approach during the nineteenth century.[348] A fundamental pedagogical change, however, was afoot in the world of legal education; the controversial case method of law teaching, utilized at Harvard Law School, was gaining momentum.[349] Indeed, near the end of the nineteenth century, the Vanderbilt Law School faculty indicated that it was beginning to incorporate the case method into its existing teaching model: "The method of instruction is partly by text-books, partly by lectures, and partly by the examination and discussion of selected cases."[350]

The Vanderbilt Law School faculty also demonstrated a desire to expand the academic program. For four academic years, 1888–92, the faculty offered instruction for "post-graduates and young practicing lawyers."[351] Rather than develop a particular course of study, the faculty indicated that it would design an appropriate program for interested parties.[352] The short duration of the offering and the lack of any fuller description of the program indicate that it may not have been a successful venture.

The trajectory of the academic program at Vanderbilt Law School during the final quarter of the nineteenth century was clearly upward. The faculty's aspirations for a more rigorous intellectual environment were demonstrated by efforts to first encourage and then require a longer period of study, to create a more demanding classroom experience, and to consider establishing minimal admissions standards. While the School was not a national leader academically, by all accounts the University administration and the Law School faculty were serious about providing as fine a legal education as their circumstances would allow.[353]

INFRASTRUCTURE

Vanderbilt Law School's early academic program was entwined with the School's financial, facility, and library infrastructure. An examination of these fiscal and physical factors facilitates an understanding of the constraints within which the lessees operated.

Finances. Vanderbilt University's financial arrangement with the Law School lessees, beginning with the 1875 lease,[354] was simple. The lease specified that the three lessees—Baxter, Malone, and Reese—were entitled to tuition receipts, guaranteeing $1,000 per lessee per annum over the next three academic years.[355] Although the lessees could look to the University to make up any shortfall during this three-year, start-up period, the University's financial guarantee expired at the end of the 1877–78 academic year.[356] Thereafter, the lessees depended solely on tuition for compensation. Law School enrollment data and tuition rates signal how the lessees fared financially throughout the remainder of the nineteenth century.[357] Enrollment totals for the years of the lease are shown in Figure 1.[358]

Enrollment and tuition figures for the initial three years of Vanderbilt Law School's existence under the lease (1875–78) indicate that a total tuition revenue of $8,600 should have been produced,[359] an amount almost match-

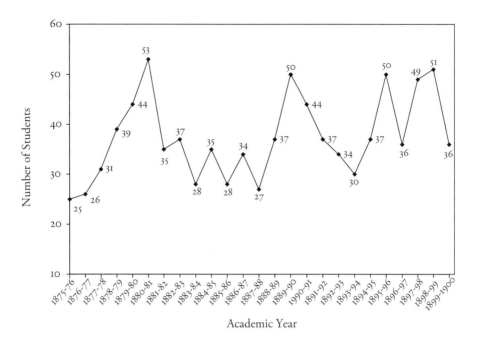

Academic Year

ing the $9,000 guaranteed by the University for that period. Further, annual tuition for Vanderbilt Law School was $100 from the 1878–79 academic year through the remainder of the lease.[360] With an average annual enrollment of almost thirty-nine law students per academic year during that period, the initial $3,000 target for annual income seemed manageable. In reality, a different picture emerged.[361]

The University bursar reported to the Board of Trust that cumulative income from law student fees from 1875–78 was only $5,877.75.[362] Similarly, fees paid by law students in the 1878–79 school year totaled $2,171.50,[363] even though full tuition from the thirty-nine enrolled students would have yielded tuition income of $3,900.[364] Several factors may account for this revenue deficiency.

First, the Law School allowed students to attend class prior to paying tuition. This practice occurred notwithstanding announcements mandating the advance payment of tuition.[365] In reporting on the Law School's deficit in 1877, Board of Trust President McTyeire projected—incorrectly, as it turned out—that the Law School would become "self-supporting" the following year since "some who gave tuition notes a year ago have paid them."[366] Collection of law student debts continued to be a problem.[367] For example, the bursar reported in 1879 that he had received $129.25 from law students for overdue amounts from prior years and that unpaid law student obligations approaching "several hundred dollars" had been turned over to a local attorney for collection.[368] Similarly, a decade later, the following entry appeared in the "Resources" section of University financial records: "Notes of Law students for tuition [$]435."[369]

Second, scholarship and tuition remission programs may also have reduced revenue somewhat.[370] This factor does not, however, appear to have had a significant negative financial impact on the Law School. It is doubtful that early University scholarship or tuition remission programs, which were expressly or apparently designed primarily for students in other departments, decreased Law School tuition receipts significantly, if at all.[371] Moreover, the Law School did not establish its own full tuition scholarship program until the beginning of the 1890s, and this program was limited to two or three senior students each year.[372]

Third, the Law School prorated tuition for those students who did not maintain their enrollment for the full year.[373] Enrollment statistics may have included law students who were in attendance for only a semester, and tuition apparently was charged on a semester rather than an annual basis.[374] Furthermore, University records refer to fees that were refunded to law students[375] without clarifying whether this return of fees was a refund for students who did not complete a semester or the functional equivalent of a scholarship or loan program.

In addition to tuition revenues falling short of expectations based on the number of students enrolled, enrollment patterns themselves at Vanderbilt Law School during the nineteenth century contributed to financial and planning concerns. These patterns were not only irregular (year-to-year fluctuations of more than twenty percent were not uncommon), but overall growth was painfully modest.[376] The average enrollment in the first five academic years of the lease (1875–80) was thirty-three; the average for the last five academic years of the lease (1895–1900) was only forty-four.[377] These somewhat discouraging enrollment figures and their import for Law School revenue were increasingly on Chancellor Kirkland's mind as the end of the lease drew near.[378]

Facilities. Vanderbilt Law School occupied three separate facilities during the nineteenth century.[379] In the Law School's opening year (1874–75), Professor William Reese conducted all classes off campus in a single classroom in a commercial building.[380] For its second academic year (1875–76) and its initial year under the long-term lease, the Law School moved to campus where it stayed until 1889.[381] During this on-campus period, Vanderbilt Law School was housed in the University's principal building, which was then known as "Main."[382] As early as 1880, the law faculty appealed to the Board of Trust for additional quarters, noting that its existing room in

Main was "too small" to accommodate Law School classes adequately.[383] The Law School was at some point allowed to expand within Main,[384] but the modest size of the Law School's area in this building apparently was a continuing problem.[385]

Eventually a solution to the Law School space issue was reached.[386] The University decided to construct an office building in Nashville's business/legal district to provide accommodations for the Law School, the Dental School, and commercial tenants.[387] The project, which reportedly was not a successful investment from a financial perspective, was finished in 1889.[388] Vanderbilt Law School moved into its new off-campus quarters in time for the start of the 1889–90 academic year.[389] The structure, referred to originally as the Law and Dental Building and later as the Law Building when the Dental School departed the premises,[390] would house the Law School until the beginning of 1916.[391] The Law School initially was allocated "The Law Lecture Room," as well as two additional rooms for housing the law library.[392] Attorneys rented much of the other office space in the building.[393] While the new site separated the Law School from the rest of the University, the law students' classes were now just a short distance from the courts and many law offices.[394] Moreover, access to the Law School was more convenient for faculty members as they shuttled between practicing law and teaching.[395]

By 1896, the condition of the Law School's accommodations in the Law and Dental Building had become an issue. Law students petitioned the law faculty to restore the School's quarters to their "proper condition."[396] Dean Malone seconded the students' petition, noting the "dilapidated and disreputable appearance of the Law lecture room."[397] Chancellor Kirkland agreed that the lecture room required "considerable work" and advised the Board of Trust that "[s]omething must be done."[398] The Board responded by having the lecture room renovated before the beginning of the 1896–97 school year.[399] As a means of ensuring that the Law School facilities would remain in good repair, the Law School instituted a program of requiring all students to post a $2.00 damage deposit.[400]

Law Library. Vanderbilt Law School initially did not have its own library by contemporary standards,[401] but the School did collect law books from the first academic year under the lease.[402] From the beginning, Vanderbilt law students also had privileges at the library operated by the state[403] and soon gained access to the law library maintained by the Nashville Bar Association.[404]

The Law School's library developed slowly. In 1880, the law faculty formulated a plan to create a "large Law Library" by requesting that practitioners and judges donate used legal tomes to the Law School.[405] This effort achieved a measure of early success. By 1886, more volumes had been collected than could be housed in the Law School's two bookcases in Main.[406] At that point general reference works were moved from the Law School to the University library to make room for recent donations of law books.[407] But despite these developments, the law library remained of extremely modest size.[408]

Several significant breakthroughs occurred for the law library when Vanderbilt Law School moved in the summer of 1889 to set up operations in the newly constructed Law and Dental Building. First, the University assigned two rooms for use as a law library.[409] This was a signal occasion; never before had the Law School's facilities included sufficient space to house a substantial collection of legal materials.[410] The Law School and University were thereby motivated to initiate concrete steps to develop a quality law library.[411]

Second, the law faculty sought University funding for a law librarian, contending that the creation of this position would lead local attorneys to rent space in the Law and Dental Building, entrust their law books to the care of the law librarian, and allow those volumes to be used by the Law School.[412] The law professors further argued: "With a library we feel assured we can make the Law Dept. double its attendance. . . ."[413] The Board of Trust soon approved a plan to organize and operate a law library in the new building and to hire a law librarian at a $1,000 annual salary.[414] In addition to attending to the law library, the law librarian was charged with significant supplemental administrative duties, namely managing the Law and Dental Building, except for the Dental School's area, and serving as Law School secretary.[415] Wilbur F. Barclay, a member of the Board of Trust,[416] was named Librarian of the Law Library of the University shortly before the beginning of the 1889–90 academic year.[417]

Third, the Law School rapidly assembled a collection of legal works exceeding $10,000 in value.[418] The School acquired these materials primarily through a $2,000 Board of Trust allocation, the gift of Francis B. Fogg's noteworthy personal collection, and the Nashville Bar Association's contribution of its substantial law library.[419] Also included were less extensive donations from law faculty members and other benefactors.[420] With the law faculty's purchase in 1891 of former Dean Cooper's exceptional law volume collection, the Law School's library holdings grew to approximately six thousand volumes, reportedly unsurpassed in the region.[421] The Law School continued to expand its collection; by the end of the nineteenth century, the law library's volume count had reached eight thousand.[422]

A careful look at the way the growth of the law library was financed reveals the comparatively aggressive role the law faculty played in this endeavor and the tension that developed between the faculty and the University over law library financing. The members of the law faculty were keenly interested in nurturing the expansion of the law library; they formulated plans, obtained donations, made contributions of their own, and pressed the University for financial support.[423] The University's Board of Trust, however, exhibited understandable hesitancy about committing funds for law library development given the quasi-proprietary nature of the Law School.[424]

The Board's general approach on this score is illustrated by its handling of an 1890 Law School overture calling for a substantial University financial commitment to law library expansion. The law professors proposed that the Board "invest" $6,000 to $10,000 in library purchases to create, in the words of Law Librarian Barclay, "a complete law library." The law faculty would guarantee the University a six percent annual return through the end of the lease by utilizing funds generated by library user fees and covering any shortage themselves. The Board was not persuaded and "postponed indefinitely" the matter.[425]

The Board of Trust, however, by no means ignored the financial needs of the law library. It had, after all, hired a law librarian and provided seed money for acquisition of legal volumes in order to fashion a suitable law library in the Law and Dental Building.[426] Nonetheless, strings were attached to the $2,000 allocation; the Board stipulated that the law school faculty members pay interest on that amount to the University.[427] Uncertainty eventually arose regarding this "obligation," which appeared in the University's financial records as a "Law Faculty Loan."[428] Noting that the existence of a written undertaking by the law faculty was in doubt and that the University had benefited from the existence of the law library in the Law and Dental building, Chancellor Kirkland suggested that the Board relinquish its claim to interest payments and have the entry moved to the "Library Equipment" assets category of University financial records.[429] The Board did not pursue this matter further; the arrangement remained designated as a loan on the University records until after the lease ended.[430]

Another misunderstanding regarding library financial matters developed with respect to the Law School's acquisition of the Cooper collection. In 1891, the law faculty had, on its own account, bought Dean Cooper's library for a $240 annual annuity over the duration of Cooper's life.[431] Two years later, Dean Malone advised the Board of Trust that it had been the law faculty's hope that the University would assume the obligation of making annuity payments and that he thought there had been "some informal statement to this effect by one or more of the Executive Board."[432] Nonetheless, the Board of Trust apparently did not undertake any responsibility in this regard at that point, and the law professors continued to pay the Cooper annuity.[433]

As these situations indicate, the issues of law library funding and management under the Law School operating lease were nettlesome and beyond easy resolution. Uncertainties surrounding the University–Law School partnership in maintaining a law library lingered until the end of the lease in 1900.

"REORGANIZATION": POISED FOR CHANGE

As Vanderbilt Law School's operating lease approached its 1900 termination date, Chancellor Kirkland and the Board of Trust considered alternative organizational models. Although sound reasons had existed for both sides to enter the lease,[434] the overall structure of the arrangement had significant educational, financial, and governance drawbacks.[435]

Kirkland did not wait until the end of the lease to begin campaigning for a significant change in the University–Law School relationship. In 1898 he reported to the Board:

> It will be remembered that our present contract with the Law Faculty expires in June 1900. It is very desirable that we should do everything possible to build up the Department within the next two years, so that the University can then assume direct control of the Law Department, managing it in every way as we now manage the other departments of the University with the exception of the Dental Department.[436]

At the 1899 Board of Trust annual meeting, Kirkland noted that the Law School lease would lapse the following year. While reporting that "no serious friction" had developed regarding the lease arrangement, he opined "that steps ought to be taken by this Board to assume direct control of the Law Department next year" and expressed his opposition "to any form of contract which alienates from the Board complete control of any department of university work."[437]

By the end of the century, several factors prompted a University decision to restructure its relationship with the Law School. First, the Law School's operating lease was not an attractive one financially for Vanderbilt. The University provided the Law School with teaching and library space that the University furnished, maintained, and cleaned, and for which it paid the utilities.[438] Moreover, the University had been funding a law librarian's salary since 1889.[439] But the institution never obtained any income from the lease because the lessees were entitled to tuition receipts.[440] In essence, the lease arrangement ensured that the Law School would be a financial drain on the University.

The related issue of the size of the Law School student body was also a matter of concern.[441] Chancellor Kirkland became frustrated by the Law School's inability to increase its enrollment and toward the end of the lease term was sharing this frustration with the Board of Trust on an almost annual basis: "Our enrollment ought never to be below 50, and really ought to reach 100."[442] (1896) "We have always felt that the attendance in this department was not as large as the merits of the department deserved."[443] (1898) "[W]e should not be satisfied until we have secured an attendance of at least 75 students [i]n this department."[444] (1899) Yet, the largest Law School enrollment during the nineteenth century was fifty-three students in the 1880–81 school year,[445] and the 1899–1900 academic year saw a drop in enrollment from fifty-one in the previous year to thirty-six.[446] Indeed, Kirkland phrased the question that led to restructuring the Law School largely in terms of enrollment. After noting that a "self-sustaining" law program was impossible with current enrollment levels, he stated that the issue presented the Board was how to enhance the Law School's "popularity" without impairing its "efficiency."[447]

Governance of Law School matters was yet another disquieting subject. In his plans for realigning the University–Law School working relationship, Chancellor Kirkland, taking a position consistent with a national trend in academe of that era,[448] emphasized the importance of the University having "direct control" over the Law School.[449] He may have viewed a new arrangement as a way of avoiding the uncertainties that had arisen in the areas of student discipline and financial affairs—particularly the purchases that contributed to the expansion of the law library.[450]

The Board of Trust approved a "reorganization" of Vanderbilt Law School at its annual meeting in June 1900.[451] Kirkland praised the law faculty's performance over the years ("[it] has always been of a high and thorough character"[452]), but reported that he and the Executive Committee had ascertained "certain weak points in the method of managing this department, which we think ought to be remedied."[453] Under the new arrangement, Malone was selected to continue in the position of Law School dean, although his post-lease decanal role has been characterized as being "largely

... honorary."[454] In any case, Malone's reappointment to this high-level administrative post may be read as signaling University recognition of the value of his long-term leadership and the need to establish a positive, as well as highly visible, point of continuity during a transition period.[455]

Indeed, the reconstituted plan for the Law School mandated a number of noteworthy changes:[456] (1) Appoint "an active and enthusiastic man" as Law School secretary who, in addition to teaching, would be responsible for overall administration of Law School operations.[457] Among his duties would be "judicious advertising" of the law program, which was expected to cause the Law School's enrollment to be "doubled within a few years."[458] (2) Increase the number of weekly instructional hours offered in each year (junior and senior) of the two-year program from six to a minimum of ten,[459] with moot court being an additional requirement.[460] This adjustment was designed to move the Vanderbilt Law School program toward parity in this regard with other law schools.[461] (3) Schedule class hours, not for the "convenience of the professors" as in the past, but for the benefit of the students.[462] By concentrating course offerings in a certain portion of the day for each of the junior and senior classes, law students would need to undertake only a single daily commute to the Law School; presumably they then would view recently constructed on-campus student housing as a more attractive residential alternative.[463] (4) Rearrange the Law School's space in the Law Building, including provision for a second lecture room, made possible by shifting the Dental School to another location.[464] (5) Expand the size of the law faculty to eight members and pay those individuals predetermined salaries.[465]

Financially, the new arrangement brought the Law School within the general University framework, but the law program still retained a vestige of its former quasi-proprietary nature; the law faculty members would receive a salary bonus if the Law School operations were profitable.[466] In accordance with standard University/departmental accounting practice, the Law School secretary was to collect Law School receipts and transfer those funds to the University bursar who would pay Law School obligations.[467] The University and the law faculty would evenly divide any profit resulting from the operation of the Law School, with the law faculty members' portion to be allocated pro rata on the basis of salary.[468]

Chancellor Kirkland expressed pleasure with the outcome of the reorganization, writing in 1901: "Our professional schools are no longer farmed out to those who will assume the responsibility of administering them without burden to the University or annoyance to the Board. They are now, every one of them, under the care and charge of the Board of Trust, so that one harmonious organization runs through our whole system."[469]

The major features of this reorganization offer an implicit assessment of Vanderbilt Law School during its first quarter century. While Kirkland's words of praise at the end of the lease reflected well on the lessees,[470] more important was the revised approach and direction charted for the Law School. The University committed additional funds and facilities, expanded the faculty and administrative personnel, enhanced the academic demands of the program, and oriented it more toward student needs. These changes were not the response of a disgruntled Board of Trust and Chancellor. Rather, these actions suggest an overall positive evaluation of the quality of legal education provided at Vanderbilt Law School and a judgment that increased resources would lead to a more robust Law School in the twentieth century.

✌ CHAPTER TWO
The Struggle for Respectability

THE CHALLENGE OF LEADERSHIP

The Law School began classes in the fall of 1900 with renewed energy, a university commitment of new resources, and a restructured organization that promised a brighter future.[1] The School had become a more integral part of a highly regarded University. In 1889, the United States Commissioner of Education included Vanderbilt in a tabulation of twelve endowed institutions "which, together with certain of the state universities, approach more nearly the idea of true universities than any other institutions in the country."[2] The additional resources committed by the University in the 1900 reorganization had enlarged the Law faculty and doubled the amount of instruction given to each class.[3] The new Kissam dormitory allowed law students to live on campus, becoming more active participants in the University's intellectual and social life, and lectures were arranged so that students were required to make the trip to downtown classes only once a day.[4]

Unfortunately for the School's future, one reality did not change: the Dean of the Law School remained a part-time position. Thomas Malone stayed on as dean following the reorganization in what was increasingly becoming an honorary capacity. John Bell Keeble, as part-time Secretary of the Law School, was responsible for the day to day direction of the School beginning in 1900, but he resigned the secretaryship and cut down on his teaching just two years later to devote more time to his position as Tennessee attorney for the Louisville & Nashville Railroad.[5]

Malone tendered his resignation letter on June 3, 1904:

For nearly thirty years I have devoted my best efforts to building up a Law School which should be worthy of the other departments of our great University. That we, in fact, have such a school now, we all, I think, believe, its scholarship is sound, rather than specious; its traditions are manly; and the ethical spirit pervading the student body is worthy of all commendation. . . . [the opportunity to build such an institution] I regard, as the chief good fortune of a long career. . . . It seems to me that the best service I can now render to the school . . . is to ask you to place the burden which I have so long borne upon the shoulders of a younger and more competent man.[6]

Malone had been much beloved by the students, a sentiment summed up by a former student a few years after his resignation: "He was, in my day as a student, a universal favorite with the student body. We all admired him, we all loved him. The law faculty then was a strong one. There was Baxter, Reese, Smith and Malone. The others we thought strong men, learned, all good lawyers, one of them a great lawyer, all uncommon men. But in Colonel Malone we saw all these things and—we reverenced him."[7] Despite Malone's many strengths, however, it was clear that a full-time dean was called for if Vanderbilt was to keep pace with the development of legal education in America.

Chancellor Kirkland, rather than seeking a full-time leader for the Law School, pursued Horace Lurton for the deanship. Lurton was then serving as a judge on the Sixth Circuit Court of Appeals based in Cincinnati, certainly a full-time job, and he spent half of each month in Ohio when the court was in session. Lurton understood the problems with a part-time deanship, writing to Kirkland on September 23, 1904: "I greatly regret that you are unable to get a working head for the Law Department. My time is so fully occupied that I can at most be a figure head. But if this is the very best you can do I will serve as locum tenens until you can do better, or I see that I can no longer afford to pretend to fill a place which I do not fill."[8] Two weeks later, Lurton reiterated the point in a most reluctant acceptance letter: "I am sorry you have had to fall upon me for Dean. The office needs a man who can give his whole time to the Law School. I will however serve as best I can hoping you will soon find some one to take my place."[9]

Lurton had joined the faculty on a part-time basis in 1898, teaching his Constitutional Law and Federal Procedure class in a 14-day period during which the class met every day. He served as dean from 1904 until he was appointed to the U.S. Supreme Court in 1910 by President William Howard Taft, who had served with him on the Sixth Circuit Court of Appeals. Lurton came to the job with an ambitious agenda, advocating a full three-year curriculum and increased graduation standards, so that the School could meet the standards for joining the recently-established Association of American Law Schools.[10] But Lurton's inability to tend consistently to

Law School details was a problem even before he became dean. Action at a faculty meeting on May 7, 1904, for example, was postponed and a special meeting was called for May 21, "this being a date on which Judge Lurton would be able to attend." The May 21 meeting was cancelled because of absences, and it was noted that "Judge Lurton was absent from the city" when the next faculty meeting was held on June 13th.[11]

This inconsistent pattern did not change upon his assumption of the deanship. As Kirkland reported to the Board in 1907: "Judge Lurton, who holds the office of Dean is absent from Nashville most of the time and rarely concerns himself with the Law Department. He considers his position rather a matter of form; at least, so far as administration is concerned."[12] In announcing Lurton's resignation to the Board, Kirkland's praise was faint, at best: "Judge Lurton's connection with the department has been of great value to us chiefly be [sic] reason of his wide reputation and ability as a lecturer. He has not had time to give any attention to the detailed administration of student affairs. He has, however, given a most acceptable course of lectures each year on International Law."[13]

Having recognized the danger inherent in the part-time deanships of Malone and Lurton, Kirkland's solution to the problem came in the person of Allen G. Hall. In 1903, after Keeble stepped down as Secretary of the Law School, Kirkland persuaded the Board that it was "very important that the services of someone should be secured who can give his time exclusively to the department. . . . There is at present no center for the department. . . . and in general the department has been left to shift for itself."[14] Hall became the School's first full-time faculty member in 1903, serving as Professor, Secretary, and the school's Librarian. The next year, he added duties as rental agent for the Law Building, managing the leases of excess space to attorneys and businesses, for which he received the "usual commission of 5% on all collections made."[15] His responsibilities expanded further in 1907, when the Board accepted Kirkland's recommendation that Hall be appointed Chairman of the Faculty "with all the authority usually vested in the Dean, this authority to be exercised by Hall, both toward faculty and students, at all times in the absence of the Dean."[16] As indicated above, those times were numerous.

The notion of teaching law as a career was developing in the United States between 1870 and 1900. While most law professors were still part-time teachers at the turn of the century, the appointment of full-time, salaried law professors was growing among elite university law schools.[17] Allen G. Hall was cut from that mold.

Hall, a Vanderbilt law graduate of 1885, had resigned from the practice of law in 1898 because of ill health. Following a period of recuperation, he taught at the Nashville High School until joining the Vanderbilt faculty. Despite his physical infirmities, he was vigorous in mind and spirit, and he threw himself into his Law School duties. When Lurton stepped down in 1910, Kirkland quickly recommended Hall to the Board as the School's first full-time dean, noting, "The real management of the department has been all the while in the hands of Dr. Allen G. Hall."[18] While Hall's deanship was cut short by his death in the fall of 1915, the School's achievements under his leadership were substantial.

Chancellor Kirkland would later write a brief history of the Law School in which he identified five important changes that took place during Hall's administration: (1) the casebook method of instruction was adopted; (2) the School became a member of the AALS; (3) a full-time dean was employed and provision was made for additional full-time faculty; (4) the School was moved into College Hall on campus and became an integral part of University life; and (5) the change in organization from a Department of the University into a School of Law was effected.[19] One of Hall's dreams that was not fulfilled was the creation of a graduate program in law. He secured Board of Trust approval in principle of such a program in 1907, with the authority for arranging the details of a Master of Laws program delegated to the Board's Executive Committee, upon the presentation of a course of study by the faculty.[20] This plan, however, was almost a century in its incubation. The first LL.M. students were not enrolled at Vanderbilt until 2001.

Hall's push for greater professionalism included a dramatic restructuring of the School over the summer of 1909, as part of the implementation of a new three-year degree program. Upon his request, the Board officially terminated the connection of all members of the faculty as of the end of the spring 1909 term, and asked Hall (not Dean Lurton) to recommend a faculty for the School. Hall wrote to Kirkland that March: "I think professors should be employed with the understanding that they are not 'fixtures,' but may be retired when their work becomes unsatisfactory." The restructuring resulted in the termination of only one faculty member, the promotion of a second, and the hiring of a third—with an eye toward eventually moving these two men into full-time positions.[21]

Hall also was a strong advocate of the case method of teaching, and thus the requirement that all faculty members use casebooks was another feature of the restructuring. Previously, faculty had been allowed to choose their own method of instruction, but Hall would have none of it: "No first-class Law School tolerates in its regular course the Lecture System or the use of what is known as the 'Horn-Book,' a sort of 'pony of the law,' for lazy students and teachers." The "modern method" which embraced the "Case System" would now be required in all regular courses.[22]

Hall was intense in his efforts to improve classroom work at the Law School. He kept lists of his colleagues' absences, late arrivals, and early dismissals, occasionally sending letters to faculty asking for a detailed reporting of their hours of instruction or informing them of deficiencies that he had observed.[23] He took faculty to task for giving exams that were not "creditable to this department" and for giving grades that were too high.[24] As he complained to the Chancellor in his annual report in 1915: "My impression is that the work in the Law School has not been as strenuous as in former times and that many students in all the classes are doing rather poorer work than usual. I attribute this to a number of causes: one in particular—that professors are not as exacting of students as they should be and that their examinations are not sufficiently rigid to be a real test of the student's progress and proficiency."[25]

His own rigor in the classroom was the source of student complaints, such as this resolution adopted by the Junior Class before he became dean:

WHEREAS Prof. Allen G. Hall, of the Law Faculty of Vanderbilt University adopts rules in his classes which seem to us incompatible with the dictates of ordinary justice, such as 'Not one of you, no matter what his grade may be on daily classes or on examinations, will get a 'pass' under me, if he has a single unexplained absence against him.' And again: 'No one will pass under me who leaves my class before the end of my lecture.' And

WHEREAS he, although entitled to keep us only one hour, persists in keeping us from fifteen to forty-five minutes over-time in lengthy lectures on points that often require little or no explanation. And

WHEREAS he treats us as if we were high school boys and falsifiers, rather than as grown-up and responsible young men, as is shown by such an assertion as: 'When one of you young men tell me that you are compelled to miss my lecture on account of *private business,* I take the statement *not* with a *grain* of salt but with a *barrel.*'

NOW THEREFORE, BE IT RESOLVED by the Junior Law Class

(First) That we petition Dr. James H. Kirkland, Chancellor of this University, and Judge Thos. H. Malone, Dean of the Law Department, to take such steps as will afford us the necessary relief.

(Second) That a copy of these resolutions be mailed to Dr. Kirkland, Judge Malone, and Mr. Allen G. Hall.[26]

Student dissatisfaction with Hall may have had something to do with his efforts to eliminate the "pernicious habit" that had developed for a class, as a whole, to cut a recitation "if a majority of the members desired to attend any special entertainment or for any reason wished to absent themselves."[27]

Hall's continuing health problems interfered with his ability to work from time to time. Because he was not able to do any work in February and March of 1908, substitute teachers for his classes had to be found. By November of 1908, on the advice of his physician, he had eliminated all activities except those which were required by his routine duties at the Law School. Something of a perfectionist, Hall never seemed satisfied with his work. Despite the dramatic improvements he had brought to the School, he rendered this assessment in his May 1914, annual report to the Chancellor: "Upon the whole I should say we are getting on in a fair kind of way in the Law Department, but I am by no means satisfied and am eagerly looking forward to a time when we shall be able to make some radical changes. I realize that it would take money to develop the school along the lines I have in mind."[28] In September 1914, the Board authorized the Chancellor to make arrangements to give Hall a leave to recuperate from a summer illness. Faculty member Charles H. Wilber signed faculty meeting minutes as Acting Dean, and attended the AALS annual meeting in that capacity that year. Hall returned to his duties in the spring, but suffered another relapse and died on November 28, 1915.[29] In mourning his loss, the University's obituary recognized him as "the organizer of the new school and the guide of its destinies."[30]

Almost inexplicably, Vanderbilt returned to the model of a part-time dean after the five years of Hall's deanship. It is "almost" inexplicable because one can imagine that students, faculty, and administrators alike would have preferred a more congenial atmosphere after the hard-driving Hall years. However, major law schools across the country had long since established full-time deanships, as schools moved from appointing a "faculty member who could also administer," to appointing "an administrator who could perform as a faculty member."[31] The University turned to John Bell Keeble to assume the deanship on a part-time basis, beginning as an Acting Dean on November 30, 1915. In less than four years, Kirkland would report to the Board of Trust about negligent and indifferent students, and faculty who regarded their classes as unimportant tasks, commenting: "The situation during the present year is in striking contrast with that which existed during the days of Dr. Allen Hall, who erred, if he erred at all, on the other extreme."[32]

In many ways, Keeble was a good choice for dean. An 1888 graduate of the Law School, he had been an active leader in the School as a student, although not always in ways that would have foreshadowed his becoming a dean. He denounced university disciplinary rules in an editorial in the *Observer* (the earliest of the Vanderbilt student magazines), and he led the famed protest march out of the Main Building when John Sherman, the brother of Union General William Tecumseh Sherman, spoke in the chapel at the invitation of Chancellor Garland.[33] By the time of his selection as dean, he had served on the faculty for almost twenty years as a professor who "won the admiration of hundreds of students by his great knowledge of Constitutional Law. His justice has been tempered with mercy, and there is no student who has not drawn inspiration from him."[34] Keeble had been active in alumni affairs, was a prominent, successful attorney, and had played a leading role in representing Vanderbilt in the law suit that led to the University's separation from the Methodist Church in 1914. But he was a busy man, and was in "full accord" with Kirkland's view that "ultimately the Law department should be placed in the hands of a Dean who is not engaged in active practice."[35] They both knew better, but after appointing Keeble to be Acting Dean in 1915, Kirkland then appointed him dean for a two-year term (the shortest period of time in which Kirkland thought a permanent dean could be found), and he was still dean in December 1926, when Vanderbilt was excluded from the AALS.

Words of warning about the School's drift were frequent. With Hall's death, the School had lost its only full-time faculty member. In the summer of 1916, Keeble reported "Unless we can secure the full time of a capable teacher, for the coming year, I believe it will cause the loss of prestige and students that it will require years to regain."[36] There were breakdowns in communication—covering such administrative matters as scheduling classes, teaching assignments, and accrediting association requirements—between Keeble and Professors Wilber and H. B. Schermerhorn, who at times served in the capacity of part-time Secretary of the School. Kirkland reminded the Board in 1919 that Keeble's business obligations did not allow him to devote time to the school, "save as a passing incident:" "Mr. Keeble is holding this position only because there is no one else available. He has repeatedly indicated his readiness to give it up if we can get someone suited for the position who can give his whole time to the School. My feeling is that this ought to be done as quickly as possible."[37]

By June 1926, Kirkland would report that the school was "largely in the hands of the Librarian, Mrs. Davidson, and the Assistant Secretary, Mrs. Chester," which he saw as wholly unsatisfactory. Yet, he said, "Mr. Keeble's long connection with the school, and his deep interest in it, make a radical change at the present time impossible and unadvisable."[38] But radical change did come, when Vanderbilt was expelled from the AALS at the end of that year, on December 31, 1926.

It is unclear why Kirkland and the University followed the pattern of part-time deanships through Malone, Lurton and, after the brief break of Hall's tenure, with Keeble. Could it have been a commitment to an increasingly out-of-date image of a dean that focused more on reputation and public stature than on the leadership that a dean should bring to the School? Were financial considerations a factor, leading to choices of smaller part-time salaries in the face of the resource problems that are described below? Even in persuading the Board to appoint Hall as the first full-time faculty member, Kirkland suggested that his remuneration should depend to some extent on the School's tuition revenue, and that attendance would increase in the wake of such an appointment so that the School would cease to be an expense for the University.[39] Perhaps personal relationships were key elements in these choices. Kirkland had relationships with Malone, Lurton, and Keeble in the years before naming them to their Twentieth Century deanships. Edwin Mims, Vanderbilt historian as well as friend and confidant of Kirkland's, referred to Keeble as "one of the most prominent alumni of the University," counting him among the "distinguished men" who were "special friends of the Chancellor."[40]

For whatever reason, Vanderbilt by and large stayed with the pattern of part-time leadership until it was too late. While the model was eventually abandoned with the appointment of Earl C. Arnold in 1930, by the time he came to office the School was heavily burdened by low enrollments, the AALS rebuke, insufficient financial resources, inadequate physical space, and years of Board of Trust neglect—too burdened by all of this to be able to meet the twin challenges of the Great Depression and World War II.

A NATIONAL EMBARRASSMENT

The Association of American Law Schools (AALS) was founded in 1900 with thirty-two charter members, for the purpose of improving the legal profession through legal education. Vanderbilt Law School was represented by faculty member J. C. Bradford at the meeting at which the association was created in Saratoga Springs, New York, on August 28, 1900.[41] Growing out of the ABA Section on Legal Education, the new organization would add authority to the opinions that had been expressed by that section—at least for the schools that wished to maintain membership in this select circle.[42] All of the thirty-five schools represented at the meeting were designated as charter members of the association *if* they met minimum standards for the admission of students (including a high school diploma or its equivalent) and for the length of the degree program (two years of thirty weeks of classes, soon to become three years).[43] Vanderbilt, however, was not able to meet the association's requirements until 1910 when it lengthened its degree program to three years.[44] Dean Lurton pushed the University for the longer program and membership in the AALS, arguing that it was difficult to explain to better students that Vanderbilt was a first-class school when it was not eligible to join the sole national organization of law schools. He pointed out that the Law School was the only department of the University that did not conform to the standards of its national association, and reported that all members of the law faculty were "heartily in favor" of adopting the three-year course of study as soon as possible.[45]

Strong student support also developed for the new three-year program. When the John Marshall Law Club debated the issue in 1914, the club voted unanimously in favor of the recently-adopted course of study instead of the two-year program. Cecil Sims persuasively argued the case; as the club minutes reported, "Mr. Sims' speech undoubtedly won the debate, and it was decided that this vote should be made known to Dr. Hall."[46]

From 1910 to 1925, Vanderbilt's participation in the professional organization was uneventful. But the AALS required periodic inspection visits of all schools as a condition of continued membership, and Claude Horack, a member of the University of Iowa law faculty and Secretary of the AALS, conducted such a two-day visit at Vanderbilt in October 1926. It is apparent that Vanderbilt did not take the visit seriously. Dean Keeble did not meet with Horack. Professor Schermerhorn, the faculty Secretary, had a brief interview with him, and Horack was left to examine the school's program and records with administrative staff. As Chancellor Kirkland later commented, "I am sure that Horack went away feeling personally aggrieved because of the apparent discourtesy with which his whole visit was received."[47]

Vanderbilt began to take this re-inspection visit seriously two months later when Professor Morton Hendrick, attending the AALS annual meeting as Vanderbilt's representative, sent the following telegram to Keeble the afternoon of December 29th:

```
EXECUTIVE COMMITTEE MET YESTERDAY TUESDAY CLAIMS
YOU WERE NOTIFIED TO BE PRESENT REPORTED THIS
MORNINGS MEETING TO EXCLUDE MISSISSIPPI AND
VANDERBILT AND TO PLACE WASHINGTON UNIVERSITY
ON PROBATION FOR TWO YEARS CARRIED EXCEPT AS
```

TO VANDERBILT PRIOR TO MEETING I SAW AIGLER AND
HORACK DISCOVERED CONTENTS OF REPORT THEY CALLED
SPECIAL MEETING COMMITTEE AS RESULT FINAL VOTE
ON VANDERBILT DEFERRED UNTIL FRIDAY YOU TO MEET
COMMITTEE FRIDAY MORNING NINE IMPERATIVE BETTER BE
HERE TOMORROW PREPARED TO MAKE FULL CONCESSIONS BE
SURE TO SEE ME FIRST ON ARRIVAL ANSWER.

In this way did Dean Keeble receive notice that Vanderbilt was scheduled to be expelled from the association in two days. Keeble did appear at that Friday meeting to argue the School's case, but by that time the die had been cast.

When Kirkland later reviewed the matter, he concluded that neither Keeble nor Schermerhorn had paid adequate attention to these matters, and that neither of them understood the association's requirements or had enforced them properly. In the end, he concluded, the AALS charges of general neglect were sustained by the record.[48] An illustration of the lack of administrative attention to important detail can be found in this exchange on the floor of the meeting, after Keeble arrived and declared that he was hearing some of the charges for the first time:

> Horack: "I took these cases up with the people who were in charge of your office, and they went over each case with me to find the facts. Whether they reported to you I cannot say."
>
> Keeble: "You took that up with Mrs. Davidson and Mrs. Chesney? They are merely women working in the office. You did write to us that you found some objection and that you expected to bring it up here . . ."
>
> Ira P. Hildebrand [Texas]: "Did the Secretary telegraph you before he went to your school that he would be there?"
>
> Keeble: "Yes, but I did not understand why. . . . Now, you want me to be perfectly frank. I find I was mistaken about Mr. Horack. It is not the first time I have been mistaken. I thought Mr. Horack was taking a trip."[49]

The focal point of the association's concern was the admission of students, but there were other aspects of the operation of Vanderbilt Law School that troubled Professor Horack and others. The arrangement of the class schedule and the work of students outside the school gave it the appearance of a part-time school that would not be eligible for certification as a full-time school.[50] The school's building space, the condition of the library, and the reliance on a part-time dean were other specific issues that surfaced.[51] But the proverbial "smoking gun" was the admission of students who did not meet AALS requirements. The Executive Committee's recommendation that Vanderbilt be excluded from membership was based upon its finding that the School had failed to comply with the standards on the amount of college work required for admission, and the number of special students (students who did not meet the admissions standards) who could be admitted each year.[52] A motion to substitute probation for the Committee's recommendation of exclusion failed on a 13–36 vote, and then the expulsion was approved without a vote count recorded.[53]

Vanderbilt had run afoul of two AALS standards: a new admission standard that went into effect in the fall of 1925, requiring that a student complete two years of college work prior to admission to member law schools, and a standard passed in 1922 that limited the number of special students that could be admitted who did not meet the basic admission standard. ("Special students" were not eligible to receive a law degree.) The steady rise in law school admission standards across the country were highly controversial. Many law faculties in the early twentieth century lobbied for higher admission standards, wanting to distinguish their schools from part-time and night schools.[54] Harvard led the way, requiring a college degree for law school admittance by 1896.[55] Other law schools, however, resisted the movement to increase admission standards. Yale was in the forefront of the opposition, with President Arthur Twining Hadley asserting, "I believe that we should strive to widen rather than narrow the range of those we can reach by our professional schools." His concern was that such a degree requirement for admission would make "the professions of law and medicine places for the sons of rich men only."[56] Virginia did not require a high school diploma for admission until 1903, the Board of Regents at Michigan rejected a 1908 request from the law faculty that a year of college work be required for admission, and the President of Northwestern denounced a law faculty proposal in 1916 that three years of college work be required.[57] But the pressures for heightened standards proved to be inexorable, and Vanderbilt proceeded with increasing its own admission standards, at its own pace.

In 1907, the University's Board had approved a faculty recommendation of an admission standard that required "the presentation of a diploma or certificate covering at least a High School course or the standing of an examination including as much."[58] Kirkland suggested, in 1914, the pos-

sibility of raising the Law School entrance standard to match the medical
school standard of one year of college work, observing that "the study of law
is difficult, especially as conducted under the case method of teaching, for
immature pupils fresh from High School." However, a year later he was reporting to the Board of Trust a large decrease in enrollment in the medical
school and noted that "the chief cause was the increase in requirements for
admission."[59]

One year of college work became a requirement for admission to Vanderbilt Law School in 1921, with Kirkland recommending Board approval
of Keeble's proposal. The application of the new standard was delayed until
the fall of 1923, and by then the AALS had already approved an admission
requirement of two years of college work to go into effect in 1925. Vanderbilt formally adopted the AALS-mandated two-year requirement, but its
abuse in admitting special students led to its expulsion. AALS standards
allowed up to ten percent of an entering class to be special students, students who did not meet the two-years-of-college requirement, but Horack's
inspection of the records found more than twice the number of permitted
special students in both the first-year and second-year classes.[60] While these
special students were non-degree students, they were nonetheless an attractive source of income for law schools, as only the study of law—not a law
degree—was required to sit for bar examinations.

Dean Keeble, in his public statements on the expulsion from the AALS,
addressed the violations of the association's standards. One rule required
two years of college work for admission, but it also allowed three hours
of the work to have "conditions." The second was the limit on the number of special students allowed. Keeble stated that the first standard was
violated unwittingly because of a misinterpretation of the meaning of the
word "conditions." The second rule, he said, was violated unintentionally
in 1925–26, but the fault was remedied in the following year.[61] The public
University position, as published by Vanderbilt three years later at the time
of the School's readmission to the association, was: "The School of Law had
violated only technical rules, and did not cease to be a splendid and efficient
law school."[62]

The Law School's exclusion from the AALS was a stunning blow for
Kirkland. He had long been a strong, public advocate for high educational
standards. When the Southern Association of Colleges and Schools (SACS)
was formed in 1895, it was Kirkland who drafted the statement of purpose
and wrote the by-laws. He was a member of the Executive Committee of
that association for forty years, as well as serving terms as President, Secretary, and Treasurer. In 1906, when the Association of American Universities

invited the Southern Association to meet with representatives from similar regional accrediting associations, it was Kirkland who represented SACS, and he was named Vice-President of the National Conference Committee on Standards of Colleges and Secondary Schools that resulted from that meeting. As Mims noted, "Vigorously Kirkland denounced frauds in educational work."[63]

Now, in 1926 his own Law School had been expelled from the AALS. He was forced to admit to his Board of Trust that his previous year's report to them, describing the Law School's success in meeting the new admission standards, had been "ill-advised."[64] Keeble and Schermerhorn both offered to resign. Publicly, Kirkland refused to accept their offers, saying that no good could be accomplished by accepting them.[65] But he knew a change had to be made. He wrote to Board of Trust member E. E. Barthell, asking for his help in identifying a person who could serve as a full-time dean "such as was Allen Hall." He further noted: "I do not wish Mr. Keeble to know that I am making inquiries regarding a possible successor . . . I am perfectly clear that this Law School cannot be satisfactorily administered either by Keeble or Schermerhorn or both of them."[66]

A review of the record makes it clear that Vanderbilt did, indeed, fail to adhere strictly to AALS standards. But there is evidence that the harshness of the sanction was due, at least in part, to the personal insult Horack perceived in the dismissive way in which he and his inspection visit were treated. There was close cooperation between the AALS and the ABA in the 1920s, after a period in which little progress was made in increasing standards in legal education because of conflict between the two national organizations.[67] Professors packed the 1920 meeting of the ABA Section on Legal Education and Admission to the Bar and thus gained control of the section. In the following years, the ABA and the AALS worked hand in glove, repeatedly raising standards, with one association often adopting a standard that was in place at the other organization.[68] By the autumn of 1925, conformity among the standards of the two associations had been achieved.[69] Yet, while AALS and ABA standards were essentially the same, Vanderbilt did not lose its ABA accreditation.

The ABA had published its first list of approved schools in November 1923, supplemented by a "Class B" list of schools. The Schools in Class B did not comply with the association's standards at that time, but they had announced their intent to comply in the near future.[70] Vanderbilt was not included on either inaugural list, but the next month the School was added to Class B as a result of information received after the initial publication.[71] Vanderbilt received full ABA approval in 1925. After the AALS exclusion,

the Secretary of the Section on Legal Education of the ABA made an inspection visit and the School's approval by the ABA was continued.[72] After
the list of schools approved by the ABA and AALS had become identical in
the spring of 1926, Vanderbilt became one of five schools listed by the ABA
but not the AALS by 1928.[73]

While Kirkland acknowledged the admissions failures and held Keeble
responsible, he took exception to Horack's criticism of the part-time nature
of the School's program: "This criticism of Mr. Horack was resented very
bitterly by Dean Keeble, and it seemed also very unjust to me."[74] Kirkland
concluded that it would be very difficult to secure readmission to the association as long as Horack was the administrative officer.[75] Thus he must
have been dismayed when Horack, while still Secretary of the AALS, was
named the ABA's first full-time adviser on legal education in 1927—with
the primary assignment of raising the standards of law schools and of bar
admissions—and then was elected President of the AALS in 1928.[76]

Kirkland's urgent task was to get the School back on track. He observed
that the School's one great need for more personal supervision by "responsible officers" became even greater, as "both of the women who have been
assisting in the administration of the School of Law [Ms. Chester and Ms.
Davidson], have recently resigned. . . . To students, it looks as if the whole
school were disintegrating."[77] In June 1927, Kirkland told the Board that a
full-time administrative officer needed to be found immediately to attend to
the management of the School, but only two weeks later he reported that a
satisfactory appointment could not be made at that time, and thus Professor
Morton Hendrick was recommended as a part-time Assistant to the Dean
for the coming year.[78] A year later, this picture was unchanged, as Hendrick
was extended for another year: "Mr. Hendrick does not possess the personal
qualifications that make him an attractive officer in this capacity. However,
we are not able to suggest any improvement at the present time and under
present financial conditions."[79]

While stymied on the personnel front, Kirkland and Keeble made progress elsewhere. The Law School catalogue embodied an important change,
adding the phrase "at the time of the admission to the school" to the published admissions standard that required the certification of completion of
two years of college work. By the summer of 1928, Kirkland reported that
in addition to enforcing admissions standards, the School had renovated its
law library—adding desks and stacks, better lighting, and purchasing books
to complete broken sets. The appointment of Professor John Howard Moore
as Librarian had proved to be very satisfactory and was regarded as more or
less permanent.[80] In June 1929, Kirkland noted in his report to the Board

the continued progress the School was making in complying with AALS admission requirements: "It is believed that our record is clean in this particular. It is further believed that with a similar record for the summer law school and for the entering class of 1929 we may be ready to apply to the Association for re-admission in December 1929."[81]

The readmission process actually began the next month, when Albert J. Harno, the new Secretary of the AALS, sent a questionnaire to Dean Keeble on July 15th, to be completed as part of the School's application for readmission. The School's part-time administration was still a problem, however, as Harno asked Keeble in September if Vanderbilt still intended to apply for readmission. Harno wrote that he had received no response from the School, and that the completed questionnaire had to be submitted in the near future if he was going to be able to do the required site visit and evaluation prior to the association's December meeting. Keeble, in turn, wrote to Schermerhorn: "Sometime ago, I sent you a questionnaire that Mr. Harno had sent to be filled out in order to be presented to him with an application to be admitted into the Association of American Law Schools. I have been out of the city a good deal, but it is evident that you have failed to have this filled out."[82]

Keeble died suddenly on October 10, 1929. Kirkland had lost a good friend, and was now faced with replacing a dean that he had already been unable to replace. With the important business of being readmitted to the AALS looming, he was in no mood to receive an October 26, 1929, letter from Harno, informing him that the AALS Executive Committee had deferred action on Vanderbilt's petition for re-entry until they had received more information about the Law School's library expenditures, its intentions concerning a new dean, and any plans for "more satisfactory and dignified quarters."[83] The degree to which the Chancellor's patience had been tested once too often by the association can only be fully appreciated by a reading of Kirkland's own words in a November 6, 1929, reply to Harno:

> Your first statement that Vanderbilt University has failed to comply with the requirement of the Association in the matter of library additions came as a distinct surprise to me. . . . As soon as we were excluded I authorized and instructed Dean Keeble to take steps to meet in every particular the requirements of the Association. . . . I am enclosing herewith a statement made out with the greatest of care under direction by the Bursar of the University and the Librarian of the School of Law. If necessary it can be sworn to before a Notary Public. You may depend on its accuracy. If you were furnished figures different from these

given herewith they were certainly given in error and without a clear understanding of the case. . . . In light of this report it would seem to me that your first criticism of our School of Law will have to be modified very considerably when you next make a report to the Executive Committee.

Concerning a permanent dean:

I can assure you that your concern in this matter can be no greater than our own. . . . We realize that the future of the School of Law is largely dependent on the action taken at this time. . . . You cannot be ignorant of the fact that the attitude of your Committee makes our position all the more difficult.

And on the building:

It is perhaps true that these quarters are not as dignified as might be wished. At the same time they are entirely adequate for good work, and need not affect adversely any class room work that we offer. . . . If the Association has established certain requirements in the matter of buildings Vanderbilt University will either meet those requirements or withdraw its application.[84]

On December 27, 1929, Vanderbilt was unanimously re-elected to membership in the Association of American Law Schools. Professor Harno made the motion. Professor Horack was the presiding officer.[85]

GEOGRAPHIC CAPTURE

One of Allen Hall's priorities, from the beginning of his tenure as Secretary in 1903, had been to gain admission to the Association of American Law Schools for Vanderbilt. After years of preparation and progress, he sent an inquiry in the spring of 1909 to W. R. Vance, the Secretary of the AALS, accompanied by a copy of the School's new catalogue. Hall wrote:

May I ask whether this announcement complies in all particulars with the rules of your association, so as to render us eligible to selection? I have had considerable correspondence in respect to this matter from various members of the Association of American Law Schools, and it occurs to me that it is about as hard for a Southern Law School to break into your Association as it is for a plutocrat to get into the Kingdom of Heaven. If there are any "i's" to be dotted or any "t's" to be crossed, be kind enough to advise me and we will try to cross and dot.[86]

Allen Hall never looked for excuses. If he thought that a law school in the South faced an uphill battle to achieve national respectability, then it was probably true. Cornelius Vanderbilt's founding gift for the University was made to strengthen "the ties which should exist between all geographic sections of our common country," but decades later Vanderbilt remained very much a captive of the region in which it was located.

The University of Tennessee was the only Southern law school to be admitted to the AALS as a charter member in 1900, but by 1905 that school was facing exclusion from the association because it did not yet have a three-year course of study. At the organizational meeting in 1900, the "older and stronger and larger" schools had agreed to a concession which gave southern schools five years to meet the three-year degree program requirement. At the 1905 meeting, rather than acting to make the AALS an association of only northern law schools—Tennessee was the only member school located south of the Ohio River—the membership referred the matter of Tennessee's continuing status to the Executive Committee for consideration with a report expected the next year.[87] Tennessee was financially unable to sustain a third year of instruction, and its AALS membership was suspended until 1913, when a three-year program was adopted.[88]

The difficulties associated with a law school's location in the South were explicitly addressed again on the floor of the AALS annual meeting in 1926 when Vanderbilt's exclusion was being considered. Keeble raised it himself, talking about low educational standards in the South in general, and in Tennessee in particular, and of a law school's obligation to "not go too rapidly beyond the exigencies of the community that we serve."[89] J. Nelson Frierson of South Carolina moved that Vanderbilt be placed on probation for one year, stating that exclusion would cast "an unjustifiable slur upon the whole South."[90]

Even those voting in favor of Vanderbilt's exclusion acknowledged the "Southern problem." The comments of H. W. Arant, of Kansas, articulated that point of view:

> I was for a time connected with a Southern law school. I was born in the South, and I know all about it—all about the difficulties of which Dean Keeble has spoken. . . . I know the difficulty that the Southern law school has in getting money, and I know something about the small

salaries that are paid in Southern law schools from rather intimate contact with those salaries. . . . I wished many times during the four or five years that I tried to do my bit in elevating legal education in the South that something of this sort might have happened that would jar the University into a realization that in some way or other somebody had to be shaken loose from more money than they were spending, and, Dean Keeble, I would have welcomed some such thing as this when I was associated with that Southern institution.[91]

These brief glimpses of the workings of the AALS illustrate a fact of life in the first half of the twentieth century for universities and law schools located in the South. The economic, educational, social, and cultural realities in the region presented enormous obstacles for those schools who were trying to establish academic respectability on the national scene. By almost any economic indicator the South lagged behind the rest of the country. Per capita income in the region was only 62% of the national average in 1920, and efforts to secure northern investment for economic development largely failed. Measures of educational achievement at all levels were similarly lower.[92] In a candid moment with his Board of Trust, Chancellor Kirkland voiced what was widely understood: "We have frequently compared our work with that of large and flourishing institutions in other parts of the country, with great universities like Harvard, Princeton and Chicago. In reality we have never been in a position to compare ourselves with these institutions."[93] As he acknowledged later, even if Vanderbilt achieved his goal of becoming the best law school in the South, that would place it only among "the good law schools of the entire country."[94]

While Vanderbilt deans could claim that the Law School was "one of the few truly national schools in the country," citing the large number of states represented in the student body,[95] records from that era make clear that the benchmarks used to evaluate the School's operation were drawn from the South. When the School's enrollment plummeted to 83 students in 1928/29, this was reported as a decline similar to that in other southern law schools.[96] Vanderbilt was constantly operating under what were perceived to be regional constraints concerning the amount of tuition they could charge, which in turn affected the size of faculty salaries they could offer, and the level of admission requirements they could sustain.[97] Speaking at a Vanderbilt Symposium on Higher Education in the South in 1938, Herschel Whitfield Arant, at that time Dean of the Ohio State University College of Law and Secretary of the AALS, was blunt in speaking to his Nashville audience: "It is hardly too much to say that, until twenty-five years ago, with the exception of the University of Virginia, there was no law school in the South that had been generally recognized as a first-class law school."[98] Vanderbilt was very much a product of that region.

Vanderbilt's general disadvantage of being located in the South, in terms of developing and sustaining a high quality academic program, was compounded by the particular disadvantage of operating a law school in the state of Tennessee. In 1902, Tennessee was probably the "most amply served" state in the nation, with one law school for every 225,000 residents.[99] This hyper-competitive market was the result of a diploma privilege, which allowed judges and the faculties of law schools to issue licenses to practice law, and the lack of any regulation in the state as to what constituted a "law school." This combination led to institutions such as the Nashville College Law School (sometimes called the National College of Law), which began offering law degrees by correspondence in 1899, "doing little more than selling degrees."[100]

The diploma privilege, on the books in Tennessee since 1859, was repealed in 1903 when the legislature created a Board of Law Examiners that consisted of three members appointed by the state Supreme Court, and required all applicants to pass the board's examination.[101] The Tennessee Bar Association had been actively lobbying for this change for sixteen years, with James C. McReynolds among the leaders of the effort.[102] Another step was taken in 1919, when the Tennessee Supreme Court revised the rules under which the Board operated. The new rules required, as a prerequisite to taking the state bar exam, a high school education and at least one year of studying law in a reputable law school or in the offices of a reputable lawyer who had been a member of the state Supreme Court bar for at least five years. In an effort to deter fraud, the rules stipulated that the board be given at least a month to consider an application, and the board revised its processes, providing the names and addresses of all applicants to the state and local bar associations "to expose one to the public to see if his moral character could withstand critical public scrutiny."[103]

While these changes could only work to Vanderbilt's advantage in its efforts to recruit a student body of an adequate size, the School still found itself competing in a regional market—with competitors who had lower admission standards, shorter degree programs, and usually lower tuition rates. Vanderbilt's response was to strengthen the quality of its academic program and to emphasize that difference to prospective students. The deans and faculty were intent on improving the quality and rigor of a Vanderbilt Law School education for their own purposes. But it was also the case that public recognition of the quality of the school's education was important for the recruitment of students. The School's membership in the Association of American Law Schools was an ingredient in the School's larger strategy: Vanderbilt had to market itself as providing an education that was worth the additional time and money required of students—students who could obtain a law degree for less money, in less time, at Cumberland Law School and other schools in the region.

Vanderbilt was especially keen to distinguish itself from Cumberland, which was clearly the leading competitor among the non-accredited schools in the area (Cumberland would receive ABA approval in 1949). By 1920–21, Cumberland was the only law school in the country that still had a one-year program for earning a law degree.[104] While Cumberland had declined from its nineteenth century peak when it enrolled more students than Harvard, it still registered twice as many students as Vanderbilt in the 1920s, charging them less tuition for the entire degree than Vanderbilt did in each of its three years. When asked by the registrar of the University of Missouri Law School in 1920 if transfer credits should be accepted from Cumberland, Vanderbilt's registrar responded that Vanderbilt did not allow credit for the work done there, while commenting that Cumberland did give a "thorough drill" to students preparing to take the Tennessee bar exam—implying, of course, that Vanderbilt sought to do much more in its educational program.[105]

The regional context presented Vanderbilt with two cross-currents that had to be navigated. On the one hand, the economic and cultural realities of the South posed significant obstacles to efforts to create an academic program that would rival those of major schools in other parts of the country. On the other hand, competition for students with unaccredited schools in the region, and especially in Tennessee, made it imperative that Vanderbilt develop an educational program that clearly offered more than could be found in those competing institutions. The Law School would not successfully overcome these regional obstacles until after World War II.

STANDARDS AND STUDENTS

In the early 1900s, the national legal education establishment defined the improvement of educational quality as the adoption of the case method of instruction. While a few law faculties challenged the case method of teaching that had emerged from Christopher Columbus Langdell's Harvard of the late nineteenth century,[106] Hall and Kirkland hitched Vanderbilt to that bandwagon. In 1902, a report to the ABA indicated that "only twelve law schools adopted the case method, thirty-four maintained unequivocally the textbook system, and forty-eight schools admitted some sort of mixture."[107] But in those early years of the twentieth century the tide had already turned in favor of the case method.[108] By 1908, thirty schools had adopted this approach to instruction.[109] In 1912, nearly every course at Yale was taught with casebooks and the faculty passed a resolution allowing an instructor to use the case method in any course, even a first-year class, if he had the permission of the dean.[110]

Vanderbilt Law School announced its purpose, in the 1901/02 catalogue, as giving "the student a liberal training in the fundamental principles of every important branch of the profession, and not merely to give him a license to practice law in Tennessee." The focus was on preparing graduates to succeed as lawyers, not just to attain admission to the bar. The program described in that catalogue relied on a combination of the case method and a more traditional reliance on textbooks, in an effort to generate "a familiarity with general rules and principles" as well as "the application of those rules and reasons." The School's 1905/06 catalogue was the last one to defend the School's reluctance to adopt wholesale the case method on the grounds that "a familiarity with general rules and principles is essential."

Vanderbilt had been using the case method as part of its program as early as 1896 when the first catalogue reference to this pedagogical approach appeared, and thus the School was well within the national mainstream. Other law schools that introduced the case method in that decade included Columbia, Northwestern, Cornell, Wisconsin, Hastings, Chicago and Stanford.[111] The case method was introduced at Richmond School of Law in 1905, but the claim that it was the first law school in the South to use that approach[112] overlooks the earlier introduction of the method at Vanderbilt.

An assessment of the materials used between 1901 and 1904 yielded the conclusion that the use of the case system varied depending on who was teaching in a given year. "Cases" were a part of the reading in as many as eleven courses in 1902/03, but that had dropped to four courses by 1904/05 with the departure of James C. McReynolds from the faculty.[113] Dean Malone was said to have relied in part on the case system approach in his classes, but his son, a member of the faculty during those years, said of his father's teaching style: " . . . he thought that this growth [of law] was based on broad principles which could be summarized; and that these ultimate principles—rather than myriad exemplification—should be stressed."[114]

By 1908, Hall reported to the Chancellor that the lecture method was being abandoned, stating that "there is a tendency on the part of members of the Faculty to use Case Books more extensively. The Faculty has not adopted any exclusive method. . . . I am convinced that it [the case method] is for *most subjects* the best method of legal instruction."[115] The pre-dominance of the case method, in the context of some variety, was reflected in the School's public statements. The 1913/14 catalogue announced that the case method was not "the only" means of instruction, as each faculty member was given liberty "to choose the method best suited to develop his particular subject." Two years later, the ascendance of the case method appeared clearly in the catalogue's statement that the School "is committed to the 'case system' of instruction, and most of the professors pursue this method exclusively." Following "the leading American law schools," Vanderbilt adopted the policy because it "enables teachers to so conduct their courses that the student may acquire not only knowledge of the rules, but also the ability to deal with legal problems." Dean Hall was a strong advocate of moving exclusively to the case method, reporting to the Chancellor in 1915 that eighteen courses were taught exclusively by the case method, eight courses by a combination of the textbooks and casebooks, and commenting, "It is not wise to have two systems of instruction prevailing in the Law School."[116]

In addition to the gradual adoption of this newly-emergent method of instruction, the faculty periodically acted to enforce and elevate academic standards: failing a significant number of members of the Senior class, dismissing students for failure to attend class, refusing to review final grades with unsuccessful students, and not allowing students to pledge a legal fraternity during their first semester of law school.[117] Upon assuming the deanship, Hall worked mightily to make other changes that would take the program to a higher level. In his first semester as dean, Hall sought to reverse existing practices, even in the face of pressure from the Chancellor, when Oscar F. Noel applied to attend classes at the law school. Noel had been enrolled in the academic department at Vanderbilt and played on the football team in 1905 and 1906. He subsequently transferred to Yale where he received his law degree. Noel was then applying to return to Vanderbilt in 1910 because he wanted to play on the Vanderbilt team that fall which was scheduled to play Yale. (Noel was surely motivated, at least in part, by his failure to make the football team at Yale.) Hall saw this case as emblematic of larger problems: "Our School has suffered much in the past because it seemed to be the dumping ground for all 'incompetents' who desire to participate in the athletic and fraternity life of the University, to the exclusion of every thing else." He said he did not believe that a Yale law graduate could sincerely desire to take law classes at Vanderbilt ("It seems to me rather absurd that he should wish to enter Vanderbilt Law School when we can offer him only work which he has just covered in one of the most famous law schools in the United States."), and said he would not allow Noel to take work at the School unless Kirkland ordered him to do so.[118]

Kirkland responded, stating that Noel would instead be matriculating in the academic department and asking Hall to allow Noel to take law courses. The Chancellor pointed out that law students were allowed to take work in the academic department and asked Hall "to return this courtesy."[119] The student newspaper praised Noel's performance in the game against the University of Tennessee two days later. The following week he played right tackle in the 0–0 tie against Yale in New Haven, and he was then declared ineligible to play by the Southern Intercollegiate Athletic Association.[120] It is unclear if he ever attended any Law School classes. That same semester, Hall allowed Malvern Ulysses Griffin to enroll in the Law School only on the condition that he not play football that season. Griffin, an "All Southern" tackle the previous year, had been barred from playing football by the academic department because of low grades and Hall was emphatic that comparable standards be enforced in his school.[121]

The administrative reorganization of 1900 and the return of the School to the main campus in 1915 were both aimed at enhancing the Law School's academic program. The Chancellor and others expected that a heightening of standards and seriousness of purpose would result from a greater integration into the University academic environment and increased oversight by the University administration. These expectations were fulfilled as activities beyond the classroom became an important feature of the law students' life in the University setting.

The John Marshall Law Club was created in 1906. This new club was seen as a threat to the existing campus literary and debating societies, the Dialectic Literary Society and the Philosophic Literary Society, which dated back to 1875 and 1876, respectively. The Marshall Club was similar to the existing clubs in its debating and oratorical emphasis, but it was organized by and for law students. Initially, the older societies were apprehensive that the new group would weaken them by drawing law students away from their membership, and policies were adopted that excluded the Marshall Club from annual events. But in 1909, following a published call in the Vanderbilt *Observer* for the Marshall Club to join the Dialectic and Philosophic Societies in sponsoring the University's literary magazine, the restraint was loosened and the three groups joined together in oratorical and publishing ventures.[122]

Tau Kappa Alpha, an intercollegiate oratorical and debating fraternity, was installed at Vanderbilt in May 1910 by John H. DeWitt, a Nashville attorney and a TKA member from Harvard. Students from the Law School and the College of Arts and Science were charter members, including G. W. Follin, a college student who later served as president of the organization for all three of the years that he was enrolled in Law School (1911–1914). Papers presented at fraternity meetings ran from the usual fare—"Judicial Recall" and "Statewide Prohibition"—to the more exotic, such as "The Gastronomic Pabulum and its Duplicate Relation to Metaphysical and Psychiatric Phenomena."[123] Another charter member of Tau Kappa Alpha was A. M. Harris, an adjunct professor of oratory in the College. Keeble arranged for Harris to teach a required course in Public Speaking in the Law School in 1916, to the astonishment of Professor Wilber, the School's Secretary, who had already made up the class schedule without any awareness of this arrangement until Harris came by to teach his course when school opened that fall.[124]

In the early years of the century, some uncertainty about University regulation of law students remained. Chancellor Kirkland notified Dean Hall that the law students who were members of "general fraternities" would be governed by new campus-wide rules, and the Law School faculty agreed that the rules governing College fraternities would also govern those of the Law School. [125] With the move back to campus in 1915, law students were integrated into the University Student Council, which represented all of the schools on the West Campus, managed student publications, and took the lead in directing student activities.[126] However, when the College's Dean of Students, Madison Sarratt, placed three law students on probation during that first year back on the main campus, Dean Keeble sought clarification of the new arrangements, asking Kirkland if Sarratt had the power to expel a student from the Law School "for any cause that seems to him to be sufficient," or if such a decision still remained with the faculty of the School. Kirkland responded that the authority of the Dean and the faculty had not been impaired, and that if Sarratt determined that a student should be dismissed, he would apprise the School of the facts and a decision could be made there.[127] Even so, Law students at least claimed to be unaware the disciplinary reach of the central University offices. The Dean of the College found it necessary to write to Law Professor Charles Turck in 1922 about confusion that had arisen concerning University regulation of law students' activities: "Students matriculated in the Law School are saying that they never heard of this before. Please consult with Dean Sarratt and as soon as possible make this ruling of the School of Law public."[128] The Board of Trust acted in 1925 to complete the integration of student affairs, appointing Madison Sarratt to a new University-wide position of Dean of Men, lifting his appointment out of the College and explicitly giving him responsibility over the behavior of all the students at the University. Only placing all students under the same codes and administrative officers, argued Kirkland, would avoid "disorganization and disaster."[129]

Over time, the School's vision of its mission expanded beyond just preparing graduates to succeed as attorneys. Keeble captured this spirit in his annual report in 1919, as he addressed the role that "a real law school" could play in preserving the nation's form of government and fundamental social principles: "Discontent, disorder, revolution, chaos, in my judgment, can be materially prevented by a systematic and thorough training of men in a well balanced and well conducted law school. Just as the aim of the medical college of today is to inculcate principles of preventive medicine, so that of the law school is, or should be, the prevention of political and social disease."[130]

Despite these efforts at curricular and extracurricular improvement, within the Law School and the University, Chancellor Kirkland was quite dissatisfied with what he saw at the Law School in 1923, as he reported to the Board of Trust:

> With the increased preliminary requirements for the study of law it is hoped that the law students will become more stable and show less disposition to experiment with their professional education. At the present time, a great many young men seem to go into law without due consideration, and readily drop it after the slightest effort. This is shown by the fact that twenty-two students, which is almost ten per cent of the attendance, withdrew from the law school at or before the close of the first half year. During the last academic year there were eighty-one students in the first year class. In the present second year class there are only forty-three students, which shows a loss of nearly half. . . . in striking contrast with the permanence of the students enrolled in the School of Medicine.[131]

As in other areas, Kirkland saw some backsliding in the instructional program in the years following Hall's death. He commented in 1925 on a report he had received from Dean Keeble: "What is needed is less lecturing with more individual work on the part of the student, more papers, more themes, and more practical work of other kinds. All of this requires a larger teaching force and more attention from the faculty."[132]

While Vanderbilt worked to keep pace with developments across the country in academic programming, it was not only slower than most national schools to broaden its student body to include women, it was also the last law school in Tennessee to enroll a woman. The University of Tennessee admitted a woman in 1903, and Cumberland admitted two in 1905.[133] Vanderbilt's first female graduate was Clara Marie Weber, of Bridgewater, South Dakota, who received her Bachelor of Laws degree in 1919—graduating first in her class—one year before the ratification of the Nineteenth Amendment giving women the right to vote.

Nadine Helm may have been the first woman accepted as a student to Vanderbilt Law School. She wrote to Allen Hall on November 10, 1907, and again on November 27th, saying she wanted to pursue the study of law, but had noticed that there were no women among the students listed in Vanderbilt's catalogue. She asked if the School did admit women. Hall responded that although several women had applied, none had matriculated because none of them had met the School's admission standards. Thus, he wrote, the question had never been presented to the Faculty or the Chancellor. He asked her to read the entrance requirements in the catalogue that he was sending her, and if she was satisfied that she met the standards, he told her, "I would be glad to present the matter in a formal way to the authorities of the University with a view of establishing a precedent either of accepting or rejecting female applicants."[134]

Ms. Helm had graduated from the Alabama Girls' Industrial School in May 1906, with a concentration in English. She had taken additional course work at George Peabody College for Teachers in the summer of 1906, and then began teaching first grade. She wrote back to Hall on December 3, 1907, and again on January 13, 1908, informing him that she was confident she met the standards. Hall notified her on January 18, 1908, that a policy decision had been made and that she could matriculate.[135] Apparently, however, she never enrolled.

While Hall was willing to accept a female student, he was certainly not seeking them out. When he received a mailing from Crane & McGlenen, "College Agents," with a price list of what it would cost to get a list of high school graduates from different states, Hall responded by asking what it would cost to get a list of only male graduates from specified states. That's what he ordered, and he then complained when the list that was sent to him contained the names of both boys and girls.[136]

Lucy L. Jones of Roswell, New Mexico was the first woman to enroll in the Law School, registering in the category of "Irregular and Special Students" for only one year in 1915/16. Clara Weber, the youngest of eleven children of a German immigrant, entered the following year. She had only a high school education, while twenty-three of her twenty-six male classmates had attended college. Yet, at the end of her first year she received one of the two scholarships awarded to the students with the highest first-year averages; she received the Callaghan & Co. Prize for the highest average at the end of the second year; and she was awarded the Founder's Medal at graduation, at that time given to the student regarded by the faculty as the "best lawyer" in the class.[137] She also was chosen as the student body secretary and treasurer, and the yearbook representative.

Weber returned to Bridgewater, after graduation, to practice law. She and her husband, Leroy Allan, moved to Georgia where they operated a small manufacturing business, and then moved to California. She was proud of her Founder's Medal, often showing it to house guests until her death in 1979.[138]

Weber began her course of study at Vanderbilt in 1916, two years before the American Bar Association admitted its first woman.[139] When she graduated, there were 1,068 women enrolled in American law schools, although only 381 of them were in schools approved by the AALS.[140] In the early twentieth century, the legal profession was largely closed to women, as only 1.4 percent of attorneys were women in 1920. Most of the law schools that admitted women enrolled only one or two a year,[141] and Vanderbilt was no exception. The next two women to graduate were Mary Ryan and Grace Wilson who completed their work two years after Weber in 1921. Wilson married Cecil Sims, a 1914 Law School graduate whose name appears often in the School's history. Her son, Wilson Sims, and her family endowed two awards for Vanderbilt Law students in her name, honoring her on her ninetieth birthday

Theresa Scherer Davidson graduated in 1922, after completing her first year of law school at Ohio State University. She had earned her B.A., Phi Beta Kappa, and her M.A. at Oberlin, and transferred to Vanderbilt when her husband, Fugitive poet Donald Davidson, came to the University to join the faculty in the English Department. Ms. Davidson earned the award for the highest grade point average in her second year class. She served as Law School Librarian after graduation for two years, from 1925–27, and was caught up in the AALS controversy. While Keeble's comment to the AALS was that she and Ms. Chester were "merely women working in the office," Kirkland reported to the Board that the management of the school was largely in the hands of these two women. Ms. Davidson later earned her Ph.D. in classics and taught Roman Law and Classics at Vanderbilt off and on for a decade after that, in addition to practicing law.

When Pauline Lafon graduated in 1936, she was only the tenth woman to graduate from Vanderbilt. After practicing law in Arkansas, she returned to Nashville, married Albert Gore, and her involvement in his political career would delay her returning to the practice of law until 1971 when he left the U.S. Senate. She presented the Florrie Wilkes Sanders Lecture at the School in 1994, and received the Distinguished Alumnus Award in 1999. Their son, Albert Gore, Jr., took a leave of absence from the Law School in the spring of his second year in 1976 to begin his own political career. He won election to the U.S. House of Representatives that year, went on to the U.S. Senate, served two terms as Vice-President of the United States, and never returned from that leave of absence.

Despite their achievements, routine acceptance of women at Vanderbilt Law School was slow in coming. In 1949, when Vanderbilt installed its chapter of the Order of the Coif, graduates dating back to 1912 when the national organization had been established, who would have qualified for Coif membership, were offered membership in the Vanderbilt chapter and invited to the installation. No women were on the list;[142] among those excluded were Clara Marie Weber and Julia Reese, the Founder's Medalist in 1934. Year after year, the faculty meeting minutes included the list of the "men" who had completed the requirements for the degree that year—even though some of those graduates were named Pauline, Mary, Catherine, Virginia, and Lillian. Finally, in 1956, a list of "persons" who had completed the degree requirements was presented to the faculty. Among those "persons" were Doris Blossom Garman who had won the Morgan Prize that year for the most outstanding writing on the *Law Review*, and Doris Ann Dudney, the Founder's Medalist and first woman Editor-in-Chief of the *Vanderbilt Law Review*.[143]

A SHORTAGE OF RESOURCES

A lack of adequate resources was the major headwind that Vanderbilt Law School faced in its struggle to achieve national respectability. In fact, the survival of the School was continually in doubt during the first half of the twentieth century because of financial pressures. The aspects of the School's program that were most visible to external constituencies such as prospective students and the legal education community were the School's faculty and the building that housed its program. The School had begun the century with a faculty composed only of practitioners who were teaching on a part-time basis. This arrangement, however, proved to be unstable, resulting in rapid turnover. At one point Chancellor Kirkland commented, "It would almost seem as if the University Law Faculty is a recruiting ground for large corporations and the general government."[144] To remedy this problem, Vanderbilt endeavored to build a more solid faculty base, improving the academic credentials of those they appointed and increasing the full-time component of the faculty.

A dramatic change in the expectations regarding the educational background of faculty members occurred in the first decade of the century. In 1901/02, five of the eleven faculty members had no formal education beyond high school. When Lurton assumed the deanship four years later, he did not have a higher education degree, but five of the six faculty members serving under him had law degrees, and two of those had additional academic degrees. The only faculty member, other than Lurton, without a law degree was John W. Judd. Judd joined the faculty in 1904, having served as President of the Tennessee Bar Association, as assistant counsel for the L&N Railroad, and on the Supreme Court of Utah. He was the last faculty member to be appointed without some kind of post-secondary degree. William K. McAlister became a member of the faculty in 1910 and later served for seventeen years on the Tennessee Supreme Court; he was the last faculty member of that era to be appointed who did not have a law degree.[145]

Accompanying the elevation of educational credentials was the somewhat slower movement to full-time appointments. Improved finances, AALS requirements, and aspirations to improve the academic program led to the development of a full-time faculty over a thirty-year period. A precipitating event in the movement toward a predominantly full-time faculty seems to have been the resignation of Charles Lawrence toward the end of the 1912/13 academic year. When Hall had organized the restructuring of the faculty in 1909, his original recommendation had been that Lawrence be made a full-time faculty member, the second one after himself. Hall's plans were scaled back in his final proposal—probably after a conversation with Kirkland discussing budgetary issues. In the scheme finally approved in 1909, Lawrence was promoted from instructor to assistant professor, his teaching hours were increased, and Edward T. Seay was added to the faculty with the intention of eventually increasing both of their appointments to full-time positions.[146]

Lawrence had received his B.A. from Vanderbilt in 1884, and his LL.B. in 1886 at the age of twenty. He served as a part-time faculty member until 1913 when he resigned his position to go to Washington to serve as Special Assistant to Attorney General James C. McReynolds. Kirkland took note of his leaving, and commented on the rumor that another faculty member was departing (Percy D. Maddin also left in 1913), when he brought the issue to the Board of Trust. Kirkland was not only concerned about turnover. He was also aware of the growing national trend of law schools to move from a practitioner-professor model to the scholar-professor model that Langdell had established at Harvard. Kirkland's interest was not in following fashionable trends but in improving educational quality:

> These experiences raise the question whether we can continue to fill such vacancies from the Nashville bar. Aside from the uncertainty of tenure, there are disadvantages in having too much work in the hands of active practitioners. Sometimes the loss of hours is a serious matter and classes become dissatisfied under the impression that their interests are neglected.
>
> Law Schools are finding it desirable to secure the services of instructors devoting themselves exclusively to teaching. A number of such men are already at work in the different schools of the country, and experience seems to show that the instruction of students does not suffer by being taken out of the hands of practicing lawyers.[147]

Charles H. Wilber was appointed as the second full-time faculty member that summer. He was recruited from the University of Idaho School of Law, where he had served as Associate Professor and Secretary. His tenure at the school was short—he resigned his position in the summer of 1918 to serve in World War I, entering an officers' training camp, and he died in the influenza epidemic on October 15, 1918. But during his brief time at the School, he validated the full-time professor experiment. He was a hard worker who satisfied the high standards of Dean Hall, not missing a single recitation during his first year, and his performance led Hall and Kirkland to conclude that an additional full-time faculty member should be hired to teach classes that were being taught by various members of the local bar.[148]

These aspirations were put on hold during the enrollment downturn caused by World War I. An increased reliance on part-time faculty members during the war years, however, convinced Kirkland that more full-time faculty should be appointed as quickly as possible to replace the practitioners who were primarily interested in other things, often missing classes and demoralizing students. For Kirkland, the chief difficulty was financial: "It is next to impossible to get a suitable man for less than $4,000 per annum."[149] Financial concerns had to take a back seat on this issue, however, when the AALS adopted a new regulation that which went into effect in 1919 that required a School to have three full-time faculty members. At that point, Vanderbilt did not even have a full-time dean.

When classes opened in the fall of 1920, Vanderbilt was in compliance with a full-time faculty of H. B. Schermerhorn, Edmund C. Dickinson, and Charles J. Turck. Dickinson, who had previously taught at Florida and

Alabama law schools, left after only two years to teach at the University of West Virginia School of Law. His position as the third full-time faculty member was filled by the same Charles Lawrence whose departure had spurred the hiring of full-time faculty. Lawrence had completed his tour of duty in Washington, rejoined the Vanderbilt faculty, and remained until poor health forced his retirement in 1931. Turck, a Columbia law graduate who had taught at Tulane Law School, stayed not much longer than Dickinson. He departed in 1924 to become Dean of the University of Kentucky Law School. He later served as President of Centre College, and then President of Macalester College.

Schermerhorn, on the other hand, became a fixture on the faculty. He earned his law degree from the University of Pennsylvania, a master of laws from Temple, and for twenty years practiced in Philadelphia and taught on the Temple and the Washington and Lee law school faculties. He had served as a part-time member of the Vanderbilt faculty prior to World War I, resigned in November 1918 to go to Paris to practice law with the Coudert Brothers firm, and returned to assume a full-time position in 1920. In addition to his scholarly activities (he authored a treatise, *Essentials to the Principal Actions in Tort at Common Law*), Schermerhorn was very involved in local musical, dramatic, and artistic activities. He was considered the most cultured member of the faculty, as evidenced by his *Virginia Law Review* article that consisted of extracts of a translation of the Roman advocate Quintilian's Institutes of Oratory. He taught at the Law School until Saturday morning, January 26, 1935, when he died walking from the building just after teaching a class.

Three full-time faculty was progress, but this number was, after all, the minimum required to maintain AALS membership. Vanderbilt was moving toward a faculty that was dedicated principally to their educational responsibilities, but compared to the mainstream, it was at the back of the pack. The School was keeping up, but just barely. Part-time faculty provided much of the School's instruction prior to 1930, and some of the instructors brought considerable attention to the Law School. Foremost among these was James C. McReynolds. McReynolds completed his four-year program in the academic department in three years, graduating as Founder's Medalist in 1882. He returned to Vanderbilt to join the law faculty in 1899, teaching commercial law, insurance, and corporations until 1903. He was appointed to the University's Board of Trust in 1907, and was the longest serving member of the Board at the time of his death in 1946.[150]

McReynolds left the faculty when he was appointed Assistant Attorney General of the United States in 1903. He was subsequently named Attorney

General by President Woodrow Wilson, who then nominated him for the U.S. Supreme Court where he served from 1914 until 1941. The vacancy McReynolds filled on the Court was the one caused by the death of his former Vanderbilt faculty colleague, Horace Lurton. McReynolds was a staunch conservative, who became most well-known as an adamant opponent of Franklin Roosevelt's New Deal. His teaching was highly technical rather than theoretical, and Dean Keeble would write of him years later, "no man who has ever been in the faculty made a greater reputation as a teacher in the same length of time."[151] McReynolds left $10,500 to the Law School endowment in his will.[152]

Another faculty member who was more well-known for his work outside the classroom was Dan McGugin. McGugin was the head football coach for Vanderbilt University for three decades, beginning in 1904. He learned law and football at the University of Michigan, where he played football for, and then was an assistant to, coaching legend Fielding Yost. His first team at Vanderbilt was undefeated, outscoring its opponents 452–4, as McGugin ushered in "The Golden Age of Vanderbilt Football," as his first ten years were called by Mims. But Mims also insisted that McGugin was "worthy in every way to take his place among the outstanding administrators and scholars of the University."[153] At the end of the 1907 season, McGugin was added to the Law School faculty to teach Constitutional Law and Commercial Law, and he decided to move his legal practice from Detroit to Nashville.[154] The highly successful teams of this era drew heavily from the law student body. Their participation contributed to the team's athletic and financial successes, which enabled Vanderbilt to build the first stadium in the Southeastern Conference,[155] the "voluminous concrete bowl" that was dedicated as Dudley Field in 1922.

Coinciding with the growth in the faculty was the relocation of the Law School to the main campus in 1915. The Law and Dental Building became known as The Vanderbilt Law Building when the Dental Department moved out in 1901. That move allowed the Law School to expand into vacated space that was especially needed for the growing library. Annie B. Warren, who served as law librarian for fourteen years, began creating a card catalogue for a collection that was approaching 10,000 volumes. While there were certainly larger law school libraries, this was a substantial collection. In 1908, only thirty-three law schools had collections as large as 5,000 volumes—a threshold that Vanderbilt had passed seventeen years earlier with the acquisition of Judge Cooper's Library.[156] The University considered the building on Cherry Street to be an investment, but it turned out to be a miserable one. Kirkland called the building "our most unsatisfactory investment" and "a dismal failure."[157] Some rooms went unrented, payments were not collected on others, and repair and maintenance charges mounted. After years of effort, Vanderbilt sold the building in a lease/purchase arrangement to the Commercial Club (later the Nashville Chamber of Commerce), and the Law School moved to the third floor of College Hall (later to be named Kirkland Hall) over the Christmas holidays in 1915.

Kirkland was hopeful that the building vacated by the Law School would disappear from the University's financial report, but over the years the University loaned the Commercial Club $25,000 for renovation and another $10,000 for furniture; it then forgave three months of rent because of the amount of time required for the renovation, and another month of rent because of a fire. As payments from the Commercial Club became past due, the Board instructed the Chancellor to threaten legal action; an elevator accident resulted in a lawsuit being filed against the University. In 1939, the Chamber of Commerce relinquished the lease, and the University eventually traded this white elephant for the Halcyon Apartments—which it intended to dispose of at the first favorable opportunity.[158]

The relocation to the main campus was, on the whole, a considerable improvement for the School. The advantages of housing the School in the downtown area in 1889 were seen to have diminished, as "electric cars [a trolley line] have brought the West Campus so near the heart of the city that distance is no longer a factor."[159] The move back to the main campus brought students closer to their academic work, allowed them to board on campus, and to be more integrated into campus life.[160] The School's 1915/16 catalogue noted that the change removed the School from the "many use-less diversions of the 'down town' section." While it was not so convenient for the part-time faculty whose practices were downtown, Kirkland viewed the move as helping unite the Law School with the College of Arts and Science.[161]

Resource constraints continually plagued the Law School. In those early days, financial stability was all about enrollment. The School had no en-dowment. The first endowment of any amount dedicated to the Law School appeared in 1924, and the first substantial endowment was created in 1944, when the Board provided matching dollars for a Law School fund drive. There was no annual fund, as the School was not allowed to solicit non-endowment gifts designated for the School until 1958. There was no support from foundations or similar organizations, as those did not become a factor in the School's financial picture until 1956. In those days, Law School reve-nue was tuition income. Period.

The twentieth century began with Chancellor Kirkland declaring his belief that the enrollment of the Law School, which had averaged about forty-five students in the previous five years, could be doubled within a few years.[162] This assessment turned out to be overly optimistic, as the annual enrollment did not exceed eighty until the post-World War I boom years, and averaged only about sixty in those first two decades. A number of factors appeared to restrain the enrollment growth that the University wanted. The lengthening of the degree program from two years to three years in 1910, in order to earn admission to the AALS, put the School at a competitive disadvantage in the region in the eyes of students looking for the shortest path into the profession. The University was quite open in its views that the Law School "had to compete with many shoddy institutions which have no standards of admission and only short time requirements, and are conducted for revenue only."[163] The advent of World War I sharply reduced the number of available students. Perhaps the most surprising cause for stagnation in enrollment figures was the role that Allen Hall played in suppressing student registrations.

Beginning in his years as Secretary and then Chairman, Hall's drive to increase the Law School's reputation led him to reject some promising applicants and counsel others away from the School. Vanderbilt did not require even a year of college work for admission until 1923. Yet, Hall told applicants as early as 1907 that they should only enter a professional course of study after they had done college level academic work first, writing to one student, "If you really mean business, my advice to you would be to attend a college somewhere for two or three years and then take up the question of making a professional man out of yourself." He wrote to another applicant that he was too young to go to law school: "It is a long, hard pull to succeed at the law and one needs the years between the age of twenty and thirty to apply to building up his business and to private study." Even though University policy permitted students to take academic and law work contemporaneously, he encouraged applicants to finish their academic work first before thinking about law school, and he rejected an appeal from the Dean of the Academic Department to work out a class schedule that would accommodate students wanting to take work in both schools. To an applicant from Louisiana, he wrote, "I think it will be best for you to go to Tulane," because of that state's legal system. To an applicant from Virginia who wanted to practice law in Tennessee, he wrote that he would "be as well off at the University of Virginia as you would be at the Vanderbilt University," because Vanderbilt did not focus on the law of Tennessee. Transfer applicants were met with a dismissive skepticism about whether their prior work would be acceptable for Vanderbilt credit.

Thus, it is not surprising that the School's enrollment the year that Hall assumed the duties as Secretary was fifty-six, and the enrollment the last year of his deanship was fifty-five. The financial consequence of this stagnation was almost constant deficits. The School ran only three surpluses prior to the end of World War I, so the University was regularly transferring general funds to the Law School to balance the books, occasionally driving the University-wide annual budget into a deficit. In 1913, Kirkland announced to the Board, "The Law Department really needs some special endowment."[164] Two years later, Kirkland put all of the University's professional schools on notice. Observing that all of the professional schools, including the Law School, were a part of the University "with the understanding that they would be no tax on the resources of the University," the Chancellor declared:

> To put the whole matter in a few words the time has come in our history when Vanderbilt University must clearly measure its resources and study its obligations. Work that cannot be supported adequately will in the end have to be dropped. Each professional school should, as far as possible, rest on its own foundation and be supported out of its own funds. Far reaching efforts should be begun to secure support of this character so that in after years, if the necessity arises, the Board of Trust can with clear conscience abandon such parts of its work as it can no longer sustain, feeling that an honest effort has been made and due notice given to the Alumni and the public at large.[165]

A Committee was appointed to look into raising an endowment for the Law School, but it reported back in 1918 that an endowment "sufficient to protect the integrity of the School of Law . . . could not be raised at this time."[166] In the meantime, Dean Keeble had been appointed to a University committee, as had several key Board of Trust members, to raise funds for the endowment for the College of Arts and Science to match a challenge grant from the General Education Board. Such a diversion of resources, in this case the time and energy of the Law School dean, away from development efforts for the Law School was a pattern that would be frequently repeated in the future.

The first endowed funds dedicated to the Law School were received in 1924. Dr. Herman L. Martin, Rabbi of Fort Washington Synagogue in New York, contributed $500 for a medal to be given to the best student in the freshman law class. This medal was a memorial to his son, Archie Martin, who was a member of the fall 1923 first-year class and died suddenly on

November 24, 1923. Dr. Martin desired to have his son's name perpetuated in the place where he last worked, and after giving $25 for the first year's medal, he established this permanent endowment.[167] The Archie B. Martin Memorial Prize is still awarded each year to the student in the first-year class who earns the highest grade point average.

A post-war boom in enrollment began in 1919/20, as the number of students registered shot up to 137. The resulting surpluses eased the financial crisis. For the first time, the Law School budget was called upon to pay "for its share of heat and light" in the amount of $1,000, and then later to also pay a proportionate share of such overhead items as janitorial services, care of the grounds, and insurance. A self-supporting law school appeared to be within reach. While the University-wide cost per student was $383 in 1923, that expense was only $95 in the Law School, and law students' tuition payments were averaging $159 each, or 167% of actual cost.[168] The urgency of an endowment drive disappeared, and there was even talk of using the accumulating surpluses to build a new building for the Law School.

The Law School's financial climate changed dramatically with the expulsion from the AALS, an event Kirkland had not foreseen two years before the expulsion when he stated, "Altogether the School of Law seems to be in a perfectly safe condition to weather any storms incident to the next few years."[169] Certainly the expulsion would be a blow to the recruitment of students. There were also concerns that the robust enrollments of the 1920s were achieved through lax admissions practices that could not be continued if AALS standards were to be met. The summer after losing AALS membership, Kirkland told the Board that "one of the greatest needs of Vanderbilt University is the securing of at least a half million dollars for the School of Law." The funds could be used to appoint a full-time dean and a full-time secretary, and to erect a suitable building.[170]

A year later, the price tag and the urgency had increased, as enrollment had dropped fifty percent, partly as a result of rejecting many applicants who could not be admitted with the more rigid enforcement of admission standards. The Law School's accumulated surpluses were quickly consumed, and the University was again in the business of subsidizing a deficit operation. While a $500,000 endowment would "save us from disaster," Kirkland declared, a $1 million endowment was needed to put the School on a firm foundation. The Board viewed the situation with alarm, and recommended that Board members meet with Law faculty and alumni to develop a plan. But the meeting produced no plan, the Chancellor thought the half million could not be raised without finding an individual who would contribute half of it, and he concluded at the Board meeting in 1929, that "The School of Law must be endowed or it must die."[171]

This proclamation should not be interpreted as just hyperbole from a Chancellor who was trying to open the wallets of wealthy Board of Trust members. The University had closed its School of Pharmacy in 1920, and its School of Dentistry in 1926—both of which traced their origins back to 1879. Vanderbilt had practically ceased giving a Ph.D. earlier, announcing in its 1918 catalogue, "courses leading to the doctorate will not be organized."[172] The School of Religion was barely surviving the 1915–30 period.[172] When Dean Keeble died in the fall of 1929, the University was truly at a crossroads regarding the future of its Law School.

✎ CHAPTER THREE

The Recovery of Stature and Reputation

INTRODUCTION

That the School of Law be continued." The death of Dean John Bell Keeble presented the Board of Trust with a moment of decision regarding the Law School, and this was the resolution they adopted at their February 3, 1930, meeting.[1] The Board's decision, and the commitments that accompanied it, were not business as usual. Rather, in historian Conkin's words, "the board reached a rather daring decision—to try to build a prestige school."[2]

The exclusion from the AALS makes it all too easy to overlook the accomplishments of Keeble during his deanship. He presented a summary view of his deanship in a letter to Kirkland on July 11, 1927. He had held the school together during World War I, when he had no full-time faculty, student enrollments were small, and it looked like the school might be closed. Student enrollment had rebounded and was larger in 1927 than when he took office, even as entrance requirements had increased. On his watch, he wrote, the School had accumulated surpluses and broadened the curriculum, and instruction was stronger than at any other time in the School's history.

By 1930, however, the challenges facing the School were immense. Enrollment was painfully low, financial resources were meager, and the public perception of the quality of the School had been shaken by the AALS exclusion. A perception of excellence would be required to distinguish Vanderbilt from lower-cost schools in the region. Moreover, any effective response to these challenges would have to be achieved in the context of the gathering Depression.

A NEW DEAN AND A NEW COURSE

Earl C. Arnold—who was named Vanderbilt Law School's sixth dean in 1930—said, later, that he was surprised. The letter that surprised him, dated December 23, 1942, was brief:

> Dear Dean Arnold:
> I was delighted to learn yesterday afternoon that the Association's committee has nominated you to membership on the executive committee. The Association is to be congratulated on having your experience and judgment in its service in the unusually difficult year ahead.
> Best wishes to you.
> Sincerely yours,
> Elliottt E. Cheatham[3]

Professor Cheatham, a faculty member at Columbia University School of Law, was giving Arnold his first notice that he was being elected to serve in one of the two at-large seats on the Executive Committee of the Association of American Law Schools. This event was a landmark moment in the history of Vanderbilt Law School, symbolizing its complete rehabilitation in the professional association which had expelled the school thirteen years earlier, and marking the school's recognition as an important player among the nation's law schools.

At the same time, this triumphant moment also must have been poignant for Dean Arnold, for he was already aware of discussions within the University's Board of Trust that would lead to the closing of the School's doors. Contingency plans were being made, and when implemented the Board would suspend the operation of the Law School until the end of World War II.

The major currents in the Law School's development through the first three decades of the Twentieth Century had combined in 1926 to bring the school to its most embarrassing moment when it was excluded from the AALS. However, the reversal of those same currents led to a renaissance that could be rightfully called the "Arnold revolution." For thirty years, the University had hesitated to embrace fully the professionalism that was emerging in legal education across the United States. Additionally, the University found itself unable or unwilling to provide adequate financial resources to the School, and equally unable or unwilling to escape the negative consequences of being held captive to its location in the American

South. These deficiencies resulted in pressures and practices that stalled in-dividual efforts to achieve academic respectability.

The expulsion from the AALS, however, also served as a wakeup call—a call heard clearly by Chancellor James Kirkland, the Board of Trust, and the faculty. In aggressive and imaginative ways, the University moved to make amends on a variety of fronts. But the combination of the Great De-pression and the beginning of World War II proved to be greater obstacles than the School could overcome. The final judgment of these innovations was to be the familiar refrain of "too little, too late." Despite the consider-able efforts of Dean Arnold, his faculty, and University administrators, the Vanderbilt Board of Trust decided on February 7, 1944, to discontinue the Law School's operations.

The University's first response to Keeble's death in 1929 was to appoint Edward T. Seay as Acting Dean, less than a week after Keeble's death, for the remainder of the 1929/30 academic year.[4] Seay had been Keeble's partner in the firm of Keeble and Seay, was the Law School's Founder's Medalist in the class of 1891, and had been the Speaker of the Tennessee state sen-ate when the act abolishing the diploma privilege was passed in 1903. He joined the faculty in 1909 as part of the staffing up for the three-year degree program, after teaching in the spring of 1908 as a substitute in the Law of Damages course during Dean Hall's extended illness. Hall was impressed with his work and suggested to Kirkland that they keep him in mind as new faculty members were needed, noting that "he would make an excellent permanent member of the faculty."[5] When Seay was appointed to a regular part-time position for the fall of 1909, Hall planned to gradually increase his role to a full-time appointment.

Seay was the sitting dean when Vanderbilt was readmitted to the AALS. During his ten-month term as acting dean, he continued the enforcement of stricter admissions standards, and oversaw the conclusion of Professor Moore's thorough reorganization of the law library, including the comple-tion of the State Reports of forty states to connect with the National Re-porter System, and the purchase of new stacks, furnishings, and equipment. Seay continued teaching on the faculty until 1932, when he resigned, yield-ing to health concerns and the demands of his law practice. He became a member of the Vanderbilt University Board of Trust in 1937, and of the Board of Library Trustees of the Joint University Libraries in 1939, serving in both capacities until his death on August 19, 1941.

Earl C. Arnold was Dean of the School when the 1930/31 school year began. The Board of Trust had approved his selection in early February, subject to an agreement to terms between him and Chancellor Kirkland, and Kirkland reported to the Board in April that the acceptable arrangements had been made. Arnold was an important figure in American legal education, the first Vanderbilt dean with such a background. After receiving his law degree from Northwestern, he had been in private practice for six years and then served as assistant to the solicitor for the U.S. Department of Agriculture. He then became a law professor, teaching sixteen years successively at the University of Idaho, the University of Florida, the University of Cincinnati, and then for the seven years prior to coming to Vanderbilt, at George Washington University. A member of the American Law Institute, he had published numerous articles in major law journals, such as the *Columbia Law Review*, the *Cornell Law Quarterly*, and the *University of Pennsylvania Law Review*, and he wrote *Outlines of Suretyship and Guaranty*, a 600-page treatise published by the leading American law textbook publisher, Callaghan and Company. In short, he brought credentials and experience unlike anything seen before at Vanderbilt Law School.

Arnold also brought skills as a shrewd negotiator. He accepted the offer of the deanship only on the condition that the Board of Trust agreed to furnish the School with "all necessary funds and facilities for at least five years."[6] He negotiated a good deal for himself (a $7,000 annual salary, with guaranteed annual increases of $100), but his primary focus was on the School's needs. The Board of Trust had already re-established a quasi-endowment for the School, using $265,000 from profits of the sale of University-owned securities, and it agreed to loan funds to the School in the amount of each year's deficit for five years until funds could be raised to repay the loan. Arnold pushed for more, including substantial raises for professors Schermerhorn, Moore, and Hendrick, as well as for an authorization for the continuation of the summer school. In the middle of his first year, the Board approved his recommendations that an additional full-time faculty member be appointed, that yet another round of significant salary increases be approved for Schermerhorn, Moore, and Hendrick, and that a salary increase be given to the School's Assistant Secretary, Helen Sonnenfield. All of this was being approved as the signs of the deepening Depression were becoming clear.

Publicly, Arnold set modest goals. He wrote in the University's alumni magazine:

The present administration contemplates no radical changes in the school or its program. The first administrative officer, Dean Malone,

planned wisely; Dean Hall and Judge Lurton, his able successors, up-
held these standards; while the administration of Dean Keeble was that
of a wise, far-seeing lawyer. Judge Seay maintained these same ideals.
With such wise leadership in the past, any radical changes are unneces-
sary. However, the school must keep abreast of the times. As the standards of law schools are raised, Vanderbilt's standards will be raised.[7]

He did point out that entrance requirements were being enforced more
rigidly than ever before, with no admission of any of the special students
who had caused the school to run afoul of AALS standards. Meeting the
ABA and AALS standards was to be seen as a necessity, not a "cause for
congratulation." In the curriculum, more time and emphasis was to be
given to such "so-called practical courses" as Pleading, Evidence, and Trial
Practice—exceptions to the case method that the faculty valued in the curriculum: "It is our conviction that instruction should not consist merely of
theory nor should it be given by instructors who are theorists only."

One of Arnold's innovations was the creation of Lincoln's Inn. Arnold's
assessment in 1931 was that it would be useless—at that time and perhaps
for five more years—for Vanderbilt to petition the national Order of the
Coif honorary society for the establishment of a chapter at Vanderbilt. The
faculty thus established a local society, adopting all of the regulations of
the Order of the Coif, until the day that a Coif chapter was approved.
Schermerhorn worked out the ritual for the organization and suggested that
it be called Lincoln's Inn, after one of the four inns of court in London. On
February 6, 1931, the faculty met to form the society and to elect the three
students with the highest averages in the Class of 1931 (Warner J. Geiger,
David M. Keeble, and Charles E. Shaver).[8] A chapter of the Order of the
Coif would not be established at Vanderbilt until 1949.

Arnold worked aggressively and tirelessly, usually behind the scenes, to
bring higher legal education standards to the state of Tennessee. He sought
to create public recognition of what he saw as the lower quality of education
in the non-accredited law schools, and to promote more exacting standards
for admission to the bar in the state. He used his national connections to
bring the state's legal education into the glare of the ABA's spotlight, and
worked locally to recruit like-minded attorneys to attend important conven-
tions of the Tennessee Bar Association—while disingenuously denying that
he was participating in these behind-the-scenes maneuverings.

There can be no doubting the sincerity of Arnold's attempts at reform or
the energy that he poured into his efforts to revitalize the Law School. He

was, however, navigating against two powerful currents. The first was the Great Depression, an economic drag that weighed on the School from the moment he took office. The second was the onset of World War II which would decimate the school's enrollment and finally force the suspension of operations in 1944.

In the latter years of his deanship, he also encountered a change in Vanderbilt chancellors which may have further increased the odds against success. Kirkland submitted his letter of resignation on January 2, 1937, completing his forty-five years as Chancellor.[9] Kirkland had long been a forceful and vocal supporter of the Law School, in Board of Trust meetings and in public. In just the previous year, for example, he had responded to criticism of Arnold and his faculty by some Board of Trust members who blamed them for the lack of growth. This criticism, in Kirkland's eyes, was largely or entirely unwarranted:

> When Dean Arnold came to the School seven years ago it was just emerging from the black list in which it had been placed by the Association of American Law Schools for serious deficiencies that had occurred under the old faculty during the administration of Mr. Keeble. By efforts of the Dean and faculty it has been placed in a very creditable position. It has suffered immensely from the physical location on the top floor of College Hall. Perhaps no other law school of equal rank in the South has been treated with so much indifference. Dean Arnold has made himself highly respected and esteemed as an important citizen of Nashville.[10]

When Kirkland's retirement was announced, Arnold wrote, speaking for himself and the Law School faculty: "We all feel as if we have been attending a funeral because at this meeting of the Board Chancellor Kirkland submitted his resignation to become effective the 1st of next July."[11] Arnold knew he was losing an advocate in Kirkland. The question was who would follow.

Oliver C. Carmichael brought a new emphasis to the job when he assumed the Chancellorship in July of 1937: a commitment to the centrality of the College of Arts and Science and the Graduate School, and a focus on Southern regional leadership.[12] A former Graduate School Dean, he emphasized that the real core of any great university must be the arts college and the graduate school, and he voiced his concern about a danger that the public might begin to think of Vanderbilt as primarily a medical school. He was not opposed to improving the professional schools, but any such improvement would be a secondary effect that resulted from the strengthening of the core. He presented this view to the Board in a "Statement of Needs and Program of Development Proposed for Vanderbilt University" in June 1939. A comment by Chancellor Emeritus Kirkland highlighted the shift in priorities articulated by Carmichael: "What is new in this program is a very adequate recognition of the primary need in the life of the University of the College of Arts and Science and the Graduate School."[13] The Law School would not be expecting new direct assistance from the University as it struggled to keep its doors open.

DEPRESSION ERA FINANCES

At the outset of the Arnold deanship, the Law School's finances appeared to be sound. The University established a quasi-endowment of $265,000 for the School, and committed to cover any deficits for a five-year period even while allowing those deficits to grow by enlarging the size of the faculty and increasing faculty salaries. In addition, a committee headed by Board of Trust President Frank C. Rand had been established to launch a development campaign for the School. The Board had also authorized a $50 increase in tuition, to $200, at the earliest practicable date.

The action on the tuition increase demonstrates, however, that the School's financial picture had not changed all that much. The Board had first acted to actually raise tuition by the $50 immediately. By the time Arnold had finished his negotiating for the deanship, the action was changed to authorizing the increase at the earliest date practicable. Two conclusions can be drawn from these decisions: (1) In spite of the other changes that had been made, increasing tuition income was deemed to be a critical part of any plan to put the Law School on sound financial footing. (2) The state of the Law School and its enrollment was such in 1930 that an immediate 33% increase in the tuition rate was viewed with some concern, at least by the incoming dean, who would be wary that a higher tuition rate might suppress enrollment growth.

Despite whatever reservations Arnold may have had, the tuition increase did go into effect in 1929/30, and tuition was raised again to $235 in 1931/32. But that was the last tuition rate increase until the Post-World War II period. Enrollment dropped every year until it hit sixty-five in 1933/34. After a slight rebound in the mid-Thirties, a gradual decline began again. After forty-six students registered in the Fall of 1941, Japan attacked Pearl Harbor, the United States entered World War II, the draft age was lowered to twenty, and there was no longer anything gradual about the decrease in the number of students, or in the growth of the school's deficit.

In the first years of Arnold's term, the quasi-endowment (which had grown to $328,000 by 1931) generated enough income to balance the Law School's books, and even create a reserve that covered small deficits for a few years. The University weathered the early Depression years well, with Kirkland reporting in the summer of 1931: "Vanderbilt University is meeting the present financial crisis and general depression with less embarrassment than most institutions. . . . So far as Vanderbilt is concerned we escaped all financial loss brought about through the collapse of certain institutions in Nashville. . . . In our list of bonds there has been no failure to pay dividends."[14] The effects of the Depression, however, were already appearing in the Law School's catalogue, as the faculty actively discouraged "the registration of those students without funds to pay tuition and expenses for several months."[15]

In the preparation of the 1933/34 budget, all schools at Vanderbilt were instructed to cut their expenditures by at least ten percent. There was a specific mandate to reduce the salaries of Professors of Law by ten percent, a reduction that Dean Arnold voluntarily applied to himself even though the University was contractually bound to increase his salary.[16] By that year, the value of the quasi-endowment had dropped to $189,000, the small reserve was depleted, no new funds had been raised for the Law School, and the University was covering a $13,000 deficit. While this was considered technically a "loan" from the reserves of the College, it was understood that this was a loan "which in all probability will never be paid."[17]

The "general condition of the country" was seen as discouraging students from entering into a long period of legal training, driving even more of them into inferior schools where they could finish the course of study in a year or two, or into night schools where a legal education could be pursued without interfering with daytime occupations.[18] Vanderbilt responded, too late, by setting aside funds for ten scholarships for first-year law students beginning in 1940. Few of them were ever awarded for lack of qualified applicants. By 1941, the annual deficit had reached $25,000.

The planned help from fund raising never came. The original intention of the Board of Trust Committee was to raise $500,000 to $1,000,000 for the Law School. By 1934, Kirkland was discussing with Arnold the needs of an endowment of $1 million to $2 million, even as Kirkland acknowledged that launching a campaign for a Law School endowment had been impossible. A letter had been sent to the school's living alumni and Board of Trust members. The University mailed 1,293 letters, but only fifty-one replies were received, and just seven of those indicated a willingness to give at the suggested level of $50.[19]

When the University's original five-year commitment to Arnold expired, the Board deferred taking any action. Kirkland interpreted this as a willingness by the Board to continue covering the Law School's deficit as long as the School's shortfall did not bring the overall University budget into the red. "My opinion further is that when the income of the University is reduced to the point where it will not support all of our present commitments, the Trustees will feel obligated to suspend the School of Law until such time as outside assistance can be secured."[20]

If the Depression era had not presented such huge obstacles, the University's response to the Law School crisis could be considered a failure of leadership. The first committee that the Board of Trust appointed to study the Law School's future was replaced by a second one, which did not meet. The chair of the second committee resigned, a new chair (now Chancellor Emeritus Kirkland) was appointed, and still that committee did not meet either. Kirkland's response to being named committee chair was to comment, "There is no use in appointing a committee on the basis that was described by Sir Josiah Stamp—that separately they say they do not see anything that can be done, and then meet and pass a formal resolution that nothing can be done."[21] As the School of Religion fund drive that had preempted any earlier development effort for the Law School came to an end, a Law School campaign was again preempted, this time by a new development effort for the University Library that was prompted by a $1 million matching gift from the General Education Board.[22] Dean Arnold wrote to Professor Hendrick that he feared that the library fund drive and "considerable agitation to develop a Graduate School" (consistent with Carmichael's overall plans for the University) meant that a campaign for a law school endowment "seems sidetracked for a number of years."[23]

It was during this period that Law School alumni began to develop their views that the School was considered a "stepchild" of the University,[24] or treated as "a child chained in an attic room."[25] Perhaps the most visible sign of this perceived neglect was the housing of the school. While the top floors of Kirkland Hall were not quite "an attic room," it was widely believed that the School's reputation and enrollment suffered considerably from a lack of adequate space. In 1933, for every dollar paid in Law School tuition, the University was spending $2.30 to educate a law student. Even so, or perhaps because of this reality, Dean Arnold was renewing the appeal for a law building with adequate space, equipment, and provision for library expansion, noting that the current arrangement did not allow for any large increase in the number of students.[26] Kirkland, and then Carmichael, agreed that the lack of a Law School building contributed to enrollment woes. By 1939, Carmichael had concluded that failure to solve the building problem would leave the School "seriously crippled" and that thought should be given to making sacrifices elsewhere in the University in order to fund new facilities for the Law School.[27]

The Law Library continued to grow modestly in the relatively small space allocated to it, adding about 350 volumes annually. A significant step was taken in the development of the library in 1939, in response to a new AALS standard that required "a qualified librarian, whose principal activities are devoted to the development and maintenance of an effective library service."[28] Lillian Catherine McLaurin assumed the position of Law Librarian on a full-time basis on August 1, 1939, a year before the AALS mandate became effective. She had graduated from the Law School just that year, having previously earned her bachelor's degree at Vanderbilt as well. She would be taking coursework at Peabody College in the summers in pursuit of a master's degree in library science. Since Davidson had left the School, the librarian position had been filled by a succession of three faculty members. While she did not have a professorial rank, "Lillian C. McLaurin, Law Librarian" is listed by Dean Arnold as one of the "members of our law faculty" in a letter to Henry B. Witham, Dean of the College of Law at the University of Tennessee.[29] The faculty had decided that McLaurin could be asked to meet with the faculty when library problems were under consideration, "and that when she does she shall have a vote."[30] She served as Law Librarian until she was granted a leave of absence in the spring of 1942 to join the defense effort with the Tennessee Valley Authority.

A landmark event in the development of the Law Library was the signing of the trust indenture in 1938 that established the Joint University Libraries (JUL). The indenture read, in part:

> The intent of this instrument is to establish the Joint University Libraries, including the proposed joint library, the Peabody College Library, Scarritt College Library, and the general departmental and school libraries of The Vanderbilt University as a cooperative enterprise of the three constituent institutions mentioned above. The scope of the organization herein provided for shall be the library services and library resources of these institutions.[31]

The Law Library was clearly one of Vanderbilt's school libraries that were to be subsumed under the new organization, an arrangement that would raise questions and occasionally create friction for decades to come. As Dean Arnold had reminded Chancellor Kirkland just two years earlier, "Under the requirements of the accrediting bodies our library must continue to be administered by the Law School. . . ."[32] Yet the new arrangement for "special library units," including the Law Library, would call for funding to be reviewed and recommended by a new joint faculty advisory committee, and for the Law Library collection to be restricted to instructional and reference materials, with "all primarily research materials" to be housed in a new, central joint library.[33] The effect of the arrangement would be dealt with in the post-war years.

In the summer of 1939, the match for the library gift that created the JUL had been completed, and Fred W. Vanderbilt had died, leaving an unknown amount to the University from his estate (more than $2,000,000 was anticipated). The Board drew up a list of $11 million in endowment and building needs, including $400,000 for a Law School building and $1,000,000 for Law School endowment. The Vanderbilt estate was approved as a source for matching contributions to any gifts for one of the purposes identified in this Expansion Program.[34]

If the School were to receive any support from this program, of course, the matching funds would have to be raised. For decades, Chancellor Kirkland and then Chancellor Carmichael constantly warned that the school could not continue without major development successes. The failure of the Board of Trust to secure funding for the Law School was not due to an absence of Law School graduates on the Board, as numerous law alumni served as Board members during this period. In 1921, for example, University Alumni Trustees were added to the Board's membership for the first time, with two of them chosen in that initial year upon nomination by postal ballots through the Alumni Association. Both of the inaugural alumni trustees selected were Law School graduates: Edward East Barthell of Chicago, class of 1888, and Robert Trimble Smith of Nashville, class of 1886. Other law alumni who served on the Board included Fitzgerald Hall, the son of Dean Allen Hall, who taught at the Law School from 1916 through 1927; Judge Horace Henry White, an 1887 graduate who served on the Board from 1908 until 1946; Emory Marvin Underwood, who was elected Alumni Trustee in 1922 and served until 1960; and James Martin Souby, who also began his membership as Alumni Trustee, serving from 1930 through 1964. Nonetheless, financial contributions to the Law School were not forthcoming.

One notable addition to the School's endowment was made in 1941. The estate of Lily Cartwright Bell named the Law School as the recipient of $3,500 for student financial support.[35] The award that was endowed with this gift was announced in the 1950 catalogue with language from Ms. Bell's will:

> The endowed memorial to my husband, Bennett Douglas Bell, I wish to be placed in the Vanderbilt School of Law, the interest from the endowment to be given annually to the student in the senior law class, who is not only well versed in the law, but who shows the highest conception of the ethics of the profession, and who would strive to "Do justly, love mercy and walk humbly with God," as did the one in whose memory the prize is given and whose name it bears, Bennett Douglas Bell.

The faculty took seriously the selection of the recipient of the award named after Judge Bell.[36] The multiple faculty meetings devoted to the selection process in the early days were replaced by multiple email exchanges in later years.

Overall, however, the contributions that were needed to support the School were not made. Arnold's bitterness over this state of affairs is revealed in a story that Dean John Wade would tell of a visit Arnold made to campus years after he retired. Wade said that he and another faculty member were talking with Arnold about their plans and hopes for the School, when the former dean replied:

> Vanderbilt has never placed the Law School high on its list and it never will consistently do it. You'll get promises and maybe some results, and then they'll put you off and then other more important needs will come along and then if you keep relying on the promises you'll break your heart in disillusionment. The only way to keep an unbroken heart is to reconcile yourself to sucking the left hind teat.[37]

The actual closing of the School, rather than just the threat of closing the School, would be required before significant financial resources would be dedicated to the Law School.

MEETING REGIONAL CHALLENGES

On the occasion of the inauguration of Oliver C. Carmichael as chancellor in 1938, Vanderbilt University hosted a Symposium on Higher Education in the South. Herschel Whitfield Arant, Secretary of the AALS and Dean of the Ohio State University College of Law, made a presentation on legal education that presented a snapshot of the conditions Vanderbilt faced in the South generally, and in Tennessee more particularly.[38] The following could be considered his summary conclusion: "I hope I may not be considered to be a bad-mannered guest when I say that the situation in this state, which appears to me to be by far the worst in the South, if not in the whole country, constitutes a challenge to the Bench and Bar of this state."

Arant delivered a bill of particulars: In the fourteen southern states, no law school required a college degree for admission. Schools accounting for 43% of law student enrollment in the South required no college credit at all. Every one of the nation's states that did not prescribe any period of legal study as a condition of admission to the bar were in the South, a condition he labeled as "less than disgraceful." He stated: "As long as low standards of admission prevail and as long as the legal profession is overcrowded, I think it is safe to predict that lawyers without much practice will continue to start law schools, believing that if they cannot make a living practicing, they can make one running a law school."

Tennessee was singled out for special attention. Even though the education prerequisites for taking the Tennessee bar exam had been increased, effective in 1934, to require two years of law school or law office study (rather than one year), only 18% of the law students in the state were studying in ABA-approved schools. The state with the next lowest percentage was Maryland at 34%, followed by Georgia and Texas with 43%. Walter P. Armstrong, a Vanderbilt Law School alumnus and past-president of the Tennessee Bar Association, responded to Arant's presentation by explaining why Tennessee had more law schools per capita than any other state in the Union:

> [T]here is no restriction in Tennessee on the formation of a law school or the conferring of degrees. The incorporation of an educational institution with full degree-conferring power is just as simple as the formation of any private corporation. Five persons may get together as the incorporators, may organize a non-profit educational institution with a board of trustees consisting of the immediate family of the founder. They may present him the entire proceeds from the school and still maintain their standing as a non-profit organization.[39]

If Vanderbilt Law School was going to flourish, things had to change.

Earl Arnold, usually working behind the scenes if not behind closed doors, mounted an aggressive campaign to bring about reform in Tennessee's bar admissions standards. His co-conspirator in this effort was Dean Henry Witham of the University of Tennessee, the only other one of the twelve law schools in the state that was approved by the ABA. While Arnold undoubtedly believed in the importance of a highly-qualified bar, he also believed that his efforts to increase enrollments at Vanderbilt were hampered by competition from schools which required much less of applicants to enroll and much less of students to graduate. This campaign was eventually successful when the Tennessee Supreme Court, in 1938, adopted rules that required applicants for admission to the state bar to present to the Board of Law Examiners sufficient proof that they had at least two years of law school education, which followed at least two years of work in college.

Arnold's work coincided with major national developments. In 1927, the ABA's Section on Legal Education had secured funding from the association's executive committee to hire an Advisor on Legal Education, and Iowa law professor H. Claude Horack was named the first full-time advisor to the ABA Council of the Section on Legal Education and Admissions to the Bar. When he returned to teaching in 1929, he was succeeded by Will D. Shafroth.[40] The ABA's Section on Legal Education had made a standing offer to conduct state-wide studies of law schools with the goal of enlisting local bar support for higher standards. In 1937, the Tennessee Bar Association requested that such a survey be made. But by 1937, the TBA's request was only the visible culmination of years of preparatory work that had been quietly going on out of public view.

Vanderbilt strongly advocated higher standards. In the 1932/33 catalogue, the school stated that it "militantly supports the requirements for admission to the bar in each state as proposed by the American Bar Association." Many of Arnold's efforts to secure the adoption of such standards, however, were not visible to the public. He drafted legislation, anonymously, that would require higher standards for admission to the bar in Tennessee.[41] In 1934, he and Witham were developing lists of names to send to Shafroth, as work on the survey had already begun. Witham had been called upon to secure persons to provide answers to the surveys for all of the state's schools,[42] and the two deans were selecting recipients for the ABA questionnaire who would provide "what Mr. Shafroth wants."[43] What Shafroth and the deans wanted was public evidence of what they saw as the deplorable state of legal education in Tennessee.

The next year, Arnold secured a list from the ABA of "disapproved schools" stating: "I am very anxious to have a supply of these on hand and send them out to prospective students."[44] He also tried to get an article written by the ABA's Robert L. Stearns on unaccredited law schools published

in a Tennessee newspaper. He succeeded when the *Nashville Banner* ran the
article on June 26, 1935, after it had been rejected by the *Nashville Tennessean* and the assistant City Editor for the *Banner*. It was finally accepted by
the *Banner*'s City Editor, even though he expressed disapproval of it because
he feared it would anger Cumberland Law School constituents.[45] Arnold
continued to try to bring the spotlight of public opinion to the subject, and
even to get the U.S. Supreme Court involved by suggesting that the Court
could adopt the ABA standards as a prerequisite for practice before that
Court.[46]

But on February 1, 1937, he was despairing of his efforts. "I am sitting
in sackcloth and ashes this morning," he wrote to Shafroth. The report of
a committee appointed by the Tennessee Supreme Court had proved to be
disappointing, leading Arnold to conclude, "I doubt if the Supreme Court
will do anything towards increasing the requirements for admission to the
bar within the next five years."[47] The influence of the unapproved Tennessee
schools was very strong, he noted, and they were fighting increased standards at every turn. The Supreme Court was reluctant to act for fear that a
displeased legislature would deprive the court of its discretionary power by
passing a statute which would specify rules for admission to the bar.[48] Still,
Arnold was not giving up the fight, continuing in his letter to Shafroth:
"While I would not want my name mentioned in connection with any agi-
tation, I believe that if the American Bar Association could center its attention on some state such as Tennessee, it would be very effective."

The tide turned quickly. The Supreme Court took a step in early 1937
by requiring that applicants for the bar present evidence of a high school
education (and not just its equivalent), prior to the study of law. An observer
at the time noted that this was an important modification of the rules,
commenting that he had personal knowledge of numerous occurrences that
"smacked of fraud"—instances in which commercial law schools had assumed that an applicant had the equivalent of a high school education
because of age, business experience, or because he paid his matriculation
fee.[49] In June of that year, the Tennessee Bar Association adopted the resolution requesting the ABA to survey the law schools in Tennessee. In relaying
this information to Shafroth, Arnold commented that the new TBA President, George H. Armistead, Jr., was very much in sympathy with increasing
the standards.[50] The survey, and the resulting report by Will Shafroth and
H. C. Horack of Duke Law School published in the *Tennessee Law Review*,[51]
set the stage for decisive action.

The bulk of the report was comprised of assessments of the twelve law
schools in the state.[52] The schools surveyed (and their enrollment figures)

were: Chattanooga College of Law (73), East Tennessee Law School (10), John Randolph Neal College of Law (74), National College of Law and Commerce (12 to 15), University of Tennessee College of Law (84), Cumberland University Law School (217), University of Memphis Law School (136), Southern Law University (83), Andrew Jackson University (31), Kent College of Law (11), Nashville Y.M.C.A. Night Law School (111), Vanderbilt University School of Law (70). In addition to sections on the individual schools, the report commented on the "deplorable" condition of legal education in Tennessee: the "primitive" requirements for admission to the bar, the commercialized nature of many of the schools where the profit-motive overrode the welfare of students, the short length of many of the programs which led to students receiving "only half of a legal education or less," and the way Tennessee's lack of regulation of educational institutions resulted in "legal education racketeering."[53]

The TBA had requested a "disinterested" survey,[54] but it is difficult to imagine a less disinterested process than the one that Arnold, Witham, and Shafroth had designed. The report that was delivered was at least as much window dressing for a *fait accompli* as it was "the most important document in twentieth century legal education in Tennessee."[55] Arnold walked a tightrope in the twelve months leading up to the 1938 Tennessee Bar Association annual meeting. He wanted to do whatever he could to secure passage of higher standards: writing letters, suggesting the distribution of addresses and reports, encouraging other reformers, developing proposals, and working to turn out sympathetic voting members at committee meetings and the TBA state convention.[56] He had offered this suggestion to Shafroth on how the ABA should conduct its inquiry of Cumberland Law School: "Let me suggest to you sub rosa, that when you investigate the situation at Lebanon that you get in touch with Professor Cassiday. He is a new man. He was formerly at the University of San Francisco. He was in here to see me some time ago and gave me a great deal of inside information about that school."[57] At the same time, Arnold thought his efforts would be counterproductive if they became public.[58]

Cumberland Law School, as the most successful of the non-approved schools in Tennessee, was a prominent target for the advocates for higher standards.[59] When the state supreme court had earlier amended its rules, in 1932, to require two years of legal study rather than one for admission to the bar, Shafroth commented to Arnold, "This should do a great deal toward either improving Cumberland or eliminating it from the picture."[60] When the Shafroth/Horack survey was published, the response of A. B. Neil, the part-time dean at Cumberland and judge on the Second Circuit Court in Nashville, demonstrated the extent to which Arnold's agenda had been served. Neil wrote that the "alleged survey . . . did me the gravest injustice and was an irreparable injury to Cumberland University. . . . It would be impossible within a limited space to discuss all of the many damaging insinuations and false conclusions which are unsupported by any fact." Neil did address some of the particulars in the report, referring to the authors' "deep-seated venom," their "malicious libel," and calling them the "Fuehrers in the field of education."[61]

The report faulted Cumberland on almost every front: no administrative oversight; inadequate faculty, library, and curriculum; non-existent standards; out-of-date teaching methods; and the diversion of funds from the law school to support the college. It was this diversion of funds (the School was "as much a commercial venture as if its profit went into the pocket of one man") that the report's authors blamed for the low quality of the school: "students who attend the school are not getting the legal education which they are led to expect and for which they are paying." On the other hand, the report concluded that the University of Tennessee "ranks well among the better law schools of the South," and that Vanderbilt's "excellent reputation through the South is well deserved."

The role that Arnold had chosen for himself in orchestrating these results from behind the scenes is illustrated by an exchange of letters between him and Neil following the vote at the 1938 TBA annual convention to endorse higher standards. Neil wrote to Arnold:

> Upon my return to the City on yesterday from a short trip to West Tennessee, Mr. Seth M. Walker told me that during the State Bar Association meeting some irresponsible person, or persons, had attempted to connect you in some way with the report of Will Shafroth and H. C. Horack. I wish to assure you that no true friend of Cumberland University has ever thought for one moment that you had any part in it, either directly or indirectly. In the heat of discussion, doubtless many things were said on both sides that should have been omitted. I was not present at any session of the Association. I have always entertained the highest respect for Vanderbilt School of Law, and for you personally, although I've not had the pleasure of your acquaintance.[62]

Arnold had urged the ABA to take the action that resulted in the survey, had chosen respondents to the survey for other schools, had advocated its publication in full in the *Tennessee Law Review*, had developed and circulated a counter-proposal to the members of the Committee on Legal Education and Admissions to the Bar to head off an effort to derail the report's recommendations, and had strategized with Dean Witham to increase attendance at the convention by those who favored the report. Nevertheless, Arnold wrote in reply:

> It [the rumor] never affected me in any way and in fact I took it somewhat as a joke, although I did not want myself placed in a false position. There was no foundation in fact for such a statement. The Survey Committee came to our School without any warning and visited our classes as they did in every other school in the State. I never corresponded with either of the Committees concerning the findings and I did not send in any vote as a member of the Tennessee Bar Association on the question as to whether standards in this State should be raised. . . . Of course, I favor high standards but I have taken no active part in any fight to bring about any abrupt change. We have our own problems at Vanderbilt that take all of my energies. It has been my policy since coming to this School to avoid controversial matters so far as possible and to devote my energies to building up the School.[63]

Arnold and Witham had won. At the 1938 TBA convention, 291 of the 330 ballots cast favored at least a two-year pre-legal college and a two-year legal education requirement for admission to the bar.[64] The Supreme Court accepted the recommended change, and Tennessee became one of thirty-nine states to adopt the two-year standard for pre-legal college education. As for the length of legal education standard, forty states were already requiring three years of legal study, a step Tennessee would not take until 1948. Cumberland joined Vanderbilt and Tennessee in 1947 in requesting adoption in the state of standards that matched the ABA's standards,[65] and beginning in 1948, applicants for admission to the bar were required to be graduates of a law school accredited by the ABA or approved by the state board of law examiners.[66]

The 1938 Supreme Court ruling did not go into effect until June 15, 1940, and it did not directly affect Vanderbilt, as the School had long required the ABA minimum of two years of college and three years of legal education. But schools such as Cumberland were already suffering as twenty-eight states had adopted the ABA standards as their own by 1936,[67] and now the new rules in Tennessee established requirements that the graduates of many of the state's law schools could not meet.[68] The expectation was that the 1940 change would boost prospects for increasing enrollment at Vanderbilt,[69] but the slide continued.

ACADEMIC RESPECTABILITY

Earl Arnold quickly built a school that Kirkland was proud of, as the Chancellor reported to the Board in June 1934:

> The faculty is harmonious and composed of good teachers and hard-working investigators. Some of them are doing outside research work. The students are orderly, and contribute their fair share to the on-going of University life on campus, active in many of the important interests that lie outside the class room. Dean Arnold cooperates constantly with the alumni office, and is active in trying to build up friends for the School of Law among the alumni, often visiting remote points and making addresses before colleges, rotary clubs, and bar associations. He has also thoroughly identified himself with the life of Nashville, and is regarded as an important and worthy citizen.[70]

Vanderbilt clearly followed what was identified as the Harvard model in the late 1920s of subordinating research to the training of practitioners.[71] But some of the faculty were actively engaged in research and publication, as Arnold indicated. Of the fifty-two Vanderbilt University non-medical faculty members who had published work in the period 1930–35, six of them were in the Law School. Their work included a book written by Myles O'Connor, who had joined the faculty in 1918, and a number of articles and reviews, including articles in the Michigan, Pennsylvania, Virginia, Georgetown, Tulane, and Tennessee law reviews. Productivity continued through 1940, and then dropped off sharply as the school moved toward closing.[72]

H. W. Arant confirmed the progress that Kirkland had noted. In 1937, after his re-inspection site visit, he relayed the conclusion of the AALS Executive Committee that the school had "undoubtedly greatly improved since it was readmitted to this Association."[73] Arant reported to Chancellor Kirkland that he thought the addition of another full-time teacher would enable Vanderbilt "to take its place as one of the two or three best law schools in the South. I covet this position for Vanderbilt."[74]

Soon after Arnold's arrival, the faculty had taken a number of steps to address deficiencies that had been observed earlier. Among the changes in academic rules adopted in September 1930 were the abolition of conditional grades, approval of credit for work done at other schools only if they were members of the AALS or approved by the ABA, refusal to admit students who were ineligible to continue their studies at another school, and an increase in substantive and procedural requirements for the admission of a special student.[75] The law school's catalogue in 1931/32 actively discouraged the application of special students, a reversal of the approach of just a few years earlier which encouraged business people and others with legal interests to register as special students.

The faculty not only made admission more difficult, they also raised the bar for students to remain in School. In October 1930, they adopted a grading curve that was harsh by modern standards: A, 10%; B, 25%; C, 45%; D, 10%; F, 10%—with a C average required for graduation.[76] When ABA Advisor Shafroth expressed his concern that Vanderbilt had not dropped any students or denied graduation to any students in the three previous years for academic reasons,[77] Arnold was able to reply by communicating the new standards which he described as being "as modern as will be found in any law school."[78]

The continued tightening of academic standards, for admission and for remaining in school, surely created yet another obstacle to meeting the Board's goal of increasing enrollment. Rules were changed so that being late to a class counted as an absence.[79] In response to criticisms that grading requirements had not been severe enough in the past, several students were failed at the end of the Fall 1937 term, and in June 1938 the School told nine students—over 20% of the first- and second-year classes—that they could not return,[80] even in the face of mounting deficits. By 1941, Carmichael could report that no Vanderbilt graduate had failed a bar exam in "about five years."[81]

Vanderbilt resisted trading quality for balanced budgets. Apparently, Board of Trust member Barthell was so discouraged about inadequate tuition receipts that he discussed with Arnold the prospect of hiring a large number of adjuncts and teaching larger classes by abandoning the case method as a way of balancing the school's budget.[82] But the school was going in the opposite direction. Barthell's inquiry led to an interesting exchange, probably set up by Arnold in order to use national standards to derail Barthell's suggestions. Arnold raised Barthell's ideas in a letter to Arant in his capacity as Secretary of the AALS. Arant expressed surprise that the questions were even asked, "I would not have supposed that a Dean of any American Law School could have any doubt about most of the matters concerning which you inquire." On the specific inquiry about moving from the case method to the textbook method of teaching exclusively, he said that "no such backward step has ever been taken or even seriously considered by a member school. However, I entertain no doubt as to what would happen if such a step were taken."[83] As Arnold communicated to Barthell, in all probability a school that made such a change would be dropped from AALS membership for failing to follow "those standards and practices generally recognized by member schools as essential to the maintenance of a sound educational policy."[84] Barthell responded: "In my opinion, if the Secretary of the Association correctly expresses the views of the Association, then the Association needs investigating."[85]

Arnold and Carmichael were attempting to bring an increased professionalism and rigor to the faculty's work, which sometimes resulted in a clash of expectations. Interactions with Professor Morton Hendrick provide a glimpse into the evolving culture at the School. Hendrick joined the faculty in 1926, having taught for two years at Drake Law School, following several years in practice. When he and Professor Lawrence had made an arrangement to re-allocate their own teaching loads and compensation in 1930, Dean Arnold and Chancellor Carmichael made it clear that such matters were not open to private negotiation among individual faculty.[86]

Hendrick again found himself the subject of administrative attention when he delayed his return from a leave of absence. Hendrick had been granted a leave for 1937-38 because his father was seriously ill, and he then received an extension for a second year which he requested, as he put it, with the "Roosevelt Depression coming before I was ready for it."[87] As the time approached for him to return, Hendrick wrote to Arnold that he was not feeling well, and in a series of communications he pushed his anticipated arrival date back to September 1, then to September 15 (the date of the first faculty meeting), then to September 25 (the first day of classes). Arnold's and Carmichael's increasing irritation led to a telegram from Arnold to Hendrick: "University authorities concerned over delayed arrival after two years of leave. . . . Am instructed to advise that if health hampers work expected you should resign. . . . Fear continued uncertainty will bring immediate action by Board. Wire collect." The same day, Hendrick wired back: "Wire exact date of faculty meeting I will be there"[88]

This incident provoked Arnold to communicate to Hendrick a range of expectations of faculty members, some of which had arisen or become more definite during his two-year leave. Arnold included a summary statement of the changing environment in a letter to Hendrick:

> The University feels that we are paid beginning September 1st although there may be no meetings or assigned work to do. After all, a teacher must exercise some initiative and do considerable research work. In fact the Board is going to insist hereafter that we do more research work, spend more time in our offices where we are available to students, and really give our entire time to the University as we would certainly do if

we were working for a private concern. . . . While the faculty is paid in installments, the Board feels that it is really a twelve months job and, with the exception of a reasonable summer vacation, a man ought to spend time in research in connection with his work and in improving himself as a scholar and as a teacher. More emphasis on this work outside of class room will be evident in the Board's attitude from now on.[89]

Carmichael appeared at a faculty meeting a week later, reinforcing the expectations that faculty would be available for consultation with students and that they would engage in research.[90]

Financial constraints prevented major expansion of the curriculum in the 1930s, but incremental improvements were made. Legal Ethics was offered for the first time in 1931/32 as an elective, and became a required first-year course the following year.[91] Elective courses became a more prominent feature in the curriculum, an experimental course in Labor Law was introduced, and more emphasis was given to courses in public law. But even Arnold described such changes as "tinkering with the curriculum,"[92] and little could be done to address the acknowledged desire to enhance education in the social sciences.[93]

A school the size of Vanderbilt could not offer as broad a curriculum as the larger schools. A survey of the curriculum in the nation's smaller schools was conducted in 1938, and the results of that survey shed light on the distinctive features of a Vanderbilt education. The survey was distributed to forty-eight schools, and forty-five responded.[94] Vanderbilt's required first-year course of study was typical for the time, with two exceptions: a course in Constitutional Law (required in the first year by only three other schools in the group), and Legal Ethics (required by only two others). Vanderbilt students were given more flexibility in their upper-class coursework than was true at most schools. The only two required second or third year offerings were Trial Practice and Practice Court, and Appellate Practice and Practice Court—and these courses were not even available at many other schools. Another distinctive feature of the Vanderbilt curriculum were courses offered by Professor William Armstrong Hunter: Trade Regulation (listed by five other schools), Equity Pleading (listed by three), and Drafting of Legal Instruments, which appeared at no other school.[95]

Hunter had been a faculty colleague of Arnold's at George Washington, and came to Vanderbilt directly from a Research Fellowship at Harvard to fill Schermerhorn's position. Hunter also supervised Vanderbilt students' work with the Nashville Legal Aid Society, interviewing witnesses and assisting in the preparation of cases. Vanderbilt students began legal aid work in the summer of 1939; only five schools responded to the survey by saying that their students regularly participated in legal aid work or other apprenticeship training.

Toward the end of the decade, the faculty began to unravel, prompting Chancellor Carmichael to comment in 1940, "Since 1937 the School has been somewhat disorganized," noting specifically the two year leave of absence for Hendrick, a leave for Terry Kirkpatrick after which he resigned, and the fluidity of the appointment status of Lowe Watkins.[96] The beginnings of the unsettled state of the faculty could be traced to the death of Schermerhorn on January 26, 1935. A faculty colleague of nineteen years, he was not only a source of stability but was highly regarded, as indicated by the resolution adopted by the faculty that read, in part: "In faculty and student groups, and by large numbers of the people of Nashville, he was held in peculiar esteem and affection."[97] Myles O'Connor retired in 1938, after serving on the faculty at three different times dating back to 1902. Kirkpatrick resigned in August 1939, at the end of a year's leave, immediately before the beginning of classes. The uncertainties surrounding Hendrick's leaves of absence in 1937/38 and 1938/39 have already been discussed. Roy Robert Ray was appointed as a visiting professor to fill in for Hendrick, and then he departed after one additional year; Robert Cook similarly filled Kirkpatrick's slot on a temporary basis during his leave in 1938/39.

Tracking the faculty status of Lowe Watkins gives some evidence of the disorganization that worried Carmichael. Watkins had earned an M.A. and Ph.D. in economics at Vanderbilt, a few years after graduating from the Law School as Founder's Medalist in 1924. He was initially hired as a last-minute replacement, when Kirkpatrick did not return from his leave, on August 16, 1939, for classes that started that fall, becoming the first Law School faculty member to hold a Ph.D. His appointment was changed to a part-time position for 1940/41, but in the spring of that year he was approved for a position on the faculty of the College of Arts and Science to teach a course in Constitutional Law during a faculty member's illness, and then he was also approved to step in to fill the shoes of Thomas H. Malone, Jr, who had died on March 21, 1941. Malone, an 1896 graduate of the school and the son of Dean Thomas Malone, had been teaching on a part-time basis since 1923, and was recognized as a "thorough scholar, a successful lawyer, and a rare personality."[98] He had joined Clarence Darrow in the defense of John Scopes when the evolution-teaching case was appealed to Tennessee's Supreme Court. Watkins served in a part-time capacity for the next two years, before his position again became a full-time appointment in 1942-43. The range of his teaching was immense, as he taught seventeen different courses including Administrative Law, Business Associations, Constitutional Law, Contracts, Bankruptcy, Domestic Relations, Labor Law, Public Utilities, Taxation, Torts, and Trade Regulation.[99] He would continue his faculty work when the School re-opened after the war, with a re-appointment to a part-time position.

CHAPTER FOUR

A Casualty of War

The Doors Close

A ny prospects for a near-term reversal of the Law School's fortunes ended with the attack on Pearl Harbor on December 7, 1941. Many American law schools continued operation through World War II, but these schools had large enough enrollments to survive the temporary but significant decreases in the number of students. Vanderbilt's enrollment had shrunk to the point that there was no such margin. While all schools had struggled with the economic challenges of the Depression, Vanderbilt faced the additional obstacles to maintaining a substantial enrollment brought on by its lack of a law school building, increased academic standards that made admission more difficult and attrition more frequent, a resource base that hampered program development, and spreading student discontent.[1]

The registration figures tell the story. The Law School opened in the fall of 1941 with forty-six students, a decrease of only nine from the previous year.[2] But seven of those students departed during the year to enter military service, and the draft age was lowered to twenty. Only twenty-one students enrolled for the fall 1942 semester, and by February 1943 only twelve students were still registered.[3] In fall 1943 twenty-two students were reported to be enrolled, but two withdrew within a few days, and of the remaining twenty only seven were full-time students, one of whom graduated in December.[4] The often-delayed decision on the School's operations could not be delayed any longer.

Chancellor Carmichael had openly discussed closing the School with the Board of Trust as early as February 1942. He was concerned that the School would lose its standing and accreditation, and that it would be difficult to revive the School after the war if it closed. He expressed hope that the AALS would suspend some of its standards during the war, and concluded, "I have no recommendation to make at this time, but it is likely that some drastic steps may have to be taken at the next meeting of the Board."[5] But at the next Board meeting in June, the Chancellor had no recommendations to make, and no action was taken. The February 1943 Board meeting resulted only in the appointment of a committee to study options. The dean was authorized, however, to inform students that instruction would be offered the following year, without specifying the type of program that would be available.[6]

In the summer of 1943, efforts were being made to keep the doors open. Arnold suggested the enrollment of students from the Nashville Y.M.C.A. Night Law School, which was being closed for the duration of the war. That school had been founded in 1911 by four Vanderbilt law graduates (Morton B. Adams, William P. Cooper, Lee Douglas, and Robert Selph Henry) to serve those interested in a legal education who were unable to attend classes during the day.[7] Vanderbilt's Board approved the recommendation that students who had been enrolled at the Y.M.C.A. school be allowed to enroll at Vanderbilt (with the understanding that their degrees would be granted by the Y.M.C.A. school), and some classes were scheduled at night to accommodate these potential new students. On campus, the Chancellor had appointed a committee of faculty members from the Law School and the College of Arts and Science to develop a cooperative program in law and the social sciences to benefit the Law School.[8]

When the AALS adopted Emergency Resolution No. 7, Vanderbilt's dilemma was resolved. The resolution, presented to the Vanderbilt Board in February of 1944, stated:

> Any member school which suspends instruction during the present war may retain membership and upon notice to the Secretary may assume inactive status provided (1) it spends at least $1,000 per year in maintaining accessions to its library; (2) it pays annual dues at one-half the normal rate.
>
> Such a school may resume active status upon a showing to the Executive Committee that it meets all standards of the Association; such a showing shall be made at least 60 days before reopening, and it shall contain a statement of the number of faculty, the proposed expenditures for faculty and books, and an outline of the proposed curriculum.[9]

The AALS had taken the potential consequence of loss of accreditation off the board, and the University's committee immediately recommended that the Law School be suspended effective July 1, 1944, according to the plan set forth by the AALS. The Board approved the recommendation, noting that the current year's experiment had proved that there was not any market for part-time legal instruction in Nashville, and that closing the School would save the University at least $15,000 per year.

The committee emphasized that it favored reopening the School when the war was over. The committee also made note of the fact that the Law School was the only Vanderbilt school that did not have its own endowment and urged that there be a vigorous effort to raise endowment funds for the School.[10] In adopting the committee's recommendation, the Board observed that there might be some advantage to closing the School temporarily, making possible "a new start with a new outlook." Fitzgerald Hall was added to the committee, which was charged with developing plans for the reopening of the School at a later date.[11]

Arnold opposed the closing of the School, writing to Witham the week after the decision was made, "I agree that the closing of the Law School for the duration of the war seems to me to be a mistake. . . . In fact, had it not been for a hard fight I made a year ago this action would have been taken then."[12] He had predicted that enrollment would dwindle to three or four full-time students, and thus proposed establishing an evening division for part-time students, accompanied by lower tuition and extensive advertising[13]—an alternative the Board found unfeasible. Arnold was the man caught in the middle. He had seen the problem looming for years. One of his strategies for keeping the School open had been to reduce the budget by encouraging some faculty members to accept "better jobs" elsewhere,[14] a move that may have turned out to be something of a self-fulfilling prophecy to the extent that the deterioration of the faculty had contributed to the School's demise. When the decision to suspend operations was made, the task was left to Arnold to respond to complaints from parents and students who had been told the year before that there were no plans to close the School.[15]

Even before the final decision, the School's operations were winding down. In the spring of 1942, leaves of absence had been approved for William Hunter (to serve as a Lt. Colonel in the U.S. Army), Harold E. Verrall (to serve in the regional Office of Price Administration in Atlanta), and Law Librarian McLaurin (whose leave was extended in the spring of 1943 after she enlisted in the WAVES as an ensign). In September 1942 a one-year leave was approved for Hendrick, "with the understanding that there is no commitment for re-instatement at the expiration of the leave of absence, because of the uncertainty of the present situation."[16] With Hendrick's departure the School was left with only the three full-time faculty members required by the AALS: Lowe Watkins, who was being appointed for only one semester at a time; John Howard Moore, who was unable to do any teaching for most of the spring 1943 semester because of illness; and Arnold. In June 1943 the faculty decided that there would be no award that year of the Founder's Medal nor would they award scholarships or any other prizes. The faculty did approve the law degree for one student: Raymond Marshall Briggs.[17]

The Board voted on February 7, 1944, to close the School. Subsequently, arrangements were made to allow the six third-year students who were enrolled at that time to complete their degrees. Professor Moore was to be employed full-time until January 1, 1945. Moore, who had taught at Florida and Mercer before joining the Vanderbilt faculty in 1924, was one of the two faculty members whose full-time tenure spanned the WWII reorganization, and he taught until 1949.[18] Watkins was retained on a part-time basis to help offer the coursework needed by the continuing students. A "Memorandum for the Minute Book of the Law School," signed by Moore and Watkins, records that the six students completed the work for their degrees as of December 20, 1944.[19] One of the six students was Earl Kazuo Nishimura, a "Hawaiian student of Japanese extraction," who had been allowed to continue his work only with clearance from the National Japanese American Student Relocation Council.[20]

Arnold stayed until the end. He had had several opportunities to leave, but felt that his first duty was to Vanderbilt.[21] He continued in office, even at some cost to his own health: "The strain here during the past two years has been such that much has been taken out of me. The Doctor told me to slow up last Fall, and Mrs. Arnold told me I must resign. So the action of the Board was doubtless a good thing for me, because I would have tried to keep the school going."[22] Arnold was granted a year's leave of absence beginning July 1, 1944, with the understanding that he would not resume the deanship of the School at the end of that period—in accord with his expressed wishes. He had written Carmichael in March 1944, "This does not change my present desire, already communicated to you, that some one else be selected when the Law School reopens after the war."[23] Arnold was designated Dean Emeritus, and remained interested in the School's affairs until his death in November 1949.

Moore remained employed at Vanderbilt during the closure, on a reduced salary, serving as Librarian beginning in January 1, 1945, and handling correspondence and other inquiries. The other Law School employee during this period was Ms. Sonnenfield, who worked half time on Law School library and secretarial work, and half time with the new endowment campaign for the Law School. She had served as Secretary to the Dean, or the School's Assistant Secretary, since 1927, and was named Law School Registrar in the spring of 1940. By June of 1945 the development campaign she was working on had received cash and pledges totaling $370,000—a sign of better days to come.

William V. A. Sullivan was the School's first graduate in 1875. He later served in the U.S. Senate from the state of Mississippi.

Allen G. Hall became the first full-time faculty member at the Law School in 1903. He served as dean from 1910 until 1915.

Thomas H. Malone served as Dean
of the Law School from 1875 until 1904.

Dean Earl C. Arnold guided the School
back to respectability after its exclusion
from the Association of American
Law Schools, and through the Great
Depression, until operations were
suspended in 1944.

Clara Marie Weber became the first woman to graduate from Vanderbilt Law School in 1919, shown here with classmates.

The Class of 1932 in their first year, on the steps of Kirkland Hall with Katherine Elizabeth Miller, the lone woman in the Class, front and center.

The Law Library Reading Room in Kirkland Hall in 1950, housed in the former
University Chapel (note the stained glass windows).

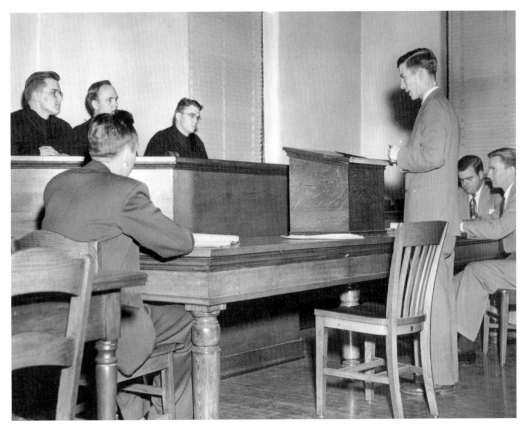

A moot court presentation in 1950: Frank Gilliland is presenting to "appellate judges" James H. Roberts, Henry McCall, and Abner McGehee. Seated (from left) are David Rutherford, Harold Dedman, and Sydney Keeble.

Law students' socializing included formal dances, as at this 1955 Law Day Dance.

Student pictures of the first two African-American students to enroll in Vanderbilt Law School in 1956, Frederick T. Work on the left and Edward Melvin Porter on the right.

Vanderbilt Law Review student editors in their office in Kirkland Hall, circa 1955. (Photographer: L.L. Tucker)

Construction of the first Law School building on campus in 1961,
with Furman Hall in the background.

Students moving the Law Library's collection to the new building in the summer of 1962.

The new home for the Law School after moving out of the top floors of the University's main administration building, Kirkland Hall, in 1962.

An early "high tech" classroom in the new building, circa 1965.

CHAPTER FIVE

Reopening the Law School

Dale Coffman was chosen to be the dean in charge of the resurrected Law School. A national search had narrowed the field of candidates to Coffman and Benno Schmidt. When Schmidt withdrew on February 8, 1946, Coffman was offered the position that afternoon and his appointment was effective on March 1.[1] Coffman's educational credentials were stellar: B.A. (Phi Beta Kappa) and J.D. (Order of the Coif) from the University of Iowa, followed by an LL.M. at Harvard, where he studied under Felix Frankfurter, and later an S.J.D. from Harvard. But he was something of a surprising choice because he was not a legal scholar,[2] having served as General Counsel for General Electric for most of his career following five years on the Nebraska law faculty.

He left Vanderbilt after only three years, but his impact on the Law School was significant. He not only presided over the reopening, he recruited an accomplished faculty (including John Wade and Morton Ferson, the first of the "recycled" faculty—faculty at other law schools who were forced into retirement by mandatory age limits at the end of distinguished careers), he established the *Vanderbilt Law Review* and the Vanderbilt chapter of the Order of the Coif, and he led a partially successful campaign in the state to raise bar admission standards.

Coffman's first order of business was to create a new faculty, one that was "well above the average." "We are well on our way toward the acquisition of such a faculty, and I have no conscience whatever in stealing the best men from the best law schools and law firms of the country."[3] His initial appointment was Rollin M. Perkins, a member of the AALS Executive Committee who had taught for thirty years on the Iowa Law School faculty. He was the author of several casebooks and textbooks and his articles had appeared in the nation's leading law reviews. Perkins was the key to Coffman's desire to have an instantly respected faculty. His strategy was to fill one of the faculty positions "with a man who has a national reputation as a legal scholar and one who has made a name for himself in the teaching side of the legal profession." Coffman identified Perkins, who had been one of his teachers, as just such a candidate: "I believe that the appointment of this man would assist in giving Vanderbilt Law School immediate recognition in the profession. . . . Mr. Perkins has had many professional honors conferred upon him and is the author of an amazing number of books and articles."[4] Coffman's assessment was shared by the dean who was losing Perkins, as Dean Mason Ladd wrote, "Perkins is an excellent teacher. There are really none better and to have a man of his ability as a teacher on your faculty almost in and of itself will give your school a good lift at the start. . . . I was sorry that I could not raise his salary to compete with your offer."[5]

Perkins was named the Frank C. Rand Professor of Law, a professorship created by the Board of Trust in June 1945 in recognition of Board President Rand's outstanding service and devotion to the University, particularly his generous contributions in securing the endowment for the Law School. This was not only the Law School's first named professorship; it was the first faculty chair in the University outside of the School of Religion.[6]

In addition to Perkins, the cohort of new faculty included Jefferson Barnes Fordham, Hugh L. Sowards, and Walter W. Dwyer. Fordham had been on the West Virginia faculty for five years and the LSU faculty for six years, following his years of practice on Wall Street. After only one year at Vanderbilt, he left to become dean at the Ohio State School of Law. He later served for eighteen years as dean at the University of Pennsylvania Law School.

Sowards was appointed as assistant professor of law. He came directly from receiving his LL.B. from Yale, where he had distinguished himself in becoming the first law student in Yale's history who was allowed to occupy a regular faculty position at the university while still a student.[7] Dwyer, who earned his LL.B. at Harvard, joined the faculty as Law Librarian and Lecturer in Legal Bibliography. He was the author of "A Visual Outline of Legal Research" which was required reading for law students at Harvard and Columbia. His brother Frank X. Dwyer, the acting director of the Library of Congress, came to Vanderbilt at the reopening to collaborate in the reorganization and cataloging of the library.

These new faculty members joined two returning faculty. Harold Verrall, who originally came to Vanderbilt in 1931 from Cornell, returned from his leave of absence, and Howard Moore continued but only on a part-time basis because of poor health. The teaching faculty was rounded out with three local attorneys who also taught on a part-time basis: Robert Sturdivant, the School's 1938 Founder's Medalist, who had done graduate work at Harvard Law School; William Wade, a chancery court judge; and Lowe Watkins, who was engaged in a tax practice at Keeble, Keeble, and McGugin.

The students who entered the Law School in 1946 were a distinctive group. Nearly all of them were World War II veterans. Compared to law students in any other era, they were older, more experienced, more disciplined, more serious about their studies—and ready to contribute to the institution. When Professor Moore's voice would not carry in the suddenly large class crammed into an amphitheatre, the students purchased and installed a sound system. They also exerted some control of the academic program. In October 1947, for example, the first-year students met and rescheduled their Torts class from a Saturday to a Friday, apparently without faculty participation, so that it would not conflict with a Vanderbilt football game.[8]

Coffman succeeded in establishing two institutions that he considered crucial to moving Vanderbilt into the mainstream of national institutions. One was the *Vanderbilt Law Review*, at a time when "practically every major law school in America publishes its own Law Review."[9] Sowards was the Faculty Editor for the initial December 1947 issue. The faculty approved the inaugural student editorial board on November 4, 1947, with Herschiel S. Barnes being named the first Editor in Chief.[10] The next semester the faculty chose new board members, including Mary E. Mann as Comment Editor, making her the first female student to hold an editorial position on the journal.[11]

The second institution Coffman worked to create at Vanderbilt was a chapter of the Order of the Coif, the national honorary society which recognized the top ten percent of each graduating class. For the inauguration of the local chapter in 1949, thirty-seven graduates of the School, who would have been eligible for Coif membership in prior years, returned in the spring of 1949 to attend the initiation of that year's top 10%. At that time, there were only thirty-eight chapters of the Order of the Coif nationwide, comprising about one fourth of the AALS membership.[12]

Coffman also worked at moving into the national mainstream by addressing Tennessee bar admission standards. When he became dean, Tennessee and Georgia were the only two states in which most of the state's law students were enrolled in schools that did not meet the minimum standards of the ABA. While 85% of law students nationally were attending ABA approved schools, Coffman estimated that figure to be 25% in Tennessee.[13] Dean Sam Gilreath of the Cumberland Law School and UT Dean William

Wicker joined Coffman in supporting an effort to raise Tennessee standards for admission to the bar to the ABA minimums, which had already been adopted in forty-two states.

Coffman authored a resolution to the Tennessee Supreme Court advocating specific increases in the state's bar admission rules which would require three years of law study in a school with at least three full-time teachers and a law library of not less than 7,500 volumes. These changes, which would have elevated the state's requirements to the minimum recommended by the American Bar Association, were quickly endorsed by the leadership of the Tennessee Bar Association which petitioned the court to adopt them. "Some law schools in Tennessee are not giving veterans and other students their money's worth," said Aubrey Folts, president of the TBA, and a poll of the association's members showed a three to one majority in favor of the changes.[14]

But the opposition quickly mobilized. Within a week, students and alumni of the Y.M.C.A. night law school had begun a letter writing campaign. Ferriss C. Bailey, the School's dean (and Vanderbilt law alumnus) stated that adoption of the new standards would mean certain closure of the school. *The Nashville Tennessean* editorialized against the revisions, and a local American Legion post condemned Coffman "for promoting and fostering this effort to destroy night schools." Folts backpedaled, saying he did not know what position the association would take on the specific proposals because he had not heard back from the committee on education.[15]

At the TBA convention later that June, the association avoided taking action on the dean's resolution by approving a simple recommendation that "standards of admission be materially increased." Because this resolution, which was passed unanimously, did not specify any particular changes, the expectation was that they would lead to no significant alteration in the bar admission standards.[16] The rules subsequently issued by the Tennessee Supreme Court contained none of the offending provisions in the dean's resolution. The changes were not, however, inconsequential as they required an increase in the number of hours of class instruction in the part-time schools, provided that law schools could not be conducted as commercial enterprises or through correspondence instruction, and required prior approval of any new schools by the Board of Bar Examiners (who would use standards such as "an adequate library," and "competent instructors") in order for a school's graduates to be eligible to take the state bar examination.[17]

Coffman resigned abruptly in the spring of 1949 in the third year of his deanship to become the founding dean at a new law school at UCLA.

His resignation had an effective date of March 1, an unusual time for a dean to depart. In the annual dean's report that Perkins filed as acting dean that spring, he called Coffman's new position "the outstanding opportunity of the day in the field of legal education," an opportunity that had been "viewed hopefully by practically every law dean in the country."[18] When Coffman left Vanderbilt to take the deanship at UCLA, Perkins stepped in and served as Acting Dean for the remainder of that academic year, and then he left to join Coffman at UCLA. Coffman took not only Perkins to UCLA, but also Verrall, the librarian Dwyer and two valued staff members. Even Red Sanders, Vanderbilt's head football coach, left for UCLA, announcing his departure on the same day that Coffman did.

Coffman's boss, Chancellor Branscomb, had concluded that Coffman was more suited to launch or reorganize a school than to handle day-to-day administration.[19] Wade rendered this assessment of Coffman's "serious drawbacks as an administrator" a year later: "I am afraid that he could not be at any one place for any real period of time without creating serious friction, both in his relations to those above him and in his relations to those below him. His methods of handling problems and reaching decisions are sometimes arbitrary and made without due regard for the various points of view involved."[20] Wade would later say that his first year on the Vanderbilt faculty, under Coffman's deanship, was the only unhappy year of his life— quite a statement from a Marine who was seriously injured in the World War II Pacific Islands campaign.[21]

Coffman's dealings with Vanderbilt continued after he left. In 1956, Ray Allen, the Chancellor at UCLA, wrote to Branscomb, describing problems that he thought would "almost inevitably result in a request that Dean Coffman resign his deanship." He asked Branscomb for his appraisal, in confidence, of Coffman's performance at Vanderbilt, an appraisal that he would use only in response to any questions his Board of Regents might ask concerning his decisions in this matter.[22] Branscomb responded with a candid itemization of "the points of difficulty."[23] Among these difficulties were Coffman's violation of University policies, a "bombastical and egotistical" approach to public relations, and one particular instance of misrepresentation. Despite Allen's assurances that anything Branscomb said would be held "in strictest confidence," reports of at least some of the contents of the letter made their way back to Coffman, including the statement that his resignation had been received on the Vanderbilt campus with some relief.

Coffman wrote to James G. Stahlman and other members of the Vanderbilt Board of Trust, asking them to write letters on his behalf that would refute what the Chancellor had said about him.[24] Stahlman was having none of it, but declined with incredible diplomacy: "By reason of my own high regard and friendship for you, I would be adverse to any effort to prove the truth or falsity of anything that might have been written or said about you during your connection with Vanderbilt."[25] Stahlman also put a little distance between himself and Coffman regarding political matters on which they may have been like-minded. When Coffman complained in his letter, "I am being attacked out here by the parlor pinks and those who do not agree with our view," Stahlman wrote simply in reply, "I am sorry that you are under attack by the parlor pinks or others in California who do not agree with your views." In yet one more foray, Coffman asked a few years later to talk with Stahlman about returning to Vanderbilt as Chancellor when Branscomb retired. Stahlman's reply was short and to the point: "I wish I could give you some encouragement with reference to your returning to Vanderbilt, but knowing the situation as I do, I would not be so unfair as to mislead you by holding out any false hopes."[26]

William Ray Forrester followed Coffman as dean in July 1949. After receiving his law degree from the University of Chicago, he practiced with a Chicago bank and a law firm, before joining the Tulane faculty in 1941. He had served as Acting Dean there, and was Assistant Dean at the time he accepted Vanderbilt's offer. He was well-liked at Vanderbilt, but returned to Tulane to be their dean after only three years as Vanderbilt's dean. When Forrester arrived, "morale was at a very low ebb" because of the departures of Coffman, Perkins, Verrall, and Dwyer—most of the full-time faculty. He plugged the holes with a visiting appointment for Herman L. Trautman, and with part-time appointments of three additional former Founder's Medalists who were members of the local bar: Edwin Hunt, Cecil Sims, and William Waller.

Forrester extended a practice of luring distinguished professors out of retirement. Coffman had recruited Morton Ferson, who came to the Vanderbilt law faculty in 1948, at the age of seventy-two, as a visiting faculty member after having served as dean at George Washington, University of North Carolina, and the University of Cincinnati law schools. Ferson was appointed as Frank C. Rand Visiting Professor of Law in 1949. He, too, joined the exodus to UCLA in 1951, but returned to Vanderbilt a year later. Forrester followed the second career precedent by recruiting Edmund M. Morgan who joined the faculty in 1950. Morgan had been pushed into retirement from his position as Royall Professor of Law at Harvard Law School, and his second distinguished career at Vanderbilt would last until 1963.

Law School enrollments were declining nationally when Forrester began his term as dean because the veterans who had been attending law school on the G.I. Bill had moved through the system. This was a positive development for legal education, in Forrester's mind, as the previous few years had seen too many students crowded into large classrooms to the detriment of the learning environment. He used this occasion to offer a vision for Vanderbilt that would guide the School beyond his deanship. Vanderbilt's education, he flatly asserted, was unsurpassed in the South, but he was not content with regional superiority in the competition for the better students and potential leaders. "The strong national schools of the North and East will also be seeking to attract such students from this area to their institutions. For my part, I believe that the Vanderbilt plan for a moderate-sized student body, with a strong faculty, offers certain definite advantages in comparison with the schools of the North and East where the number of students is very much larger and the contact between faculty and student slight."[27]

Curricular changes were also underway. Introduction to the Study of Law was added as a first-year course; practice court was extended to all three years, including the assignment of writing briefs and preparing arguments to first-year students; an advanced legal research and writing course was created for upper-class students; and Jurisprudence was introduced into the curriculum as an elective. A measure of the academic strides being made at Vanderbilt during Forrester's deanship was the dramatic increase in passage rates on the Tennessee bar exam: from 49% in 1950, to 73% in 1951 to 93% in 1952.[28] In the late 1940s, Harold Verrall began building a file on the Tennessee bar exams that the School made available to students. He collected copies of the exam for a twenty-year period, classified all questions according to law school courses, and searched the *Tennessee Digests* to identify the cases upon which the questions were founded. He found considerable repetition in the areas covered over the years.[29]

Forrester's tenure was brief, but he made a good enough impression that when Vanderbilt was engaged in the search for a Provost a dozen years later, Wade and Professor Paul Hartman each recommended Forrester to the search committee.[30] He later was a member of the Visiting Committee for Vanderbilt Law School while serving as dean of the Cornell School of Law.

Both Coffman and Forrester benefited from a new fiscal stability in the Law School. In important ways, the reopening of the School began even before it closed. A letter was sent to the Law School's 1,400 former students in February 1944, five months before the closing of the School in July. There was a gratifying response to this letter, quite unlike the similar letter in 1935 which had fallen on deaf, or at least indifferent, ears. This time, most of the respondents expressed interest in an effort to raise endowment funds, and thought that there would be a similar interest among their colleagues in a development campaign for funds designated for the School. Indeed, the initial response included contributions of $390.[31] These gifts constituted the beginning of an unrestricted endowment for the Law School.

Encouraged by the response to this letter, the Board moved immediately in 1944 to provide a resource base for reopening the School after the war. Specifically, the Board voted not only to make an effort to secure funds for the School's endowment during 1944/45, but also to provide matching funds of up to $500,000 to establish an endowment of $1 million that would be used exclusively for the Law School.[32] By June 1945, the fund drive (which had received over $200,000 in cash and pledges by February) had stalled. Kirkland commented that it was not surprising that the campaign had been difficult as it was possibly the first such campaign for a law school in the South, and he suggested that the Board consider using $130,000 of accrued interest on the F. W. Vanderbilt Estate Funds to complete the drive.[33] The next year, the Board approved such an allocation of $125,000 (in addition to the $500,000 match), thus establishing a Law School endowment of $1 million to support the post-war School.[34] The University had also used general funds to pay for a $20,000 remodeling and rearranging of Kirkland Hall space for the reopening, in the hope that future Law School operations would create a surplus to liquidate the advance.[35]

Coffman's first act as dean was to recommend an increase in tuition from $240 to $350, which was approved by the Board.[36] The G.I. Bill allowed up to $500 per year for tuition, and thus schools across the country were generally raising tuition 15% to 30% or more. Despite soaring costs, enrollments soared even higher. In 1946/47, college enrollment nationally reached 2.1 million, surpassing the previous record of less than 1.5 million.[37] Vanderbilt Law School was one of the boats lifted by this rising tide. With an enrollment target of 150, the School registered 153 students in fall 1946, 268 in fall 1947 (243 of whom were veterans), and an astonishing 354 in fall 1948. The growth was actually constrained by the limited physical facilities, as Coffman told Branscomb that the entering classes of 150 "could have been almost three times that size if we had taken all qualified applicants."[38] Tuition was increased to $400, exceeding the national median of $324, and the budget surplus grew.

Enrollment numbers, however, dropped almost as quickly as they had risen. By the fall 1951 term only 171 registered, with even fewer (128) in the following year. Simultaneously with the ebbing of the pent-up demand from World War II, the call went out for military enlistments for the Korean War and the Law School enrollment dropped below the financial break-even point of 175 students. Even with only 120 students in 1954/55, the faculty refused to lower admission standards, a position supported by Branscomb: "To lower admission standards would immediately lower the quality of the work. They have shown, it seems to me, a statesmanlike view of their task, and have a current reserve adequate to see them through a half-dozen years even at this enrollment, so that I am not disturbed by this situation."[39] A steady improvement in this picture in the following years confirmed the wisdom of the School's strategy.

CHAPTER SIX

The Wade Years

JOHN WEBSTER WADE

The way Mary Moody Wade remembered the trip, she and her husband John were on their way to Knoxville to interview for a job at the University of Tennessee when they stopped off in Nashville to visit with Dale Coffman. Coffman, whom John knew from his days as a Harvard student, was the Dean of Vanderbilt Law School at the time. Coffman offered him a job on the spot and the couple never went on to Knoxville.[1] The appointment of John Webster Wade to the Vanderbilt faculty laid the cornerstone for the institution that Vanderbilt Law School would become. A widely-experienced, but not unbiased, Elliott Cheatham would one day write to Wade, "You have made a greater contribution to legal education than any other dean of your time, transforming a barely tolerated local law school into a 'prestigious law school.'"[2]

The Law School had reopened its doors, accepting new students in the fall of 1946. Financial commitments by the University, and unprecedented success in fund raising for the School, had provided a much-needed resource base. The number of students who enrolled, fueled by post-war pent-up demand and financed by the G.I. Bill, was also unprecedented in the School's history. The initial appointments of deans and faculty were promising.

But in those early years of the reopened School there were transitional developments that bordered on turmoil. In less than six years, the School would be looking for its fourth post-War dean. By 1949, not a single faculty member from the group that welcomed the new students in 1946 remained at Vanderbilt. The rush of students in the late 1940s had dwindled: by the time Wade assumed the deanship in 1952, enrollment had declined from a peak of 354 students to 128 in the fall of 1952. The University appointed a new Chancellor in 1946, Harvie Branscomb, who trumpeted new, national aspirations for the University. Clearly the Law School was not keeping pace.

In what may have been the pivotal event in the School's history, John Wade became the Dean of Vanderbilt Law School. When he stepped down as dean twenty years later, he had planted the seeds, if not set the School's trajectory, for the rest of the century. In many ways, the nature of the School came to reflect Wade's personal characteristics: his fierce loyalty and dedication to the School, his commitment to broadening its horizons, and his personal stature as a scholar.

When Forrester announced he was returning to Tulane in 1952, it took Vanderbilt only two weeks to name John Wade as the new dean. Wade brought academic credibility to Vanderbilt Law School. He received his A.B. and LL.B. degrees from the University of Mississippi, and then earned his LL.M. and S.J.D. degrees from Harvard.[3] He was a member of the University of Mississippi law faculty for eleven years, and was Visiting Professor at the University of Texas the year before joining the Vanderbilt faculty in 1947. By that time, he had published leading articles in the *Harvard Law Review*, the *Illinois Law Review*, the *Texas Law Review*, and the *University of Pennsylvania Law Review*. He went on to author or co-author three leading casebooks on Torts, Legal Methods, and Restitution. He was the Reporter for the *Restatement (Second) of Torts,* and served on the Executive Committee of the AALS, the Council of the American Law Institute, and the Executive Committee of the American Judicature Society.

His scholarly achievements were well-recognized by Vanderbilt during his career. The University created the rank of Distinguished Professor in 1964, and has used that designation sparingly. Wade was appointed as Distinguished Professor of Law in 1971, the only member of the law faculty to hold that rank in the Twentieth Century. He received the Harvie Branscomb Distinguished Professor Award for 1976/77, an award recognizing creative scholarship, stimulating and inspiring teaching, and service to students, colleagues, the University, and society at large. (In the forty-three year history of the award, 1964–2006, Wade was the only Law School faculty member to be so honored.) He was the fifth recipient of the University's Earl Sutherland Prize for Achievement in Research, in 1980, awarded to faculty members "whose achievements in research, scholarship, or creative expression have had significant critical reception and are recognized nationally or internationally."

These achievements are remarkable. What is even more remarkable is that so much of the work was done during his deanship. He actually took on substantial administrative work beginning in 1948 when he was appointed faculty editor of the *Vanderbilt Law Review*, in an era in which the position entailed responsibilities for all phases of the publication greatly in excess of those imposed on faculty advisers in later years. Paul Sanders wrote of Wade's work: "Without question he was the person most responsible for the firm and early establishment of the *Vanderbilt Law Review* as a nationally recognized major legal publication. The reputation of the *Review,* in turn, constituted a major component in the advancement of the School within the state and throughout the region and nation."[4] Under Wade's direction, Branscomb observed, the *Vanderbilt Law Review* had come to be recognized as "one of the better law reviews of the country."[5]

Wade was not an aloof scholar, but was actively involved in his work with students. John Boult spoke for many of his student colleagues in saying that Wade not only enjoyed esteem "as America's leading authority on the law of Torts, but more importantly as a stern yet totally fair law school administrator."[6] "Stern" and "tough" were terms often used to describe Wade, and almost all contemporaneous biographical notes included references to his service as a lieutenant in combat intelligence in the U.S. Marine Corps in World War II, where he saw action in Saipan, Tinian, and Iwo Jima. (He pulled some strings to get into the Marine Corps, after being rejected by the Army for high blood pressure and by the Navy for poor vision.) Through his sternness, however, an affection for his students showed through, as in this note card posted on a bulletin board in the fall of 1967: "To my beloved students: It is a distinct honor to have been selected as Teacher of the Day by the Good Guys of WKDA, and I greatly appreciate the part which you played in bringing it about. May I say, in return, that you are not just the students of the day, but the students of the century! JWW." A similar note was posted several years earlier by Mary Moody Wade, after the dean had undergone a five-hour operation, thanking those students who had donated pints of blood in his name.

Wade devoted himself completely to the School.[7] Symbolic of his stature was the ceremony in which he personally handed out over 450 diplomas on October 10, 1969. Following national trends, the basic law degree at Vanderbilt was changed from the LL.B. to the J.D. in 1967, and the next year the change was approved retroactively for all alumni.[8] At the time, over eighty-five percent of the ABA accredited schools had adopted the J.D. as their first professional degree, and most had granted the degree retroactively. The J.D. Investiture Ceremony in October 1969 was the largest gathering of Vanderbilt Law alumni in the School's history, as almost half of the living alumni returned to campus. Wade presented diplomas to alumni whose graduation dates ran from 1912 to 1967, with more than 750 alumni and guests in attendance.

Wade served as dean for two decades, yet wanted the end of his deanship to be a non-event in the life of the School. Provost Nicholas Hobbs attended a Law School faculty meeting in September 1970 to inform the faculty that Wade had earlier expressed his desire to the Chancellor to limit his deanship to about twenty years, and had now decided it was time to announce his intention to the faculty. Wade said he would remain as dean until a successor was named, rejecting notions that he was resigning for reasons of ill health, displeasure, or lack of interest, and reiterating that he now wanted to return to teaching and research.[9]

Wade wrote to the Law School Development Council, "We do not wish to publicize the event beyond that which is obviously necessary. My thought is that it should be treated as a part of the orderly development of the Law School, and that the publicity can come with the announcement of the new dean."[10] Wade was not one to look backward, as was evident in the last two paragraphs of his final annual report as dean:

> This is the last Dean's Report I shall prepare. When the time arrives to prepare one next September, Dean Knauss will have been in the office for seven or eight months.
>
> The Law School has made some progress during the 20 years I will have been in office. But to think of recounting some of the ways would be to look backward. I believe it is far more important to be looking forward and anticipating the real surge to the front which will be taking place with an able, resourceful and considerate new dean. He will inherit an excellent faculty and a capable staff. I expect to be very proud to be serving as a faculty member in the Vanderbilt Law School as it moves forward in the future.[11]

Robert L. Knauss was appointed in the summer of 1971, taking office in early 1972.[12] Wade did indeed continue his teaching and research at Vanderbilt, and he assumed emeritus status in 1981, although he continued to teach from time to time at the Law School through the 1988/89 academic year.

OUTGROWING THE REGION

Harvie Branscomb became the University's fourth chancellor in September 1946. The dramatic shift in vision that he brought to the University is illustrated by comparing the title of the Symposium that marked Carmichael's inauguration in 1938 ("Higher Education in the South"), with the title of Branscomb's address to the Board at the end of his first year as Chancellor: "Vanderbilt and our International Responsibilities." The University and Law

School of Carmichael's day had cultivated a regional focus. The publication that was developed for the University's most prominent fund raising effort during Carmichael's years as Chancellor was titled "Vanderbilt University and the South."[13] Statements of the Law School's mission were regional in scope.[14] Carmichael expressed concern that the Law School might actually be enrolling too many students from outside the South, thus undermining its regional significance.[15] Albert Ewing, Jr., a prominent Law School alumnus, was likely speaking for many of his colleagues as he wrote to the Chancellor on the occasion of the School's closing:

> I believe that whenever possible only Southern Professors should be employed at the Law School as well as in the University, but that in no instance should ability and character be sacrificed to this end. . . . Vanderbilt is a Southern University notwithstanding its origin and present financial support. If it cannot remain Southern in character its influence for the welfare of our State and Nation will be greatly lessened if not destroyed. I believe that Vanderbilt should not seek to imitate Harvard, the University of Chicago, Yale, or any other Institution.[16]

The Vanderbilt of the first half of the Twentieth Century had remained largely a southern institution, for better or for worse. But when the School's doors were reopened, the regional character of the School was challenged. Throughout his term as Chancellor, Branscomb spoke and wrote on international education, and brought a wide range of new programs to the University intended to make national and international impacts. The days of focusing primarily on Vanderbilt's place in the South were gone. The University provided its Law School with a base from which to pursue national stature. In 1949, Vanderbilt was elected as the thirty-sixth member in the Association of American Universities. The only other southern schools among the thirty-six were Duke, Virginia, North Carolina, and Texas, and with the exception of "two technological schools," Vanderbilt had the smallest student enrollment in the association.[17]

Three major developments that supported the School's national ambitions transpired in the first decade of Wade's deanship: (1) the receipt of substantial funding from the Ford Foundation; (2) an expanded student recruitment program, energized by the appointment of John Beasley; and (3) the construction of a building for the Law School. The Ford Foundation's first large grant to the Law School was a $200,000 award in 1956 to found the *Race Relations Law Reporter.* The *Reporter* would be a unique publication, printing statutes, court decisions, administrative rulings, and other legal developments bearing on "racial matters" on the Federal, state, and local levels. Vanderbilt began publishing the *Reporter* with an initial three-year grant, with Professor Paul Sanders serving as the first Director.

The *Race Relations Law Reporter* was established to present in complete, objective fashion the primary legal materials of the time dealing with the subject of race. It began when there were no commercial reporting services in the field, and the publication catapulted Vanderbilt onto the national scene. At one time the reporter had a circulation of over 6,000, second only to the *Harvard Law Review* among legal publications.[18] The Ford Foundation continued to fund the *Reporter* until 1968 when the foundation decided to enforce its policy of not supporting any program for an indefinite period. The foundation did, however, later make an additional grant to enable the School to publish a more limited *Race Relations Law Survey* for three more years, ending in 1972.

Branscomb met with Henry Heald, President of the Ford Foundation, in the late 1950s to make a plea for substantial support for the Law School. While Branscomb's pitch was regional—that the key to a more effective and forward-looking public leadership in the South was better lawyers, which meant better legal education—this approach was a strategic choice rather than a departure from his larger vision. The Chancellor tailored his message in light of his assessment of the words that would bring success with the Ford Foundation.[19] Branscomb closed his presentation by stating that no law school between Charlottesville, Virginia, and Austin, Texas, had achieved distinction, and from that one could draw only one conclusion: "that we had an obligation to develop a great law school at Vanderbilt University, but we needed help." As Branscomb described the end of the meeting, he paused for questions, and after a long silence just added lamely, "Well, that is what I wanted to say." Heald replied, "We'll kick the idea around a bit," rose from his chair, and said good-bye.[20] Kick it around, they did. The first result of the meeting was a 1958 Ford Foundation grant of $350,000 to the Law School to provide support over a seven-year period for new faculty positions, student financial aid, research support, the *Vanderbilt Law Review*, and a series of institutes, lectures, and seminars.[21]

Another Ford Foundation grant was announced in 1960, with $4 million allocated to Vanderbilt University on the condition that the University matched the grant with $8 million in additional gifts. The Foundation informed the University that this grant was the result of discussions that were originally begun in connection with the needs of the Law School, and thus "the development of this School should be given priority."[22] As a result, $300,000 was immediately applied to the Law School building fund, and

another $600,000 was allocated to the Law School over a five-year period
to pay for two new faculty positions, increased faculty salaries, a research
and publications fund, student scholarships, and enhancement of the Law
Library.[23]

The changing of the Law School's aspirations is captured in capsule
form in the report filed in 1965 at the end of the Ford Foundation Seven-
Year Grant.

> [The grant] was made to a small law school with high scholastic stan-
> dards but very inadequate physical facilities, somewhat local in its ap-
> peal but with aspirations for affording strong regional leadership. Pres-
> ently, at the expiration of the grant, the law school. . . . having achieved
> regional leadership, now has aspirations for attaining true national
> eminence.[24]

The financial support from the foundation proved to be essential in the
School's efforts to pursue those aspirations.

By the beginning of Wade's deanship, the Law School had accumulated
reserves of $176,000 from the days of over-enrollment. After several years of
drawing down the reserves through deficit operations, Wade was able to return the School to surplus budgets in the early 1960s. Prudent management
(the School's year-end financial results were regularly better than budgeted),
and substantial increases in tuition rates were part of the story, but the
dominant feature of the School's financing was the support from the Ford
Foundation. However, five-year grants and even seven-year grants come
to an end. In the last two years of the Ford grants, over forty percent of
the Law School's budget was supported by soft money. Professor Hartman
commented on this "unhealthy situation," reporting that this "precarious
method of financing" had consumed much time and effort for every faculty
member.[25] By 1966, the Law School was facing structural annual deficits of
over $100,000, and the School relied on University funds to close its books
each year through the end of Wade's deanship.

In his last meeting with the Board of Trust as Chancellor in 1963,
Branscomb reported on the Law School. His remarks both noted the progress that had been fueled by the Ford Foundation and foreshadowed the
work that was yet to be done.

> The School of Law, having been the cause of concern for a number of
> years, is now vigorous, growing, and reflecting credit on the University.

The expiration of certain grants will cause temporary problems. The creation of the post of Assistant Dean and the acquisition of Mr. Beasley for the position will enable the Dean's Office to meet its expanded responsibilities, and relieve Dean Wade, whose outstanding work as a teacher should not be crowded out by administrative duties. We can be happy about the work and the prospects of this School.[26]

John S. Beasley II was appointed Assistant Dean and Assistant Professor of Law in August 1962. He would prove to be a very effective teacher, and he became the School's recognized authority in Oil and Gas Law. But it would be as Assistant Dean, and then Associate Dean, with the recruitment and admission of students in his portfolio, that John Beasley would extend the School's national reach, thus leaving his mark in the Law School's history.

Beasley's extraordinary success was rooted in his belief in and his love for Vanderbilt. He earned his Vanderbilt B.A., Phi Beta Kappa, in 1952. His Vanderbilt J.D. followed two years later, in a B.A./J.D. bridge program. He was the Executive Director of the Alumni Association for the four years prior to his joining the Law School faculty. He left the Law School in 1971 at the end of the Wade deanship, but even in this professional "sabbatical" from Vanderbilt he served as national chair of the Law School Fund Campaign. He returned to Vanderbilt to serve for sixteen years as the University's Vice-Chancellor for Alumni and Development, as well as National Alumni Director of the Centennial Campaign, Special Assistant to the Chancellor, and staff secretary to the search committee that recruited Chancellor Joe B. Wyatt. Named Vice Chancellor for Alumni and Development, Emeritus, in 1999, Beasley continued to play an active role in the life of the Law School and the University, serving as Counselor to the Chancellor in his "retirement." No one who ever heard him speak had any doubt about his passion for this School. When he spoke, audiences were captivated. As Dean Dent Bostick would later observe, "John Wade would not have been the success he was without John Beasley."[27]

Vanderbilt had long engaged in efforts to recruit students. Dean Arnold had reported on his visits, and occasionally those of other faculty members, to many of the colleges in Tennessee. Dean Forrester reinstituted a program for visiting colleges in the surrounding region, with his visits to Bowling Green College and Western Kentucky State College as the School moved toward a comprehensive college campus recruitment program.[28] Forrester also addressed the fact that the School had no scholarships for students at that time, requesting of Chancellor Branscomb that the Law School be given a fair allotment of the general University funds that were allocated to scholarships.[29] Notice of scholarships available to law students began to appear in the School's catalogue the following year.

But Vanderbilt's recruiting program advanced by leaps and bounds beginning in the early 1960s. A report on recruitment visits in 1959/60 lists forty colleges and universities that were visited, reflecting a systematic recruitment program organized by first-year Assistant Dean Kenneth L. Roberts. Fifteen of those schools were in Tennessee, nearly all of them in the southeast region, and no Ivy League schools were included.[30] Roberts was succeeded in the Assistant Dean position the next year by Gilbert S. Merritt, Jr. When Merritt, who had earned his bachelor's degree at Yale, suggested that he make a couple of trips to eastern universities, Wade agreed, and he was soon reporting on his visits to Harvard, Yale, Wesleyan, Williams, Amherst, Dartmouth, and Princeton.[31] Beasley, who was charged with simultaneously expanding the size and improving the quality of the class, described his new job as picking up Merritt's briefcase and his pace. During the fall of 1963, in Beasley's second year, Vanderbilt faculty members visited ninety-one colleges and universities, most of them outside the southeast region, including all of the Ivy League schools and only two in the state of Tennessee.[32] The figures increased in the years to follow, with most faculty members making annual recruiting trips for the School.

John Beasley went on the road in his Plymouth Fury to meet potential applicants face to face. This approach maximized the impact of his incredible charm and persuasive powers, and allowed him to take the measure of the students whose potential may not have been fully reflected in grade point averages and LSAT scores. As Wayne Hyatt, one of the self-described "Beasley's Bastards," portrayed the group, they were "students whose future was likely to be better than their past."[33] Their response to the opportunity Beasley gave them was affection for the man and loyalty to the School. As alumni, they set out to make good on Beasley's wager, through success in the profession and with support for the School through their dollars and service. Hyatt himself was an example of this: adjunct faculty member, chair of the alumni building committee, member of the Law School Alumni Board, recipient of the School's Distinguished Service and Distinguished Alumnus awards, and member of the University's Board of Trust as President of the University's Alumni Association. A classroom in the School is named for Hyatt and his wife Amanda.

Scholarships came to play a larger and larger role in the competition for outstanding students. While $40,000 of the Ford Foundation Four Million Dollar Grant had been designated for Law School scholarships, overall financial aid funding levels were below that of Vanderbilt's competitors as Wade complained in 1963, "We have no scholarships exceeding tuition ($800)."[34] A major breakthrough occurred in 1966, when the Justin and Valere Potter Foundation established the Patrick Wilson Merit Scholarships, named in memory of the son of Mr. and Mrs. David K. Wilson. Patrick had planned to enter the Vanderbilt Law School in the fall of 1965 but was killed in an automobile accident in France on August 28, 1965. The scholarships were "all-expense awards" given to five entering students, initially in the amount of $2,500 for each of three years at a time when tuition was $800 per year.[35] The impact of the new program extended beyond the students who actually received the awards and enrolled. In the fall of 1966, for example, five of the fifteen Patrick Wilson candidates who had been brought to campus received the award, and eight of the other ten also enrolled. A substantial number of Nashville law firms began to supply full tuition scholarships.

Another development that coincided with Beasley's recruitment efforts was the construction of a new building that the School moved into in 1962. The Law School had reopened in 1946 with great fanfare, a substantial endowment, a new faculty, and a large number of students. But the long-anticipated Law School building was not a part of the package. Carmichael considered the School's arrangement on the upper floors of Kirkland Hall to be "reasonably adequate"[36] and he continued to push for a long-term solution in a joint Law-Social Sciences building. But as soon as he left the Chancellorship, discussions of a joint facility ceased. For another decade, the University equivocated on the issue. University officials acknowledged that the physical arrangements for the School were "entirely inadequate."[37] When Branscomb arrived, he recognized the "acute need," telling the Board, "A law school building, the cost of which may be estimated at $400,000, must be actively sought. . . . The provision of this should not be long delayed."[38] Yet, a year later when the Board decided what to do with funds remaining from the Frederick W. Vanderbilt estate, a Law School building was not even mentioned; and four years later Branscomb concluded that the University had a physical plant that largely met its needs: "To be sure, we could use a Fine Arts Building, an additional chemistry laboratory, but no formidable necessities lie before us. I draw the conclusion that we are in a position to eliminate special campaigns and to direct alumni giving to un-restricted support of the University."[39]

Talk of a law building continued,[40] but the talk turned to action only when John Wade negotiated the conditions under which he would remain at Vanderbilt. Wade was approached by Duke Law School in its dean search, and Wade informed Branscomb that a Law School building would have to be constructed if he were to stay.[41] When he was offered the Duke deanship in 1957, he told the Chancellor that the question that loomed largest in his mind was "the future of the Vanderbilt Law School." Branscomb presented the issue to the Board which raised salaries for Wade and the eight full-time faculty members, increased the library budget, and created new scholarships for law students, even though the School had budgeted a $40,000 deficit that year.[42] These improvements were welcomed, but the new building remained the key.

At its next meeting in May 1957, the Board resolved that "the time has come to provide for the School of Law the physical facilities which it has long needed" and a building fund was created.[43] Cecil Sims was tireless and persuasive in his role as building campaign chair, describing the Law School as "the best in the South with the poorest facilities of any law school in the United States, and the only accredited law school that has no building."[44] Even with the campaign under way, Wade and the faculty had to fight what they considered to be substandard proposals, including one to adapt the existing Wesley Hall for their use.[45] Branscomb captured the faculty's mood with this anecdote that he told at the Building Dedication:

> This building began in the minds of the Law School faculty I do not know how long ago. I can only report that some six or eight years ago I proposed to the Dean of the School of Law that we place an elevator in Kirkland Hall so that the older members of the faculty would not have to climb the stairs. He conferred with his faculty and a few days later brought back to me their reply. They had discussed the matter, he said, and had concluded, first, that they did not have any older members of their faculty and, second, that the only elevators that he could get them interested in talking about were the ones that were in the proposed new Law School building.[46]

Wade wrote to Branscomb in 1959, commenting when yet another disappointing proposal had been made, and making clear what his understanding had been:

> It may well be that the cost of building a nationally great law school is less than that required for building a great school in one of the other three professions. But not this much less! The implication that the University is content with a good law school while it expects to build and maintain nationally outstanding schools in the other professions is, I

am sure, not intended. Certainly we in the Law School are not prepared to accept this premise. It is not at all what I have understood, or what I have led the law faculty to believe the University has in mind.[47]

In December 1960, with $811,000 in hand or pledged, the Board authorized the expenditure of $1.1 million for the construction of the new building.[48] Wade was getting the building he wanted. He referred to "our goal of regional pre-eminence and national eminence" in writing to Harold Vanderbilt on behalf of the faculty, to express appreciation for the "action of members of our Board of Trust in contributing an unprecedented sum as an initial impetus to the new capital-funds drive."[49]

The Law School moved in the summer of 1962, and the new building was dedicated on April 6, 1963. Sims presented the building on behalf of the alumni at the dedication ceremony. He was introduced by Branscomb, who identified Sims' loyalty and services to the School for nearly four decades, as "probably its greatest assets," noting that Sims had taught and inspired its students, found jobs for its graduates, fought its battles, and "corrected its chancellor," in addition to chairing the building fundraising committee.[50] Sims had also played a major role in securing the funding base for the School's revival in 1946, which led Dean Knauss to observe in 1972, "Mr. Sims was primarily responsible for the reopening of the Law School after World War II."[51]

The dedication of the new building could have been a moment of satisfaction, a time to savor the arrival at a major milestone on the way to becoming a major national institution. Not so for John Wade, who spoke at the ceremony: "A law school should be a place of intellectual ferment. Instead of becoming fat and complacent and lazy, we expect to remain lean and hungry. . . . We can and will be a better law school."[52] Even Wade, however, could take satisfaction in the strides the School had already taken, as he told the Board, "[W]e wrought better than we knew."[53]

Wade viewed the *Vanderbilt Law Review* and the *Race Relations Law Reporter* as the two most effective instruments in promoting the School's national stature.[54] Events related to each of these publications, however, signaled competing agendas that would create conflict during the Wade years, and result in broader tensions and aggravations in the deanships to follow as Vanderbilt pursued a more national strategy.

One signal of the School's changing aspirations was the creation and then termination of the *Law Review*'s Annual Survey of Tennessee Law. In 1953, recognizing Vanderbilt's close relationship with the legal profession in the state, the *Law Review* instituted the Annual Survey, an issue dedicated to the description of the year's developments in the state as a service to the local bar. Twelve years later, the faculty voted to terminate the Survey, in passing the following motion by a 7–4 vote: "That the Vanderbilt Law School discontinue now the treatment of legal developments in Tennessee on a systematic and organized basis as a unified segment of the *Vanderbilt Law Review*, leaving it to the discretion of individual members of the faculty to write and publish articles on Tennessee law or related problems whenever they so desire."[55] A survey of the state's legal developments no longer matched the national reach of the faculty's more expansive vision: "Vanderbilt is transforming itself into a national School of Law, and the survey of local law is scarcely compatible with that new ambition."[56]

In a similar move, the Tennessee Practice and Procedure course, which had long been taught by adjuncts William Harbison and Robert Sturdivant, disappeared from the catalogue in 1974/75. Harbison was a Founder's Medalist in the class of 1950—widely believed by students and alumni to have accumulated the highest grade point average of any graduate under the numerical scheme used until the late 1980s—and he went on to serve on the Tennessee Supreme Court. He began teaching on a part-time basis at the Law School immediately upon graduation, and taught the required Professional Responsibility class later in his career. In 1968, an old academic title that had fallen into disuse at Vanderbilt was officially revived by the Board of Trust. The title was Adjunct Professor, to be granted to part-time instructors who had served with distinction as Lecturers and who possessed all of the qualifications for a regular faculty position. The Board approved the re-establishment of the position and bestowed it initially on only one faculty member at the University: William J. Harbison.[57] The student body selected Harbison as the recipient of the Law School's outstanding teacher award in 1972/73—a remarkable achievement for a part-time teacher.[58]

Yet another sign of Vanderbilt's broader self-image was Wade's lack of attentiveness to the regional environment. Dean Arnold's deanship had been consumed by the politics of Tennessee standards for admission to the bar and by competition with non-accredited schools in the state. For Wade, these were simply non-issues, with the exception of an unsuccessful effort in 1961 by the Vanderbilt, Cumberland, and Tennessee deans to secure adoption of a standard that would allow students to be admitted to the bar in the state only if they had graduated from a school with at least three full-time faculty members.[59]

At this point, Cumberland's decline had changed the legal education landscape in the state. In May 1961, both the ABA and the AALS deferred action on suspending the school's approved status only with the assurances that the 1961 summer quarter would be the last session in the Lebanon, Tennessee, location. Thus, Cumberland was engaged in public talks about merger with Memphis State University, the University of Tennessee, and Howard College in Alabama.[60] Apparently Vanderbilt was also a party to such merger discussions, as Cecil Sims and Sam Gilreath at Cumberland reached the point of a handshake of agreement—which ultimately foundered on the issue of which Cumberland faculty would be retained after the merger.[61] Cumberland's merger with Howard College (now Samford University) was agreed to in June 1961.

Broadening Vanderbilt's horizons did periodically create controversy, as occurred with the founding of the *Race Relations Law Reporter*. In its second year Wade reported that the publication was succeeding as "an objective and impartial reporting of the primary legal materials. . . . [D]espite the highly emotionalized tinge of the whole subject matter not a single letter of criticism has ever been received from anyone who has inspected an issue."[62] Always the shrewd lawyer, Wade's inclusion of the phrase "from anyone who has inspected an issue" both masked the controversy that arose when the University accepted the grant, and undercut as uninformed reactions the objections that had been received.

When the Ford Foundation grant was announced Sims Crownover, a prominent local alumnus and 1936 Founder's Medalist, wrote to Chancellor Branscomb—expressing opinions that were symptomatic of the tensions that came with the School's pursuit of its national ambitions. Crownover, who would soon be in the forefront of the protest against the Law School's integration, sent copies of the letter to both of the local newspapers as he voiced views that remind twenty-first century readers of the climate in 1955:

> I was shocked to read that the Vanderbilt University School of Law had accepted a $200,000 grant from the Ford Foundation's Fund of the Republic. . . . It is my honest opinion that Vanderbilt University should immediately retract any acceptance of this grant. . . . [T]he history of the Fund of the Republic is that of a left-wing organization, devoted to the objectives of discrediting the national campaign against Communism and by holding anti-Communists up to public contempt. . . . I believe that you will be highly commended if you and the Board of Trust see fit to reverse this decision, the implications of which are among the most serious the University has ever confronted.[63]

James G. Stahlman responded immediately, as President and Publisher of the *Nashville Banner*, a member of Vanderbilt's Board of Trust, and as

Crownover's friend, writing to "My dear Sims." After acknowledging his valued friendship and shared views about protecting things that are fundamental to the preservation of American institutions and liberties, he took exception to Crownover's position: "If you had made as thorough an investigation of the reasons for Vanderbilt's acceptance of the $200,000 grant from the Fund of the Republic as you insist the University should have done before accepting the grant, I do not believe that you would have written such a letter." Stahlman went on to argue that Vanderbilt could do "a sounder, saner, more objective and, therefore, more serviceable" job than any other institution, that the project would bring credit and prestige to the Law School, and that the grant came with no strings attached. He closed by adding, "I am more than distressed that you have seen fit to make copies of it public to the *Nashville Banner* and the *Nashville Tennessean*."[64]

While the School made strides in moving toward the national stage during the Wade years, the financial basis for sustaining a prominent position was lacking. Much of the growth in academic programming had been achieved through temporary funding, such as the Ford Foundation grants. A number of factors accounted for the failure to provide a permanent financial foundation to support the School's aspirations. Considerable time and energy were devoted to the highly successful solicitation of foundations which did give a jump-start to the School's program. The capital campaign for the building was completed under Wade's deanship. But the School was not permitted to suggest to its alumni that they could make their contributions to the Law School, instead of the University, until 1958,[65] and it was not until 1968 that the Law School was allowed to solicit its own alumni who had also graduated from one of Vanderbilt's undergraduate schools. Most of the pre-World War II Law School alumni fell into this hands-off pool. In 1963 nearly half of the Law School's alumni made annual contributions to Vanderbilt, but only a small proportion of those gifts were designated for the Law School.[66] In 1966/67, of the $245,000 donated to the University by Law School alumni, only $8,000 went to the Law School.[67] The cumulative result was virtually no growth in the School's endowment from the reopening until the end of the Wade deanship.

Wade himself had a deep aversion to personally soliciting funds from individuals.[68] He did, however, create structures and enlist the help of others in the cause. The first law alumni association was organized on April 18, 1953 (Law Day) by Alfred T. Adams, Sr. and Charles C. Trabue, Jr. Trabue, the grandson of Dean Thomas Malone, was elected the first president of the Vanderbilt Law Alumni Association, serving in that capacity from 1954 to 1956.[69] When each Vanderbilt school was appointing a Committee of Visi-

tors in 1968, Wade moved beyond that structure to create a second committee focused on development. Even though he was able to attract people of
such stature as Erwin Griswold, Roy Wilkins, Griffin Bell, and Dean Rusk
to the School's committees, the resource base remained problematic.

Part of the story of the Law School's financial woes was the University's
failure to deliver on what had been understood to be a commitment to
the Law School's endowment in the $55 Million Campaign in the 1960s.
The Law School had anticipated that at least $4 million would be added
to the Law School's endowment during that University campaign. When
the fund drive ended and no money had been added, disappointment and
recriminations followed. Alumnus Edwin O. Norris sought to approach his
friend William S. Vaughn, President of the Board of Trust in 1970, asking
that the Board allocate $4 million from the campaign to the Law School.[70]
Norris's work coincided with the death of Harold S. Vanderbilt, who left $10
million to the University with matching conditions. While no simple transfer resulted, Norris's efforts apparently did lead to the University's creating
a 3-for-1 match for endowment contributions that was established when
Robert Knauss was appointed as Wade's successor.

The Law School was transformed during the Wade years, despite the
limited development successes. While Wade was dean, the entering class
grew from 31 to 156. When the new building was opened in 1962, Wade
noted that the School could "admit a class of almost any size we desire."[71]
The enrollment did increase annually, from 268 that fall to 460 full-time
students in 1971/72, even as the annual tuition grew from $800 to $2,200.
The average LSAT score of the entering class had doubled to the ninetieth
percentile by 1971. In that last year of the Wade/Beasley era, the number of
applicants doubled from the year before.[72]

The School's national reach was reflected in the geographic diversity of
the student body. A geographic base of twelve states exploded to forty-two
states and foreign countries. The number of colleges represented likewise
soared from 12 to 151. The percentage of incoming students from Tennessee
decreased from 57% to 20%, with about half of the students coming from
outside the South. The percentage of Vanderbilt graduates in the first-year
class dropped from 47% to 16%. Beasley reported in September 1969 that
the top five feeder colleges were Vanderbilt, Yale, Dartmouth, Virginia,
and Duke, and that the only problem with students was the small number
of black students in the School.[73] Vanderbilt was averaging only about one
African-American graduate per year in the late sixties and early seventies.

The full-time faculty increased in the Wade years from eight to twenty-
two, the number of courses offered annually grew from thirty-seven to

ninety, and library holdings tripled. The School had added a clinical program, the Transnational Legal Studies Program, and a second student-edited publication (*The Vanderbilt Journal of Transnational Law*), the Urban and Regional Development Center, an intensive first-year writing program, and a steady diet of conferences, lectures, institutes, and symposia.

In sum, there were many features of the Law School's move from regional aspirations to the national stage. However, if one event, if one day, were to be highlighted as symbolic of this transformation, for Chancellor Branscomb it was October 20, 1956, the day that the University affirmed the admission of African-American students to the Law School: "On the whole, I think it was an historic day for Vanderbilt. While one must yield to the temptation to dramatize events, I suspect that on Saturday last this institution decided to be a university national in its interests and thinking, rather than a regional institution."[74]

BREAKING THE COLOR BARRIER

In the nineteenth century, Vanderbilt Law School had begun to enroll Native American students and a small number of international students from Asia. In the early twentieth century, students with Latino names such as Octavio Acevedo, Xavier Christ, and Joseph Rodriguez were registered.[75] Breaking such racial and ethnic barriers took place, apparently, without incident. But this prior experience did nothing to prepare the School, the University, and the alumni for the admission of African-American students.

Frederick T. Work and Edward Melvin Porter registered for the fall term at the Law School in 1956. In so doing, they made Vanderbilt the first integrated private law school in the South. Work was a graduate of Fisk University, where he had been an all-conference basketball player, and the son of two professors—one of whom was that university's internationally-known composer and director of the Fisk Jubilee Singers, John W. Work. Porter graduated from Tennessee State University where he had been President of the student government association, after four years of military service. They became the School's first African-American alumni when they graduated in 1959. Vanderbilt Law School did not arrive at this point easily or without controversy.

The application to the Law School in 1949 by an African-American student, Robert E. Williams of Nashville, was brought to the attention of the Board of Trust. Chancellor Branscomb was instructed to send the following reply to Williams: "This is to acknowledge receipt of your registered letter of May 25 addressed to me, and your letter of June 7 addressed to the

School of Law. This is to advise you that Vanderbilt cannot entertain your application for admission to the School of Law."[76] Branscomb proposed a qualifying phrase which would have stated that his application could not be entertained "at this time," but the phrase was stricken from the letter by the Board.[77]

From that point forward, the Law School moved slowly but inexorably toward integrating the student body, pushed and pulled by factors both external and internal to the University. In 1950, the faculty of Yale Law School introduced a proposal to add an integration standard for AALS membership, to be considered at that year's annual meeting. The Yale proposal was sent to committee at the AALS meeting; a similar resolution was subsequently approved at the December 1952 meeting. The Vanderbilt faculty had reservations in 1951 about taking a position contrary to University policy. They decided that Vanderbilt should abstain on such votes, unless "circumstances arising at the meeting make it unwise to abstain, then the delegates are authorized to take whatever action they believe to be most consistent with the views on the subject known to be entertained by the Chancellor and law faculty."[78] In response to memos from Forrester in late 1951, Branscomb revealed both his personal commitment to integration ("achieving the ends which you and I both wish to achieve"), and his insistence that Vanderbilt not be forced by external forces to integrate (the "right handling of the segregation issue" might require withdrawing from the AALS).[79]

Just as Forrester, and then Wade, passed along information to Branscomb about the progress of integration at other schools, Branscomb passed along news of such developments to the Board and even instigated the writing of a letter by the Divinity School faculty in the fall of 1952 expressing their belief that black students should be admitted.[80] The University of Tennessee had admitted African-American students in 1951, leading Branscomb to comment to the Board: "It is my understanding from our legal counsel that laws still stand upon the statute books of Tennessee requiring a completely dual system of education. We will want Mr. Sims to comment on the legal phases of this problem. I doubt, however, that it is practical for us to avoid the problem by pleading this legal situation. The public is not likely to be convinced that what is legal in Knoxville is illegal in Nashville."[81]

The U.S. Supreme Court announced its decision in *Brown vs. Board of Education* in May 1954, and the Law faculty pressed its case, presenting a memorandum to the Board the following semester—which was passed over without action. At the next Board meeting, Branscomb read yet another letter from Dean Wade, reminding the Chancellor that the issue of integration had been pending for some time and asking his advice as to how the school should respond "in the event we receive an application for admission from a qualified Negro student."[82] A memorandum, attached to the letter, clearly and eloquently laid out grounds for the response that a unanimous faculty hoped they would receive:

> [W]e have come to the mature and considered opinion that the wisest course would be to permit the admission of a qualified Negro applicant in accordance with the normal selective admission policies of the Law School. . . . We feel that the recent Supreme Court decision should have particular significance for a law school. While the precise holding applies only to state-supported schools and not to a private university like Vanderbilt, we believe that a school which seeks to instill a feeling of respect and reverence for the law and legal institutions, must demonstrate a concern not only with the strict letter of the law but with its true spirit, involving its underlying purpose and objective. The principle of legal equality of education in the Constitution as now declared by the Supreme Court in the Segregation Cases, is quite clear and unmistakable.[83]

The memorandum also referred to the results of a student referendum which showed a majority of Law students in favor of integration, with two-thirds of the student body stating that they personally would have no objection to integration.

Following a long discussion, Cecil Sims offered a motion at the May 6, 1955, Board meeting that was adopted with no dissenting vote cast: "That the Chancellor be authorized to advise the faculty of the School of Law that it is the sense of this Board that they should not decline to admit a student otherwise in their opinion considered qualified solely because of race, creed, or color."[84] The Board would later characterize this action as merely applying a policy that had been established in 1953, when Joseph A. Johnson, Jr. had been admitted to the Divinity School because there was no institution of a similar type in Nashville. In the Law School's case, the Board relied on the fact that there was not a school in the city that was accredited by the American Bar Association.[85] Wade credited the ease with which Sims' motion passed to a peculiar set of circumstances at Vanderbilt: "There was never any regulation of our Board of Trust in connection with the admission of Negroes. The School had always depended upon the statutes of Tennessee which prohibited them. Since the statutes are now unconstitutional, the Board of Trust was able without taking any action at all to say that the matter was within our own discretion."[86]

In October 1955, Wade informed the AALS Special Committee on Racial Discrimination that its report could publicly identify Vanderbilt as being prepared to admit African-American students voluntarily.[87] Branscomb concurred in this public announcement, making Vanderbilt the only one of the sixteen AALS segregated schools that was prepared to integrate voluntarily. Wade contacted the President of Tennessee State University, and Branscomb (the Chancellor from Alabama) and Wade (the dean from Mississippi) visited the President of Fisk University, asking them to encourage their best students to take the law school admissions test and to apply to Vanderbilt.[88] (Vanderbilt strongly encouraged, to the point of requiring, these African-American applicants to take the test, and the School reimbursed them for the cost. The Law School would begin requiring the test of all applicants the following year.) On September 19, 1956, Vanderbilt Law School was integrated.

On campus, the enrollment of Work and Porter was almost a non-event. "Not a ripple of concern was visible in the student body, either in the School of Law or elsewhere."[89] No students protested to the dean or chancellor; none withdrew over the issue. Initially, Work and Porter experienced their classmates as not particularly friendly, as they found themselves the subjects of stares and whispered conversations. They were asked to limit their activities to the Law School. They could not live on campus (they did not want to). They were not to eat in the dining halls or participate in campus student organizations. But the atmosphere improved quickly and they noticed no open hostility after the first few weeks. One student reported to Wade at the beginning that he could not study sitting next to Porter. Wade's response was that he should try again, and if he still couldn't maybe he should go to school someplace else. Porter and the hostile student later became good friends.

In fact, Work and Porter reported[90] developing several "good friendships" with "superb colleagues" by the start of their second year. Porter had a previous experience with integration, as he was serving in an all-black outfit at Fort Dix when President Truman ordered the desegregation of the armed services. He soon found himself with no inhibitions about visiting the bookstore or the dining hall—not because any restrictions had been formally lifted but because Wade had told him not to let those barriers stop him from doing what he wanted to do. Work, too, found the environment to be increasingly cordial, and he was elected Presiding Moot Court Judge in this third year. A low profile approach, on both sides, may have contributed to an incident-free transition. As Porter would later write to Wade, "[M]any times problems which confronted me at Vanderbilt were never revealed because I tried to do my best to keep from bringing them up."[91]

A different story unfolded off campus. When the registrations became publicized there was a flood of negative mail, and three official alumni clubs passed statements censuring the Chancellor and the Board.[92] A new Independent Association of Alumni and Friends was formed, dedicated "to guiding Vanderbilt University in the direction of conservative principles as opposed to socialistic and communistic principles and that as a part of this program we would oppose the admission of negroes to any department of the University."[93] The coincidence of the first volume of the *Race Relations Law Reporter* being published in the year that Vanderbilt admitted its first two African-American students "gave rise to the report that the Ford Foundation's promise to grant funding for the *Reporter* had been used to bribe Vanderbilt to become the first private university law school in the South to desegregate its student body."[94]

The matter came to a head at the time of the Board of Trust meeting that fall. Branscomb and Board President Harold S. Vanderbilt left the October 20 session of the Board meeting in order to meet with the directors of the Alumni Association. At that Alumni Association meeting, a motion to disapprove of the Board's action died for lack of a second. Later that day, the Law School's alumni association met to consider a resolution "to deplore the admission of Negroes and to request that no more be admitted." The president of the association was certain that the motion would pass and urged Wade not to speak at the meeting, for fear of having a stronger resolution introduced. Wade insisted on making a report on the matter, and following his presentation the resolution was tabled by a vote of 56–12. Eddie Morgan offered his own commentary on Wade's appearance before the group: "His frankness and sincerity were impressive. On the whole, it was one of the most artistic performances I have ever seen. . . . The result was a complete triumph for the Dean."[95]

Wade was continually looking for ways to push against racial boundaries. John Boult tells this story from his law student days:

> One of the new black law students was a former basketball All-American at Fisk University in Nashville, who had later played a couple of seasons with the Harlem Globetrotters. That winter, Vanderbilt's basketball team was leading the Southeastern Conference and had a crucial home game against Kentucky, the conference's perennial powerhouse.

A few days before the game the dean of the law school called me and another senior law student to his office. He told us he had three tickets to the Kentucky game and that he would like for us to go to the game along with Fred Work, the black law student who wanted very much to see the game. Elmore Holmes, of Memphis, and I escorted our fellow law student to the game and when we took our seats I think Elmore and I were both a little dismayed to suddenly realize that the very tall black fellow seated between us was the only black person in the arena. Before that moment, the all white hue of the crowd at Vanderbilt's Memorial Coliseum, the finest college basketball venue in the south in those days, had never truly registered with either of us. From that time I could never again fail to notice public gatherings of all white people.[96]

John Work wrote to Wade, after his son's graduation, to express his gratitude for Wade's efforts on his son's behalf, recalling: "Frederick tells of your attending an interdepartmental basketball game in which he participated. I have the feeling that your attendance at that game was not entirely due to your love of basketball."[97] Work's white classmates insisted that he play in the game which was a product of a challenge to the law students by Vanderbilt's medical students. Wade, whom Work thought was nervous about what might happen, attended practices as well as the game.

Work and Porter continued to be trail blazers after leaving Vanderbilt, Porter going to Oklahoma City, Work to Gary, Indiana, each to practice law. Porter had accepted a job in Chicago during his third year. One evening a busload of students from Oklahoma came into Deborah's Place, a prominent black restaurant where he was working as night manager. They were returning from an NAACP meeting in New York City, brimming with enthusiasm in the wake of that event, and they persuaded Porter to return to Oklahoma and become involved in the Civil Rights movement there. Porter was elected president of the Oklahoma City chapter of the NAACP in 1961, less than two years after graduating. He remained active in the Civil Rights movement, later serving as Vice-President of the Oklahoma State Conference of NAACP Branches. He was elected as the first African-American member of the Oklahoma state senate, serving for twenty-two years from 1964 to 1986.

Work was accepted into the LL.M. program at Yale, but he deferred enrollment because he could not support his wife, and soon a child, on the fellowship that had been offered. Disappointed that he seemed to be the only member of his graduating class without a job, despite making good grades, he read about the bustling economy in Gary, Indiana. And thus this

Nashvillian who had just navigated one foreign culture experienced another culture shock as he started his career in that Midwestern steel mill town. Acclimating to the new environment, he was elected judge of the municipal court seven years after arriving. He was the city's first African-American judge and he held the position for ten years. In 1968, Work became the first African-American to win nomination to a state-wide office in Indiana, when he was chosen at the Democratic state convention for the position of judge in the Second District Appellate Court. He would also serve as the President of the Lake County Election Board, and was honored by the Gary chapter of the NAACP with its Benjamin Hooks Award.

The next African-American did not graduate from Vanderbilt Law School until 1964, at which time Isaiah Cresswell and Janie Greenwood Harris graduated—Ms. Harris becoming the first African-American female graduate. She was aware of her unique position in the School's history, but she does not recall ever hearing it mentioned during her student days. As one of only three women, and two students of color, she felt somewhat isolated, although she found all of the faculty quite willing to meet with her. Her days were filled with studying and working in the library, where librarian Mary Green and associate librarian Pauline Woodard provided a welcoming environment.

The Law School did not limit its Civil Rights activities to the admission of students. A plaque in the Law School building makes note of the place where Underwood Auditorium[98] once stood, and memorializes a 1962 event. The plaque reads:

> On December 28, 1962, from this spot (which was then the site of the stage of Underwood Auditorium), the Rev. Martin Luther King, Jr. spoke on The Ethical Demands of Integration. Following the speech, which was part of a conference organized in the wake of the University's expulsion of Vanderbilt Divinity student James Lawson, the university announced that the Law School could no longer schedule events without central administration approval. That policy has long since been abandoned, and the University now celebrates Rev. King and his legacy each year in January.[99]

King's speech and the University's reaction to the speech illustrate the tugs and pulls that accompanied the Law School's effort to take its place on the national stage.

The Southern Regional Council and the Fellowship of Southern Churchmen organized the conference, which gained national attention and brought favorable national publicity to Vanderbilt because King spoke for the first time on the Vanderbilt campus.[100] Undoubtedly, this is what the Law School intended. Branscomb and the University, on the other hand, were quite displeased. In response to a decision by a "minor official" in the Law School to allow "a controversial outside organization" to use space in the new Law School building, Branscomb distributed a memo to all University officers, stating that all requests for the use of University facilities must be approved by the Executive Committee of the Board of Trust, which met monthly.[101]

The Law School faculty extended its activities beyond the campus borders. In 1963, the faculty gathered signatures of law faculty from Southern schools for "A Statement of Law and Race Relations." The initiative began when Professor Elliott Cheatham invited his Vanderbilt colleagues to sign on to the statement that would be circulated across the region for signatures and then sent to major newspapers. The statement attacked "the false idea that our national laws may be disregarded and put aside by State officials or private citizens." When the statement was released on July 7, 1963, it was signed by 104 deans and professors of law from southern schools, including every member of the Vanderbilt faculty.

Attacking the use of interposition and similar concepts by George Wallace and other Southern governors, the statement drafted by Cheatham and edited in consultation with his Vanderbilt colleagues was bold. These officials, they wrote, "inflict a grave injury to our country at home. These men inflict an even greater injury to our country abroad. They discredit it and give aid and comfort to our mortal enemies in these dangerous times. These thoughtless persons, while not in the camp of our enemies, do our enemies' work. . . . This argument leads on to anarchy for it implies that every person is entitled to interpret the law for himself and act accordingly."[102]

The statement was picked up by the Associated Press and received national publicity. Letters poured in from across the country, pro and con, from New York to California, from Florida to Michigan. Among the responses were some very hostile comments from some of the School's most influential and prominent alumni. That summer Wade was named to the Executive Committee of the new national Lawyer's Committee for Civil Rights Under Law, which was formed following a White House conference. Wade was one of forty-six signers of a statement by that group, charging that the "manifest illegality" of Governor Wallace's conduct sought to "substitute the rule of force for the rule of law." When the letter was published in the *Birmingham News*, the listing of the Executive Committee had been rearranged with Wade listed as the first signer, apparently because of a typographical error.[103]

Shortly thereafter, Wade received a memo from Lloyd N. Cutler asking for public support for a forthcoming statement by forty Birmingham lawyers to be published in the *Birmingham News*. This time, however, Cheatham advised Wade not to act publicly: "Reluctantly I have come to the conclusion that on balance it would not be wise for you to indorse publicly the Birmingham statement. You are something like a trustee of your influence and position as Dean in Vanderbilt University (as I am of the lesser status as professor of law). The influence and position, coming from University connection, should be used only rarely in public matters."[104] Nevertheless, on October 3, 1963, Wade wrote to Cutler: "I wired the following message to the *Birmingham News* last Monday: 'Last Sunday's 'Public Statement' by a group of Birmingham lawyers should be commended as a forthright yet restrained description of the proper role of law in the current crisis in Birmingham and Alabama. John W. Wade, Nashville, Tennessee.' "[105]

Students followed the faculty's lead in the 1960s. In 1965, the law student body voted decisively (203 to 91, at a time when the student body numbered 357) in favor of a resolution that publicly chastised the segregated local bar association: "that the racially discriminatory practice of the Nashville Bar Association is detrimental to the profession, repugnant to the spirit of the Law, opposed to the basic concept of equal justice under the Law, and results in the perpetuation of the very evils which members of the legal profession have sworn to oppose."[106] The local media seized upon the students' action and the next month the NBA voted 260–175 to admit African-American attorneys.[107] In 1968, the students sent a resolution to the Mayor and Governor in the aftermath of Martin Luther King's assassination "urgently requesting that as a first step toward meaningful peace and racial dignity, all units of the Tennessee National Guard be immediately withdrawn from the Negro community, unless their presence is very clearly warranted."[108] VBA President Andrew W. Bolt sent a letter to all members of the U.S. House of Representatives urging them to vote for the Senate version of the 1968 Civil Rights Act, and to implement the recommendations of the Report of the National Advisory Commission on Civil Disorders.[109] And in March 1970, the student body approved a resolution that opposed President Richard Nixon's nomination of G. Harold Carswell to the U.S. Supreme Court.

Rita Sanders Geier was a law student, and a part-time instructor at Tennessee State University, who took more direct action. In 1968, she filed suit against the state of Tennessee and the U.S. government, charging segregation in the state's higher education system. Her suit was prompted by the expansion of the predominantly white University of Tennessee at Nashville, which she claimed resulted in the duplication of programs available at the predominantly black Tennessee State University in the same city. Her suit changed the landscape of higher education in Tennessee and was finally dismissed, upon the request of Ms. Geier and all other parties, in 2006 following a determination that the state had met the requirements of the consent decree that had resulted from the suit.

Thus were the Wade years a time of change, even turmoil, reflecting social developments of the time. Integration was the issue that provoked the most open conflict. But the institution was changing in other ways as the School struggled with the tension between maintaining strong ties with alumni and prospective students in the immediate geographic region, and devoting time and energy to reaching more distant national and international communities. As the School was changing its size, program, complexion, and aspirations, Wade chose "Stability and Change Through Law" as the theme for the 1963 building dedication ceremony. The School needed its own source of stability during this time of change, and found it in a core group of faculty.

INSTITUTION BUILDERS

Financial resources were a constant obstacle to building a faculty, an obstacle that was only overcome by loyalty to Vanderbilt and dedication to the challenge of building a first-class school. As noted earlier, the entire initial post-World War II faculty was gone by 1949. Coffman reported on recruiting difficulties in 1947: "During the last year I have negotiated with at least six qualified lawyers for positions on this faculty, all of whom have declined to join us because of lack of housing facilities and insufficient compensation."[110] In two years, Coffman himself would be gone, taking three senior faculty members with him.

Five men came to Vanderbilt in the decade from 1947 to 1957, each of whom remained on the Vanderbilt faculty for more than twenty years. In addition to Wade, these were Paul Hartman, Paul Sanders, Herman Trautman, and Ted Smedley. Eddie Morgan credited the dedication and staying power of this faculty core for the School's remarkable progress: "I doubt that it can be matched anywhere in this country."[111]

Paul Sanders joined the Vanderbilt faculty as Professor of Law in 1948/49, following service on the faculties of the University of California at Berkeley and Duke law schools. Sanders was a founding member of the national Labor Law Group. He served extensively as an arbitrator of labor disputes, and received several Presidential appointments to boards and committees to deal with national emergency labor disputes. He acted as the "chief administrative officer" of the School, by faculty consensus, after Dean Wade's sudden illness and hospitalization in March 1961. He submitted the Dean's Annual Report to the Chancellor that spring, and served through the end of the academic year.[112] Sanders published his work frequently and received the School's first paid research leave in the spring of 1972, before retiring in 1974. Typical of this group, he stayed at Vanderbilt despite attractive overtures from other schools. As Morgan would write to Branscomb, "Professor Sanders is constantly rejecting invitations to greener pastures."[113]

Paul J. Hartman was appointed Assistant Professor of Law in the fall of 1949. He had taught at Virginia and Wake Forest, after experience in private practice, and had come to Vanderbilt directly from the S.J.D. program at Columbia. A nationally recognized authority in state and local taxation, he retired from full-time service in 1976, but continued to teach through the fall of 1988. He served as Acting Dean at the Law School for 1964/65, while Wade was on leave for that year as the Meyer Visiting Research Professor at Columbia—a paid leave that carried no teaching responsibilities, thus enabling Wade to engage full time in his research and writing. For many students, Wade was the brain of the School and Hartman was its soul. Hartman was honored with the University's Thomas Jefferson Award in 1968 for distinguished service to Vanderbilt through extraordinary contributions as a member of the faculty in the councils and government of the University. He chaired a variety of University committees, and was a National Vice-Chairman for the University's $55 Million campaign in the 1960s. Hartman's teaching was legendary and the School named its outstanding professor award in his honor in 1975. Wade described Hartman as "a tough teacher, demanding of students and exacting in his grading. Students pretend to fear being called on, but most of them look forward to it as an exciting adventure, and after the experience is over, they savor it."[114] Alumni honored him by establishing a student loan fund in his name upon his retirement.

Herman Trautman also joined the faculty in 1949/50 as a Visiting Professor, having been identified as "an exceptionally talented man in the classroom" by Forrester. He was named to a permanent position as Professor of Law the following year, a position he held until his retirement in 1977. He received his law degree at the University of Indiana and practiced law in that state until he entered military service in World War II. In 1954/55, Trautman was awarded a Ford Faculty Fellowship and was a Graduate Fellow at Harvard Law School. Trautman's expertise was in the area of taxation, a topic on which he lectured and wrote widely, and testified before Congress.

Ted Smedley came to Vanderbilt from the Washington & Lee law faculty to serve as associate director of the *Race Relations Law Reporter* in 1957. Two years later, he took on the duties as Director, in addition to Professor of Law. His directorship of the *Reporter* and then the *Survey* lasted until 1972, although as he pointed out later, the initial grant had been for a two-year period: "They (and we!) had the idea most of the problems would be solved in that time. That seems a little humorous now."[115] Wade viewed Smedley as an ideal director: well organized, with a passion for accuracy and objectivity, a strong sense of duty, and a remarkable capacity for perseverance.[116] As a professor, Smedley was the prime proponent of what the School called the "Vanderbilt method," a pervasive teaching of the subject of professional responsibility throughout the Law School curriculum.[117] He retired in 1978, although he continued to teach occasionally into the mid-1980s.

This core group of faculty defined Vanderbilt Law School for many students. Some of the students may have thought Sanders was murky, Trautman was pretentious, or Hartman was brutal. But they also thought that they were all good teachers. And there was no doubt that each of them was dedicated to building Vanderbilt into the best school they could.

By intent or happenstance, Vanderbilt experimented with a practice of hiring a recent graduate to provide administrative assistance to the dean, and to do some teaching.[118] After one-year terms in this rotation by Ken Roberts[119] (1959/60), and Gil Merritt[120] (1960/61), the practice came to an abrupt end with the appointment of Robert N. Covington in 1961/62. More than forty-five years later, at the time of this writing, Covington remains on the Law School faculty. His contribution to the school was immense, as testified to ten years after his initial appointment by Elliott Cheatham:

> In Professor Covington's last year as a student in the School, the Faculty of Law voted to establish an introductory course for entering students. On his graduation he was appointed to the faculty and was given the very difficult assignment of planning the course and supervising the preparation of materials for it. The course on Legal Methods and the accompanying casebook are the result. The course is, probably, the most useful addition to the curriculum in the 1960s and the credit for it goes primarily to him. . . . Professor Covington has carried numerous onerous burdens as a member of the faculty team. In my view no one else, except Dean Wade himself, has contributed more to the School of Law in the 1960s than Bob Covington.[121]

In a less academic venture, in 1968 Covington organized The Resurrection and Restatement of the Pigboy Crabshaw's Up-Tight, All-Night, Out-of-Sight, South Twenty-First Street Ambulance-Chasing and Marching Society Jazz Band, Ltd. The shorter name of the group was The Statutory Grapes. The Dixieland band, which received front-page notice in the *Wall Street Journal*, was composed of four law faculty members, six law students or graduates, and a member of the Medical School faculty.[122] The band cut and sold an album, with all proceeds going into a need-based scholarship fund for law students. Covington taught the first class in the new Law School building in 1962, and a room in the expanded building was named in his honor four decades later.

While the core of long-timers on the faculty anchored the School and its academic program, some members of the faculty, of course, did leave. Vanderbilt's was not a faculty without alternatives, and those who stayed did so out of loyalty. The School's shoestring operation, with its reliance on temporary grants, was vulnerable to raids. In the spring of 1954, for example, Wade reported that of the full-time faculty of eight, four were considered for deanships during the year and three were offered professorships at substantial increases in salary.[123] Only William Warren accepted, going to Ohio State after three years as an assistant professor at Vanderbilt. Branscomb's statement to the Board in May 1957 reflected a typical theme during those years:

> We have done virtually nothing to assist this School for a period of eleven years. Nevertheless, the School has grown in stature and in reputation. The unhappy proof of this happy fact we experienced this spring, when four of the eight full time members of the faculty received invitations for appointments to other schools at salaries considerably in advance of our present scale. The Dean of the School received over the course of two weeks invitations from three of the major universities of the country for appointments to their staffs. That these members of the faculty remained here is evidence of their commitment to the task of building at Vanderbilt a School of Law of high quality and wide influence.[124]

In 1966, six faculty members received offers from other institutions with salaries "substantially in advance of current salaries." Wade reported that the School's faculty salaries were "substantially below those of institutions with which we wish to compare ourselves, and even behind those of institutions which we have long regarded as not in our class." [125]

Thomas Roady, when he decided to leave Vanderbilt in 1966, wrote a letter that offered an assessment of the challenge.[126] Roady had come to Vanderbilt in 1956, having previously served as Acting Dean at the Washington University Law School in St. Louis, and on the law faculties of the University of Tennessee and University of Missouri law schools. He noted Vanderbilt's failure to move rapidly ahead with respect to the size of the faculty and staff, improvements in the library, and the development of a graduate program. Most disheartening to him was the continued loss of promising young faculty members, due to these conditions and low faculty salaries. He listed among these losses in recent years, Joel Handler to Illinois, Hodge O'Neal to Duke, Jim Kirby to Northwestern, Leo Raskind to Ohio State, Daniel Gifford to the State University of New York at Buffalo, and Graham Parker to Osgood Hall in Toronto. (Hodge O'Neal was a particularly significant loss. While he was only at Vanderbilt from 1956 to 1959, in 1958 he published *Close Corporations: Law and Practice,* a treatise that established a field that he would shape for decades to come.) "In fact," Roady commented, "the only two really outstanding young men we have managed to keep for any length of time have been Bob Covington and John Beasley, and they have a special loyalty to the school which probably accounts for their still being with us." Unless the situation was improved, meaning unless substantial financial resources were committed (his estimate was a $6 million addition to the Law School endowment), he concluded that the school should be prepared to lose Hal Maier, Karl Warden, Richard Strecker, Nathaniel Gozansky, and Ray Patterson.

Maier joined Covington and Beasley as those having a "special loyalty" to Vanderbilt, and he remained until his retirement in 2006. Strecker and Gozansky, however, were gone in two years, and Patterson not long after.[127] Seven other faculty members left in the three-year span from 1968 to 1970, including James H. Cheek, III. A 1967 alumnus, Cheek had come to Vanderbilt as a faculty member and Assistant Dean immediately after receiving his LL.M. from Harvard. He left for private practice after just two years, but would continue to teach as an adjunct for thirty-five years. A recipient of both the Distinguished Service and Distinguished Alumnus awards, he helped shape the development of the nation's corporate and securities law through his chairmanship of the ABA committee on securities law, as an advisor to the ALI's project to develop a Federal Securities Code, and as secretary of the ABA's Corporate Laws committee which rewrote the Model Business Corporation Act. He chaired the National ABA Task Force on Corporate Responsibility formed in response to Enron's bankruptcy.

Karl Warden left in 1980, going to the University of North Dakota to be dean. Vanderbilt lost a unique contributor in Warden. To enhance his teaching and research, he sought out experiences not usually encountered by faculty members. With the help of a grant from the Ford Foundation, he submerged himself, incognito, into Denver's skid row, the Colorado state penitentiary, three mental institutions, a welfare department, a parole department, and over forty other local and state agencies.[128] He was convinced that these first-hand experiences would be of value to his work, as he believed that his predominantly middle-class students needed to know more about the people whose lives would be affected by their future decisions.

The faculty as a whole was open to new pedagogical approaches as the School attempted to move beyond the case method, in response to what Wade identified as the need for a "revolution" in law teaching. New curricular elements included more individual work on the part of students through seminars and internships, perspectives courses like Jurisprudence and Legal Process, and the "utilization of nonlegal materials in the curriculum and the proper portrayal of the relationship of law to the other social sciences."[129] The quality of education provided by a dedicated faculty combined with successes in student recruitment and admissions to create outstanding professional results for students. It was not unusual for a hundred percent of the students in a graduating class to pass the Tennessee bar exam, and in many years there were more employers requesting Vanderbilt graduates than the School could supply.[130]

The care and commitment that the faculty brought to the instructional process can be seen in the School's week-long orientation program before the first-year classes began. The faculty conducted sessions, accompanied by assigned readings, on such topics as An Introduction to Court Structure, Anatomy of a Lawsuit, Techniques of Law Study, Law and the Legal Profession, The Purpose and Function of Legal Education, and three or four sessions on An Introduction to Case Analysis. Chancellor Alexander Heard made a presentation on The University Honor System. This orientation program constituted a substantial academic overlay—in addition to the sessions introducing students to the school, the library, the faculty, student organizations, and meetings with faculty advisers.

The faculty so dedicated to teaching produced three hallmarks of the curriculum that could only have been achieved through intensive faculty labor: (1) a first-year writing course that was taught by every member of the faculty, when instruction in the subject was being left to recent graduates at many law schools; (2) a Legal Methods course that had been developed through a collaborative faculty effort and resulted in a leading casebook in the field; (3) the "pervasive approach" to teaching legal ethics, bringing into each course a concern for the basic problems facing all lawyers.[131]

The new legal writing course was added to the curriculum in the fall of 1961. The course was organized in small groups and taught and graded by every faculty member, including the dean. Unanimous faculty action linked the course sections to advisor/advisee groups, thus yielding not only personalized writing instruction but enhanced student/faculty relations. For a while, beginning in the second year of the program, the Legal Methods and Legal Writing courses were merged.[132]

As was the case with most law schools, Vanderbilt's curriculum evolved as the practice of law evolved. Thus, new courses were appearing in such subjects as Labor Law, Trade Regulation, Administrative Law, and Taxation. A notable feature of the curriculum was the Practice of Law course first offered by Cecil Sims in 1950.[133] Years before the ABA would require a professional responsibility course in the wake of Watergate, Sims was teaching students about the problems confronting lawyers in the practice of the profession, attempting to bridge the gap between study in a law school and the responsibility attorneys would be assuming after graduation. The course was not required, but about eighty-five percent of the third-year students attended his Saturday morning lectures.[134] Sims was a firm believer in the broad education of attorneys. When asked in class if it was important for a lawyer to know Latin, he replied, "No, but it is important for him to have forgotten it."[135]

In 1955, the course became The Profession of Law, as other members of the faculty joined Sims in teaching the class, and Cheatham's *Cases and Materials on the Legal Profession* became the text for the course. The School's aim was to go beyond the regulations that governed the profession and to develop a course that "treats legal ethics in detail and inculcates in students a sense of the lawyer's obligation to serve his profession by participating in professional organizations and his obligation to serve his community by providing real leadership."[136]

By the early 1960s, Vanderbilt had begun to experiment on a large scale with a pervasive approach to teaching professional responsibility—a development that garnered national attention.[137] While teachers at other schools had included discussions of professional responsibility in other courses, Vanderbilt's program of systematically pursuing this approach on such a large scale was probably unprecedented.[138] Most of the faculty participated in this thorough infusion of ethical and professional concepts across all three years of a legal education—a cooperative endeavor that brought a distinctive Vanderbilt cast to the study of law.

A section on "Institution Builders" should not close without comment on the role the School's students played in making the School what it was in the 1950s and 1960s. The students' contributions to advancing the academic program were almost innumerable, ranging from carrying books and furniture to the new building to insuring a smooth transition to an integrated school. Many of the legal services programs were the results of student initiatives and depended on their volunteer efforts. Saturday classes were abolished as a faculty concession to student wishes. While some campuses were sites of turmoil and strife in the 1960s, Vanderbilt law students were substantial partners in the operation of the institution. When the American Bar Association established national Law Day observances in 1958, the School used the occasions as a platform for attracting national figures. The organization of the Days were turned over to the Vanderbilt Bar Association, which brought to campus such speakers as Supreme Court justices William O. Douglas and Stanley Reed, Griffin Bell, Nicholas deB. Katzenbach, and Fred P. Graham—a 1959 graduate who at that time was the Supreme Court correspondent for the *New York Times*. The students also directed a Bench and Bar lecture series, enacting a by-law to the student bar association constitution that the law library be closed during the lectures. In 1965, the faculty's speaker series was consolidated with the students' speakers series, under the leadership of the students. That same year, the *Law School Alumni Newsletter* was subsumed into the *Dicta*, the student-run newspaper—a sign of the quality and seriousness of this student publication.[139] Such an arrangement would be unfathomable to a later generation of students for whom the *Dicta* became a satirical, at times underground, commentary on life at the School.

Undoubtedly there were tensions and occasional conflict within the student body. On balance, however, the School benefited from an uncommon collegiality, a loyalty to the institution, and a dedication to the enterprise among students that paralleled the same features on the faculty side of the podium.

MAKING THE MOST OF SECOND CAREERS

Allen M. Steele, Law School alumnus and University Board of Trust member, expressed the sentiments of many when he said, "Our Law School made its reputation with distinguished professors who had retired elsewhere."[140] Vanderbilt certainly took advantage of mandatory retirement age policies at other law schools, although it was not unique among American law schools in this regard, or even the most aggressive in pursuing this strategy. That recognition goes to the Hastings College of Law. In 1959, for example, Hasting's entire full-time faculty of fifteen was past the normal retirement age, ranging in age from sixty-five to eighty-three, with an average of seventy-three. Roscoe Pound, the retired dean of the Harvard Law School, called this "the strongest law faculty in the country."[141]

Among the faculty who found new life at Vanderbilt were Morton Ferson, Blythe Stason, and Warren A. Seavy. Ferson, who was President of the AALS in 1946, actually taught in two different stints at Vanderbilt, before joining the famed Hastings faculty in 1956 at the age of eighty. Seavy, another former AALS President, was a Harvard emeritus professor who visited in 1959/60 and was "regarded by many as the outstanding exponent of dialectic teaching in the country."[142] Blythe Stason came to Vanderbilt in 1964 from a position as Administrator of the American Bar Foundation. He had previously been at the University of Michigan as a student, faculty member (1924–60), Dean (1939–60) and University Provost (1938–44), before joining the Vanderbilt faculty. A prolific author of books and articles, he wrote the Uniform Anatomical Gift Act which was adopted by states across the country in the regulation of organ transplantation. He stayed for five years, chairing the university interdisciplinary steering committee to establish the Urban and Regional Development Center. Wade identified Stason as exemplary in fulfilling a faculty member's obligations of professional service: a life member of the National Conference of Commissioners on Uniform State Laws, a consultant to the Atomic Energy Commission, and a member of the Attorney General's Committee on Administrative Procedure, and the Hoover Commission Task Force.

Each of these men made contributions to Vanderbilt in their "retirement years," but the names that are hallowed in Vanderbilt lore are Edmund M. Morgan and Elliott E. Cheatham. Eddie Morgan was, said Erwin Griswold, "universally recognized as one of the great law teachers and legal scholars of his time."[143] Ray Forrester, who recruited him, wrote in 1949 that Morgan was the foremost teacher of the law of evidence and procedure in the United States. "In fact, it is probably no exaggeration to say that he is, all things considered, the outstanding American law teacher on the present scene."[144] He joined the Vanderbilt faculty in 1950, at the age of seventy-one, "still in vigorous health" and desiring to continue his distinguished career."[145]

Morgan left Harvard under its compulsory retirement rule.[146] After teaching at the Minnesota and Yale law schools early in his career, he had returned to Harvard, his alma mater, in 1925. He served as acting dean twice (1936–37, 1942–45) and as Royall Professor of Law from 1938 until his retirement. The author of two casebooks, a treatise, and many articles in leading law reviews, he was also the Reporter for the Model Code of Evidence and the President of the AALS in 1940. In August 1965, he received the American Bar Association Medal, the highest award bestowed by the association.

Morgan was a demanding taskmaster in the classroom. "He was somewhat of the old school," according to Griswold, "not given to undue gentleness to students, either in the classroom, or in his marking of their examination papers."[147] Wrote the *Harvard Crimson*: "To students he was a short, slight, kindly man who underwent a schizophrenic change in the classroom which they claim he turned into 'medieval horror chambers' by devilish cross examinations on court procedure."[148]

Morgan requested that his Vanderbilt classes be scheduled at 11:00, to allow him to "persuade" the students to stay until 12:30 or thereabouts so that he could get in some extra time without adding to the number of class periods. In making this arrangement he asked the dean, "Do you think this is practicable, or do Vanderbilt students insist on getting official credit for all time spent in the classroom?"[149] His grading did not mellow in his "second career." One set of Civil Procedure grades he submitted contained no A's, 8 B's, 19 C's, 27 D's, and 9 F's, and he commented that he had graded each student on their best two out of three answers: "Had I graded on all three, less than 25 per cent of the class would have passed, and there would have been no grade above middle C."[150] His drill in the classroom was grueling, but he cared deeply for his students, leading him to regularly, and privately, give financial assistance to those in need, and to personally fund a prize for the student submitting the best work to the *Law Review.*

Morgan remained active during his years at Vanderbilt. He was appointed by President Truman in September 1951 to serve on the Commission on Internal Security and Individual Rights. He also chaired the United States committee that revised the Code of Military Justice, published *Basic Problems of Evidence* in 1954, chaired American Law Institute committees, gave dozens of lectures, and paved the way with his contacts at the Ford Foundation for grants that were awarded to Vanderbilt. The fact that Morgan personally paid his own secretary to assist in his numerous professional activities was a commentary both on his generosity and on the School's meager resources at the time.

In spite of his distinguished achievements, he maintained a public humility, as evidenced in a handwritten note to Dean Forrester: "Dear Ray, It is mighty generous of you and the faculty to recommend me for the Frank C. Rand professorship. I greatly appreciate the honor, though I can think of nothing I have done to deserve it."[151] When he retired, he donated his library to the School and that collection became the nucleus of the Law Faculty Library that was named in his honor.

When John Wade began recruiting Elliott Cheatham to come to Vanderbilt, Cheatham at first declined, replying that while he had once hoped to come to Vanderbilt he had already committed to join the Hastings post-retirement faculty.[152] The Hastings offer came with tenure, which Vanderbilt's offer did not, and Eddie Morgan joined in the recruiting of Cheatham.[153] When the fall of 1960 arrived, Cheatham was at Vanderbilt where he was an active teacher and scholar for eight years, and Research Professor of Law for four years after that. Cheatham had taught at Emory, the University of Illinois, and Cornell law schools before joining the Columbia law faculty in 1929, where he was named the Charles Evans Hughes Professor of Law in 1950. He was elected President of the AALS in 1942, authored the leading casebooks in both Conflict of Laws and the Profession of Law, and was a nationally respected scholar. Morgan called him "the most distinguished legal scholar that has ever joined this faculty."[154]

Cheatham's success in the classroom matched Morgan's, but with a very different demeanor, as he was once described as "the parfit gentil knight of Chaucer's tale, securing by the very force of his urbanity a degree of student preparation which others are denied."[155] Cheatham was actively engaged in Vanderbilt's affairs, often suggesting development strategies to Wade, and responding to requests for comments from the dean on a range of topics. He chaired the Curriculum Committee whose report was the backbone of the School's 1964 Planning Study, and also the ad hoc committee which created the new first-year Legal Methods and Legal Research and Writing courses.

His writing never ceased and it remained "lively and original."[156] John Wade observed of Cheatham: "He can sternly and firmly prod and redirect the lazy or recalcitrant student, the not-so-productive faculty member, or the lagging dean. At eighty, he is presently engaged in writing two books and has plans for a third. He works seven days a week, I really don't know how many hours."[157] Cheatham was notified just hours before his death on January 13, 1972, that he had been selected by the fellows of the American Bar Foundation to receive their research award, the Foundation's highest honor.[158]

Morgan and Cheatham each were appointed for a time as the Frank C. Rand Professor of Law, but the circumstances surrounding the use, and then the disappearance of, the Rand Chair are a little mysterious. The professorship was not endowed, but had been created by the Board of Trust to honor Frank C. Rand, the Board's President, in 1945. A policy soon developed at the University that did not allow a chair to be named for an individual un-less financial support was forthcoming in connection with the adoption of the name. Yet, just six weeks after the Board of Trust's affirmation of this policy was cited by Branscomb (in 1951, in rejecting a proposal for a Wood-row Wilson Professor of International Relations in the College of Arts and Science), the Board approved Morgan's appointment as the Frank C. Rand Professor of Law.[159] Morgan held the chair until his appointment for 1963/64 was cancelled because of ill health. Elliott Cheatham was then named the Rand Professor beginning in 1964, and when he changed to part-time status in 1968, Stason was the Rand Professor for his final year, resigning in the summer of 1969. At that time, the Rand Professorship disappeared from Vanderbilt records, without formal announcement, and the practice of ap-pointing retired faculty to full-time positions also came to an end. From that point forward, the School's reputation would be made by the teaching and scholarship of younger faculty, whose careers would be shaped by stan-dards that were evolving at Vanderbilt as they were nationally.

Law students' socializing included "Blackacres" at which kegs of beer appeared
on Friday afternoons in the courtyard of the new building, as on this Friday in 1976.

Bob Covington, the longest serving professor in the School's history, during 1964 registration with students (from left) Judson Harwood, Otto Gerlach, and Jesse Zellner.

Dean John Wade presented Associate Dean John Beasley with his J.D. diploma. The ceremony on October 10, 1969,

Martha Craig Daughtrey,
first female faculty
member in 1972, later
served on the U.S. Sixth
Circuit Court of Appeals.

John Wade, listening to Sandra Day O'Connor, at the dedication ceremony for the
expanded and renovated building in October 1982. Surrounded by Herman Trautman,
Paul Hartman, Charlie Warfield (Class of 1949), Andy Shookhoff (Class of 1977), Karl
Warden, and Divinity School Dean Jack Forstman.

The School's Founder's Medal has been worn by the top graduate each year since 1876, as Mary Crossley does here in the 1987 commencement ceremony. Ms. Crossley, also Editor-in-Chief of the *Vanderbilt Law Review*, was named dean of the University of Pittsburgh Law School in 2005. (Photographer: David Hildebrand)

Robert Belton (left) became the School's first African-American faculty member in 1975, visiting here with the 1991 Martin Luther King Jr. Lecturer Haywood Burns, Dean of the City University of New York Law School. (Photographer: Anthony Lathrop)

Alumni became an important part of the School's financing. Jim Cheek, Class of 1967, is shown here presenting the gifts and pledges accumulated at the 1992 Reunion.

The School's outstanding teacher award is named for Paul Hartman and Don Hall. Hartman, center, is enjoying a moment at a Law School reunion event with Hall and his wife Nancy, circa 1991.

CHAPTER SEVEN

Opportunities and Challenges

INTRODUCTION

Vanderbilt Law School, at the end of the Wade deanship, was clearly focused on occupying a place among the nation's elite law schools. Thus, the story of the following thirty years is the story of how this pursuit of prestige and elite status entangled the Law School, inevitably, in certain conflicts and tensions. A school cannot be all things to all people, and choosing some routes to maintain and enhance the School's standing required departing from or declining to take other paths. In this, Vanderbilt was not unique. Indeed, in many ways Vanderbilt during this period reflected and reinforced broader national trends.

CHOOSING AMONG PRIORITIES

Law professor James F. Blumstein chaired the Ad Hoc University Committee on Appointments, Renewal, and Tenure, which issued its report (the CART report) on January 27, 1984. The implementation of this report would change the Vanderbilt landscape, but not without controversy. Law professor Donald J. Hall was one of thirteen members of the Law School faculty who signed a memorandum to Chancellor Joe B. Wyatt expressing concern about the report's recommendations.

Blumstein and Hall each came to Vanderbilt in the fall of 1970, as newly appointed assistant professors of law, and over the course of their careers they would come to epitomize the different sides of one of the most contentious matters in the School's history. The CART Report brought to the surface the tension between the relative emphasis on, and importance of, teaching on the one hand, and research and publishing scholarship on the other. The latter is the coin of the realm for schools seeking national and international recognition, while the former had been the heart of what made Vanderbilt Law School distinctive through most of its history.

A number of developments made this clash of cultures inevitable. The increased valuation of research may well have begun with a passion among faculty members to understand better what they were teaching. These impulses were reinforced by the general shift nationally in the second half of the twentieth century for university-based law schools to model themselves more along graduate school lines than trade school lines. Certainly teaching faculty had long been interested in the how and why of the law they were teaching. The difference was that universities and law schools were finding ways and resources to allow, support, and reward faculty pursuit of these interests. This shift was especially pronounced at schools like Vanderbilt, as the University was working to establish its reputation as a national research university. In this national competition for elite recognition, published scholarship became more and more the "gold standard," at least in part because that was a product that could be evaluated on a nationwide basis in a way that outstanding teaching could not be.

John Costonis captured this national movement in his first year as dean at Vanderbilt in the self-study prepared in 1985 for the Southern Association of Colleges and Schools. In 1981, the ABA's Accreditation Committee of the Section on Legal Education and Admissions to the Bar found that Vanderbilt had "made a conscious decision to maintain a small student body with a distinctive student-faculty environment and to commit its energies to an extraordinary degree to its teaching function." Four year later, Costonis painted a different picture. While stating that the line between teaching and research was often so fine as to be invisible, he also noted "some shift in emphasis from the teaching to the research and publication function" which had increased the national visibility of the faculty. "It is important that the proper balance be struck on these two essential faculty activities, and in this respect Vanderbilt is probably no different than any other major law school."[1]

In the immediate post-War years Vanderbilt Law School had been frank about its efforts to recruit an excellent faculty. Coffman said that he had "no conscience whatever in stealing the best men from the best law schools and law firms in the country." But he was looking for "lawyers who are interested in the teaching side of the profession," which he distinguished from professors teaching in law departments of universities.[2] A program approved by the faculty in 1950 is evidence of the emphasis the faculty placed on the quality of their teaching. Each faculty member would visit at least two classes of each of his colleagues. Following the visits, a constructive criticism would be written, and the unsigned reports would be delivered to each faculty member to give him the benefit of frank suggestions from colleagues.[3] Even so, a survey of law schools in Tennessee in 1949, conducted by Elliott E. Cheatham while still at Columbia, noted that "To an unusual degree the faculty members have contributed to the law through research," but they continue to give their first priority to teaching.[4]

The faculty was mindful of the School's emphasis on teaching, as recognized in a 1963 Curriculum Committee report: "The American faculty of law has been predominately a teaching faculty, giving greater emphasis in the selection of its members and in their work to the teaching function than do the faculties of most university schools and colleges. It has been so at Vanderbilt to a marked degree."[5] This "marked degree" of seriousness about teaching became a Vanderbilt hallmark over the years, and affected how the faculty chose its new colleagues. When John Costonis became dean at Vanderbilt, he was worried by one feature of the faculty appointments process at the School. He observed that the faculty quickly dismissed candidates for faculty positions—often after they had been in the building for only a couple of hours—who came to campus with sterling credentials and exceptional research accomplishments. This was a pattern he had not experienced in the law school faculties he had previously served on, such as those at New York University and the University of Pennsylvania, and he was concerned that quick decisions were being made on the basis of personal first impressions and who the faculty "liked." What Costonis came to understand was the faculty's concern for teaching. Typically, a visiting faculty candidate would make a presentation to the faculty at 9:00 A.M. on the first day on campus. After that presentation, and the questions and answers that followed, if the faculty were not convinced that the candidate would be a strong classroom teacher, they lost interest, no matter how strong the candidate's paper record was.

While not abandoning its heritage of good teaching, the School had begun to grant more prominence to research and publication in the early 1960s. The same Curriculum Committee report that acknowledged the School's traditional emphasis on teaching also commented that that predominance had come at a cost to research, writing, and publication. Recommendations were made to promote more faculty research and publication. In his building dedication address in April 1963, Dean Wade had already sounded the theme: "Law Schools must encourage their faculty members to engage in research by affording the necessary funds, the time, and the facilities."[6] Even so, Wade considered research and publishing to be "complementary" to the faculty's teaching, which should receive "paramount emphasis."[7]

The faculty responded to Wade's urgings. In the five years leading up to a 1971/72 University-wide planning study, there was an outpouring of casebooks and articles in some of the nation's leading law reviews.[8] Robert L. Knauss was brought to Vanderbilt as dean in the spring of 1972 in part to address issues of faculty research productivity. Knauss succeeded Wade as dean, coming from the University of Michigan where he had been Vice-President for Student Services for the University, and Professor of Law in a highly regarded law school. He had earned his J.D. degree from Michigan, following a bachelor's degree from Harvard, and was active as a publishing scholar in the fields of business associations and securities regulation. He informed the faculty, at the meeting at which he was introduced as dean-elect, that the tenure process would be handled "with vigor,"[9] and the School's first paid research leave was granted to Paul Sanders in the spring of 1972.

When Knauss arrived he was surprised by how little the faculty was publishing and he made a strong push to increase research and published scholarship. He pursued faculty appointments with this in mind, and attempted to address the administrative burdens on faculty that diverted their time and energy from research. He announced the closing of the Summer School, with the last regular session being held in 1974. The money that had been spent on summer teaching salaries was placed in a fund to provide summer grants for faculty research.[10] But, as Conkin observes in his Vanderbilt history, "in the early 1970s the quantity of faculty publications began to decline."[11] While twelve to sixteen faculty members were publishing every year in the early 1960s, the number was smaller a decade later (even as the size of the faculty grew), and more book reviews and reports were appearing among the listed publications.[12]

Knauss notified the faculty on January 16, 1979 of his resignation—effective with end of semester.[13] At that time, University President Emmett Fields lauded Knauss for improvements during his deanship in the scholarly standing of the faculty and the geographic diversity of the student body, concluding that the Law School was assuming national status as a result.[14] Knauss sensed that the dynamics between Vanderbilt's deans (who had enjoyed considerable autonomy) and the University central administration were changing, and he decided that seven years as dean was enough. His connections with Vanderbilt extended through two years of leaves of absence while he was a Visiting Professor at the newly-formed Vermont Law School, before he accepted the position of dean at the University of Houston Law Center in 1981.

C. Dent Bostick followed Knauss in the deanship, first as Acting Dean for 1979/80 while Knauss was on leave, and then with a five-year appointment as Dean effective July 1980. Bostick had first come to Vanderbilt as a visitor in 1968 from the University of Florida faculty. His deanship was successful in many ways, but two related events would dramatically change the environment in which he worked. The first of these was the appointment of Joe B. Wyatt as Chancellor of the University in July 1982. When he addressed the Board of Trust in his first meeting with them, Wyatt said a few words, generally complimentary, about each of the individual schools at Vanderbilt. His *only* comment on the Law School was, "We have seen the number of law students swell nationwide in recent years, and we now have approximately twenty times as many lawyers as Japan but only half as many engineers and scientists. That is a matter for concern."[15] These could not have been encouraging words for the Law School's dean.

More consequential for Bostick's deanship, and the Law School, was Wyatt's appointment of the CART committee in April 1983. Wyatt had come to campus in the aftermath of a lawsuit brought against the University by English professor Elizabeth Langland over her denial of tenure. He concluded that there were serious flaws in the processes through which the University handled faculty appointments, renewals, and tenure decisions, and thus he informed the Board that he had appointed a committee, with Blumstein as the chair, to make recommendations that would address that process.[16] His actual charge to the committee, however, was broader than what he had presented to the board, as the committee was charged to consider and make specific recommendations not just on process issues but on the "criteria and standards" related to the appointment, retention, renewal, promotion, tenure, recruitment, and productivity of faculty of national and international standing.[17] The result was a comprehensive set of recommendations related to tenure standards and procedures, faculty appointments, and faculty renewal.

A period of comment and response followed the issuance of the Committee's report in January 1984, and the next fall the Chancellor asked the CART committee "to reconvene and reconsider their recommendations, taking into account those suggestions made by faculty members who were not in total agreement with the Committee's report."[18] Among those faculty members "who were not in total agreement with the Committee's report" were ten members of the tenured Law School faculty, and three emeritus faculty members.[19] These thirteen signed a public memorandum that was addressed to the Chancellor and "the University Community," in which they objected to (1) "the radical change in the tenure standard," which they said changed the standard "from teaching excellence *or* scholarly excellence to scholarly excellence alone;" (2) defining scholarly excellence "in terms of national notoriety, with no emphasis on the actual merit or value of the scholarly work itself;" and (3) "the creation of ad-hoc and standing university-wide committees to enforce the new standards."[20] While several issues were raised in the eleven-page memo, the heart of the matter seemed to be the first issue: "the report recommends that every unit of Vanderbilt University be prevented from adding to its tenured faculty any candidate who is a truly outstanding teacher and a competent, though not nationally recognized, scholar." Their concern was that the committee's recommendations would devalue the Law School's teaching excellence which was nationally recognized and the source of its success in providing an outstanding educational experience.

The portion of the CART report that drew this opposition stated that a decision on tenure should focus on research and scholarly creativity and productivity, teaching effectiveness, and total professional contribution:

> National distinction through past achievements in published research is a *sine qua non* for appointment or promotion to a tenure position. In addition, a department or school recommending a candidate for appointment or promotion to a tenure position must present convincing evidence that supports its informed judgment that future productivity will likely continue. . . . In addition to satisfying the Research standard, a candidate must satisfy the Teaching standard. Thus, in order to qualify for appointment or promotion to a tenure position, a candidate must demonstrate effectiveness in teaching, which is an essential criterion to satisfy in order for the candidate to warrant an award of tenure.[21]

In September 1986 the Board approved policies, based on the CART committee recommendations, which incorporated both the change in standards and the creation of new University committees.[22] While policies flowing from the CART report addressed a wide range of issues, "Foremost among these policies was the requirement that tenure not be granted to any faculty member whose research was not judged to be 'excellent.'"[23] In making these changes the Board moved in the direction of Jim Blumstein's vision.

Blumstein was appointed University Professor of Constitutional Law and Health Law and Policy in 2003. The title of University Professor had been used rarely since it was created in 1970 to recognize "exceptional scholars whose work lies in two or more fields or disciplines."[24] In 1992 he was awarded the Earl Sutherland Prize for Achievement in Research at Vanderbilt to honor faculty "whose achievements in research, scholarship, or creative expression have had significant critical reception and are recognized nationally or internationally," the only Law School faculty member other than Wade to have received the award since its inception in 1976. Blumstein was elected to the Institute of Medicine of the National Academy of Sciences. As the author of several books and dozens of articles, and the recipient of a number of research grants, his career exemplified the emphasis on research and publication championed in the CART Report.

Don Hall, on the other hand, opposed the report's elevation of the research standard for tenure, fearing the impact that change would have on the school's tradition of outstanding teaching. He received the Teacher of the Year Award in 1973/74, before the School initiated the Paul J. Hartman Outstanding Professor Award, named for its inaugural recipient, in 1975. When students cast their ballots for the Hartman Award in subsequent years to recognize excellence in teaching, they chose Hall in eight different years, spanning four decades. In the fall of 2004, the award was renamed the Hall-Hartman Outstanding Professor Award. When the University inaugurated the Vanderbilt Chair of Teaching Excellence Award in 1994, Hall was one of the two initial recipients. When the Tennessee Bar Association created its Outstanding Law Professor Award for the state's four law schools, Hall was the first honoree.

Hall was certainly not the only outstanding teacher on the faculty. Nicholas Zeppos was named a Hartman winner in five years over just an eight-year span, before he moved on to Kirkland Hall as Associate Provost, later becoming Provost and Vice Chancellor for Academic Affairs. Alumnus Carlton Tarkington endowed a Chair in Teaching Excellence in the Law School, and the first recipient of the Tarkington Chair in 2003 was Thomas R. McCoy, who received the Hall-Hartman Award seven times before he and Hall retired together in 2007.

Similarly the faculty was composed of a number of publishing scholars in addition to Blumstein. The School's endowed chairs have been used to recognize this contribution to the profession, and inaugural holders of the Law School's endowed chairs and professorships have included Charles O. Galvin, Harold G. Maier, Donald Langevoort, Robert Thompson, Suzanna Sherry, Rebecca Brown, Randall Thomas, Robert Rasmussen, John Costonis, and Kent Syverud.

The tension between research and teaching at Vanderbilt, as at most law schools, was a matter of emphasis rather than a choice between irreconcilable options. The vast majority of the faculty took both of these endeavors quite seriously. For example, Blumstein received the Hartman teaching award in 1982, and Hall produced multiple editions of a criminal procedure casebook. Vanderbilt's faculty were not one-dimensional in their interests. Among the chair holders, Bob Rasmussen demonstrated the balance between teaching and publishing, winning the outstanding professor award six times before leaving in 2007 to become dean at the University of Southern California Law School. Provost Tom Burish, in his assessment of the impact of the CART Report a decade after its implementation, gave voice to the aspiration to appropriately acknowledge both enterprises:

> Previously, faculty members could receive tenure if they were judged as 'competent' in research, as long as they were considered 'excellent' in teaching. The teaching standard put forth by CART requires 'highly effective teaching' by all who receive tenure, whereas previously merely being 'competent' in teaching was sufficient if their research was 'excellent.'
>
> Thus, the CART policy eliminated the tradeoff between outstanding teaching and outstanding research. For the past decade at Vanderbilt, to earn tenure, faculty members have had to be outstanding in both.[25]

In July 1984, in the midst of the CART approval process, Bostick announced that he would be returning to the teaching faculty at the end of the upcoming academic year. His five-year term as dean was coming to an end and he had been on the losing end of conflicts with the Chancellor not only on the CART Report, but on a faculty tenure recommendation and an entry-level faculty appointment. Bostick remained on the faculty until his retirement in January 1992.[26] In a sign of Chancellor Wyatt's endorsement of the new direction in faculty standards, none of the faculty members who signed the memorandum that opposed the CART Report were named to the search committee to identify Bostick's successor.

An important ingredient in the promotion of scholarly research and publication is a program of faculty research leaves. Even after the beginning of paid faculty research leaves in 1972, such leaves were awarded less often than once a year through the Knauss and Bostick deanships. John J. Costonis became Dean in 1985. In an effort to strengthen the faculty's production of scholarly research, he instituted a regular research leave policy, eventually establishing eligibility every eight years for faculty members actively engaged in publishing. The number of leaves averaged about three per year during his deanship. Costonis also substantially increased summer research grants and expanded the size of the faculty, which enriched the curriculum and allowed for a reduction in the teaching load for each faculty member.

As Acting Dean in 1996/97, David F. Partlett announced an improvement in the policy, reducing the eight-year cycle for research leaves to a seven-year cycle. Partlett had been appointed to the faculty as Professor of Law in 1988, and was added as a co-author to Wade's *Torts: Cases and Materials* in 1994. While at Vanderbilt, he chaired the University Faculty Senate, received the Law School's Distinguished Service Award in 1997, and the University's Thomas Jefferson Award in 1998.[27] He departed in 2000 to assume the deanship at Washington & Lee School of Law, and later became the dean at Emory Law School.

Kent D. Syverud began his tenure as Dean and Garner Anthony Professor of Law in the fall of 1997. He had been on the University of Michigan law faculty for a decade, where he had also served as Associate Dean for Academic Affairs. The coming of Kent Syverud to the Vanderbilt deanship brought a dramatic change in the research leave picture, as he created a policy of pre-tenure leaves, extended leaves to faculty beyond the tenured and tenure track faculty, and instituted "mid-term" leaves including those supported by the funding of the FedEx Research Professorship. As a result, faculty research leaves increased until they averaged about ten per year in the last three years of his deanship.

Of course, this number of leaves could only be supported by an increase in the size of the faculty, and thus it was the School's success in faculty hiring during this time that made this dramatic enhancement in research support possible. In 1967, the School reported a student-faculty ratio of twenty-seven to one, even though the ABA accreditation standard at the time provided that schools should "make every effort to maintain a student-faculty ratio of not more than twenty to one."[28] By the end of the century, that ratio had dropped to sixteen to one. A larger faculty contributed to the research and publication effort by reducing teaching loads, permitting more research leaves, and allowing faculty to teach more in their areas of specialization—all without reducing the range of curricular offerings available to students. A larger number of publishing faculty also increased national awareness of the work the faculty was doing, a factor that became increasingly important in the assessment of schools in the last decades of the century.

MINING A LARGER TALENT POOL

The transitions in deanships illustrated the types of "growing pains" the School experienced in the years after Wade stepped down. Bob Knauss was given a less than hospitable reception among some alumni, especially local alumni, when the School reached beyond its traditional base for a new dean. For some alumni, John Beasley was the "favorite son" candidate in that search, although Beasley says he didn't consider himself a candidate. The dean following Knauss was Dent Bostick, a southerner and a member of the faculty. His appointment satisfied some constituencies but was not welcomed by those who thought a different choice would have been more in line with the aspirations of a national, research institution. Then John Costonis came in as dean to advance scholarship and national aspirations, but he ran afoul of those who thought, fairly or not, that the message of this brash northeasterner was condescending or dismissive of the School's past achievements.

John Costonis served as Dean and Milton R. Underwood Chair in Free Enterprise from 1985 through 1996, an eleven-year tenure that was the longest of any post-World War II dean except Wade. Costonis was a well-known land use scholar and teacher, who had been offered a tenured position on the Vanderbilt faculty in 1976, an offer he had declined. Coming from the NYU Law School faculty, after time on the faculties at Illinois, Pennsylvania, and the University of California at Berkeley, Costonis expressed an appreciation for Vanderbilt's strength in the region but he wanted to reach out and broaden the School's constituencies.[29] Some diversification at the School merely followed larger national trends, but Costonis made a concerted effort to broaden the School's reach and progress was made on his watch, before he left in 1996 to serve as Executive Director of the Quantum Foundation, and then as Chancellor of the Louisiana State University School of Law.

Securing a geographically more diverse student body had been a goal of the faculty from the time the School reopened in 1946.[30] But the attainment of this goal would create friction and dissonance for many of the School's supporters. The tension between honoring southern roots and reaching for national acclaim was felt in various ways by members of the Vanderbilt community. In May 1962, Branscomb stated that Vanderbilt University was widely expected to take a role in national educational leadership, yet "This does not mean that we need cease to be Southern. . . . It does not mean that we will sacrifice our historic traditions."[31] The first of the "Assumptions for Vanderbilt University," presented at a Board of Trust planning retreat in 1965, reveals a continuing concern for regional connections as the school marched toward national and international greatness: "The University will develop toward national and international distinction and thereby most effectively meet its regional responsibilities."[32] In the end, the School moved away from Cecil Sims' vision of developing "leadership in the South from students with Southern backgrounds."[33]

Justin Wilson gave voice to the misgivings that many of the School's supporters felt along the way. He supported the School following his graduation in 1970—as a member of the alumni board, a financial contributor, and an Adjunct Professor of Law. The Patrick Wilson Scholarship program established by his family was a valuable contribution to the School's development. When he participated in the Vanderbilt Oral History Project, however, he expressed misgivings about the change in the School's aspirations that undoubtedly reflected the views of other Nashvillians and Tennesseans. "[W]hen I grew up we associated Vanderbilt with Nashville, and as a Nashville school, and not as a national school, and I understand very fully the desire of the university to speak of a national university, although I'm not sure at all that I really fully agree with it." Wilson believed that Vanderbilt's identity as a Southern school had diminished considerably, to the point that it was his perception when he was in law school that Vanderbilt discriminated in its admissions decisions against local applicants.[34] The issue was still on the minds of University trustees at a Board retreat in February 1998, as one of the discussion items was how the University could move aggressively to become a top ten national university, without losing what was valued about its "Southerness."[35]

The Law School responded to concerns such as Wilson's from time to time, as illustrated by an article in the School's alumni magazine in 1977. Then-Associate Dean Bostick wrote about how the criteria of excellence and diversity played out in the admissions process. He defended the emphasis placed on the LSAT, described how the School was looking for outstanding undergraduate grades "particularly from schools in all parts of the country known for high standards," and acknowledged that many rejected applicants were "supported actively by alumni and friends of the law school." These rejected applicants were "undoubtedly well-qualified for law school," but the School was looking for the "diverse educational, cultural, and geographical backgrounds" that were essential ingredients in legal education.[36]

Costonis addressed this issue in terms of two "concurrent missions." "The first focused on the traditional values that have meant so much to graduating students. I speak here of excellent teaching, a strong sense of professional ethics, and the School's historic roots in Tennessee and in the South generally. . . . The second mission is oriented more to the future; it seeks to build on an already firm base to achieve broadscale national excellence."[37]

The focus on wider horizons that began in the Wade years continued. A sign of the changing focus was the re-assignment of the Weldon B. White Prize. The White Prize, honoring the one-time Justice on the Tennessee Supreme Court, was originally endowed to recognize the student who prepared "the best written study of some aspect of the law of the State of Tennessee."[38] As the School's focus shifted, and fewer and fewer students were producing any papers on Tennessee law, the award's designation was eventually changed at the beginning of the twenty-first century to recognize the graduating student who submitted the best research paper in fulfillment of the School's advanced writing requirement, on any subject matter, taking the place of the existing "Dean's Award."

One way the Law School wanted to achieve greater diversity was in the admission of female students. About ten to twelve women students were in the student body each year through the 1960s, as the total enrollment approached 400. The 1970s was the breakout period for women students. In 1976, Chancellor Heard noted the increase in the number of enrolled women law students from 14 in 1970 to 114 that year. He commented further on the surge of activity generated by those students: The Women Law Students Association had sponsored a well-attended Southeastern Regional Conference on Women and the Law, and had published a 46-page booklet, *Tennessee Women and the Law,* that sold over 2,000 copies. For the second year in a row, a woman had been elected President of the Vanderbilt Bar Association, women were active in student recruitment and on student/faculty committees, and a course on Sex Roles and the Law had been added to the curriculum.[39] These changes did not come easily, or without controversy. The coverage in the student newspaper of the organization of the Women's Law Students Association in the fall of 1971, for example, prompted a spate of contentious articles and letters by students and recent alumni. Among those debating whether the paper had engaged in "good satire" or "outright slander" was the "Vanderbilt Association of Male Chauvinist Pigs."

The rapid increase in the number of women students created some stress in the School's operation, highlighted perhaps by the women's liberation of a restroom. The fall semester of 1973 presents a snapshot of the changing times. That semester sixty-two women enrolled in the School, a jump from thirty-eight the prior year, and twenty-four and fourteen the two years before that. This growth created strains not anticipated in the Dean's Office. The students complained that the single restroom for female students, with only one stall, was simply not adequate. They were not satisfied with the administration's decision to allow them to also use a staff women's restroom located in the administrative area next to the dean's suite. Taking matters into their own hands, the women students chose the most centrally located men's room in the building, put up their own sign designating it as a women's room, and began using it. The male students did not surrender their turf easily, and there followed a two-week period during which students of both genders used the facility. The Dean finally officially ratified the conversion of the restroom to a women's room.

A watershed in the composition of the student body had been reached. The upward trend in enrollment continued as women comprised 30% of the student body in 1980, 39% in 1993, and 48% in 2003. With their larger numbers, women moved out of their marginalized status. Doris Dudney was the first Editor-in-Chief of the *Vanderbilt Law Review* in 1955/56. In the twenty-three years between 1982/83 and 2004/05, seven women were elected to the position—three in the first five years of the new century.

The School also made strides in increasing racial and ethnic diversity in the student body. More than a decade after Work and Porter achieved their breakthrough as the first African-American graduates, the School was averaging only one black graduate a year in the late sixties and early seventies. An abrupt change came at the beginning of Knauss's term as dean. Twelve African-Americans enrolled in the fall of 1972, and the figure was thirty-five in the following year, "constituting a larger number than any other law school in the South."[40] The number of African-American graduates peaked at twelve in 1978 and 1979, but by then the number in the first-year class had begun to decrease. In response to this decline, the faculty adopted an explicit affirmative action policy in 1980 that applied to Law School admissions and the award of scholarship assistance.[41]

A breakthrough of sorts occurred at the beginning of the Costonis deanship when the number of African-American students in the entering class doubled from seven to fourteen in 1985 and 1986. As scholarship aid to students increased from 14% of tuition to 24%, the number of minority students continued to grow until the 1991 entering first-year class included twenty-one African-Americans and twenty-two other minority students. A critical mass had been established.

The proportion of minority students in the student body increased from 16% in 1993 to 23% in 2003. By spring 2004, African-Americans comprised 12.4% of Vanderbilt's student body, the highest percentage of any of the schools ranked in the *U.S. News* Top Twenty Schools.[42] In that same semester, however, another race-related problem appeared. A number of black students mounted public protests after looking at the students who had been chosen for membership on the School's three student-edited publications in the previous two year's competitions and seeing no black students. Changes in the competition process and selection criteria were adopted by the faculty, shifting some weight from grade point averages to scores in an anonymous writing competition. Eight new African-American members were selected by the three publications in the next annual competition.[43]

In addition to diversity in the student body, a broadening of the School's constituencies was evident in the changing composition of the faculty. The Law School honored Rebecca L. Brown and Nancy J. King in the spring of 2003, in what was a culmination of a process that began in 1972. Brown was named the Allen Professor of Law, and King was named the Lee S. and Charles A. Speir Chair in Law. They were the first women faculty members at Vanderbilt to move through the faculty ranks and be awarded a chair. Martha Craig Daughtrey was the first woman to be appointed to a full-time faculty position at Vanderbilt, but she departed after three years, before being considered for tenure. Allaire Urban Karzon received tenure, but was never promoted to Professor of Law. Margaret Howard was the first woman to hold the title Professor of Law, but her success came haltingly and through a contentious process. Her dissatisfaction at Vanderbilt led to her departure in 2001 to accept a faculty position at Washington & Lee Law School. Suzanna Sherry was the first woman to hold a chaired position at the Law School as the Cal Turner Chair in Law and Leadership. Hers was a lateral appointment, as she was named to that chair when she came to Vanderbilt from the University of Minnesota in 2000. Thus, the chair ceremonies honoring Brown and King were the occasion of the first promotion of women through the faculty ranks to a named faculty appointment, and in that sense exemplified progress over a period spanning almost a century.

The story begins in 1914, when Mrs. Annie Mary Elliott, Librarian of the Law Department, was one of the first two women at the University to be listed on the Vanderbilt Faculty Register.[44] Elliott, who was also secretary to Dean Keeble, served in that capacity until she resigned in 1921 and was replaced by Mrs. Ellen Douglas Chester.[45] And, as noted earlier, Law Librarian Lillian McLaurin was considered a faculty member for some purposes during the Arnold years. The picture began to change in the early 1970s as the number of women in the profession was increasing significantly. Dean Wade reminded the faculty in 1971 that the School was committed to diversifying the faculty, emphasizing that "no prospective faculty member would be excluded on the basis of sex or race."[46]

The national climate had changed dramatically. In 1970, the Women's Equity Action League filed a class action sex discrimination law suit against all U.S. universities and colleges for their faculty hiring practices. The next year, the Professional Women's Caucus brought a similar suit specifically against law schools. The Department of Health, Education, and Welfare informed the presidents of all American colleges and universities of their responsibilities not only to practice nondiscrimination but to engage in affirmative action to rectify inequalities that existed in their employment practices. At its 1970 annual meeting, the AALS voted to prohibit sex discrimination among member schools, and in 1972 the extension of Title VII of the Civil Rights Act of 1964 and the passage of Title IX of the Higher Education Act increased the legal pressure on universities.[47]

Martha Craig Daughtrey, a member of the Vanderbilt class of 1968, joined the faculty as Assistant Professor of Law in 1972. There were 16 women among the 150 students who entered the Law School that fall. Daughtrey had developed a habit of breaking barriers. She had already been the first female Assistant U.S. Attorney in Tennessee, and in her position as Assistant District Attorney, the first woman to prosecute a case in Nashville's criminal courts.[48] Daughtrey, also a Vanderbilt Phi Beta Kappa undergraduate degree holder, had performed a trial run in the classroom by co-teaching a criminal procedure course with Karl Warden before John Wade called in the spring of 1972 and offered her a full-time appointment. During her three and a half years on the faculty, she felt she was carrying a burden as the School's first and only female faculty member, and she found confrontations in the faculty lounge to be especially unpleasant.[49] Her tenure committee had already been appointed when she was nominated to the serve on the Tennessee Court of Criminal Appeals. She joined the court in January 1976, and then later served on the Tennessee Supreme Court—the first woman to serve on each of these courts. In 1993, she was named to the U.S. Court of Appeals for the Sixth Circuit where Gil Merritt (Class of 1960), the U.S. Attorney who hired her right out of law school, was serving as Chief Judge.

Patricia Eames was appointed as Associate Professor of Law in 1974, following fifteen years of practice as a labor lawyer. She was the only other woman on the faculty when Allaire Urban Karzon came to Vanderbilt in 1977 as Associate Professor of Law, and Eames departed for Antioch School of Law after Karzon's first year. The students selected Eames for the outstanding professor award in her last year, and Karzon was the recipient two years later. A Yale law graduate, Karzon came with extensive experience in the corporate world, most recently as Vice-President and Counsel for RCA Corporation in New York. In the spring of 1983, the faculty voted to approve tenure and a promotion to Professor of Law for Karzon, but when the Board of Trust acted, tenure was granted but not the promotion.[50] She continued to teach as a popular tax professor until her retirement in 1995, but she remained at the Associate Professor rank—a consequence, some thought, of the changing scholarship standards in the faculty promotion process.

Margaret Howard was a tenured faculty member at St. Louis University School of Law when she visited at Vanderbilt in 1981/82. She accepted a permanent position, and she stayed on as an Associate Professor but without tenure. When her candidacy for tenure came before the faculty in 1984, the report of the faculty committee recommended that she be given a two-year tenure track renewal at the same rank. At the faculty meeting at which that report was considered, however, the faculty voted to replace the committee's recommendation with a recommendation that Professor Howard be granted tenure.[51] The faculty's recommendation was forwarded to Chancellor Joe B. Wyatt, who was serving as Acting Provost because the Provost's position was vacant. As was reported to the Board, "The Chancellor, in his capacity as Acting Provost and in consultation with Professor Blumstein, concluded that Professor Howard had not met the standards for the granting of tenure and offered her an additional two-year contract."[52] (At that time, Professor of Law Blumstein was also serving as Special Advisor to the Chancellor for Academic Affairs.) Howard accepted the two-year contract, but filed a grievance with the Senate Ethics Committee and retained counsel, leaving the University's General Counsel to speculate that they faced a potential sex-discrimination case.[53]

Eighteen months later, the Board approved the Chancellor's recommendation that Professor Howard be awarded tenure. Wyatt had set up a tenure review process that entailed a review of Howard's work by three individuals who had not been a party to the original Howard deliberations: newly-arrived Dean Costonis, and emeritus faculty members Wade and Hartman. Chancellor Wyatt's judgment, upon receipt of the ad hoc committee's report, was that during the intervening time, Professor Howard had produced substantial additional research that had been judged to be of high quality by distinguished outside reviewers.[54] Thus, Professor Howard was tenured in 1986, and subsequently promoted to Professor of Law in 1992. While she stayed at Vanderbilt another nine years, and was selected by the students for the Hartman Award in 1999, strains remained. She announced her decision to leave Vanderbilt in a memo addressed directly to the student body, perhaps as a sign of her disaffection from the School's faculty and administration. She wrote to the students: "If I were able to make this decision solely on the basis of my students, I assure you that I would be at Vanderbilt until someone carried me out in a box."[55]

Suzanna Sherry had established a national reputation as a distinguished scholar in just eight years on the Minnesota faculty when she was recruited to join the Vanderbilt faculty in 2000. With her appointment to the Cal Turner Chair in Law, she became the first woman to fill a named faculty position at the School. Three years later, the installation of Brown and King—who had had started their teaching careers at Vanderbilt in 1988 and

1991, respectively—brought the story to its conclusion. Both were accomplished scholars. The University created Chancellor's Awards for Research in 2003, and Brown and King were the two Law School faculty members to receive that honor in the first four years of the awards. Brown won the AALS Scholarly Papers Competition in 1993, and King received a major research grant from the Department of Justice in 2006. At that time, seventeen of the School's forty-six faculty members were women.

The Law School began to alter the all-white composition of its faculty when Carlton H. Petway was appointed to a part-time Lecturer in Law position in 1969. An Assistant District Attorney with a law degree from North Carolina Central School of Law, he taught criminal law administration beginning that fall. By the early 1970s, Vanderbilt was under the same pressure to address race disparities in the composition of the faculty as it faced in the area of gender. The first response was the appointment of Kenneth U. Jordan in 1974 to a full-time position with the title of Clinical Instructor in Law.

Upon graduating from the segregated high school in South Pittsburgh, Tennessee, in 1962, Jordan enrolled at the University of Tennessee as one of the first three "regularly enrolled" African-American students—meaning that they were the first black undergraduates allowed to live on campus. The other two dropped out, but Jordan persevered and graduated in 1966. After serving as an Air Force Captain, including a tour of duty as a squadron commander in Southeast Asia, he entered Vanderbilt Law School in 1971, graduating in 1974. Pat Eames had received a federal grant for an EEOC clinic and Dean Knauss asked Jordan to serve as her assistant in that clinic. A semester later, as part of his effort to reduce the administrative burden on tenured and tenure track faculty, Knauss asked Jordan to add Assistant Dean to his portfolio—a position with wide-ranging responsibilities including student organizations and counseling, the School's physical plant, and personnel duties. He left the Law School in 1976 to accept the position of Opportunity Development Officer for the University, where he was responsible for monitoring compliance with Vanderbilt's Affirmative Action Plan and with federal regulations related to affirmative action and equal opportunity. In that position, Jordan continued his annual student recruitment trips to the Upper Midwest as part of the Law School's efforts to diversify the student body. He later served as Vice President and General Counsel at Meharry Medical College, commanding general of the Tennessee Air National Guard, and Chief of Staff of the U.S. Department of Justice Management Division.

Another African-American, Charles W. Quick, served briefly on the faculty as a Visiting Professor in 1975. Quick, who was Professor of Law at the University of Illinois, taught current constitutional problems that fall. A more significant appointment in 1975 was the appointment of Robert Belton as Clinical Instructor in Law and Director of the Equal Employment Opportunity Commission Project. Belton's background included a J.D. from Boston University, five years of service as an attorney at the NAACP Legal Defense and Education Fund, and five years of private practice in Charlotte, North Carolina. He had been plaintiffs' counsel in such landmark civil rights cases as Griggs v. Duke Power Co., and Albemarle Paper Co. v. Moody. After two years in the clinical position, Belton was appointed to a tenure track position, being named Associate Professor of Law in 1977, and promoted to Professor of Law in 1982. He focused on labor and employment law in his long career at Vanderbilt, and was elected to the Executive Committee of the AALS in 1991. He received lifetime achievement awards from the Minority Group Section of the AALS, and from the Napier-Looby Bar Association in Nashville. For many of his years at Vanderbilt, Belton was the only person of color serving on the full-time law faculty, and he was advocate, advisor, and mentor for many of the minority students who came through the School. Eventually the School also made progress on this front in broadening its constituencies, and in the fall of 2006 the school reported eight minority faculty members—including Belton in his thirty-second year at the School—in its annual report to the ABA.

A SCHOOL . . . NOT AN OLYMPICS[56]

A law school, like a university, needs to understand what it values before it can decide how or whether to compete, and what altruistic behavior it wants to encourage. More to the point, a law school, like a university, should not surrender the definition of what it values to the market or to *U.S. News and World Report*. It should attempt to influence the world, the market, and the rankings to value what it values, or else it is in the end going to surrender control of its destiny to others who may care very little where that destiny leads.[57]

Kent Syverud, in the first month of his deanship at Vanderbilt, challenged the faculty to focus on where the School had been and where it might be going, drawing on the distinction between being a school and being an Olympics. When a dean warns his faculty not to fall prey to a particular temptation, that usually means he thinks there is a real temptation to be avoided. For years the Vanderbilt faculty had looked at their J.D.

program, at what went on in their classrooms, at the success their graduates experienced, and concluded that they were offering a legal education second to none. The *U.S. News and World Report* rankings came along and told them that their school was second to fourteen, or even seventeen, other schools.

The temptation to be an Olympics instead of a school, to focus on winning a competition rather than enhancing an academic program, has become intense among law schools since the creation of the *U.S. News and World Report* rankings in 1990. Law School rankings existed before *U.S. News* got into the business. One of the earlier rankings systems was the Gourman Report, but its validity was questionable. When Board member Charles Trabue noted that the 1977 Gourman Report had placed Vanderbilt Law School in the top fourteen law schools in the nation and suggested that such good press be used in publicizing the School, Chancellor Heard had other thoughts. Since Gourman's rating criteria had been kept secret, and the evaluation of other Vanderbilt schools had been "capricious," the Chancellor's view was that the Law School's rating should be accepted gratefully but not given "unbridled publicity."[58]

A quick look at the Gourman rankings confirms the caution voiced by Chancellor Heard. Not only is there no explanation in the reports of the method used, the results raise doubts. For example, in the 1983 rankings, Vanderbilt is still included among the group of fourteen "distinguished" law schools, ranking fourteenth among that group. The report also ranks each school on several sub-factors: Administration, Curriculum, Faculty Instruction, Faculty Research, and Library Resources. Vanderbilt ranked fourteenth in each of the individual categories. In fact, all fourteen of the top schools had precisely the same ranking in each of the individual categories as they had in their overall score.[59]

U.S. News and World Report launched its more prominent and more widely-accepted ranking of law schools in March 1990. Many sources other than this weekly news magazine have ranked law schools for various purposes since 1990. Vanderbilt, for example, was ranked No. 4 in The National Jurist's list of Best Law Schools in 1997.[60] Bruce Leiter, a faculty member at the University of Texas, has developed a wide variety of listings in his Educational Quality Ranking project. Among these were rankings in 2003 of Faculty Quality (Vanderbilt ranked eighteenth) and Teaching Faculty (eighth).[61] But the *U.S. News* rankings were clearly the most well-known.

The *U.S. News* rankings became a significant impetus for schools to take an Olympics approach to their business. Virtually all deans of American law schools signed an annual letter calling the rankings "inherently flawed," an "unreliable guide" that was "unworthy of being an important influence" on the choices prospective students made.[62] Yet many of these same deans became involved in questionable practices of dubious educational value in efforts to secure higher rankings for their own schools.[63]

The Law School faculty was not the group most susceptible to being tempted by an Olympics-style approach to education that was driven by ratings and rankings. In March 1997, a first-year student stormed into the office of Anne Brandt, Vanderbilt's Assistant Dean for Admissions and Student Affairs. That year's edition of the *U.S. News* rankings had just been released, showing that Vanderbilt's ranking had dropped from sixteenth to seventeenth. The student was irate about the School's "plummeting" in the rankings, concluding his tirade by saying that he would never have come to the School if he had known his degree was going to be devalued in this way. Later that day, the magazine issued a press release, stating that their editors had discovered a mistake in calculation and issuing a corrected rankings that showed Vanderbilt as No. 16, the same as the year before.[64] Thus, when another student appeared in Dean Brandt's office the following day to file the same complaint, she was able to turn an irate customer into a satisfied student with that small bit of news. The reality, however, that a one-place difference in an external scale made so much difference to these students speaks volumes about the impact the ratings game has had for some constituencies.[65]

Deans, of course, played the rankings game, as Knauss did in 1978 when he wrote that he thought Vanderbilt was "one of fifteen schools in the top ten,"[66] and Bostick did as Acting Dean, stating the school ranked in the nation's top twenty.[67] Kent Syverud arrived with aspirations of moving the School up one place in the rankings each year for five years, but at the end of his deanship the School's ability to maintain its relative standing was met with a measure of relief and satisfaction. Vanderbilt's relative position in the *U.S. News* rankings was remarkably stable, ranging from a high of fifteen to a low of eighteen during the first fifteen years of the published ratings.[68] There were, of course, indicators other than rankings that reflected Vanderbilt's more prominent place on the national stage. In 1974, D. Allen Gates, III, a member of the class of 1972, became the first Vanderbilt graduate to serve as a clerk on the U.S. Supreme Court, appointed to clerk for Justice Harry Blackmun. Vanderbilt's entering classes, as measured by such indicators as LSAT scores and college grade point averages, were consistently in the top tier. Graduates were increasingly hired by major law firms across the country. Vanderbilt competed with "Top Twenty" law schools in the recruitment and retention of faculty.

With national prestige becoming an increasingly important issue for the School, it is worthwhile to examine what affected rankings. The first answer is resources. "First," said Alexander Heard in 1972, "with private universities, over the long run, the most significant determinant of institutional quality is the institution's wealth. With private universities, over the long run, the most significant determinant of institutional quality is the volume of financial resources that it has at its disposal. . . . It isn't *only* that, it isn't *all* that, but that is the central feature in my view."[69]

Each of the Law School's deans had to address the resources issue in their own context. Knauss had been given the kind of incentive that Wade had asked for when the Board agreed to contribute $3 from University funds for each $1 raised for the Law School's endowment.[70] Wade had begun an endowment drive in 1969/70, but the School's unrestricted endowment in 1971 was very little more than the $1 million that had been established at the end of World War II. Perhaps first and foremost Knauss was hired to raise money. As Chancellor Alexander Heard reported to the Board, Knauss was "eager to engage in the fund raising that the Law School requires to offset its failure to receive in the University's recent capital campaigns the endowment that is necessary for the school's further progress."[71] The development drive that started in the spring of 1972, chaired by alumnus Reber Boult, was the School's first campaign that was independent of a larger University campaign.

By June 1975 the development drive was completed and the School's endowment increased from $1 million to $4.6 million with the matching funds included. Sixty-three percent of the School's alumni made contributions in 1974/75, apparently the highest percentage for any law school in the country.[72] However, giving to the School then fell off dramatically.[73] While the annual fund remained healthy, major gifts and designated giving dwindled to a trickle. Despite the success of the endowment drive, the Law School continued to run deficits through most of Knauss's term in office. Toward the end of his time as dean, Knauss had a one-word answer to the question, "What is the principal problem that faces the Law School?" The answer, in all caps, was "DOLLARS!"[74]

Bostick, on the other hand, was required to run surplus budgets in the post-reassessment environment of the early 1980s—"reassessment" being the name of a University-wide effort to bring more discipline to the University's fiscal operation. Bostick was able to create these surpluses in part because of large tuition increases and in part because of successes on the development front. While his term as dean was the shortest of the post-Wade deans, a number of fund-raising milestones were reached during this period, with considerable assistance from Board President David K. Wilson, Vice Chancellor for Alumni and Development John Beasley, and the University's Development Director Jerry Smith. These successes also reflected the strong personal relationships Bostick developed with many alumni.[75] Among the hallmarks of the fundraising during Bostick's term were the School's first endowed professorship (established by a gift from Judith Thompson), the School's first two endowed chairs (the Milton R. Underwood and David Daniels Allen chairs), the School's first two endowed lectureships (the Charles N. Burch and the Cecil Sims lectures), the funding of a Faculty Excellence Fund to supplement faculty salaries that had been lagging, and the completion of the fundraising for a building renovation and expansion. At the same time that the School was receiving these major gifts, the annual fund increased every year, growing from $167,000 in 1978/79 to $383,000 in 1984/85.

Just as the Law School's physical facilities had been an impediment in national competition prior to 1962, it became an asset in later years. Planning for an addition to the Law School building began as early as 1974, with a half million dollar gift and pledge from Milton Underwood. In the summer of 1976, Knauss indicated to the faculty that construction might be started as early as the coming fall semester. But fund raising stalled, and various alternatives of combined facilities with the Graduate School of Management, the Institute for Public Policy Studies, or other units of the University were considered and then discarded. The Board of Trust finally approved an internal loan of $1 million in December 1978. Only $1.1 million had been raised for the building project, and $350,000 of that was a challenge grant from the Kresge Foundation that was about to expire with a deadline that was looming.[76] However, it was not necessary to use the loan. Funding was finally completed with a $1 million gift from the Massey Foundation in November 1979. The law library, which was a major beneficiary of the expansion and renovation, was dedicated as the Alyne Queener Massey Law Library on September 24, 1982, with the dedicatory address delivered by Sandra Day O'Connor.

The Law School Library had been completely inadequate for the School's aspirations when it reopened in 1946.[77] "Our library is not good," wrote Dean Coffman in his annual report. "A great number of the texts are out of date, there are serious gaps in much of the elementary, essential material, and many of the books have been almost ruined by the dry heat of the winter, and dirt."[78] The library's collection grew steadily in size and quality in the following years as it more than doubled in size in less than fifteen years. Under the leadership of newly-appointed faculty member Harold G.

Maier, serious work on creating an international law collection began in 1965. The Law Library earmarked funds in its budget for foreign and comparative law titles, the University provided funding to purchase 500 volumes that were "too expensive" to handle within the School's resources, and several hundred volumes in the field of international law were transferred from the Central Library to the Law Library "on a loan basis." The hope was that this loan would become permanent if the "faculties of the Law School and the College can come to an agreement as to whether [the] international law collection should be in Law or General Library."[79] Only three years earlier, David Kaiser, the Director of the Joint University Libraries, had blocked such a transfer because of the recataloging problems that would be created.[80]

The issue of the "autonomy" of the Library did bubble to the surface from time to time. In 1962, Branscomb expressed his concern to Wade about the insistence of the American Association of Law Libraries that law libraries be completely independent from other library systems. Branscomb was clear that he viewed such compartmentalization as educationally unwise, and that separation from the JUL was not going to happen. "If necessary, we would withdraw from the Association of Law Libraries."[81] Wade assured Branscomb, "There has never been any criticism of our set up and we do not anticipate any in the future."[82] The report from an ABA site visit just the prior year made no mention of the JUL, while referring to the "autonomous 60,000 volume library" and stating "The library enjoys autonomy."[83]

Mary Polk Green, a 1952 graduate of the Law School, served as director of the Law Library from 1959 until her retirement in 1975. She inherited a "miniature book budget" because the library had run out of space to add volumes until a new building was constructed. She oversaw the move to the new building, providing this story as commentary on the tight budget she managed: "The moving men were Vanderbilt students—graduates and undergraduates—high school students and anyone else willing to tote heavy stretcher-like book carriers. The first morning's work resulted in a fine crop of blistered hands. The library ordered the cheapest work gloves available from the Vanderbilt storeroom. These lasted one afternoon."[84]

The School adopted a new model for a library director when Igor Kavass was appointed as a tenured Professor of Law and Director of the Law School Library in 1975. Kavass had served as Professor of Law and Director of the Law Library at Duke, Northwestern, and Alabama, and on the law faculty at Monash University in Melbourne, Australia before that. He assumed the presidency of the International Association of Law Libraries in 1977 and moved the organization's offices to Vanderbilt. He shepherded Vanderbilt's transition into the age of computerized research, and dramatically expanded library collections and services. He also chafed constantly under the strictures of the Joint University Library, especially as they related to the hiring of staff. Kavass aggressively sought to protect and extend the Law School's autonomy, at times in discussions with Deputy Provost Glen F. Clanton who enforced the JUL's authority on the Vanderbilt campus—discussions in which voices were raised more than a little. Tensions eased somewhat with the dissolution of the JUL in 1979, following Vanderbilt's merger with George Peabody College for Teachers, although boundaries and procedures continued to be uncertain from time to time with the successor to the JUL, Vanderbilt's Jean and Alexander Heard Library.

Costonis came to the deanship in 1985 with his own ideas about moving Vanderbilt forward on the national scene. Resources, lots of dollars, would be needed quickly, and as a result of his negotiations during the dean search, the Law School was authorized to run deficits over the first seven years of his deanship, up to a cumulative total of $2 million. This "line of credit" was put to use immediately to increase financial aid to students, to enlarge the size of the faculty as well as increase faculty salaries and support for faculty research, and to bolster the library's collections and subscriptions. The budget was back in balance in 1992/93. The actual accumulated deficit had reached $950,000, and with surpluses in the following years, the aggregate deficit was eliminated in three years.[85] In part, the budget moved back in balance with the success of the Capital Campaign under the leadership of Assistant Dean Kay Simmons, in which over $20 million in contributions, pledges, and bequests was raised by the fall of 1995.[86] In part, however, budgets were balanced by trimming expenses. By the end of the Costonis deanship the School was maintaining its sixteenth position in the *U.S. News* rankings with a ranking of thirty-eighth in the resources section of the ratings (a figure which fell to forty-seventh the following year).

One obstacle Costonis encountered was the termination of the Patrick Wilson Scholarship program. The program had never been endowed. Following the advice of Chancellor Branscomb, the Potter Foundation funded the program annually and retained a role in the selection process. The awarding of the highly-valued scholarships became an indicator of the School's "growing pains," as some faculty became concerned about the proportion of Wilson Scholars that were Southern, white, male Protestants. Costonis pushed for more funding and an endowment, but in November 1986 the School was notified by the trustees of the Potter Foundation that the annual support for the program would be ending. With the termination of the Patrick Wilson program, Costonis sorely needed a replacement—both to continue the recruitment of excellent students and to repair the impression that he had "lost" the merit scholarship program. Help came from an unanticipated source. Ucola Collier Katzentine died on June 2, 1986, and she bequeathed one third of her estate to Vanderbilt Law School for scholarships in honor of her late husband Arthur Frank Katzentine, a 1924 graduate of the Law School. The amount was $1.1 million, and was used as the founding gift for the creation of the John W. Wade Scholarship program. The Katzentine donation and the opportunity to honor the former dean spurred additional fundraising. By 2001, the combined book value of the Katzentine bequest and other donations to the Wade Scholars Program was $2.5 million, with a market value of almost $7 million. The Patrick Wilson program lived on in spirit, as in September 1993 the ninety-eight former Patrick Wilson Scholars established the Patrick Wilson Scholar's Scholarship Fund to endow a full-tuition scholarship.

The first resource challenge Kent Syverud faced when he became dean in 1997 was the Law School's building. The School had long since outgrown the facility that had been enlarged in 1982, and the needs were pressing. Planning had actually begun in May 1987,[87] but a succession of plans and scenarios took on a more urgent tone when the American Bar Association found Vanderbilt out of compliance with ABA standards on physical facilities at the end of the Costonis deanship.[88] Early plans for a $6 million addition had been revised to an estimated $15 million by the time Syverud arrived and hit the fundraising trail. He reported that $5.1 million had been in the building fund in April 1997, before his arrival. At the end of his first year in the deanship, Syverud reported in April 1998, that $8.5 million was in hand for the building, and he was able to report $16 million in gifts and pledges just eight months later.[89]

A faculty building committee, chaired by Tom McCoy who had also chaired the 1982 building committee, continually expanded the desired building program, raising the sights almost as quickly as the funds were being raised. But Syverud kept finding the money. As a result, the Law School building received a complete makeover, and the total square footage increased 70%, in a $24.5 million project that was completed in 2002. While every School function benefited from the building enhancement, the project's principal focus was on space for students—especially the state-of-the-art classrooms (the square footage devoted to classrooms increased 70%, with little increase in the number of seats). The new building also provided larger and improved study and social space and offices for student organizations. For many alumni, the new grand facility reflected and encouraged what they saw as the growing grandeur of the institution.

Syverud also brought a different decanal style to the management of resources, as he and Costonis represented two ends of a continuum that ranged from the broad delegation of responsibilities in the Costonis deanship to the much more hands-on approach taken by Syverud. Costonis focused on assembling the best faculty and administrative team that he could recruit. He then saw his principal job to be providing the resources that the faculty and administrators needed to succeed. He often drew an analogy from his days of running paint crews as a student: it was his responsibility to hire good painters and then to make sure they had the paint they needed in their buckets. For Syverud, the way a school became excellent was to be excellent in every facet of its operation. He led by example, becoming involved in decision making on wide range of administrative detail. He brought with him an unrelenting insistence on excellence, on providing Vanderbilt students with the best academic program and environment that the School could possible provide, and on the highest quality in each constituent piece of the whole of the Law School.

The proper use of resources is as important as having adequate resources. If a School is to heed Syverud's warning about being a school rather than an Olympics, that school will invest its resources in the things that reflect its own values. All schools aspire to excellence in scholarship and teaching. Syverud posed the question of whether the School valued anything different from what all other schools value in their pursuit of high ratings.

A distinguishing feature of the Vanderbilt culture had been a civility among faculty, a collegiality among students, and a sense of community between these two groups. As Provost Zeppos commented upon the hiring of Syverud, the new dean would be bringing "a belief that a law school is a community, not a set of discrete groups that happen to be in the same building."[90] As a school, rather than a sporting competition, one goal would be to nurture this community and not just devote resources to compete in the same events that other schools had entered. The strategic plan embraced at the outset of the Syverud deanship was for Vanderbilt to become "the most student-centered of the first-tier national law schools," while also addressing a concern among some faculty that the students' comfort not stand as an obstacle to mounting a rigorous academic program: "Vanderbilt's history suggests that it is a civil and supportive atmosphere throughout the Law School that makes it possible to impose upon students extraordinary rigor and demands in class and in clinics."[91]

Vanderbilt's faculty and administration believed they had succeeded in maintaining a distinctive environment among Top Twenty law schools, and that belief was bolstered by external evidence, such as the 1994 survey by *The Princeton Review* that ranked Vanderbilt fourth nationally in "Quality of Life."[92] Maintenance of this community feel over the years may have been aided by the Southern location, the small, intimate size of the School, and conscious choices in the recruitment of faculty and students. Visiting faculty and new faculty hired away from other law schools regularly commented on the civility of faculty discourse. While other law schools were known to engage in divisive argumentation, Vanderbilt was relatively serene, steering a fairly steady, moderate middle course, often by consensus rather than forced compromise.

The congeniality in faculty interaction was paralleled by a collegiality in the student body. Institutional efforts were made to avoid the cut-throat competition that was alleged to permeate other top-ranked schools. The admissions office emphasized this theme in its recruitment of students, and the atmosphere seemed to be perpetuated by the self-selection among applicants who found the pitch appealing. The School made efforts to promote collegiality and community within the building. A faculty "Open Door" policy permitted students to drop by without prior appointments; free coffee and doughnuts were served to students during exams; faculty were encouraged to attend Friday afternoon "Blackacres"—named after the courtyard where students gathered around kegs of beer (and alternative beverages). One particularly noteworthy function was an annual senior trip to the Jack Daniel Distillery, located in Lynchburg, Tennessee about seventy miles down the road.

In the early 1980s, faculty attendance on the Jack Daniel's trip had begun to wane, but the occasion was still very popular among students. After a day of libation at the distillery one spring, the students and a small number of faculty members were returning on two Greyhound buses when a student in the second bus decided to "moon" passing cars on the interstate. He chose the emergency exit window, and when he pressed up against the window it popped out, spilling him onto the highway. . . with the bus traveling sixty miles per hour. Amazingly, he escaped serious injury. Don Hall, the associate dean who was more or less in charge of the trip, was in the lead bus. When he climbed into the ambulance with the somewhat bloodied student, the student's first statement was, "Dean Hall, I have a paper due Monday. Do you suppose I could get an extension?" The Jack Daniel's trip survived even this incident. It was finally discontinued two years later when intoxicated students who had been returned to the School chose to disassemble a number of loose-leaf reporters in the Law Library, sprinkling their contents like giant snowflakes from a balcony overlooking the reading room.

It would be a mistake to think that Vanderbilt students were all about doughnuts, beer, and whiskey. Student organizations were formed over the years which not only brought speakers to campus but which provided opportunities for law students to present their own original work to classmates and faculty members. In 1974, the University's lawyers encountered an example of the students' engagement in academic pursuits. In the early 1970s, Vanderbilt University was benefiting from an urban renewal program that was being challenged by residents in the affected neighborhood. In the spring of 1974, the University's lawyers appeared before a panel of the Sixth Circuit Court of Appeals in Cincinnati to argue their case, only to find the judges reading, and then asking questions about, a just-published student note in the *Vanderbilt Law Review* that opposed the University's position.[93] Seven student authors, led by Special Projects Editor Charles Fels, contributed to "The Private Use of Public Power: The Private University and the Power of Eminent Domain,"[94] addressing a topic that received renewed public interest following the U.S. Supreme Court's 2005 decision in *Kelo v. City of New London.* The students' intellectual independence was demonstrated again in 1987, when the sponsor of a *Law Review* symposium on the privatization of prisons withdrew its funding. The sponsor disagreed with the composition of the symposium's panel of authors, but the *Review*'s editorial staff, headed by Editor in Chief Mary Crossley, refused to bow to pressure to alter the makeup of the panel.

While there are a variety of legitimate and admirable ways that resources can be used to strengthen academic programs and enhance students' educational experience, over the years Vanderbilt focused first on development of an outstanding faculty. When Chancellor Heard identified financial resources as the most significant determinant of institutional quality, the point was not just to have the money, but to use it effectively. For him, the most effective use of resources in the pursuit of greatness was to invest in the faculty: "I think that the ultimate quality of the institution is going to depend inescapably . . . on the quality of the faculty. . . . The quality of the faculty is the most important point of leverage that we have in shaping the future."[95]

The priority of faculty excellence remained the University's first focus two decades later. "Vanderbilt's ability to attract and retain distinguished faculty members will determine its reputation and the quality of its programs," stated Bronson Ingram, the President of the Board, when reporting on the $500 million Campaign for Vanderbilt in 1994.[96] An essay by Provost Burish distributed to the Board four years later concurred: "The faculty is the single most important resource of an outstanding university. The quality of a university is linked more closely to the quality of its faculty than to any other measure."[97]

Measuring faculty quality is hardly a science. Communications from Vanderbilt law deans regularly extolled the quality of the faculty. Senior faculty were pleased with the entry-level appointments that were made, and with their own success in mentoring these young men and women through the more rigorous tenure processes. There was similar satisfaction with lateral hires, and the faculty took note of how often other law schools attempted to recruit faculty away from Vanderbilt, and how often those other schools failed. Anecdotal testimony from alumni, and from other academicians, was positive.

National aspirations are also often related to size. A school's reputation is enhanced when it has more faculty members who are visible in their scholarship and publications. It is plausible to think that the more high quality specialized programs a school has, the more widely known its academic programs will be. Thus, a national reputation is likely affected by both faculty quality and quantity. At the risk of falling into the Olympics trap, it could be pointed out that the element in the *U.S. News* methodology that may most closely track faculty quality is the reputation rank among legal academics. On this score, Vanderbilt's ranking did increase from twenty-first in the first *U.S. News* survey in 1990 to seventeenth in 2001. The size of this increase, however, may also reflect national realities—that to a large extent Vanderbilt was running very hard just to stay in its relative place.

Fiscal realities usually dictate that increasing the size of the faculty requires increasing the number of students who are paying tuition. Such growth, however, can create a new tension. As the student body had reached 430 students in 1971, Dean Wade conveyed his vision to the Board of Trust, a vision that did not focus on reputation, but on educational excellence. And for Wade this aspiration had implications for the School's size: "We do not want to change in size. We do not feel we can grow much larger without changing the nature of the school to a very large degree. We like to think we provide a custom-made education rather than an assembly line education. What we want to do is consolidate, refine, and to improve our present programs."[98] Vanderbilt Law School did grow however, registering 641 students in the fall semester of 2005—an increase of almost fifty percent in the intervening thirty-four years.[99] At that point, the school began efforts to reduce the size of the entering J.D. class.

Thus springs the tension between a small school that focuses on the core of a J.D. program, and a somewhat larger school that not only has a larger faculty, with the potential of a larger impact on the national scene, but that also offers a wider variety of educational opportunities to its students. An argument can be made that the "custom-made" education that Wade advocated can be more fully realized in a larger program that provides students with more academic alternatives. That is certainly the route Vanderbilt took as the traditional, academic-year J.D. program was supplemented with a host of new options for students.

MODERNIZING THE ACADEMIC PROGRAM

The scope of the Law School's teaching and research expanded dramatically in the second half of the twentieth century. The number of courses listed in the catalogue grew from 43 in 1950, to 83 in 1975, to 146 in 1999. The mere increase in the length of the course list, however, does not begin to tell the story of the transformation of the academic program. Adjectives like interdisciplinary, transinstitutional, clinical, and transnational became everyday descriptors of an academic environment that was moving beyond a small, case-based, traditional J.D. program. The pace of this diversification accelerated toward the end of the century, following national trends as specializations, joint degree and certificate programs, and other niche-creating vehicles expanded dramatically across the country.[100]

While there were explorations of interdisciplinary possibilities prior to World War II[101], especially in the work of Lowe Watkins, explicitly interdisciplinary courses that were often team-taught began showing up in the curriculum in the 1950s and 1960s. Among these were a Jurisprudence course taught by Dean Forrester and Sam Stumpf in the Divinity School (Stumpf would later join the Law faculty); Law and Accounting offered by Charles Crouch in the Department of Business Administration; Medical Jurisprudence, taught by Law and Medical School faculty, headed up by Paul Sanders who also had an appointment as lecturer in the School of Medicine; and a Regional Economic Development Seminar, taught for five years by Associate Professor of Law Leo Raskind, who had a Ph.D. from the London School of Economics in addition to his Yale law degree. Soon to follow were law courses on the economics of crime, law enforcement and justice, accounting, law and anthropology, and corporate strategy—all of which were taught or co-taught by professors of economics, accounting, psychiatry, and management. All Law School faculty members were urged in a 1966 Curriculum Committee report to "review continuously possible ways in which the knowledge and manner of approach employed by scholars in other fields of learning might be used to improve the depth of instruction offered in a particular field."[102]

The Urban and Regional Development Center, with support from a $350,000 Ford Foundation grant in 1969, had its beginnings in the basement of the Law School building. The Center, later to become the Vanderbilt Institute for Public Policy Studies, brought faculty from law, economics, political science, and sociology together in multidisciplinary teaching and research, offering interdisciplinary seminars that were open to Law students. Law faculty played important roles in the development of the institute: Blythe Stason co-authored the original grant proposal, James Blumstein directed the center for two years, and Bob Knauss chaired the advisory committee that oversaw the transition from center to institute.[103] Law faculty would continue their involvement: directing centers at VIPPS, serving as investigators on its research grants, offering courses that were considered to be "VIPPS courses," and approving a dual appointment for Assistant Professor of Law Randall McCathren, who would spend half of his time at the institute.[104] On the other hand, Law School deans sometimes came to see VIPPS as a competitor for faculty time and for funding, both for gifts from Law School alumni and overhead from grants.

In the 1970s, joint degree programs were approved with the Owen Graduate School of Management, the Divinity School, and the Graduate School. This model, which granted credit toward the J.D. degree for work done in other schools at Vanderbilt, was later expanded to include a joint J.D./M.D. program, and a J.D./M.P.P with the public policy degree program at Peabody College. The Law School joined the Divinity School, the Medical School, and the Management School in fashioning the Cal Turner Program in Moral Leadership. The program, endowed in 1994 by Cal Turner, Jr., and named for his father, was created to foster the understanding of moral behavior, ethical practices, and individual responsibility in the professions. One of the two endowed chairs in the program was established at the Law School—Suzanna Sherry was the inaugural holder of the chair—and Dean Syverud was the first Law School instructor in the program's team-taught Professions and Society course.

Gordon Gee became Vanderbilt's seventh Chancellor in 2000 (and also a tenured member of the Law School faculty). Upon his arrival, he identified finding ways "to foster greater cooperation between units" as one of his five goals for his first five years in office.[105] At that time, three Law School faculty members had joint appointments with their tenure home in other schools: Ellen Wright Clayton in Medicine, Carol Swain in Political Science, and Paul Edelman in Mathematics. Three Law faculty members had secondary appointments in other departments (in History, Political Science, and Religion), and eight faculty members had earned Ph.D. degrees. These figures would quickly increase.

The interdisciplinary spirit on campus was reflected in, and fed by, the creation of an Academic Venture Capital Fund to provide support for "transinstitutional initiatives."[106] The Law School was fast out of the box, collaborating with the Owen Graduate School of Management to create a Law and Business Program in 2001. Randall S. Thomas, with a J.D. and a Ph.D. in economics from Michigan, came to Vanderbilt the prior year from the University of Iowa and was named the John Beasley II Professor of Law and Business. In addition to directing the Law and Business certificate program, Thomas also designed and directed the newly approved LL.M. program and the Vanderbilt-in-Venice summer program. Robert S. Thompson did much of the heavy lifting in the Law and Business program and directed the New York Stock Exchange Directors College. He had also joined the Vanderbilt faculty in 2000, having been recruited from the Washington University School of Law in St. Louis, where he crossed paths with former Vanderbilt faculty member Hodge O'Neal. Thompson joined in, and then carried on, O'Neal's work on close corporations.

The creation of a certificate program in Law and Business was part of a cluster of initiatives during the Syverud deanship that moved the School beyond a traditional, academic year J.D. program. After almost a century of proposals and plans, an LL.M. program was finally created, and with that a joint-degree program was approved for LL.M. students with the University's master's-level program in Latin American Studies. The faculty fashioned a small program, designed for foreign attorneys who planned to return to their home countries.[107] A third student-edited publication, the *Journal of Entertainment Law and Practice* (later renamed the *Vanderbilt Journal of Entertainment and Technology Law*), received approval after almost thirty years of student efforts to create a third journal.[108] Classes moved back into the summer months, for the first time since the Summer School had been discontinued in 1974, with the creation of a study-abroad program in Venice and the establishment of a full range of summer externships that included classroom components. The expansion of externship offerings was a piece of a larger emphasis on enhancing experiential learning possibilities for students.

The appointment of Junius Allison as Professor of Law in 1971 had signaled the beginning of the integration of clinical work into the academic program at the Law School. The School had long had an interest in this "practical" side of a student's education. As early as 1930, Dean Arnold had been making contacts with the Legal Aid Society in Nashville, but it was only in the summer of 1939 that senior law students began interviewing witnesses and assisting in working up cases for the society.[109] The program had to be reconstituted after the closing of the School. The title "Legal Aid Clinic" made its first appearance in the 1957/58 Law School catalogue, heading a section that read in its entirety: "Under an arrangement with the Nashville Bar Association, certain upperclassmen in the Law School are assisting in the operation and conduct of the Nashville Legal Aid Clinic. The experience is proving of practical value to the students, and their participation is rendering a useful service."[110]

The School began a "complete legal services program" in 1968, coinciding with the peak of the national Great Society programs. Professor Donald Stacy and Neil Cohen, Legal Aid Society President, had developed programs to provide legal assistance to indigents through Central State Mental Hospital, the State Penitentiary, Legal Services of Nashville, the Metro Public Defender's Office, and other programs.[111] By 1970, almost a hundred law students were providing legal aid on a volunteer basis through the Legal Aid Society to Nashvillians.[112] When Allison, formerly Director of the National Legal Aid and Defender Association, joined the faculty in 1971, he assumed responsibility for these activities and academic credit was approved for students' clinical work outside the classroom.[113] Students worked in district attorneys,' public defenders,' and Legal Services offices, as well providing services to numerous Nashville non-profit agencies. The expansion of these opportunities was supported by grants from the Council on Legal Education for Professional Responsibility, and Nashville's Law Enforcement Assistance Agency office.

Five years later, the faculty adopted sweeping changes in the clinical program, including the creation of live client clinics in civil law, criminal law, and juvenile law, and approval of credit for work in an internship program and with the School's student-run Legal Aid Society. The faculty also approved the recommendation that the clinic be staffed by a director with faculty status, two full-time instructors, and adequate support staff.[114] The Director hired pursuant to this action was Frank Bloch, who joined the faculty in 1979 with a J.D. from Columbia, a Ph.D. in Politics, and experience in the California Rural Assistance Program where he had been directing attorney. When Bloch stepped down as the clinic's director in 2001, he was replaced by Susan Kay, who had joined the clinical faculty in 1980, a year after graduating from the Law School.

Almost immediately after the 1977 faculty action to establish the new clinic, the program came under scrutiny by the University. The University's President, Emmett Fields, initiated a reassessment program in 1978, to identify ways in which Vanderbilt funds could be used in more effective ways. The high cost per credit hour of clinical instruction caught the eye of a University-wide Reassessment Panel. Seeking to save dollars in some programs in order to fund priorities in other areas that had been identified by the panel, the group recommended "Consideration of the continued utility of funding the Clinical Education Program at its present level of cost."[115] The Law School faculty's response was clear. It strongly endorsed continued support for the clinic, sending a report of its action to President Fields.[116]

The tug and pull on the Vanderbilt campus mirrored a national debate about how much financial support should be devoted to the activities that were sometimes called "skills training." An ABA task force produced a report in 1992, known as the MacCrate Report, which recommended that law schools develop or expand instruction in a variety of legal practice skills.[117] Costonis weighed in on the subject in an article published in the *Journal of Legal Education.*[118] For him, the issue was economic rather than pedagogic. He argued that the type of education being proposed in the MacCrate Report, however noble, was beyond the financial capabilities of law schools. While Costonis never contemplated any reduction in clinical work at Vanderbilt, he also did not envision the kind of expansion that was to come. In a short period of time, under Syverud and Associate Dean Kay, the School moved from running three live-client clinics to offering seven clinical courses that included transactional and policy clinics.

One other area of educational emphasis that expanded the horizons of Vanderbilt law students was international law. Long before "globalization" became the word of the day, Vanderbilt was establishing strength in the field. Harold G. Maier had completed his LL.M. at Michigan and was doing graduate work at the University of Munich when he was appointed in 1965 to establish an international law curriculum. Acting Dean Hartman reported to the Board: "For many years Vanderbilt Law School has felt the need to enrich our curriculum by offering courses in the area of International and Comparative Law. . . . Based on all available evidence, Mr. Maier appears to be a most outstanding prospect for developing these extremely important and complex fields of law."[119] Maier was an immediate hit with the students, who dedicated the 1969 Law Day to him for the second time in three years. He went to work developing courses and expanding library holdings, and in 1973 was named the first Director of the Transnational Legal Studies Program.[120] Elements of the program included a coherent collection of courses, with an initial slate of ten courses taught by six faculty members (in Maier's first year, there were three international courses, all taught by him).

New extracurricular activities for students included the International Law Society, the Jessup International Moot Court Competition Team, and the Transnational Studies Council. In its first year of competition in 1967, Vanderbilt's Jessup team won the national championship when it defeated the team from Harvard in the final round. The team (coached by Maier and composed of Alvin Adams, Charles Pitman, John Hossenlopp, Elizabeth Culbreth, and Daniel McAllen) reflected the changing demographics of the student body, as the five students came from New York, Iowa, Pennsylvania, North Carolina, and New Jersey. The School's second student-edited journal, *The Vanderbilt Journal of Transnational Law*, published its first issue in January 1972. The predecessor to the *Transnational Journal* was *The Vanderbilt International*, a Xeroxed "bulletin" produced by the students in the International Law Society with funds provided by the Vanderbilt Bar Association beginning in 1967/68. A credible international law program was made possible with the appointment of a second international law scholar in 1972, Jonathan I. Charney. Charney and Maier went on to have distinguished careers, including such notable achievements as Charney's editing the *American Journal of International Law*, Maier's service as Counselor on International Law to the Legal Adviser of the U.S. State Department, and the naming of each of them to endowed chairs at Vanderbilt—the Lee S. and Charles A. Speir Chair in Law, and the David Daniels Allen Distinguished Chair in Law, respectively. Charney, whose career was cut short by his death in 2002, received the Alexander Heard Distinguished Service Professor Award in 1999—the only Law School faculty member to receive the honor established in 1983 to recognize contributions to the understanding of problems of contemporary society.

Overall, the School's educational program expanded. While the teaching load for members of the tenured and tenure-track faculty was reduced, other types of faculty resources to teach the curriculum grew. The number of adjunct faculty was significantly increased, providing students with more specialized offerings, often more directly related to experience in practice. The first-year legal writing program became staffed in the 1990s by part-time instructors who focused their attention on that single instructional activity, with assistance from the School's professional librarians. A clinical professorial faculty track was established in 1988, providing a career path for the development and advancement for those faculty members. The variety of Visiting Professors of Law increased, as short courses (usually spanning a week or less on the calendar) were introduced into the curriculum. This development allowed the School to offer courses to students that were taught by faculty who were not be able to come to campus for a full semester.

In summary, the watchwords for the Law School's response to an ever-changing legal profession were "more" and "different." More and different kinds of faculty. More and different kinds of courses. More and different approaches and alternatives for students who were preparing themselves to enter the practice of law. There is no doubt that William Sullivan received a custom-made education as the sole graduate in the Law School's first graduating class in 1875. While John Wade believed that keeping the School small and keeping the program narrowly focused was the way to maintain a custom-made approach to legal education, Vanderbilt made choices available to the students who registered in 2000 that allowed them to custom-make their own education.

Epilogue

A Future Even Greater Than Its Past?

This book begins with the words by Paul Sanders about aiming for the stars that are found in a Law School video that was shot in 1998. The last words on that video are spoken by Dean Kent Syverud: "Our task now is to insure that Vanderbilt Law School is an institution with a future even greater than its past."[1] A future even greater than the past is, of course, the goal of most institutions. Whether Vanderbilt Law School achieves this goal in the twenty-first century is a judgment that observers many years into the future will be positioned to make. While it is much too early to assess what this century holds for the Law School, it is possible to take note of the major elements that are in place.

The first of these ingredients is a new dean. Kent Syverud stepped down as dean after eight years in the office, leaving a considerable legacy. He taught a heavy load for a modern day dean, regularly teaching the first-year Civil Procedure class as well as electives. He served as Editor of the *Journal of Legal Education* for five years, as President of the American Law Deans Association, and of the Southeastern Association of Law Schools, and was Chair of the Board of Trustees of the Law School Admissions Council when he resigned. Major achievements during his deanship included the renovation and expansion of the building, the creation of the LL.M program, the Law and Business certificate program, the Venice summer program, and the filling of seven new faculty chairs. Alumni endowed a scholarship in his name and the Garner Anthony Professorship that he had held was renamed the John Wade-Kent Syverud Professorship. Syverud had planned the transition long in advance, and began a well-deserved year's leave of absence in the summer of 2005. Not many months into his leave, however, he was recruited by Washington University Law School in St. Louis to be their dean, a position he assumed in January 2006.

The first holder of the John Wade-Kent Syverud Professorship was the man who replaced Syverud as dean, Edward L. Rubin. Rubin came to Vanderbilt in 2005 from the University of Pennsylvania Law School where he had been the Theodore K. Warner, Jr. Professor of Law since 1988. Rubin was a nationally acclaimed scholar who had taught a wide range of subjects including administrative law and commercial law. He had previously spent six years on the faculty at the Boalt Hall School of Law at the University of California, Berkeley, three of those years as an associate dean.

Rubin came to Vanderbilt with an ambitious agenda to reform legal education. He told the faculty, during the search for a new dean, that he had no interest in being dean at Vanderbilt, or at any other law school, unless the faculty was interested in a substantial transformation of the academic program. He set forth his assessment of the state of legal education, and the kinds of reform that were called for, in a *Vanderbilt Law Review* article in his second year as dean.[2] In that article, Rubin argues that it is time to develop a new law school curriculum for the twenty-first century, to replace the antiquated curriculum that is based on Christopher Langdell's nineteenth century approach with an up-to-date, well-designed approach to legal education.

The second element was the University's senior leadership. Rubin expressed confidence in the possibility of achieving his grand goals, in part, because of this leadership team. Gordon Gee had come to Vanderbilt as the University's seventh Chancellor in 2000. David H. Williams, II, had come in the same year as Vice Chancellor for Student Life and University Affairs, General Counsel, and Secretary of the University. Nicholas Zeppos, Provost and Vice Chancellor for Academic Affairs, was named to that position in 2000, having initially joined the Law School faculty in 1987 after doing civil appellate work for the Department of Justice. A scholar in the fields of administrative law and legislation, he had served in the Law School as Associate Dean for Research, and in the University positions of Associate Provost and then Vice Chancellor for Institutional Planning and Advancement. All three of these senior administrators—Gee, Williams, and Zeppos—were tenured members of the Law School faculty. In addition to their duties in Kirkland Hall, all taught at the Law School on occasion, and Williams taught tax law regularly. All were supportive of the new dean and were in positions to assist him in the pursuit of his agenda

The third element in place was the development of a structure within the University that could enhance the School's resource base. Vanderbilt had long maintained an every-tub-on-its-own-bottom (ETOB) approach to finances. Unlike some universities which utilized a pooled income system which relied on the central administration to distribute funds to the various schools and offices as it saw fit, Vanderbilt's system had allowed schools, by and large, to retain the income they raised through tuition, gifts, and other sources and to use that income for needs within the school. When Gordon Gee addressed the Faculty Assembly in the fall of 2000 for the first time after becoming Chancellor, he signaled his intention to redesign the University's financial model. "We hide behind an ETOB model," he said, "with each division its own financial center—a highly decentralized budgeting system." His plan was to create a more flexible budget, "with central funding available for investment in academic priorities that transcend school and departmental lines."[3] On April 7, 2005, he again addressed the Faculty Assembly, speaking of the "post-ETOB economic model" that was guiding the University's development. Emphasizing the transformation that was occurring, he declared "We must make ourselves 'post-post-ETOB,' not only in our structures but also in our thinking."[4] The new model meant that the University's administration was accumulating funds at the center that were then allocated across the University for new "transinstitutional initiatives," as well for programs within Schools and other units.

As mentioned earlier, the Law School and the Owen School were early beneficiaries of the new model, receiving funding from the new Academic Venture Capital Fund to create a Law & Business Program. The arrival of Dean Rubin with his plans to transform the Law School's academic program provided new opportunities for the University to invest in developments in the Law School. One of these opportunities was to provide seed money for a new set of interdisciplinary centers. The first of these new programs, joining the Law and Business program, were the International Legal Studies program (a successor to the Transnational Legal Studies Program) directed by Larry Helfer who came to Vanderbilt in 2004 from the Loyola Law School in Los Angeles; and the Cecil D. Branstetter Program in Litigation and Dispute Resolution (the first of the new programs to be endowed)[5] directed by Richard Nagareda who was recruited in 2001 from the University of Georgia and was named to the Tarkington Chair of Teaching Excellence in 2006. Plans were underway to fully develop additional centers in such fields as regulatory law, law and human behavior, intellectual property and entertainment law, constitutional theory, and social justice.

W. Kip Viscusi and Joni Hersch came from Harvard Law School to Vanderbilt in 2006 as the Law School launched a Ph.D. program in law and economics—the first program of its kind.[6] Viscusi had been the John F. Cogan, Jr. Professor of Law and Economics and director of the Program on Empirical Legal Studies at Harvard, where he had taught since 1996. His Vanderbilt appointment was as University Distinguished Professor of

Law and Economics. Hersch's faculty appointment also reached across disciplines as she had secondary appointments in the Owen Graduate School of Management and the economics department in the College of Arts and Science, in addition to her primary appointment as Professor of Law.

As 2007 dawned, the law faculty had set about exploring a range of curricular innovations, including restructuring the first-year curriculum, offering year-long capstone courses in areas of specialization (such as those represented by the new interdisciplinary centers), and seeking ways to broaden experiential learning and integrate it more fully with the rest of the curriculum. Many of the elements that characterized any top-tier law school were in place: an accomplished faculty, a talented student body, effective admissions and career services operations, a substantial resource base, and a strong administrative team headed by associate deans Chris Guthrie and John Goldberg. Dean Rubin's vision was to redesign the curriculum in a way that would secure for Vanderbilt a distinctive place among the nation's leading law schools. As was often the case throughout the School's history, financial resources will play an important role, as will the faculty's work on curricular reform, in determining how the School moves forward into the new century.

POSTSCRIPT: In the summer of 2007, Bob Covington retired, Gordon Gee left Vanderbilt to become president of The Ohio State University, and Nick Zeppos was named Vanderbilt's Interim Chancellor.

Appendix

VANDERBILT LAW SCHOOL DEANS

1874–1875	William F. Cooper
1875–1904	Thomas H. Malone
1904–1910	Horace H. Lurton
1910–1915	Allen G. Hall
1915–1929	John Bell Keeble*
1930–1945	Earl C. Arnold
1946–1949	L. Dale Coffman
1949–1952	William Ray Forrester
1952–1972	John W. Wade
1972–1980	Robert L. Knauss
1979–1985	C. Dent Bostick**
1985–1996	John J. Costonis
1997–2005	Kent D. Syverud
2005–	Edward L. Rubin

*	Acting Dean, November 1915–1916
**	Acting Dean, 1979–1980

ACTING DEANS

Edward T. Seay, October 1929–1930
Rollin M. Perkins, March–June 1949
Paul J. Hartman, 1964–1965
David F. Partlett, 1996–1997

Notes

INTRODUCTION

1. "Vanderbilt University Law School: A Future Even Greater than Its Past," videotape (Arlington, Virginia; Paul Wagner Productions), 1998.
2. "Address of Dr. Garland, Chancellor of Vanderbilt University on Founder's Day," *The Christian Advocate,* June 10, 1876, p. 9.
3. "Law School Aims to Be the Best," *Vanderbilt Alumnus,* 56, no. 5 (May–June 1971), p. 11.
4. John Wade, "The Law School—Its Relationship to the University, Present Needs, and Its Future," (unpublished, undated, circa 1960).

CHAPTER ONE

1. *See Schools of Law*, U.S. NEWS & WORLD REP., Apr. 15, 2002, at 64, 72 (including Vanderbilt Law School in its grouping of "The Top Schools" and ranking it number seventeen in a field of 175 law schools).
2. *See generally* Mark B. Riley, *Looking Back: First Dean Laid Sound Foundations,* VAND. LAW., Winter 1981, at 8; William H. Fligeltaub, Vanderbilt Law Department 1875–1904: Survival Without Stagnation (Jan. 1976) (unpublished Senior Writing Requirement paper, Vanderbilt University Law School) (on file with Professor James W. Ely, Jr.). These two works are the only prior writings primarily devoted to an analysis of Vanderbilt Law School's program of legal education during this period.
3. EDWIN MIMS, HISTORY OF VANDERBILT UNIVERSITY 78–85 (1946) (discussing dire state of Southern colleges and universities in the post–Civil War period). *See generally* MORTON KELLER, AFFAIRS OF STATE: PUBLIC LIFE IN LATE NINETEENTH CENTURY AMERICA (1977) (analyzing post–Civil War developments).
4. PAUL K. CONKIN, GONE WITH THE IVY: A BIOGRAPHY OF VANDERBILT UNIVERSITY 11–12 (1985); HISTORY OF NASHVILLE, TENN. 413 (J. Wooldridge ed., 1890).
5. CONKIN, *supra* note 8, at 15–18; MIMS, *supra* note 7, at 14 ("Central University [Vanderbilt University's original name] was a mere castle in the air until the Commodore transformed it into a substantial structure."); JNO. J. TIGERT IV,

Bishop Holland Nimmons McTyeire: Ecclestical and Educational Architect 182 (1955); Announcement of Vanderbilt University, First Session, 1875–6, at second page numbered 8 (1875).

6. *See* Conkin, *supra* note 8, at 53–54; Mims, *supra* note 7, at 95–96.

7. *See infra* notes 77–83, 136–33 and accompanying text.

8. Concern about the cost of legal education in the South continued long after the Civil War ended. *See Report of the Committee on Legal Education and Admission to the Bar,* Proceedings of the Eleventh Annual Meeting of the Bar Association of Tennessee 60 (1892) [hereinafter *Committee Report for the Eleventh Annual Meeting*] (opining that "Southern lawyers must content themselves, for the present, with such legal education as the very moderate wealth of their section will afford").

9. *See* Announcement of Vanderbilt University, First Session, 1875–6, at 39 (1875); *see also* Announcement of Vanderbilt University 1876–7, at 53 (1876).

10. *See* David J. Langum & Howard P. Walthall, From Maverick to Mainstream: Cumberland School of Law, 1847–1997, at 60, 83 (1997).

11. *See* 1 Vanderbilt University: Minutes of the Board of Trust and of the Executive Committee, pt. 1, at 100–01 (May 1, 1877) (on file with Jean and Alexander Heard Library, Vanderbilt University) [hereinafter VU:BOTM] [Volume numbers cited for VU:BOTM are from the title pages of these volumes]; Register of Vanderbilt University 1876–7/Announcement 1877–8, at 57 (1877) [hereinafter Register 1876–77]; *New Publications,* Christian Advoc., June 23, 1877, at 8 (indicating that other University departments also lowered tuition at this time); Christian Advoc., Aug. 25, 1877, at 15 (announcement of the opening of the academic year at Vanderbilt University, which also appeared numerous times in the *Christian Advocate* during September through December of 1877).

12. Register of Vanderbilt University 1877–8/Announcement 1878–79, at 57 (1878) [hereinafter Register 1877–78].

13. *See* Register of Vanderbilt University 1878–9/Announcement 1879–80, at 65 (1879) [hereinafter Register 1878–79] through Register of Vanderbilt University 1899–1900/Announcement 1900–1901, at 100 (1900) [hereinafter Register 1899–1900].

14. Langum & Walthall, *supra* note 14, at 83–84.

15. In 1893, the University of Tennessee Department of Law lowered its annual tuition to $50 from $100. This move apparently resulted in increased enrollments at that institution. Julia P. Hardin, *Polishing the Lamp of Justice: A History of Legal Education at the University of Tennessee, 1890–1990,* 57 Tenn. L. Rev. 145, 148, 150 (1990); Lewis L. Laska, A History of Legal Education in Tennessee, 1770–1970, at 391 (1978) (unpublished Ph.D. dissertation, Vanderbilt University) (on file with Peabody Library, Vanderbilt University).

16. *See* Report of the Commissioner of Education for the Year 1878, at 570–

71 (1880) (reporting tuition for thirty-seven law schools with twenty-six having tuition less than $100, seven (including Vanderbilt) having tuition of $100, and four (including Cumberland) having tuition above $100).

17. *See* 2 Report of the Commissioner of Education for the Year 1899–1900, at 1986–91 (1901) (reporting tuition for ninety-five law schools with seventy-four having tuition less than $100, fourteen (including Vanderbilt and Cumberland) having tuition of $100, and seven having tuition above $100).

18. *See* Kermit L. Hall, The Magic Mirror: Law in American History 211–13 (1989); Robert Stevens, Law School: Legal Education in America from the 1850s to the 1980s 23 (1983); James Summerville, Colleagues on the Cumberland: A History of the Nashville Legal Profession 48–49 (1996) (discussing economic developments nationally and in Nashville during this period).

19. *See generally* Lawrence M. Friedman, A History of American Law 633–54 (2d ed. 1985) and Keller, *supra* note 7, at 349–53 for discussions of the evolution of the legal profession in the latter portion of the nineteenth century.

20. Friedman, *supra* note 23, at 619, 634; Hall, *supra* note 22, at 212, 216 (noting that change in "the social composition of the bar" in Southern states did not proceed as rapidly as it did in other regions).

21. Friedman, *supra* note 23, at 619, 634–35; Hall, *supra* note 22, at 214–16; Stevens, *supra* note 22, at 25.

22. Friedman, *supra* note 23, at 648–52; Hall, *supra* note 22, at 214–16; Keller, *supra* note 7, at 352–53; Alfred Zantzinger Reed, Training for the Public Profession of Law 204–16 (1921). The cited authorities discuss the significance of the founding of the American Bar Association. *See also* Albert J. Harno, Legal Education in the United States 72–78, 80–88 (1953) (considering work of the ABA's Committee on Legal Education and Admission to the Bar and its Section on Legal Education during late 1800s).

23. *See* Friedman, *supra* note 23, at 634–35; Hall, *supra* note 22, at 211–13; Stevens, *supra* note 22, at 25.

24. *See* Friedman, *supra* note 23, at 606–07; Hall, *supra* note 22, at 211–12; Stevens, *supra* note 22, at 24; Robert H. Wiebe, The Search for Order 1877–1920, at 117 (1967).

25. *See* Friedman, *supra* note 23, at 607, 640–42; Hall, *supra* note 22, at 212–14; Stevens, *supra* note 22, at 22–24; William G. Thomas, Lawyering for the Railroad: Business, Law, and Power in the New South 36–38 (1999).

26. *See* Summerville, *supra* note 22, at 46–48, 57–59; Laska, *supra* note 19, at 168.

27. *See generally* Laska, *supra* note 19, at 168–214 (discussing the Committee's work and the Association's activity).

28. *See Report of the Committee on Legal Education and Admission to the Bar,* Charter, Constitution and By-Laws, Together with the Proceedings of the Bar Association of Tennessee at Its First Annual Meeting 60–61(1882).

29. *See Report of the Committee on Legal Education and Admission to the Bar*, The
     Bar Association of Tennessee: Second Annual Meeting 41–44 (1883).
     Subsequent Committee reports occasionally were highly critical of examinations
     conducted by certain judges. *See Report of the Committee on Legal Education and
     Admission to the Bar*, Proceedings of the Eighth Annual Meeting of the
     Bar Association of Tennessee [1889], at 39–43 (1890); *Report of the Committee
     on Legal Education and Admission to the Bar*, Proceedings of the Twelfth
     Annual Meeting of the Bar Association of Tennessee [1893] 31 (1894) ("It
     is well known that, in many instances, this examination is a mere farce."). For
     discussion of problems with oral examinations given by judges, see Laska, *supra*
     note 19, at 160–67; Fligeltaub, *supra* note 6, at 9–10.

30. *See Report of the Committee on Legal Education and Admission to the Bar*,
     Proceedings of the Third Annual Meeting of the Bar Association
     of Tennessee 12–13 (1884) (supporting recommendation of the previous
     year); *Report of the Committee on Legal Education and Admission to the Bar*,
     Proceedings of the Sixth Annual Meeting of the Bar Association
     of Tennessee [1887] 23 (1888) (calling for examination by Tennessee Supreme
     Court); *Report of the Committee on Legal Education and Admission to the Bar*,
     Proceedings of the Seventh Annual Meeting of the Bar Association
     of Tennessee [1888] 100 (1889) (resubmitting recommendation of previous
     year); *Report of the Committee on Legal Education and Admission to the
     Bar*, Proceedings of the Fourteenth Annual Meeting of the Bar
     Association of Tennessee 36–38 (1895) (noting that the committee prepared
     and submitted a bill to establish the State Board of Law Examiners); *Report of
     the Committee on Legal Education and Admission to the Bar*, Proceedings of
     the Sixteenth Annual Meeting of the Bar Association of Tennessee
     16–19 (1897) (proposing statute to create State Board of Law Examiners); *Report
     of the Committee on Legal Education and Admission to the Bar*, Proceedings
     of the Seventeenth Annual Meeting of the Bar Association of
     Tennessee [1898] 12–15 (1899) [hereinafter *Committee Report for the Seventeenth
     Annual Meeting*] (supporting legislation recommended in the previous year and
     opining that the proposal "be so amended as to deprive the law schools of the
     State of the power to grant license to practice law"); *Report of the Committee on
     Legal Education and Admission to the Bar*, Proceedings of the Eighteenth
     Annual Meeting of the Bar Association of Tennessee 10–12 (1899)
     [hereinafter *Committee Report for the Eighteenth Annual Meeting*]. *See generally*
     Fligeltaub, *supra* note 6, at 11–12 (discussing reasons for legislature's reticence to
     enact such measure).

31. 1903 Tenn. Acts ch. 247; *see also* Summerville, *supra* note 22, at 60; W.
     Raymond Blackard, *Past and Present Requirements for Admission to the Bar in
     Tennessee*, 14 Tenn. L. Rev. 135, 135–42, 149 (1936); Laska, *supra* note 19, at 206–
     14. This statute also eliminated "the diploma privilege." *See* Laska, *supra* note 19,
     at 211–13; *infra* notes 44–48 and accompanying text.

32. *See Committee Report for the Eleventh Annual Meeting, supra* note 12, at 59–70 (Edmund Baxter chaired committee); *Committee Report for the Seventeenth Annual Meeting, supra* note 34, at 12–15 (Thomas Malone chaired committee); *Committee Report for the Eighteenth Annual Meeting, supra* note 34, at 10–12 (J. M. Dickinson chaired committee); *see also Report of the Committee on Legal Education and Admission to the Bar*, Charter, Constitution and By-Laws, Together with the Proceedings of the Bar Association of Tennessee at Its First Annual Meeting 49 (1882) (Andrew Allison, a committee member who read the report, became a Vanderbilt Law School faculty member several years later.).

33. Summerville, *supra* note 22, at 60.

34. *See* Reed, *supra* note 26, at 102–03 (noting that seventy-five percent of the states had "central boards of bar examiners" by 1917); Stevens, *supra* note 22, at 25.

35. Summerville, *supra* note 22, at 48–49. *See generally* Don H. Doyle, Nashville in the New South 1880–1930, at 19–62 (1985) (discussing Nashville's economic expansion in the latter part of nineteenth century); Thomas, *supra* note 29, at 37–38 (analyzing railroads' impact on the development of corporate law practice in the South).

36. *See infra* notes 167–69 and accompanying text.

37. *See infra* notes 200–98, 216 and accompanying text.

38. *See* Burton J. Bledstein, The Culture of Professionalism: The Middle Class and the Development of Higher Education in America 190–91 (1976); Friedman, *supra* note 23, at 606–09; Reed, *supra* note 26, at 183–99, 203; University of the State of New York, College Department Second Annual Report 1899, 2 Professional Education in the United States 154 (Henry L. Taylor preparer, 1900) (Law Introduction written by James Russell Parsons) [hereinafter Professional Education]; *see also* Stevens, *supra* note 22, at 73 (discussing bases for university–law school affiliations); Peter deL. Swords & Frank K. Walwer, The Costs and Resources of Legal Education 32–33 (1974) (exploring reasons for shift from apprenticeship system to law school training); W. G. Hammond, *American Law Schools, Past and Future*, 7 S. L. Rev. 400, 405–11 (1881) (ascribing "remarkable growth of law schools" principally to the adoption of codes of practice and procedure, and the construction of a network of railroads).

39. *Educational Miscellany*, Christian Advoc., Nov. 19, 1881, at 7.

40. Friedman, *supra* note 23, at 620; Stevens, *supra* note 22, at 26–27. *See generally Admissions to the Bar*, Cent. L.J., July 2, 1874, at 320–21 (criticizing diploma privilege).

41. 1859–1860 Tenn. Pub. Acts ch. 73 (1860). This statute did not specifically require a student to graduate in order to receive the benefit of the diploma privilege. Instead, it gave in-state law school faculties "the same power to grant license to practice law in the courts of this State, that the Judges of the Courts now have." *Id.* Thus, a law school faculty presumably could grant a license to

a student who did not meet graduation requirements. Indeed, the Vanderbilt law faculty publicized this possibility for a period. *See, e.g.*, REGISTER 1876–77, *supra* note 15, at 56–57; REGISTER OF VANDERBILT UNIVERSITY 1882–83/ANNOUNCEMENT 1883–84, at 61–62 (1883) [hereinafter REGISTER 1882–83]; *see also* Riley, *supra* note 6, at 10; Fligeltaub, *supra* note 6, at 11; *infra* notes 339–37 and accompanying text.

42. 1903 TENN. ACTS ch. 247 (1903); *see also* Blackard, *supra* note 35, at 136–37; Fligeltaub, *supra* note 6, at 10–12 (discussing the history of the diploma privilege in Tennessee).

43. *See* LANGUM & WALTHALL, *supra* note 14, at 101–02; Lewis Laska, *A Review of David J. Langum & Howard P. Walthall, From Maverick to Mainstream: Cumberland School of Law, 1847–1997,* 30 CUMB. L. REV. 493, 499 (2000) (book review); Laska, *supra* note 19, at 104–05, 198–213; *Committee Report for the Eighteenth Annual Meeting, supra* note 34, at 12. The diploma privilege was repealed by the 1903 bar examination statute discussed in the immediately previous subsection. *See* Laska, *supra* note 19, at 211–13; *supra* notes 31–38 and accompanying text.

44. *See* Laska, *supra* note 19, at 206, 210; Fligeltaub, *supra* note 6, at 12; *Committee Report for the Seventeenth Annual Meeting, supra* note 34, at 12–15 (noting that Malone chaired the committee that recommended the elimination of the diploma privilege). Vanderbilt faculty member J. M. Dickinson joined Malone in this endeavor. *See* Fligeltaub, *supra* note 6, at 12; *Committee Report for the Eighteenth Annual Meeting, supra* note 34, at 10–12 (noting that Dickinson chaired the committee that strongly endorsed the committee's previous recommendation to repeal the diploma privilege).

The diploma privilege may have put Vanderbilt, with its two-year law program, at a competitive disadvantage against Cumberland, with its one-year course of legal study. *See* 3 VU:BOTM, *supra* note 15, at 11 (June 17, 1895); 3 *id.* at 201 (June 13, 1898); Fligeltaub, *supra* note 6, at 15–16; Laska, *supra* note 19, at 207–08; *supra* notes 309–13 and accompanying text. *See generally* LANGUM & WALTHALL, *supra* note 14, at 101 (noting Cumberland's opposition to the bar examination statute), 103–04 (describing the enduring nature of Cumberland's one-year law program).

45. *See* HARNO, *supra* note 26, at 88–90; REPORT OF THE TWENTY-THIRD ANNUAL MEETING OF THE AMERICAN BAR ASSOCIATION 569–75 (1900); Law School Curriculum 10–12 (undated), Centennial History Project, Box 25 (unpublished memorandum on file with Jean and Alexander Heard Library, Vanderbilt University) [hereinafter Law School Curriculum].

46. REPORT OF THE TWENTY-THIRD ANNUAL MEETING OF THE AMERICAN BAR ASSOCIATION 569–70 (1900); Law School Curriculum, *supra* note 49, at 11.

47. AALS DIRECTORY OF LAW TEACHERS, 2002–2003, at 179; PROCEEDINGS OF THE TENTH ANNUAL MEETING OF THE ASSOCIATION OF AMERICAN LAW SCHOOLS 41 (1910); *see also* 5 VU:BOTM, *supra* note 15, at 51 (June 15, 1908) (noting that

the AALS demanded "certain entrance requirements and a three year course" and that Vanderbilt Law School was "eligible on the basis of entrance requirements, but not in respect of time"); Bob Holladay, *The Case History of Vanderbilt Law School*, VAND. LAW., Spring/Summer 1999, at 14–15 (noting that entry into the AALS was made possible by the implementation of a three-year program); John Bell Keeble, *The Law School and Some Men Who Have Helped to Make It*, 3 VAND. ALUMNUS 200, 201 (1913).

    Accreditation by the American Bar Association was not an issue then. The ABA did not begin its program of accreditation until the 1920s. *See* STEVENS, *supra* note 22, at 115, 173.

48.   PROCEEDINGS OF THE FIFTH ANNUAL MEETING, ASSOCIATION OF AMERICAN LAW SCHOOLS 33–39 (1905).

49.   *See generally* Riley, *supra* note 6; Fligeltaub, *supra* note 6; discussion *infra* "Reorganization": Poised for Change section.

50.   *See* SUMMERVILLE, *supra* note 22, at 59; W. Raymond Blackard, *Law Schools in Tennessee*, 14 TENN. L. REV. 267, 268 (1936); Laska, *supra* note 47, at 499; Laska, *supra* note 19, at 109. For discussion of the Cumberland program, see LANGUM & WALTHALL, *supra* note 14, at 97–111, 117; N. Green, *The Law School of Cumberland University*, 2 THE GREEN BAG 63 (1890); Laska, *supra* note 19, at 109–34.

51.   *See* LANGUM & WALTHALL, *supra* note 14, at 97–111, 117.

52.   *See* Blackard, *supra* note 54, at 268; Laska, *supra* note 47, at 499; Laska, *supra* note 19, at 166.

53.   In addition to Cumberland and Vanderbilt, one authority lists eight other law schools that operated in Tennessee during the period from 1875 to 1900. Blackard, *supra* note 54, at 269. This group includes the University of Tennessee School of Law, founded in 1890. *See* Hardin, *supra* note 19, at 148. The list, however, does not include the law school at Neophogen Male and Female College that operated in Gallatin, Tennessee briefly in the mid-to-late 1870s. *See* WALTER T. DURHAM, A COLLEGE FOR THIS COMMUNITY 55, 61, 71 (1974); REED, *supra* note 26, at 433; Laska, *supra* note 19, at 157–59. For historical analysis of Tennessee law schools and legal education in the state, see generally Laska, *supra* note 19; Clyde Conley Street, A History of Legal Education in Tennessee (1941) (unpublished M.A. thesis, University of Tennessee) (on file with Alyne Queener Massey Law Library, Vanderbilt University).

    For statistical data regarding the growth in the number of law schools in other Southern states during the latter portion of the nineteenth century, see REED, *supra* note 26, at 446.

54.   *See* Blackard, *supra* note 54, at 268; Laska, *supra* note 47, at 499; Laska, *supra* note 19, at 166.

55.   One listing of law schools operating in Tennessee in 1899 identifies six law schools—Cumberland, American Temperance University, Central Tennessee College, Tennessee, Vanderbilt, and University of the South. PROFESSIONAL

EDUCATION, *supra* note 42, at 168. Another study indicates that nine unidentified law schools were in operation in Tennessee in 1900. REED, *supra* note 26, at 446. Still another compilation identifies ten institutions as conducting law programs in Tennessee in 1900—Cumberland, Vanderbilt, Central Tennessee (Walden), Tennessee, Southern Normal University, University of the South, American Temperance (American), Union University, Chattanooga College of Law, and Southern Law College. Blackard, *supra* note 54, at 269.

56.   CONKIN, *supra* note 8, at 23. For the story of the founding of Vanderbilt University and the critical financial support provided by Cornelius Vanderbilt, see *id.* at 3–22; LUCIUS SALISBURY MERRIAM, HIGHER EDUCATION IN TENNESSEE 107–18 (1893); MIMS, *supra* note 7, at 13–44; TIGERT, *supra* note 9, at 173–203.

57.   *Bishop Wightman's Address at the Laying of the Corner Stone of The Vanderbilt University*, CHRISTIAN ADVOC., May 9, 1874, at 6.
      Because the high aspirations of those who founded Vanderbilt were clear, Governor Porter's comment in his address at the 1875 university inauguration must have sounded as a grand understatement: "Gentlemen, the mission of this University is above mere commonplace." *Synopsis of Addresses on the Inauguration of Vanderbilt University*, CHRISTIAN ADVOC., Oct. 16, 1875, at 9. In fact, expressions of lofty expectations for the University were the order of the day. Thus, by December of 1875, the phrase "Harvard of the South" had appeared in print in reference to Vanderbilt. *See Another $100,000 for Vanderbilt University*, CHRISTIAN ADVOC., Dec. 25, 1875, at 8 (suggesting that Vanderbilt needed to achieve a certain level of funding to attain a Harvard-like position in the region).

58.   *Address of Dr. Garland, Chancellor of Vanderbilt University on Founder's Day*, CHRISTIAN ADVOC., June 10, 1876, at 8, 9 [hereinafter *Address of Dr. Garland*].

59.   CONKIN, *supra* note 8, at 4; HISTORY OF NASHVILLE, TENN., *supra* note 8, at 647–48; MERRIAM, *supra* note 60, at 107.

60.   HISTORY OF NASHVILLE, TENN., *supra* note 8, at 647–48; MERRIAM, *supra* note 60, at 107.

61.   CONKIN, *supra* note 8, at 5–6; MERRIAM, *supra* note 60, at 108.

62.   *See* HISTORY OF NASHVILLE, TENN., *supra* note 8, at 412–13; MERRIAM, *supra* note 60, at 109–11.

63.   1 VU:BOTM, *supra* note 15, pt. 1, at 1 (Jan. 26, 1872); MERRIAM, *supra* note 60, at 110–11.

64.   1 VU:BOTM, *supra* note 15, pt. 1, at 1 (Jan. 26, 1872); MERRIAM, *supra* note 60, at 111.

65.   CODE OF BY-LAWS AND CHARTER: THE VANDERBILT UNIVERSITY 24–27 (2000) [hereinafter VU CHARTER]; State v. Bd. of Trust of Vanderbilt Univ., 129 Tenn. 279, 296, 164 S.W. 1151, 1155–56 (1914). The Circuit Court of Davidson County, Tennessee, Judge Nathaniel Baxter presiding, issued the decree. VU CHARTER, *supra*, at 25–27. In 1871, the Tennessee legislature had authorized the state's

chancery courts to grant corporate charters. 1870–1871 Tenn. Acts ch. LIV (1871).

On August 19, the judge certified the copy of the charter obtained by the Vanderbilt Board of Trust to be "a true and perfect copy of a decree" issued previously on August 6. *See* 1 VU:BOTM, *supra* note 15, pt. 1, at 8 (Aug. 21, 1872).

66.   *See* VU Charter, *supra* note 69, at 24, 27–28; Announcement of Vanderbilt University, First Session, 1875–6, at second page numbered 8 (1875); Merriam, *supra* note 60, at 116; *Bd. of Trust of Vanderbilt Univ.*, 129 Tenn. at 307–09, 164 S.W. at 1158–59.

67.   Chancellor Landon Garland, who fashioned the university's academic structure, had studied law for a short time. Conkin, *supra* note 8, at 39–40.

68.   *See* Reed, *supra* note 26, at 183–87; Stevens, *supra* note 22, at 73; *supra* notes 23–28 and accompanying text.

69.   1 VU:BOTM, *supra* note 15, pt. 1, at 30 (Jan. 15, 1874); 1 *id.* at 37–38 (Apr. 29, 1874); *see also* Riley, *supra* note 6, at 8. For discussion of the Law School's first academic year in operation, see *infra* "A False Start" section.

70.   J. H. Kirkland, *Twenty-Five Years of University Work*, 1 Vand. U. Q., May 1901, at 86, 87. Kirkland succeeded Garland as chancellor in 1893. *See* Edwin Mims, Chancellor Kirkland of Vanderbilt 93–96 (1940).

71.   *See* discussion *infra* "A False Start" section.

72.   *See* discussion *infra* The "Lease" and The "Lessees" sections.

73.   *See* Holladay, *supra* note 51, at 14 ("A law school for Vanderbilt wasn't exactly an afterthought, but it wasn't a primary objective either.").

With regard to the formation of the University, Chancellor James Kirkland stated: "In the beginning the question had been raised whether Vanderbilt should not devote itself exclusively to graduate, or university work. This question was wisely decided in the negative, for it was seen that the South was by then no means ready for an institution organized on such a basis." Kirkland, *supra* note 74, at 89; *see also* Announcement of Vanderbilt University, First Session, 1875–6, at 11–12 (1875) (discussing rejected notion that Vanderbilt should offer solely graduate programs).

74.   *But cf.* Holladay, *supra* note 51, at 14.

75.   *But see* Conkin, *supra* note 8, at 24 (opining that the Law School and the Medical School constituted "window-dressing," allowing Vanderbilt to become a university even though its "guiding purposes remained those of a church-related liberal arts college").

The trustees' subsequent deeds, in fact, matched the rhetoric espousing a comprehensive educational institution that was to comprise professional programs. By 1887, Vanderbilt had added Pharmaceutical, Dental, and Engineering departments. *See* History of Nashville, Tenn., *supra* note 8, at 417; *Vanderbilt University: The Lines of Work Pursued There, and the Inducements Offered*, Christian Advoc., July 2, 1887, at 4.

76. *See* REED, *supra* note 26, at 183–87, 192; SWORDS & WALWER, *supra* note 42, at 35–36; Mary Kay Kane, *President's Address: Recommitting to Teaching and Scholarship*, [AALS] NEWSLETTER, Feb. 2001, at 1, 3.

77. *See Address of Dr. Garland, supra* note 62, at 8, 9 (noting that "departments of Law and Medicine . . . are usually self-sustaining").

78. *See* FRIEDMAN, *supra* note 23, at 608–09; REED, *supra* note 26, at 183–87, 192; STEVENS, *supra* note 22, at 35; SWORDS & WALWER, *supra* note 42, at 35–36; Kane, *supra* note 80, at 3; Fligeltaub, *supra* note 6, at 3; *see also* Riley, *supra* note 6, at 8–9; discussion *supra* "External Influences" section; discussion *infra* The "Lease" section. *See generally* Mark Bartholomew, *Legal Separation: The Relationship Between the Law School and the Central University in the Late Nineteenth Century*, 53 J. LEGAL EDUC. (forthcoming 2003).

79. Fligeltaub, *supra* note 6, at 3.

80. Vanderbilt's law and medical departments of this era have been described as "two appended proprietary, administratively autonomous professional schools." CONKIN, *supra* note 8, at 24.

81. *See* Law School Administration: Deans second through seventh unnumbered pages (undated), Centennial History Project, Box 25 (unpublished memorandum on file with Jean and Alexander Heard Library, Vanderbilt University) [hereinafter Law School Administration: Deans] (discussing control of law student activities as an issue on which the Law School and the University differed from time to time); *see also infra* notes 292–90 and accompanying text.

82. The Medical School was also in operation during the 1874–75 school year. MERRIAM, *supra* note 60, at 118; MIMS, *supra* note 7, at 97; Kirkland, *supra* note 74, at 87.

83. The University launched its academic program in early October of 1875. CONKIN, *supra* note 8, at 55; James G. Wharton, *Opening Date: October 1875*, 35 VAND. ALUMNUS, Jan.-Feb. 1950, at 8, 8–9; *Dedication and Inauguration of the Vanderbilt University*, CHRISTIAN ADVOC., Oct. 9, 1875, at 8.

84. CONKIN, *supra* note 8, at 55. For other discussions of the Law School's 1874–75 academic year, see MERRIAM, *supra* note 60, at 118–19; MIMS, *supra* note 7, at 97–98.

85. *See* 1 VU:BOTM, *supra* note 15, pt. 1, at 30 (Jan. 15, 1874).

86. *See* 1 *id.* at 37–38 (Apr. 29, 1874).

87. *See id.*; *Meeting of the Board of Trust of Vanderbilt University*, CHRISTIAN ADVOC., May 9, 1874, at 9; *Vanderbilt University Law Department*, REPUBLICAN BANNER, Aug. 19, 1874, at 3 & Sept. 2, 1874, at 3 (advertisement); *Vanderbilt University. Law Department*, CHRISTIAN ADVOC., July 18, 1874, at 13 (advertisement).

    Judge East was heavily involved in the organization and early growth of the University, serving as one of its incorporators and as a Board of Trust member from the institution's inception until 1893. *See* VU CHARTER, *supra* note 69, at 25; *Vanderbilt Commencement*, CHRISTIAN ADVOC., June 29, 1893, at 9.

88. *See* 1 VU:BOTM, *supra* note 15, pt. 1, at 37–38 (Apr. 29, 1874); VU Charter, *supra* note 69, at 25.

89. *See* John W. Green, Lives of the Judges of the Supreme Court of Tennessee 1796–1947, at 194–97 (1947) (chapter on Cooper); Summerville, *supra* note 22, at 31–32, 57–58, 139, 150; Samuel C. Williams, *History of the Courts of Chancery of Tennessee*, 2 Tenn. L. Rev. 6, 21–22 (1923) (noting high quality of Cooper's opinions as chancellor and emphasizing his impact as a judge and legal commentator on field of equity); *Judge William Frierson Cooper: Paper Read by John Bell Keeble Before Tennessee Bar Association in Chattanooga*, Nashville Am., Aug. 2, 1909, at 5 (eulogizing Cooper); *Brilliant Son of Tennessee*, Nashville Banner, May 8, 1909, at 1 (reporting Cooper's death); Proceedings of the Seventh Annual Meeting of the Bar Association of Tennessee 5 (1888) (listing "presidents since organization"). *See generally* Louise Davis, *The Revealing Cooper Diaries (First of Two Parts): A Man Who Went Where the Action Was*, Nashville Tennesseean Mag., Oct. 26, 1969, at 10; Louise Davis, *The Revealing Cooper Diaries (Last of Two Parts): 90 Years of Passion & Patriots*, Nashville Tennesseean Mag., Nov. 2, 1969, at 12.

90. *See* Merriam, *supra* note 60, at 46; Laska, *supra* note 19, at 143–51; *see also* Reed, *supra* note 26, at 424 (listing the University of Nashville as having a law school in 1854–55).

91. *See* VU Charter, *supra* note 69, at 27–28.

92. 2 VU:BOTM, *supra* note 15, at 121 (June 11, 1891); Register of Vanderbilt University 1890–91/Announcement 1891–92, at 65 (1891) [hereinafter Register 1890–91]; Conkin, *supra* note 8, at 120; *see also infra* notes 422–22 and accompanying text.

93. *See* Conkin, *supra* note 8, at 19, 36, 41; History of Nashville, Tenn., *supra* note 8, at 415.

94. 1 VU:BOTM, *supra* note 15, pt. 1, at 44–45, 49 (May 3, 1875).

95. *Vanderbilt University Law Department*, Republican Banner, Aug. 19, 1874, at 3 & Sept. 2, 1874, at 3 (boldface removed). This advertisement also appeared in the *Christian Advocate*. *See Vanderbilt University. Law Department*, Christian Advoc., July 18, 1874, at 13.

96. *See* discussion *supra* Economy subsection in External Influences section (considering the effect of the economy on Vanderbilt Law School); *see also* Laska, *supra* note 19, at 510 (opining that "adverse economic conditions (the Panic of 1873) cut into enrollment").

97. *See supra* notes 54–56 and accompanying text.

98. 1 VU:BOTM, *supra* note 15, pt. 1, at 49 (May 3, 1875).

99. 1 *id.* Obviously, this was an unsettling situation for those involved. Nonetheless, an aggressive modern public relations specialist might discern an upside to the situation—with four students and eight faculty members, Vanderbilt Law School started out with perhaps the most favorable student/faculty ratio in the history of legal education.

100. *See* 1 *id.* at 49–50; Conkin, *supra* note 8, at 55; Riley, *supra* note 6, at 8; *see also* Kirkland, *supra* note 74, at 87.

101. *Vanderbilt University: Opening of the Law and Medical Departments*, Republican Banner, Oct. 4, 1874, at 4 (noting the building's College Street location); *see also* Law Department, at 6 (undated), J. T. McGill collection, Box 6, File 99 (unpublished memorandum on file with Jean and Alexander Heard Library, Vanderbilt University) [hereinafter Law Department] (indicating that the Law School's second-floor classroom was situated in a College Street structure that later housed the Fourth National Bank).

102. *See* 1 VU:BOTM, *supra* note 15, pt. 1, at 50 (May 3, 1875); Law Department, *supra* note 105, at 15 (listing seven law students in 1874–75).

103. Green, *supra* note 93, at 98 (indicating in a chapter about Reese's father, William Brown Reese, that Reese was "Jr."); Riley, *supra* note 6, at 9; *Judge Wm. B. Reese: Death of the Well-Known Lawyer and Scholar*, Daily Am., Oct. 25, 1891, at 4 [hereinafter *Judge Wm. B. Reese*].

104. *Judge Wm. B. Reese*, *supra* note 107, at 4 ("He attended the law department of Cumberland University at Lebanon, Tenn., and was admitted to the bar about 1854."). The authors have been unable to locate further information about Reese studying law at Cumberland.

105. *See* Keeble, *supra* note 51, at 200; Edward E. Barthell, *The Best Features of My College Life*, 3 Vand. Alumnus 147 (1918) (extolling virtues of Reese).

106. *See* Barthell, *supra* note 109, at 147; H. B. Schermerhorn, *History of the School of Law*, 17 Vand. Alumnus 178, 178 (1932).

107. *See* 1 VU:BOTM, *supra* note 15, pt. 1, at 50 (May 3, 1875); Riley, *supra* note 6, at 8.

108. 1 VU:BOTM, *supra* note 15, pt. 1, at 49 (May 3, 1875).

109. 1 *id.* at 50; *The First Diploma in Law*, 8 Vand. Alumnus 72 (1923).

110. *See* Conkin, *supra* note 8, at 120, 122; Merriam, *supra* note 60, at 130; Riley, *supra* note 6, at 10; *Committee Report for the Eleventh Annual Meeting*, *supra* note 12, at 65; *see also infra* notes 310–11 and accompanying text.

111. *See Vanderbilt University Law Department*, Republican Banner, Aug. 19, 1874, at 3 & Sept. 2, 1874, at 3 (advertisement); *Vanderbilt University. Law Department*, Christian Advoc., July 18, 1874, at 13 (advertisement). This advertisement recognized early graduation provided the student's "previous reading will justify it." *Id.*

112. These announcements stated: "In exceptional cases the degree may be fairly won in a single year. Everything depends on the student." *See, e.g.*, Register of Vanderbilt University 1880–81/Announcement 1881–82, at 60 (2d ed. 1881) [hereinafter Register 1880–81]; Register 1876–77, *supra* note 15, at 56.

113. *Commencement of the Law Department of Vanderbilt University*, Christian Advoc., June 5, 1875, at 8.

114. *See* Schermerhorn, *supra* note 110, at 181.

115. *See Commencement of the Law Department of Vanderbilt University, supra* note 117, at 8.

116. *Id.; The First Diploma in Law, supra* note 113.

   A number of medical students received Vanderbilt degrees in February 1875, a few months before Sullivan's graduation. They had completed the first year of their medical education while the two-year medical school was being run solely under the auspices of the University of Nashville. Beginning in 1874, the Medical School operated under the banners of both universities. Thereafter, medical students had the option of obtaining a degree from Vanderbilt, the University of Nashville, or both institutions. *See* CONKIN, *supra* note 8, at 54; MIMS, *supra* note 7, at 96–97; James H. Kirkland, *Vanderbilt School of Medicine Had Precarious Beginning 60 Years Ago*, NASHVILLE BANNER, July 18, 1937, at 10; *Medical School to Mark Hundredth Anniversary*, 14 VAND. TODAY, Feb. 1975, at 1.

117. Riley, *supra* note 6, at 12; BIOGRAPHICAL DIRECTORY OF THE U.S. CONGRESS 1774–1989, at 1895; *Law School Directory*, 3 VAND. ALUMNUS 205, 205 (1918) (entry for Sullivan).

118. *See The Vanderbilt*, CHRISTIAN ADVOC., Apr. 3, 1875, at 1; *see also The Cornelian Literary Society of the Vanderbilt Law School*, CHRISTIAN ADVOC., June 5, 1875, at 8 (noting that the society would continue to operate when the Law School reopened in the fall).

119. CONKIN, *supra* note 8, at 143–45; Frederick W. Moore, *The Twenty-Fifth Anniversary of the Opening of Vanderbilt University and Presentation of Kissan Hall*, 1 VAND. U. Q., Mar. 1901, at 6, 11, 20.

120. 1 VU:BOTM, *supra* note 15, pt. 1, at 44–45 (May 3, 1875); 1 *id.* at 58 (May 4, 1875); 1 *id.* at 59 (May 11, 1875); Riley, *supra* note 6, at 8.

121. *See* 1 VU:BOTM, *supra* note 15, pt. 1, at 59 (May 11, 1875); 1 *id.* at 59–60 (May 12, 1875); 1 *id.* at 61 (May 25, 1875). Three faculty members—Nicholson, Spofford, and Stokes—did not formally resign. The Board asked Board President McTyeire "to write to Judge Nicholson, Judge Spofford and Col. Stokes, informing them of this action ["lease" agreement], and thanking them for the use of their names in the original organization." 1 *id.* at 61.

122. 1 *id.* at 61–62 ("Lease of Law Department"); CONKIN, *supra* note 8, at 55; Riley, *supra* note 6, at 8.

123. *See* CONKIN, *supra* note 8, at 24; *see also supra* notes 73–76 and accompanying text.

124. *See* CONKIN, *supra* note 8, at 24, 120; Holladay, *supra* note 51, at 14.

125. *See* CONKIN, *supra* note 8, at 42, 53–54; MIMS, *supra* note 7, at 95–96 ("[I]t was quite clear that no idea of financial outlay was entertained in connection with the establishment of the Divisions of Medicine and Law."); *Address of Dr. Garland, supra* note 62, at 8, 9 (noting that "departments of Law and Medicine . . . are usually self-sustaining").

126. *See supra* notes 66–68 and accompanying text.

127. *See* CONKIN, *supra* note 8, at 24; *see also supra* notes 60–62 and accompanying

text. Indeed, the Law School was restructured roughly in accordance with the organization of the Medical School, which carried the Vanderbilt name but was wholly run by the medical faculty under a contractual arrangement with the University. See Mims, *supra* note 7, at 96–98. The University's agreement with the Law School, however, apparently gave the University greater authority to regulate the operations of that department than it had under its contract with the Medical School. *See* Conkin, *supra* note 8, at 54–55.

128. *See* Merriam, *supra* note 60, at 120 ("The professors of the Vanderbilt law faculty have been men actively engaged in the practice of law, and this fact necessarily has had much to do with shaping the character of the school.").

Of the three, Reese seems to have had the least extensive local practice and committed the most time to the law school venture. *See Judge Wm. B. Reese, supra* note 107, at 4 ("As a lawyer he never acquired a large practice, but he was recognized as one of the most accurate and logical jurists the State has produced."); Schermerhorn, *supra* note 110, at 178 (Reese's "health obliging him to retire from active practice of the law, he devoted his entire time to the work of the Law School"). *See generally* H. A. Hood, The Law School Faculty: The Part-Time Faculty, 1875–1920, at 1–19 (1973) (unpublished First Draft (Corrected)), Centennial History Project (on file with Jean and Alexander Heard Library, Vanderbilt University and with Vanderbilt Law School in Howard A. Hood, Law School History Drafts of Centennial History Project) (discussing the impact of the "part-time character of the faculty").

129. *See* Friedman, *supra* note 23, at 609; Harno, *supra* note 26, at 100; Professional Education, *supra* note 42, at 155; Reed, *supra* note 26, at 182–84; Kane, *supra* note 80, at 3; Riley, *supra* note 6, at 9; Fligeltaub, *supra* note 6, at 33, 40.

130. *See Judge Wm. B. Reese, supra* note 107, at 4.

131. Black's Law Dictionary 889 (6th ed. 1990).

132. *See* Friedman, *supra* note 23, at 608–09; Reed, *supra* note 26, at 183–87, 192; Stevens, *supra* note 22, at 35; Swords & Walwer, *supra* note 42, at 35–36; Kane, *supra* note 80, at 3; Fligeltaub, *supra* note 6, at 3; *see also* Riley, *supra* note 6, at 8–9. *See generally* Bartholomew, *supra* note 82.

133. The lease is set out at 1 VU:BOTM, *supra* note 15, pt. 1, at 61–62 (May 25, 1875). For discussion of the lease provisions, see Conkin, *supra* note 8, at 55; Merriam, *supra* note 60, at 119; Mims, *supra* note 7, at 98; Riley, *supra* note 6, at 8; Fligeltaub, *supra* note 6, at 2–3; H. A. Hood, Law School Finance, 1874–1973, at 4 (1973), Centennial History Project, Box 25 (unpublished First Draft on file with Jean and Alexander Heard Library, Vanderbilt University and with Vanderbilt Law School in Howard A. Hood, Law School History Drafts of Centennial History Project); Laska, *supra* note 19, at 511–12.

134. Such an arrangement for compensating law professors was widespread in that era. Kane, *supra* note 80, at 3; Fligeltaub, *supra* note 6, at 34.

135. This right was "subject to the ratification of the other lessees and of the Vanderbilt University." 1 VU:BOTM, *supra* note 15, pt. 1, at 62 (May 25, 1875).

136. 1 *id.* at 62.

137. *See* Friedman, *supra* note 23, at 608–09; Reed, *supra* note 26, at 183–87; Stevens, *supra* note 22, at 35; Fligeltaub, *supra* note 6, at 3. *See generally* discussion *supra Legal Education* subsection in External Influences section; Bartholomew, *supra* note 82.

138. *See* Kirkland, *supra* note 74, at 95; Riley, *supra* note 6, at 9; Fligeltaub, *supra* note 6, at 40–41.

139. *Judge Wm. B. Reese, supra* note 107, at 4; *see also supra* notes 107–08 and accompanying text (describing Reese).

140. *See Judge Wm. B. Reese, supra* note 107, at 4 ("He attended the law department of Cumberland University at Lebanon, Tenn., and was admitted to the bar about 1854.") (The authors have been unable to locate further information about Reese studying law at Cumberland.); Memoir of Thomas H. Malone 92–93 (1928) [hereinafter Malone Memoir] (indicating that Malone prepared for practice by reading law in an attorney's office); Thos. S. Weaver, *Thomas H. Malone, M.A.,* 7 Vand. U. Q. 77, 93–94 (1907) (noting that Malone prepared for admission to the bar by studying with a practicing lawyer); *Judge Baxter Passes Away,* Nashville Banner, June 13, 1910, at 3 ("[W]hile he [Baxter] never went to school after he was 14 years of age, he read law while in the office of Mr. Andrew Ewing at Nashville. . . .").

141. *See* Keeble, *supra* note 51, at 200 (Malone and Baxter); Riley, *supra* note 6, at 9 (same); Schermerhorn, *supra* note 110, at 178 (same); *Judge Wm. B. Reese, supra* note 107, at 4 (noting that Reese "enlisted in the Confederate service").

142. *See* Keeble, *supra* note 51, at 200 (referring to Baxter as "Judge").

143. *See* Malone Memoir, *supra* note 144, at 111–87; Weaver, *supra* note 144, at 94–98. Unfortunately, Malone died before he wrote the Vanderbilt stage of his memoirs. *See* Malone Memoir, *supra* note 144, at 218.

144. *See* Malone Memoir, *supra* note 144, at 174–87; Riley, *supra* note 6, at 9; Weaver, *supra* note 144, at 98. Coincidentally, one of Malone's future Vanderbilt law faculty colleagues and the person who would succeed him as dean of Vanderbilt Law School, Horace Lurton, was also a Confederate soldier imprisoned at the same site at the same time. Riley, *supra* note 6, at 9; *see also* James F. Watts, Jr., *Horace H. Lurton, in* III The Justices of the United States Supreme Court: Their Lives and Major Opinions 925, 930 (Leon Friedman & Fred L. Israel eds., 1997). *See generally infra* notes 203–10 and accompanying text (discussing Lurton).

145. *See* Malone Memoir, *supra* note 144, at 33–77, 90–95; Riley, *supra* note 6, at 9; Weaver, *supra* note 144, at 85–87, 93–94.

146. *See* Malone Memoir, *supra* note 144, at 95–110; Riley, *supra* note 6, at 9; Weaver, *supra* note 144, at 94.

147. *See* Summerville, *supra* note 22, at 50; Weaver, *supra* note 144, at 100; *Judge*

Malone Passes Away, NASHVILLE AM., Sept. 15, 1906, at 6; *Judge Thomas H. Malone Dead After Long Illness*, NASHVILLE BANNER, Sept. 14, 1906, at 8.

As part of his practice, Malone represented those who obtained the charter for The Central University of the Methodist Episcopal Church South, soon to be renamed The Vanderbilt University. *See* Davidson County Chancery Court File No. 7214, Metropolitan Government Archives of Nashville & Davidson County, Tennessee; *see also* Interview by Katherine Edge, Tennessee Bar Foundation Legal History Project, with Charles C. Trabue, Jr., Nashville, TN (Dec. 10, 1999).

148. *See* SUMMERVILLE, *supra* note 22, at 50; Williams, *supra* note 93, at 22; Keeble, *supra* note 51, at 200; Schermerhorn, *supra* note 110, at 178; Weaver, *supra* note 144, at 105; *Judge Malone Passes Away*, *supra* note 151, at 6; *Judge Thomas H. Malone Dead After Long Illness*, *supra* note 151, at 8.

149. *See* Riley, *supra* note 6, at 9; Weaver, *supra* note 144, at 105–06; *Judge Malone Passes Away*, *supra* note 151, at 6; *Judge Thomas H. Malone Dead After Long Illness*, *supra* note 151, at 8; Laska, *supra* note 19, at 523.

For additional observations about the accomplished and erudite Malone, see generally MALONE MEMOIR, *supra* note 144, at i–vii (Introduction by J. M. Dickinson); Weaver, *supra* note 144, at 77–109.

150. Holladay, *supra* note 51, at 14–15; Riley, *supra* note 6, at 8–9; Weaver, *supra* note 144, at 77, 102; *see also* 1 VU:BOTM, *supra* note 15, pt. 1, at 61 (May 25, 1875) (Board's appointment of Malone to Law School deanship); 4 *id.* at 177–78 (June 13, 1904) (Malone's letter of resignation); 4 *id.* at 195 (June 14, 1904) (Board's acceptance of Malone's resignation). *See generally* Law School Administration: Deans, *supra* note 85, at first through ninth unnumbered pages (discussing Malone's deanship, citing his accomplishments, and noting instances of conflict with Chancellor Garland over Law School–University relations).

151. 1 VU:BOTM, *supra* note 15, pt. 1, at 313–14 (July 4, 1882) (Malone wrote "that the State of my health will prevent me from continuing longer my labors in the Vanderbilt Law School").

152. *See* 1 *id.* pt. 2, at 473–74 (June 15, 1886); 1 *id.* at 670 (June 17, 1889); 1 *id.* at 677 (Aug. 5, 1889).

153. *See* REGISTER 1882–83, *supra* note 45, at 61; REGISTER OF VANDERBILT UNIVERSITY 1883–84/ANNOUNCEMENT 1884–85, at 61 (1884) [hereinafter REGISTER 1883–84]; REGISTER OF VANDERBILT UNIVERSITY 1884–85/ANNOUNCEMENT 1885–86, at 60 (1885) [hereinafter REGISTER 1884–85]; REGISTER OF VANDERBILT UNIVERSITY 1886–87/ANNOUNCEMENT 1887–88, at 63 (1887) [hereinafter REGISTER 1886–87]; REGISTER OF VANDERBILT UNIVERSITY 1887–88/ANNOUNCEMENT 1888–89, at 74 (1888) [hereinafter REGISTER 1887–88]; REGISTER OF VANDERBILT UNIVERSITY 1888–89/ANNOUNCEMENT 1889–90, at 63 (1889) [hereinafter REGISTER 1888–89].

154. *See* 1 VU:BOTM, *supra* note 15, pt. 1, at 313–14 (July 4, 1882).

155. *See* 1 *id.* at 314.

156. *See* REGISTER 1883–84, *supra* note 157, at 61; REGISTER 1884–85, *supra* note 157, at

60; *The Faculty List* (on file with Jean and Alexander Heard Library, Vanderbilt University) (entry for Milliken).

157.   *See* 1 VU:BOTM, *supra* note 15, pt. 2, at 373 (May 26, 1884); 1 *id.* at 412 (May 26, 1885); 1 *id.* at 464 (June 14, 1886); 1 *id.* at 505 (June 13, 1887); REGISTER 1882–83, *supra* note 45, at 61, 62; REGISTER 1883–84, *supra* note 157, at 63; REGISTER 1884–85, *supra* note 157, at 62.

158.   *See* REGISTER 1886–87, *supra* note 157, at 63.

159.   *See* REGISTER 1887–88, *supra* note 157, at 74; REGISTER 1888–89, *supra* note 157, at 63; REGISTER OF VANDERBILT UNIVERSITY 1889–90/ANNOUNCEMENT 1890–91, at 58 (1890) [hereinafter REGISTER 1889–90]; *The Vanderbilt Opening,* CHRISTIAN ADVOC., Sept. 3, 1887, at 9 (noting that Allison had served as Tennessee Bar Association president and American Bar Association vice president); HARVARD UNIVERSITY QUINQUENNIAL CATALOGUE OF THE OFFICERS AND GRADUATES 1636–1930, at 970, 987, 1213, 1216 (1930) (listing Allison as graduating from Harvard Law School in 1865).

160.   *See* 3 VU:BOTM, *supra* note 15, at 75 (June 15, 1896) (listing Law School graduates); Riley, *supra* note 6, at 9; *Noted Lawyer Dies at Home in Belle Meade,* NASHVILLE BANNER, Mar. 22, 1941, at 1, 16; *T. H. Malone Rites Today,* NASHVILLE TENNESSEEAN, Mar. 22, 1941, at 2.

161.   *Mrs. Trabue Dies: From Victorian Era,* NASHVILLE BANNER, Sept. 4, 1976, at 17.

162.   *See* REGISTER OF VANDERBILT UNIVERSITY 1894–95/ANNOUNCEMENT 1895–96, at 140–41 (1895) [hereinafter REGISTER 1894–95] (listing Law School 1894 prize-winners). "The Founder's Department Medal" was "awarded annually to that graduate . . . regarded by the Faculty as the best lawyer of his class. . . ." REGISTER OF VANDERBILT UNIVERSITY 1893–94/ANNOUNCEMENT 1894–95, at 75 (1894) [hereinafter REGISTER 1893–94].

163.   SUMMERVILLE, *supra* note 22, at 49; *Judge Baxter Passes Away, supra* note 144, at 3; *Judge Ed Baxter Crosses the Bar,* NASHVILLE AM., June 13, 1910, at 1. Baxter's father issued the court decree chartering the University. *See* VU CHARTER, *supra* note 69, at 25, 27; *see also supra* note 69 and accompanying text.

164.   *Judge Baxter Passes Away, supra* note 144, at 3; *see also Judge Ed Baxter Crosses the Bar, supra* note 167, at 1 ("Judge Baxter was largely a self-educated man.").

165.   *See* SUMMERVILLE, *supra* note 22, at 49; Keeble, *supra* note 51, at 200; Schermerhorn, *supra* note 110, at 178; *Judge Baxter Passes Away, supra* note 144, at 3; *Judge Ed Baxter Crosses the Bar, supra* note 167, at 1, 3; *Law Locals,* HUSTLER, Sept. 24, 1896, at 3. Baxter assumed the presidency of the Tennessee Bar Association in 1892–1893. TENN. BAR J., Nov. 1983, at 39.

166.   THOMAS, *supra* note 29, at 177.

167.   *See* Barthell, *supra* note 109, at 147; Keeble, *supra* note 51, at 200; *see also Law Briefs,* HUSTLER, Oct. 20, 1896, at 3 (student tribute to Baxter upon his "retirement").

168.   *See The Faculty List, supra* note 160 (entry for Baxter). Baxter apparently did not even lecture at the Law School during the 1900–01 school year. *See id.* (entry for

Baxter); 4 VU:BOTM, *supra* note 15, at 1 (June 26, 1900) (no entry for Baxter in the list of law faculty appointed for the 1900–01 academic year).

169.   *See* 3 VU:BOTM, *supra* note 15, at 143 (June 14, 1897); 3 *id.* at 201 (June 13, 1898); *Law Locals, supra* note 165, at 3; *Law Briefs, supra* note 171, at 3 (student tribute to Baxter upon his "retirement").

170.   *See* Fligeltaub, *supra* note 6, at 30–31; Keeble, *supra* note 51, at 200; *The Faculty List, supra* note 160 (entries for lessees); Announcement of Vanderbilt University, First Session, 1875–6 (1875) through Register of Vanderbilt University 1890–91/Announcement 1891–92 (1891).

171.   *See supra* notes 104–01 and accompanying text.

172.   *See* Register 1888–89, *supra* note 157, at 64; Register 1889–90, *supra* note 163, at 59; Register 1890–91, *supra* note 96, at 63; Register of Vanderbilt University 1891–92/Announcement 1892–93, at 60 (1892) [hereinafter Register 1891–92].

173.   *See* Laska, *supra* note 19, at 522–24.

174.   *See* Kirkland, *supra* note 74, at 95; Riley, *supra* note 6, at 9, 13; Fligeltaub, *supra* note 6, at 40–41.

175.   *See* Riley, *supra* note 6, at 9.

176.   *See Judge Wm. B. Reese, supra* note 107, at 4.

177.   *See* 3 VU:BOTM, *supra* note 15, at 313 (June 18, 1900) (Kirkland noting that "[t]wo of the original faculty are still in active work"). Beginning in the late 1890s, however, Baxter's involvement in the law school had decreased appreciably. *See supra* notes 172–69 and accompanying text.

178.   *See Judge Wm. B. Reese, supra* note 107, at 4 (noting that Reese "produced a work on constitutiona[l] law, which is now considered a necessity for every well-equipped lawyer").

179.   *See Judge Baxter Passes Away, supra* note 144, at 3 (noting in fourth tier of headline that Baxter was "Law Professor at Vanderbilt University" and covering this aspect of his life in two sentences); *Judge Ed Baxter Crosses the Bar, supra* note 167, at 1 (including no mention of Baxter's law school professorship); *Judge Malone Passes Away, supra* note 151, at 6 (noting only that "[f]or a period of over twenty years he was Dean of the law department of Vanderbilt University"); *Judge Thomas H. Malone Dead After Long Illness, supra* note 151, at 8 (containing one paragraph about Malone's work as dean and professor at Vanderbilt Law School).

180.   *See supra* notes 143–69 and accompanying text.

181.   *See* Holladay, *supra* note 51, at 14 ("It is hard . . . to overstate [Malone's] early influence."); Thomas H. Malone, Jr., Address Before the Malone Inn, Phi Delta Phi, and Delegates of the Provincial Convention (Dec. 8, 1922), *in* Malone Memoir, *supra* note 144, at 225 (observing that Malone "devoted his utmost energies" to his work as dean and that "[n]o case was ever more important to him than the preparation of his law lectures"); Law School Administration:

Deans, *supra* note 85, at eighth through ninth unnumbered pages (commenting on Malone's contributions).

182. *See* Kirkland, *supra* note 74, at 95; Riley, *supra* note 6, at 9, 13; Fligeltaub, *supra* note 6, at 40–41 (concluding that a "sound program" had resulted from the efforts of the lessees and others).

183. *See supra* notes 42–53 and accompanying text.

184. *See* Fligeltaub, *supra* note 6, at 33 (commenting on the law faculty's "nominal" compensation and opining that "[g]iven the purchases for the Law Library from the lessee's finances and the establishment of two $100 annual scholarships, the faculty's net salaries were virtually nonexistent"); H. A. Hood, The Law School Faculty: Faculty Salaries 52–53 (1974) (unpublished First Draft (Incomplete)), Centennial History Project (on file with Jean and Alexander Heard Library, Vanderbilt University and with Vanderbilt Law School in Howard A. Hood, Law School History Drafts of Centennial History Project) ("One may assume that the professors of that period were not getting rich from their teaching.").

185. Kirkland, *supra* note 74, at 95; *see also* 3 VU:BOTM, *supra* note 15, at 313 (June 18, 1900) (Kirkland commenting that the law professors "have seemed at all times indifferent to the question of their own remuneration").

186. *See* Riley, *supra* note 6, at 9.

187. *See supra* notes 159–59 and accompanying text.

188. *Judge Wm. B. Reese, supra* note 107, at 4.

189. 1 VU:BOTM, *supra* note 15, pt. 1, at 62 (May 25, 1875) (fifth lease provision); 2 *id.* at 170 (June 14, 1892). *See generally supra* notes 137–36 and accompanying text (discussing lease provisions).

190. 2 VU:BOTM, *supra* note 15, at 170 (June 14, 1892). Smith had already taught at the Law School. Malone and Baxter had recruited him to take over Reese's courses after Reese's death. 2 *id.*

191. *See* 2 *id.* at 197 (June 15, 1892); 2 *id.* at 202–03 (June 16, 1892); Conkin, *supra* note 8, at 120; Fligeltaub, *supra* note 6, at 32–33.

192. 2 VU:BOTM, *supra* note 15, at 202 (June 16, 1892) (letter from board member Judge Edward East to Smith).

193. 2 *id.* at 202–03 (June 16, 1892) (letter from Smith to board member Judge Edward East).

194. *See* 2 *id.* at 203.

195. *See* Register 1891–92, *supra* note 176, at 59, 62; Register of Vanderbilt University 1892–1893/Announcement 1893–94, at 59 (1893) [hereinafter Register 1892–93]; Register 1893–1894, *supra* note 166, at 73; Register 1894–95, *supra* note 166, at 75; *The Faculty List, supra* note 160 (entry for Smith).

196. 3 VU:BOTM, *supra* note 15, at 193, 201 (June 13, 1898).

197. Dickinson was the Tennessee Bar Association's president in 1889–1890 and chaired the Association's Committee on Legal Education and Admission to the Bar in 1899. Tenn. Bar J., Nov. 1983, at 39 (listing former Tennessee Bar

Association presidents); *Committee Report for the Eighteenth Annual Meeting*, *supra* note 34, at 10–12.

198. Keeble, *supra* note 51, at 200–01; Riley, *supra* note 6, at 9.

199. 3 VU:BOTM, *supra* note 15, at 201 (June 13, 1898).

200. *See generally* Riley, *supra* note 6, at 9–10 (discussing Lurton); Law School Administration: Deans, *supra* note 85, at ninth through fourteenth unnumbered pages (dealing with Lurton's career in law and his service at Vanderbilt Law School).

201. *See* Keeble, *supra* note 51, at 201 (stressing Lurton's role in developing the three-year program and in strengthening graduation standards).

202. *See* 5 VU:BOTM, *supra* note 15, at 156 (June 13, 1910); Law School Administration: Deans, *supra* note 85, at tenth through fourteenth unnumbered pages.

203. 3 VU:BOTM, *supra* note 15, at 201 (June 13, 1898).

204. *See generally* GREEN, *supra* note 93, at 213–18 (chapter on Lurton); LANGUM & WALTHALL, *supra* note 14, at 67–69 (discussing Lurton as notable Cumberland School of Law graduate); SUMMERVILLE, *supra* note 22, at 51 (commenting on Lurton); Watts, *supra* note 148, at 925–43 (treating Lurton's life and legal career).

205. 4 VU:BOTM, *supra* note 15, at 214 (Sept. 19, 1904); 5 *id.* at 156 (June, 13, 1910); Laska, *supra* note 19, at 524–25; Hood *supra* note 132, at 3; Law School Administration: Deans, *supra* note 85, at twelfth through fourteenth unnumbered pages; *see also* Watts, *supra* note 148, at 927, 935.

206. SUMMERVILLE, *supra* note 22, at 51; 5 VU:BOTM, *supra* note 15, at 156 (June 13, 1910); Watts, *supra* note 148, at 925, 933; Laska, *supra* note 19, at 524; Law School Administration: Deans, *supra* note 85, at fourteenth unnumbered page. Lurton's tenure as a Supreme Court Justice lasted only a little over four years; he died in the summer of 1914. Watts, *supra* note 148, at 927, 942; Law School Administration: Deans, *supra* note 85, at twelfth unnumbered page.

207. *See* REGISTER 1888–89, *supra* note 157, at 111 (listing Burch as receiving bachelor of laws degree); *Law Faculty*, HUSTLER, Oct. 6, 1898, at 1 (noting that Burch was "a Vanderbilt graduate"); *Law School Directory*, *supra* note 121, at 205, 209 (entry for Burch).

208. *See* REGISTER OF VANDERBILT UNIVERSITY 1898–99/ANNOUNCEMENT 1899–1900, at 89, 92 (1899) [hereinafter REGISTER 1898–99]; REGISTER 1899–1900, *supra* note 17, at 97, 101; *The Faculty List*, *supra* note 160 (entry for Burch).

209. Burch was eventually chosen to serve on the University Board of Trust. *See Law School Directory*, *supra* note 121, at 209 (entry for Burch).

210. *See* 3 VU:BOTM, *supra* note 15, at 201–02 (June 13, 1898).

211. *See* 3 *id.* at 201; *Law Faculty*, *supra* note 211, at 1.

212. *See* 3 VU:BOTM, *supra* note 15, at 312 (June 18, 1900); THOMAS, *supra* note 29, at 142–43, 157; Keeble, *supra* note 51, at 201; Riley, *supra* note 6, at 9. Dickinson apparently lectured at the Law School during the period 1901 to 1904 and then returned to serve as a professor in 1912 and 1913. *See The Faculty List*, *supra* note

160 (entry for Dickinson); Riley, *supra* note 6, at 9. Dickinson became a national legal figure. He assumed the presidency of the American Bar Association in 1907–08 and served as Secretary of War in the Taft administration. Keeble, *supra* note 51, at 201; Riley, *supra* note 6, at 9; AMERICAN BAR ASSOCIATION 2002– 2003 LEADERSHIP DIRECTORY 367 (2002) (listing past ABA presidents).

213. 2 VU:BOTM, *supra* note 15, at 16 (June 16, 1890).

214. TENN. BAR J., Nov. 1983, at 39 (listing former Tennessee Bar Association presidents and noting that Bonner was the head of the organization in 1898–99).

215. *See* 3 VU:BOTM, *supra* note 15, at 312 (June 18, 1900).

216. *See The Faculty List, supra* note 160 (entry for Waller).

217. *See Law School Directory, supra* note 121, at 210 (entry for Waller).

218. *See The Faculty List, supra* note 160 (entry for Bonner).

219. 4 VU:BOTM, *supra* note 15, at 1 (June 26, 1900); *see also* 3 *id.* at 315, 352 (June 18, 1900). *See generally* discussion *infra* "Reorganization": Poised for Change section.

Excluding Lurton, with whom a "special arrangement" had been made setting his compensation at $500, annual faculty salaries were established according to rank and the number of class hours offered. Professors were to receive $200 per hour taught each week. Adjunct professors were entitled to $150 per hour. Instructors earned $100 per hour. The dean was paid a $100 supplement, and the faculty secretary was given an extra $200. Law faculty members taught from two to four hours per week, with most offering three class sessions weekly. Thus, annual salaries were in the $300-to-$800 range. In addition, law faculty members, again excluding Lurton, were to share in any law school profit. The University and law faculty would evenly divide profits, with faculty members to allocate their portion pro rata on the basis of salary. 4 VU:BOTM, *supra* note 15, at 1 (June 26, 1900); *see also* 3 *id.* at 315, 352 (June 18, 1900); *infra* notes 470–68 and accompanying text. For discussion of this salary scheme, see Hood, *supra* note 188, at 53–54.

220. Baxter was not included on this post-lease faculty. Apparently, he returned to the faculty as a lecturer on the Law of Interstate Commerce during the period 1901 to 1904. *See The Faculty List, supra* note 160 (entry for Baxter).

221. *See generally* SUMMERVILLE, *supra* note 22, at 50–51, 58 (discussing Bradford).

222. CONKIN, *supra* note 8, at 122; REGISTER 1887–88, *supra* note 157, at 120 (listing Keeble as receiving a bachelor of laws degree); 7 VU:BOTM, *supra* note 15, at 235 (Nov. 30, 1915) (Keeble named Law School's acting dean); Keeble, *supra* note 51, at 200; *Law School Directory, supra* note 121, at 208 (entry for Keeble). Keeble served as Vanderbilt Law School dean from 1915 until 1929. CONKIN, *supra* note 8, at 261; Holladay, *supra* note 51, at 15.

223. Riley, *supra* note 6, at 10; *Law School Directory, supra* note 121, at 207 (entry for Maddin).

224. Keeble, *supra* note 51, at 201–02; Riley, *supra* note 6, at 9. *See generally* JAMES E. BOND, I DISSENT: THE LEGACY OF [ ] JUSTICE JAMES CLARK McREYNOLDS (1992); David Burner, *James C. McReynolds, in* III THE JUSTICES OF THE UNITED

States Supreme Court: Their Lives and Major Opinions 1006–17 (Leon Friedman & Fred L. Israel eds., 1997); Summerville, *supra* note 22, at 51–52 (discussing McReynolds).

225. 3 VU:BOTM, *supra* note 15, at 75 (June 15, 1896) (including Malone Jr. in the listing of Law School graduates); Riley, *supra* note 6, at 9; *Noted Lawyer Dies at Home in Belle Meade, supra* note 164, at 1, 16; *T. H. Malone Rites Today, supra* note 164, at 2; *Law School Directory, supra* note 121, at 211–12 (entry for Malone Jr.).

226. 4 VU:BOTM, *supra* note 15, at 1 (June 26, 1900); *see also* 3 *id.* at 315, 352 (June 19, 1900). Malone Jr. was a faculty member at Vanderbilt Law School for decades, teaching law there well into the twentieth century. *See Noted Lawyer Dies at Home in Belle Meade, supra* note 164, at 1, 16; *T. H. Malone Rites Today, supra* note 164, at 2.

227. Laska, *supra* note 19, at 524–25; *see also* Keeble, *supra* note 51, at 201–02; Riley, *supra* note 6, at 9.

228. *See generally* Hood, *supra* note 132, at 1–19 (discussing the impact of the "part-time character of the faculty").

229. *See* Friedman, *supra* note 23, at 609; Harno, *supra* note 26, at 100; Professional Education, *supra* note 42, at 155; Reed, *supra* note 26, at 182–84; Kane, *supra* note 80, at 3; Riley, *supra* note 6, at 9; Fligeltaub, *supra* note 6, at 33, 40.

230. Conkin, *supra* note 8, at 55; *see also* H. A. Hood, Vanderbilt Law School Students 80–83 (1972), Centennial History Project (unpublished Rough Draft on file with Jean and Alexander Heard Library, Vanderbilt University) (discussing law student participation in campus "literary societies"—"public speaking or debating clubs"). For further description of literary societies at Vanderbilt, see Announcement of Vanderbilt University, First Session, 1875–6, at 15–16 (1875).

Dean Malone reported strong "*esprit du Corps*" among law students in 1892 that he attributed, in part, to the "good fellowship produced by university athletics," noting that law students were team leaders in baseball and football. 2 VU:BOTM, *supra* note 15, at 169–70 (June 14, 1892); *see also* Laska, *supra* note 47, at 504 (commenting on law students as football players); *Law Notes,* Hustler, Oct. 5, 1893, at 4 (observing that "it seems the law class will be well represented in base ball this year").

231. *The Vanderbilt, supra* note 122, at 1. William Sullivan, the first person to graduate from Vanderbilt Law School, was the society's founding president. *Id.*; *see also supra* notes 113, 122 and accompanying text. Professor Reese apparently served as faculty advisor. *See Cornelian Literary Society of the Vanderbilt Law School, supra* note 122, at 8.

232. *See infra* notes 282–87 and accompanying text.

233. *See generally* Reed, *supra* note 26, at 313 (noting the mixed educational background of law students during this period).

234. REED, *supra* note 26, at 169 (discussing the nature of the bachelor of laws degree, commonly known as an LL.B. degree); Laska, *supra* note 47, at 504.

235. *See* REED, *supra* note 26, at 318–19; Brainerd Currie, *The Materials of Law Study*, 3 J. LEGAL EDUC., 331, 368–69 (1951); E. W. Huffcut, *A Decade of Progress in Legal Education,* 10 AM. LAW. 404, 405–09 (1902).

236. Fligeltaub, *supra* note 6, at 4–5; *see also infra* notes 300–308 and accompanying text.

237. MERRIAM, *supra* note 60, at 130; *Educational Notes,* CHRISTIAN ADVOC., Oct. 17, 1889, at 7; *Law Notes, supra* note 234, at 4 (observing "that the number of college graduates who matriculate is on the steady increase"); Hood, *supra* note 234, at 12, unnumbered page containing Table IV found between pages 13 and 14; *see also* Riley, *supra* note 6, at 10 (noting "increasing percentage of students with undergraduate preparation" in the 1890s). *See generally* REED, *supra* note 26, at 313 (noting the mixed educational background of law students during this period).

238. Average Age of Matriculates in the University, J. T. McGill Collection, Box 6, File 100 (entries for the Law School from the 1875–76 school year through the 1888–89 school year) (on file with Jean and Alexander Heard Library, Vanderbilt University); Law Department, *supra* note 105, at 15.

239. *See* PROFESSIONAL EDUCATION, *supra* note 42, at 168 (listing the law department at Vanderbilt as a school for "Men").

240. *See* VIRGINIA G. DRACHMAN, SISTERS IN LAW: WOMEN LAWYERS IN MODERN AMERICAN HISTORY 37–63, 118–30 (1998); STEVENS, *supra* note 22, at 82–83.

241. HALL, *supra* note 22, at 219; *see also* STEVENS, *supra* note 22, at 81–82. Central Tennessee College (later Walden University) maintained a law school in Nashville for African-American students during the last two decades of the nineteenth century and beyond. REED, *supra* note 26, at 425; Blackard, *supra* note 54, at 269; Laska, *supra* note 19, at 688–89.

242. During this period, the Law School listed at least seven students from Indian Territory. *See* REGISTER 1888–89, *supra* note 157, at 117; REGISTER OF VANDERBILT UNIVERSITY FOR 1895–96/ANNOUNCEMENT FOR 1896–97, at 129 (1896) [hereinafter REGISTER 1895–96]; REGISTER OF VANDERBILT UNIVERSITY FOR 1896–97/ANNOUNCEMENT FOR 1897–98 at 129 (1897) [hereinafter REGISTER 1896–97]; REGISTER OF VANDERBILT UNIVERSITY FOR 1897–98/ANNOUNCEMENT FOR 1898–99, at 129 (1898) [hereinafter REGISTER 1897–98].

243. Riley, *supra* note 6, at 12; Wm. P. Thompson, *W. W. Hastings, A Pioneer, 1866–1938,* VAND. ALUMNUS, May 1938, at 13, 13; Dollye Hefner Cravens, Standard Bearer of the Cherokees: The Life of William Wirt Hastings 3–4 (1942) (unpublished M.A. thesis, Oklahoma Agricultural and Mechanical College) (on file with Bizzell Memorial Library, University of Oklahoma Libraries) (including a quotation from a Thompson manuscript); REGISTER 1888–89, *supra* note 157, at III, 117.

244. Riley, *supra* note 6, at 12 (noting Hastings' eighteen-year congressional career);

Joe Sweat, *Cherokee Trailblazer*, 30 VAND. LAW., Fall/Winter 2000, at 8, 8–9
(observing that Hastings was a "nine-term congressman"); Thompson, *supra* note
247, at 13; *W.W. Hastings, 71, Ex-U.S. Legislator*, N.Y. TIMES, Apr. 9, 1938, at 17;
Hastings, William Wirt, 1866–1938, BIOGRAPHICAL DIRECTORY OF THE UNITED
STATES CONGRESS 1774–1989, BICENTENNIAL EDITION 1150–51 (1989) (reporting
that Hastings was a congressional officeholder from 1915 to 1921 and from 1923 to
1935), *at* http://bioguide.congress.gov/scripts/biodisplay.pl?index=H000333 (last
visited Mar. 11, 2003).

245.   *Supreme Court Commissioners*, 91 OKLA. iii (1923); *see also School of Law Notes*,
VAND. ALUMNUS, Dec. 1936, at 7, 7.

246.   *An Act to Educate Twelve Chickasaw Boys in the States, and Providing Pay Therefor*,
in DAVIS A. HOMER, CONSTITUTION AND LAWS OF THE CHICKASAW NATION
306–09 (1899).

247.   CINDY GENTRY, BATTLE GROUND ACADEMY: A MONUMENT TO EDUCATION
26–27 (1996). Apparently at Chancellor Kirkland's suggestion, the Chickasaw
students initially attended the Wall and Mooney School (now Battle Ground
Academy) in Franklin, Tennessee, to hone their Greek and Latin skills. *Id.* at 26.

248.   *See* REGISTER 1895–96, *supra* note 246, at 129; REGISTER 1896–97, *supra* note
246, at 129; REGISTER 1897–98, *supra* note 246, at 129.

249.   REGISTER 1897–98, *supra* note 246, at 141; *Law School Directory*, *supra* note 121,
at 212 (entry for Goforth). Goforth served as the first treasurer of the Vanderbilt
Law Club, "[a] literary society" that was formed in the spring term of 1896. *Law
Locals*, HUSTLER, Mar. 19, 1896, at 1.

         James W. Breedlove, another student from Indian Territory, who apparently
was not part of the Chickasaw Nation group, argued with the "affirmative" team
in a debate held at the Vanderbilt Law Club's initial meeting. The topic was:
"Resolved: that Cuban independence should be declared by the United States."
Breedlove graduated with Goforth in 1897. *Id.* at 1; REGISTER 1897–98, *supra*
note 246, at 141; *Law School Directory*, *supra* note 121, at 212 (entry for Breedlove
indicating that he engaged in the practice of law in Oklahoma).

250.   REGISTER 1898–99, *supra* note 212, at 140; *Law School Directory*, *supra* note 121,
at 212 (entry for Thompson).

251.   INDIAN TERRITORY 612, 921–22 (1901) (also published with D. C. Gideon listed
as author).

252.   *Id.* at 612.

253.   *Id.* at 921.

254.   *See* REGISTER 1888–89, *supra* note 157, at 117; REGISTER 1889–90, *supra* note 163,
at 104–05; REGISTER 1892–93, *supra* note 199, at 115.

255.   1 VU:BOTM, *supra* note 15, pt. 2, at 670 (June 17, 1889).

256.   1 *id.* at 672.

257.   *Ending the Session*, DAILY AM., June 20, 1889, at 2; *Vanderbilt Commencement*,
CHRISTIAN ADVOC., June 27, 1889, at 9.

258.   2 VU:BOTM, *supra* note 15, at 49 (June 16, 1890).

259. 2 *id.* The student had advised the Law School at the time he enrolled "that his purpose was solely to become acquainted with the general principles of law . . . to fit himself for the discharge of diplomatic duties." 2 *id.*

260. Riley, *supra* note 6, at 11. *But cf.* Fligeltaub, *supra* note 2, at 12–13 (revised version on file with authors) (opining that the "limited geographical areas for recruiting" constituted a longstanding problem).

   The following analysis of the composition of the Vanderbilt Law School student body during the nineteenth century is based on data contained in the Vanderbilt University catalogues issued from Announcement of Vanderbilt University 1876–7, *supra* note 13, through Register 1899–1900, *supra* note 17. Geographic distribution charts are on file with the authors. For annual enrollment numbers, see *infra* Figure 1 accompanying note 362.

261. *See* Riley, *supra* note 6, at 11.

262. *See id.* (noting law students' "predominantly Southern background"); Hood, *supra* note 234, at 1; Fligeltaub, *supra* note 6, at 13 (revised version on file with authors).

263. *See* Fligeltaub, *supra* note 6 (revised version on file with authors), at 13; Hood, *supra* note 234, at 1.

264. During the 1880s and early 1890s, the percentage of Tennessee students generally was in the mid-thirty to mid-forty percent range. Not only did the percentage of out-of-state students increase during this period, but the number of other states represented in the student body also rose.

265. *See* 3 VU:BOTM, *supra* note 15, at 313 (June 18, 1900); *infra* notes 445–47 and accompanying text.

266. Riley, *supra* note 6, at 11–13.

267. *Id.* at 12; *Law School Directory*, *supra* note 121, at 205 (entries for John E. Gannaway and Lytton Taylor).

268. *See* Riley, *supra* note 6, at 11–13; *Law School Directory*, *supra* note 121, at 205–13. Not surprisingly, many Vanderbilt law students of this era remained in Nashville after graduation. See Summerville, *supra* note 22, at 59 ("Vanderbilt University Law School was clearly a strong influence in the Nashville bar. . . ."); Riley, *supra* note 6, at 11 (observing that "the School's graduates became prominent in the legal communities of Nashville, the state of Tennessee and throughout the Southeast").

269. *See* Conkin, *supra* note 8, at 55 ("The Law students early gained an enviable reputation among students as free and daring, the nearest approximation to radicals on the early and very staid campus."); Mims, *supra* note 7, at 117 (observing that medical students and law students "were a law unto themselves, or outside the law"); Joseph Sweat, *Uncommon Men*, Vand. Mag., Fall 1999, at 10, 12.

270. A third illustration, which involves a law student demonstration against the administration's selection of a campus speaker, reflects the law students' independent-minded, if not confrontational, nature and also indicates how

strongly some law students identified with the region. At one point, the brother
of Union General William Tecumseh Sherman was scheduled to speak on
campus. Law students protested the event and then led a march to further
express their displeasure. MIMS, *supra* note 7, at 126; Sweat, *supra* note 273, at 12.

271.   CONKIN, *supra* note 8, at 55; *see also Vanderbilt University,* DAILY AM., May 28,
1880, at 4; *Vanderbilt,* DAILY AM., May 27, 1881, at 4; *Vanderbilt Exercises,* DAILY
AM., May 29, 1882, at 4. *See generally infra* notes 345–47 and accompanying text;
Fligeltaub, *supra* note 6, at 22–24 (discussing moot courts conducted during the
school year).

272.   Unsent letter from Landon C. Garland, Chancellor, Vanderbilt University to
Thomas H. Malone, Dean, Vanderbilt Law School (June 7, 1876) [hereinafter
Unsent Garland Letter] (on file with Jean and Alexander Heard Library,
Vanderbilt University); *see also* Law School Administration: Deans, *supra* note
85, at third unnumbered page.

273.   Unsent Garland Letter, *supra* note 276. Garland also wrote: "We know of no
University in which Moot courts form a part of the Commencement Exercises
except the Cumberland University, & in our opinion the Vanderbilt [University]
will be more honored in the breach than in the observance of their custom." *Id.*

274.   *Id.*

275.   Letter from Landon C. Garland, Chancellor, Vanderbilt University to Thomas
H. Malone, Dean, Vanderbilt Law School (June 7, 1876) (on file with Jean
and Alexander Heard Library, Vanderbilt University); *see also* Law School
Administration: Deans, *supra* note 85, at third unnumbered page.

276.   *See Vanderbilt Commencement,* DAILY AM., June 21, 1876, at 4; *Vanderbilt
University,* DAILY AM., May 30, 1879, at 4; *Moot Court,* DAILY AM., May 30,
1883, at 5; *Moot Court Debate,* DAILY AM., May 28, 1888, at 3.

    A related controversy arose in 1888, when the Executive Committee of the
Board permitted the Law School to present diplomas to its graduates at the moot
court event prior to the University's commencement, a practice the Chancellor
argued should be discontinued. 1 VU:BOTM, *supra* note 15, pt. 2, at 575 (June
18, 1888).

277.   *See Vanderbilt University, supra* note 280, at 4 (reporting that Garland and Board
President Bishop McTyeire were in attendance); *Moot Court, supra* note 280,
at 5 (noting that Garland made the announcement and that McTyeire gave the
benediction.).

278.   *Editorial,* VAND. AUSTRAL, Mar. 1879, at 3; *see also* CONKIN, *supra* note 8, at 63
(noting that efforts to publish this periodical were "[l]ed by more daring law
students"); MIMS, *supra* note 7, at 120; *Story of Vanderbilt Austral Recalled,* 8
VAND. ALUMNUS 114, 114 (1923). The *Austral* appeared each month from March
of 1879 through June of 1879. *See* VAND. AUSTRAL, Mar. 1879; VAND. AUSTRAL,
Apr. 1879; VAND. AUSTRAL, May 1879; VAND. AUSTRAL, June 1879.

279.   MIMS, *supra* note 7, at 120; *Story of Vanderbilt Austral Recalled, supra* note 282, at
114.

280. *See* MIMS, *supra* note 7, at 120–21.

281. *Editorial, supra* note 282, at 3–4. The paper's writers presumed that the rule—which resulted in "inferior accommodations with *superior* prices"—was intended to keep students enrolled in the academic department from visiting the city and was applicable only to those students "because our Board probably considered the theologians incorruptible and the lawyers too corrupt for redemption." *Id.*

282. *Id.* at 6–7.

283. *Id.* at 6.

284. 1 VU:BOTM, *supra* note 15, pt. 1, at 174 (May 28, 1879).

285. 1 *id.*

286. 1 *id.*

287. *Story of Vanderbilt Austral Recalled, supra* note 282, at 114.

288. *See* CONKIN, *supra* note 8, at 55.

289. 1 VU:BOTM, *supra* note 15, pt.1, at 62 (May 25, 1875) (sixth lease provision).

290. CONKIN, *supra* note 8, at 55; *see also* MIMS, *supra* note 7, at 117.

291. 1 VU:BOTM, *supra* note 15, pt. 1, at 176 (May 28, 1879); *see also* Law School Administration: Deans, *supra* note 85, at second through seventh unnumbered pages (discussing this conflict). Dean Malone's claim may have originated from the provision in the 1875 lease that gave the faculty "the right to the exclusive control of said Law Department." 1 VU:BOTM, *supra* note 15, pt. 1, at 61 (May 25, 1875) (fourth lease provision).

292. 1 VU:BOTM, *supra* note 15, pt. 1, at 187 (May 30, 1879); Law School Administration: Deans, *supra* note 85, at fifth through sixth unnumbered pages.

293. Volume, the title of which is obscured, containing rosters of matriculating law students at Vanderbilt during the years 1889–1907, at 8 [hereinafter Rosters of Matriculating Law Students] (on file with Vanderbilt Law School).

294. Rosters of Matriculating Law Students, *supra* note 297, at 28.

295. *See* 3 VU:BOTM, *supra* note 15, at 201–02 (June 13, 1898); 3 *id.* at 249 (June 19, 1899); CONKIN, *supra* note 8, at 122; *infra* notes 440–69 and accompanying text. *See generally* Reed, *supra* note 26, at 184–87 (discussing the trend among universities to assert greater authority over their law schools).

296. Fligeltaub, *supra* note 6, at 4–7; Law School Curriculum, *supra* note 49, at 3, 5; *see also* 3 VU:BOTM, *supra* note 15, at 143–44 (June 14, 1897); *Committee Report for the Seventeenth Annual Meeting, supra* note 34, at 14; Riley, *supra* note 6, at 10; Law School Curriculum: Admission Requirements 1–5 (undated), Centennial History Project, Box 25 (unpublished memorandum on file with Jean and Alexander Heard Library, Vanderbilt University) [hereinafter Law School Curriculum: Admission Requirements]. The Law School's announcements specifically provided that applicants were not subject to any entrance examination. *See, e.g.*, ANNOUNCEMENT OF VANDERBILT UNIVERSITY, FIRST SESSION, 1875–6, *supra* note 9, at 37; REGISTER 1897–98, *supra* note 246, at 89.

On a single occasion—in 1892, the Law School included the following statement in the Course of Instruction section of its Announcement:

"Candidates for admission to both grades . . . must have previously read Walker's American Law or its equivalent upon the institutes of the law." REGISTER 1891–92, *supra* note 176, at 60; *see also* Fligeltaub, *supra* note 6, at 6 n.18. In addition, at the very end of the century—in 1899, the Law School established the following Senior Class admission standard for students seeking a degree:

Applicants for admission to the Senior Class, who desire to become candidates for the degree of LL. B., must either have successfully passed through the Junior Class of this school, or present the diploma or certificate of graduation from some other school of law having a two years' course, or pass a satisfactory examination on all the subjects studied by the Junior Class of this school.

REGISTER 1898–99, *supra* note 212, at 89.

297. REED, *supra* note 26, at 319; Currie, *supra* note 239, at 368–69; Huffcut, *supra* note 239, at 405–06; *Committee Report for the Seventeenth Annual Meeting*, *supra* note 34, at 14 ("It is believed that no educational acquirements as conditions precedent are required by any law school in this State."); Fligeltaub, *supra* note 6, at 5; Law School Curriculum, *supra* note 49, at 3–4; Law School Curriculum: Admission Requirements, *supra* note 300, at 1–5.

298. REED, *supra* note 26, at 318–19; Currie, *supra* note 239, at 368–69; Huffcut, *supra* note 239, at 405–08.

299. Fligeltaub, *supra* note 6, at 5–6 (exploring "factors" supporting a standardless admission policy); *see also* Riley, *supra* note 6, at 10; *supra* notes 7–59 and accompanying text.

300. *See* 2 VU:BOTM, *supra* note 15, at 283 (June 18, 1894) (Professor R. McPhail Smith, reporting to Board of Trust as the Law School's "Dean Pro Tempore," opined that "many of those entering upon the study of law have lacked the proper preliminary training therefor" and stressed the importance of pre-law education that encompassed "a good smattering of Latin, a fair amount of Geometry (the finest embodiment of applied logic), and a tolerable knowledge of the history of our own country and of England."); Fligeltaub, *supra* note 6, at 6; Laska, *supra* note 19, at 518.

301. 3 VU:BOTM, *supra* note 15, at 181 (June 14, 1897).

302. *See infra* text accompanying notes 445–47; Fligeltaub, *supra* note 6, at 6–7.

303. 3 VU:BOTM, *supra* note 15, at 143–44 (June 14, 1897).

304. *See* REGISTER 1899–1900, *supra* note 17, at 97. In 1899, the Law School did establish a Senior Class admission standard. *See* REGISTER 1898–99, *supra* note 212, at 89. This standard is set out *supra* note 300.

In 1907, the Board of Trust finally established academic standards for admission of entry-level law students. *See* 5 VU:BOTM, *supra* note 15, at 45 (July 23, 1907); Law School Curriculum: Admission Requirements, *supra* note 300, at 5.

305. *E.g.*, ANNOUNCEMENT OF VANDERBILT UNIVERSITY, FIRST SESSION, 1875–6 at 37; REGISTER 1882–83, *supra* note 45, at 61–62; REGISTER 1891–92, *supra* note 176, at 59–60; Riley, *supra* note 6, at 10.

306. *E.g.*, ANNOUNCEMENT OF VANDERBILT UNIVERSITY, FIRST SESSION, 1875–6, *supra* note 9, at 37; REGISTER 1898–99, *supra* note 212, at 91; *see also* Riley, *supra* note 6, at 10.

   Terminology used to describe the degree received by nineteenth-century Vanderbilt law graduates varied. It was referred to originally as "Bachelor of Laws" (*see, e.g.*, ANNOUNCEMENT OF VANDERBILT UNIVERSITY, FIRST SESSION, 1875–6, *supra* note 9, at 37; ANNOUNCEMENT OF VANDERBILT UNIVERSITY 1876–7, *supra* note 13, at 52), then as "Bachelor of Law" (*see, e.g.*, REGISTER 1876–77, *supra* note 15, at 27, 30, 56; REGISTER 1880–81, *supra* note 116, at 60), and later as "Bachelor of Laws" again (*see, e.g.*, REGISTER 1888–89, *supra* note 157, at 65; REGISTER 1897–98, *supra* note 246, at 90, 141). The abbreviation used in certain early public announcements was B.L. (*see, e.g.*, REGISTER 1876–77, *supra* note 15, at 27; REGISTER 1880–81, *supra* note 116, at 28), but a later announcement used LL.B. (*see* REGISTER 1898–99, *supra* note 212, at 89), as did Chancellor Garland at one point early on (*see* 1 VU:BOTM, *supra* note 15, pt.1, at 68 (June 17, 1876) ("L. L. B.")). All these terms were essentially interchangeable and simply reflected variations common in the academic community. *See* REED, *supra* note 26, at 169 (discussing nature of the bachelor of laws degree, commonly known as LL.B. degree).

307. *See* Riley, *supra* note 6, at 10; Fligeltaub, *supra* note 6, at 7, 13–15.

308. *See, e.g.*, REGISTER 1876–77, *supra* note 15, at 56 ("In exceptional cases the degree may be fairly won in a single year."); REGISTER 1887–88, *supra* note 157, at 74 (noting that "a student may . . . graduate[ ] in one year"); REGISTER 1891–92, *supra* note 176, at 59–60; *Vanderbilt University! Law Department*, REPUBLICAN BANNER, Aug. 19, 1874, at 3 (advertisement recognizing early graduation provided the students' "previous reading will justify it").

309. *See supra* notes 113–16 and accompanying text.

310. CONKIN, *supra* note 8, at 120, 122; MERRIAM, *supra* note 60, at 130; REGISTER 1887–88, *supra* note 157, at 74 (noting that "many have graduated in one year"); *Committee Report for the Eleventh Annual Meeting*, *supra* note 12, at 65; Riley, *supra* note 6, at 10.

311. *See* REGISTER 1887–88, *supra* note 157, at 74; REGISTER 1891–92, *supra* note 176, at 59.

312. Fligeltaub, *supra* note 6, at 15; *see also* Riley, *supra* note 6, at 10; *supra* notes 42–48 and accompanying text.

313. *See* LANGUM & WALTHALL, *supra* note 14, at 103–04 (discussing the enduring nature of Cumberland's one-year law program); Fligeltaub, *supra* note 6, at 15–16; *see also supra* note 48 and sources cited therein (indicating that the diploma privilege may have given Cumberland, with its shorter program, some market advantage over Vanderbilt).

314. 2 VU:BOTM, *supra* note 15, at 122 (June 11, 1891) (noting that the faculty increased the number of scholarships for the senior year from the intended two

to three because of a publishing error which indicated that three scholarships were available); MERRIAM, *supra* note 60, at 130; Untitled draft document, apparently forwarded from Wilbur F. Barclay, Secretary of the Faculty, Vanderbilt Law School to Holland N. McTyeire, President, Board of Trust, Vanderbilt University 4 (undated), J. T. McGill Collection, Box 7, File 113 (on file with Jean and Alexander Heard Library, Vanderbilt University) [hereinafter Untitled Draft Document].

The number of Senior Scholarships was soon reduced to two. *See, e.g.*, REGISTER 1891–92, *supra* note 176, at 61; REGISTER 1892–93, *supra* note 199, at 61. Still another reduction was planned. In 1893, the law faculty decided to begin awarding only one Senior Scholarship. 2 VU:BOTM, *supra* note 15, at 283 (June 18, 1894) (noting that the information in the announcement needed to be amended). The members of the law faculty apparently changed their minds about reducing the Senior Scholarships to one; subsequent Law School announcements continued to declare that two Senior Scholarships would be granted. *See, e.g.*, REGISTER 1893–94, *supra* note 166, at 75; REGISTER 1895–96, *supra* note 246, at 79; REGISTER 1899–1900, *supra* note 17, at 99–100.

315. REGISTER 1891–92, *supra* note 176, at 59–60; Fligeltaub, *supra* note 6, at 14.

316. *See* REGISTER 1892–93, *supra* note 199, at 59 (allowing transfer students to satisfy one year of this requirement at another law school); 2 VU:BOTM, *supra* note 15, at 221 (June 19, 1893); 2 *id.* at 270 (June 18, 1894); Riley, *supra* note 6, at 10; Fligeltaub, *supra* note 6, at 14; Law School Curriculum, *supra* note 49, at 6.

317. 2 VU:BOTM, *supra* note 15, at 221 (June 19, 1893) (Dean Malone reporting that the law faculty expected that a firm two-year program would "seriously affect our numbers"); 2 *id.* at 270 (June 18, 1894) (Chancellor Kirkland noting that "diminution of the number of students was to be expected"); *see also* 3 *id.* at 11 (June 17, 1895) (Chancellor Kirkland expressing the desire to substantially increase the size of the Law School student body and noting: "Our Law School suffers somewhat by reason of the fact that other schools with which we compete still graduate students after only one year's study."); 3 *id.* at 201 (June 13, 1898) (Chancellor Kirkland opining that the existence of one-year law programs at rival institutions may have had a negative impact on the size of enrollments at Vanderbilt Law School); Fligeltaub, *supra* note 6, at 14–16.

318. *See* 2 VU:BOTM, *supra* note 15, at 270 (June 18, 1894); *School of Law*, VAND. ALUMNUS, Dec. 1935, at 6, 6 (charting Law School enrollment figures); *see also infra* notes 362–78 and accompanying figure and text (analyzing the issue of the size of Law School enrollments in the nineteenth century).

319. *See* 3 VU:BOTM, *supra* note 15, at 201 (June 13, 1898).

320. *See* PROFESSIONAL EDUCATION, *supra* note 42, at 155; REED, *supra* note 26, at 171.

321. *See* PROFESSIONAL EDUCATION, *supra* note 42, at 155; REED, *supra* note 26, at 171, 181–78; Huffcut, *supra* note 239, at 408 (noting that Southern law schools lagged behind the trend to increase the duration of the academic program to three years).

322. *See supra* notes 309–16 and accompanying text (discussing the law faculty's consideration of the length of the academic program).

323. *See* 3 VU:BOTM, *supra* note 15, at 201 (June 13, 1898).

324. *See* Riley, *supra* note 6, at 10.

325. Announcement of Vanderbilt University, First Session, 1875–6, *supra* note 9, at 38 ("The true object of education is not so much to fill the memory with particulars as to prepare the mind for their reception."); Announcement of Vanderbilt University 1876–7, *supra* note 13, at 52.

326. *See* Riley, *supra* note 6, at 10 (noting that this orientation "differentiated the School immediately from state institutions being established during the same period").

327. Announcement of Vanderbilt University, First Session, 1875–6, *supra* note 9, at 38–39; Announcement of Vanderbilt University 1876–7, *supra* note 13, at 52.

    Apparently, interdisciplinary work could be arranged at Vanderbilt Law School during the nineteenth century. The Law School enrolled its first joint degree candidate in 1875. Charles Pinckney Wofford of Spartanburg, South Carolina, was registered in the Law School and also in the academic department to study Latin, then geology and natural history. *See* Announcement of Vanderbilt University 1876–7, *supra* note 13, at 9, 15; Register 1876–77, *supra* note 15, at 9, 16. Wofford graduated from the Law School in 1877. Register 1877–78, *supra* note 16, at 18, 21.

328. Announcement of Vanderbilt University, First Session, 1875–6, *supra* note 9, at 38; Announcement of Vanderbilt University 1876–7, *supra* note 13, at 52.

329. *See* Announcement of Vanderbilt University, First Session, 1875–6, *supra* note 9, at 37–38; Announcement of Vanderbilt University 1876–7, *supra* note 13, at 51–52; Register 1899–1900, *supra* note 17, at 98–99. *See generally* Fligeltaub, *supra* note 6, at 24–29 (discussing the nature of the Law School curriculum during this period).

330. Register 1877–78, *supra* note 16, at 56; Register 1882–83, *supra* note 45, at 61. Later, students were required to meet the seventy-five percent standard with respect to "written examinations" or "written examinations and recitations." *See* Register 1883–84, *supra* note 157, at 62 ("written examinations"); Register 1898–99, *supra* note 212, at 91 ("written examinations and recitations").

    After a period of specifically requiring written course examinations (*see, e.g.,* Register 1883–84, *supra* note 157, at 62; Register 1888–89, *supra* note 157, at 64), the Law School, beginning in 1891, permitted oral as well as written course examinations (*see, e.g.,* Register 1890–91, *supra* note 96, at 64–65; Register 1899–1900, *supra* note 17, at 99). This policy continued until the law faculty announced a return to only written course examinations in 1901. *See* Register of Vanderbilt University 1900–1901/Announcement 1901–1902 at 102 (1901) [hereinafter Register 1900–01]; *see also* Fligeltaub, *supra* note 6, at 7–9.

331. REGISTER 1876–77, *supra* note 15, at 56; REGISTER 1899–1900, *supra* note 17, at 99 ("daily recitation").

332. *See* Riley, *supra* note 6, at 10.

333. *E.g.*, REGISTER 1876–77, *supra* note 15, at 56; REGISTER 1882–83, *supra* note 41, at 61.

334. REGISTER 1883–84, *supra* note 157, at 61.

335. *See supra* notes 44–48 and accompanying text (discussing the diploma privilege).

336. *See, e.g.*, REGISTER 1876–77, *supra* note 15, at 56–57; REGISTER 1882–83, *supra* note 45, at 61–62; *see also* Riley, *supra* note 6, at 10; Fligeltaub, *supra* note 6, at 11.

337. The new statement simply read, "The Faculty are empowered by statute to grant License to practice law in any of the courts of the State of Tennessee." REGISTER 1883–84, *supra* note 157, at 62. Eventually certain Vanderbilt faculty members assumed prominent positions in the public campaign to eliminate the diploma privilege. *See supra* note 48 and accompanying text.

338. *See, e.g.*, REGISTER 1876–77, *supra* note 15, at 56; REGISTER 1882–83, *supra* note 45, at 61.

339. *See, e.g.*, REGISTER 1876–77, *supra* note 15, at 57; REGISTER 1882–83, *supra* note 45, at 62; *see also* Fligeltaub, *supra* note 6, at 27–29 (commenting on the course materials used at Vanderbilt Law School).

340. *See* FRIEDMAN, *supra* note 23, at 610–11; HALL, *supra* note 22, at 219; Fligeltaub, *supra* note 6, at 20.

341. REGISTER 1876–77, *supra* note 15, at 56 (noting that moot court received "[v]ery great attention"); REGISTER 1882–83, *supra* note 45, at 61 (stating moot court received "[e]special attention").

342. *See, e.g.*, REGISTER 1876–77, *supra* note 15, at 56; REGISTER 1882–83, *supra* note 41, at 61.

343. *See* Fligeltaub, *supra* note 6, at 22–24 (describing moot court instruction); Untitled draft document, *supra* note 318, at 3 ("The most marked improvement in methods of instruction has been in the increased attention given to the Moot Court. . . . It is believed that at no other law school in the world is such attention given to the practical preparation of the students for the trying duties of the court room."); *see also supra* notes 275–77 and accompanying text (discussing moot court performance at graduation).

344. *See, e.g.,* REGISTER 1887–88, *supra* note 157, at 75; REGISTER 1891–92, *supra* note 176, at 60.

345. *See* discussion *supra* The "Lessees" section and Changes in Composition of Faculty section.

346. *See* MERRIAM, *supra* note 60, at 120; Riley, *supra* note 6, at 9.

347. ANNOUNCEMENT OF VANDERBILT UNIVERSITY, FIRST SESSION, 1875–6, *supra* note 9, at 39.

348. Fligeltaub, *supra* note 6, at 18–20; Law Department, *supra* note 105, at 8.

349. *See* FRIEDMAN, *supra* note 23, at 612–18; HALL, *supra* note 22, at 219–21; STEVENS, *supra* note 22, at 52–64. *See generally* WILLIAM P. LaPIANA, LOGIC AND

EXPERIENCE: THE ORIGIN OF MODERN AMERICAN LEGAL EDUCATION (1994) (analyzing the development and impact of the case method).

350. *See, e.g.,* REGISTER 1895–96, *supra* note 246, at 77; REGISTER 1898–99, *supra* note 212, at 90.

351. REGISTER 1887–88, *supra* note 157, at 77; REGISTER 1888–89, *supra* note 157, at 66; REGISTER 1889–90, *supra* note 163, at 61; REGISTER 1890–91, *supra* note 96, at 66.

352. *See* REGISTER 1887–88, *supra* note 157, at 77; REGISTER 1888–89, *supra* note 157, at 66; REGISTER 1889–90, *supra* note 163, at 61; REGISTER 1890–91, *supra* note 96, at 66.

353. *See* Riley, *supra* note 6, at 13; Fligeltaub, *supra* note 6, at 4, 40–41; Law School Administration: Deans, *supra* note 85, at eighth through ninth unnumbered pages.

354. *See generally* discussion *supra* The "Lease" section.

355. 1 VU:BOTM, *supra* note 15, pt. 1, at 61–62 (May 25, 1875). *See generally supra* notes 137–36 and accompanying text (discussing lease provisions).

356. 1 VU:BOTM, *supra* note 15, pt. 1, at 61 (May 25, 1875).

357. *See* Fligeltaub, *supra* note 6, at 33 (noting that the law faculty "suffered with nominal remuneration" and pointing out that they personally financed certain library acquisitions and student scholarships); Hood, *supra* note 188, at 52–53 ("One may assume that the professors of that period were not getting rich from their teaching."); Hood, *supra* note 137, at 5–7 (estimating mean annual Law School income in the nineteenth century at "more than $4,000," but recognizing that it "may have been less" because of unpaid student debt). The dip in enrollment to thirty in the 1893–94 academic year prompted Chancellor Kirkland to report that "[t]hese gentlemen [the lessees] do not now realize as much from fees as was guaranteed them by the University during the first three years of the operation of the department. . . ." 2 VU:BOTM, *supra* note 15, at 270 (June 18, 1894).

358. The following figure is derived from statistics presented in *School of Law*, 21 VAND. ALUMNUS, Dec. 1935, at 6, and confirmed by examination of data contained in University catalogues issued from ANNOUNCEMENT OF VANDERBILT UNIVERSITY 1876–7 (1876) through REGISTER 1899–1900, *supra* note 17. Enrollment in the Law School's opening academic year (1874–75) is discussed *supra* notes 103–6 and accompanying text.

359. Reported enrollments in those years were twenty-five, twenty-six, and thirty-one. Tuition charges were $120 the first two years and $80 the third year. *See supra* notes 13–15 and accompanying text.

360. *See supra* notes 16–18 and accompanying text (discussing tuition).

361. *See generally* Hood, *supra* note 137, at 1–8 (discussing the financing of Vanderbilt Law School operations in the nineteenth century).

362. 1 VU:BOTM, *supra* note 15, pt. 1, at 160 (May 27, 1879).

363. 1 *id.*

364. Vanderbilt Law School charged $100 annual tuition beginning in 1878 and continued doing so over the rest of the nineteenth century. *See supra* notes 16–17 and accompanying text.

365. *See, e.g.,* Announcement of Vanderbilt University, First Session, 1875–6, *supra* note 9, at 39; Register 1878–79, *supra* note 17, at 65.

366. 1 VU:BOTM, *supra* note 15, pt. 1, at 103 (June 18, 1877).

367. Law student obligations might have taken forms other than for unpaid tuition. At some point the University created a Sustentation Fund from which loans were made to students. *See* 1 *id.* pt. 2, at 606 (June 20, 1888).

368. 1 *id.* pt. 1, at 160 (May 27, 1879).

369. 1 *id.* pt. 2, at 650 (May 17, 1889); *see also* 2 *id.* at 44 (June 16, 1890) (listing "Law Dept. Bills Receivable—Notes of students [$]575" in "Resources" category of "Bursar's Statement").

370. *See* Fligeltaub, *supra* note 6, at 33.

371. *See, e.g.,* Announcement of Vanderbilt University, First Session, 1875–6, at 18–19 (1875) ("Ministers of the gospel . . . will be admitted to . . . the Academic and Biblical Departments free of tuition fees."); 1 VU:BOTM, *supra* note 15, pt. 1, at 103 (June 18, 1877) (noting that in the 1876–77 school year eighty individuals, which "included theological Students, the sons of Ministers . . . , and worthy but indigent young men," attended Vanderbilt without paying tuition); Register 1877–78, *supra* note 16, at 47 (describing Teachers' Scholarships to "non-professional Schools of the University" and Endowed Scholarships for a few students); *Educational*, Christian Advoc., July 17, 1880, at 16 (Vanderbilt advertisement proclaiming, "Six Scholarships . . . are annually awarded to successful undergraduates.").

372. *See supra* note 318 and accompanying text (discussing Senior Scholarship program).

373. In the Law School's initial year of operation under the lease, law students were allowed to pay a pro rata share of tuition for attending a portion of a semester. But the Law School also announced that "no part of [tuition] . . . will be refunded on any account." Announcement of Vanderbilt University, First Session, 1875–6 at 39 (1875). These provisions do not appear in subsequent early announcements. *See, e.g.,* Announcement of Vanderbilt University 1876–7, at 53 (1876); Register 1878–79, *supra* note 17, at 65.

374. *See* Register 1878–79, *supra* note 17, at 65 (stating that tuition for the full nine-month academic year was $100 and that tuition for each semester was $50).

375. *See* 1 VU:BOTM, *supra* note 15, pt. 1, at 160 (May 27, 1879) (stating that $180 of $2,171.50 paid by the "Law Class of the present year" was refunded "by authority of the Dean of the Law Faculty and on the Chancellor's warrants").

376. *See* Fligeltaub, *supra* note 2, at 12 (revised version on file with authors).

377. This modest growth can be contrasted with the marked increase in law school enrollments nationally during this period. The number of students enrolled in law schools increased from 3,134 in 1880 to 12,516 in 1900, and the average law

school size grew from 61 to 123 students. *See* Reed, *supra* note 26, at 198–99, 443–44.

378. *See* 3 VU:BOTM, *supra* note 15, at 11 (June 17, 1895) (Chancellor Kirkland stating his desire to substantially increase the size of the Law School student body); 3 *id.* at 201 (June 13, 1898) (Chancellor Kirkland discussing enrollments at Vanderbilt Law School and expressing "hope" that the increase in law faculty size "will cause an increase in attendance in this department"); *infra* text accompanying notes 445–47; Fligeltaub, *supra* note 6, at 7.

379. *See* Law Department, *supra* note 105, at 6; H. A. Hood, Law Sch.–Admin.– Physical Plant 1–6 (1973), Centennial History Project, Box 25 (unpublished First Draft (Corrected) on file with Jean and Alexander Heard Library, Vanderbilt University and with Vanderbilt Law School in Howard A. Hood, Law School History Drafts of Centennial History Project).

380. *Vanderbilt University: Opening of the Law and Medical Departments*, Republican Banner, Oct. 4, 1874, at 4; Law Department, *supra* note 105, at 6; *see supra* notes 104–01 and accompanying text.

381. Law Department, *supra* note 105, at 6 (undated); Hood, *supra* note 383, at 1–2 (noting that the lease required the University to provide facilities for the Law School). *See generally supra* notes 137–36 and accompanying text (discussing lease provisions).

382. Conkin, *supra* note 8, at 55; Law Department, *supra* note 105, at 6. "Main" is currently named "Kirkland Hall." Conkin, *supra* note 8, at 19, 411.

383. *See* 1 VU:BOTM, *supra* note 15, pt. 1, at 232 (May 27, 1880).

384. *See* Law Department, *supra* note 105, at 6 (stating that the Law School gained additional space in Main in 1878).

385. *See* 1 VU:BOTM, *supra* note 15, pt. 2, at 473–74 (June 15, 1886) (regarding the need for additional book space).

386. *See* Hood, *supra* note 383, at 3–4.

387. Conkin, *supra* note 8, at 110 (stating that the structure was located "on Cherry Street (presently Fourth Avenue")); *see also* Laska, *supra* note 19, at 515 (noting that the building was situated "at 311–313 Fourth Avenue North").

388. *See* Conkin, *supra* note 8, at 110, 120–21, 202; *see also* History of Nashville, Tenn., *supra* note 8, at 421.

389. *See* Conkin, *supra* note 8, at 120.

390. *See id.* at 202; Mims, *supra* note 7, at 208, 214; Hood, *supra* note 383, at 4–5; 1 VU:BOTM, *supra* note 15, pt. 2, at 675 (Aug. 2, 1889).

391. Conkin, *supra* note 8, at 202, Riley, *supra* note 6, at 10–11; Hood, *supra* note 383, at 5–7.

392. 1 VU:BOTM, *supra* note 15, pt. 2, at 675 (Aug. 2, 1889).

393. Conkin, *supra* note 8, at 110, 202; Laska, *supra* note 19, at 515.

394. Register 1889–90, *supra* note 163, at 61 (proclaiming that the "building is one of the handsomest in the city" and emphasizing its convenient location); Conkin, *supra* note 8, at 120; Merriam, *supra* note 60, at 130.

395. CONKIN, *supra* note 8, at 120.

396. 3 VU:BOTM, *supra* note 15, at 71 (June 15, 1896).

397. 3 *id.* at 105.

398. 3 *id.* at 71.

399. 3 *id.* at 143 (June 14, 1897).

400. 3 *id.*; *see also* REGISTER 1896–97, *supra* note 246, at 79 (stating that a deposit was required at enrollment and providing for refund of "[t]he whole of this deposit, or any unexpended part" at graduation).

401. CONKIN, *supra* note 8, at 55.

     The Law School's initial catalogue indicates that space in Main had been allocated for a law library. ANNOUNCEMENT OF VANDERBILT UNIVERSITY, FIRST SESSION, 1875–6, *supra* note 9, at 39. But this and the next Law School catalogue spoke in aspirational terms, referring to "a selection of ordinary Text-books *to be* attached to the School." *Id.* at 37–38 (emphasis added); ANNOUNCEMENT OF VANDERBILT UNIVERSITY 1876–7, *supra* note 13, at 51.

402. *Vanderbilt Library,* AMERICAN, Oct. 21, 1875, at 4 (noting "[h]andsome donations" of legal material to "Library of Vanderbilt University"—"seven volumes" plus a single "work"); *A Munificent Gift,* CHRISTIAN ADVOC., Oct. 30, 1875, at 8 (reporting the contribution of "seven volumes" to "the Library of the Law Department of the Vanderbilt University").

403. ANNOUNCEMENT OF VANDERBILT UNIVERSITY, FIRST SESSION, 1875–6, *supra* note 9, at 38.

404. REGISTER 1876–77, *supra* note 15, at 57.

405. 1 VU:BOTM, *supra* note 15, pt. 1, at 232 (May 27, 1880) (noting that the law faculty advised the Board that implementation of this plan would create the need for shelving space).

406. 1 *id.* pt. 2, at 473–74 (June 15, 1886).

407. 1 *id.* at 474 (two individuals donated a total of approximately one hundred books).

408. *See* CONKIN, *supra* note 8, at 120; Fligeltaub, *supra* note 6, at 34 (opining that the Law School's legal "sources were not only limited but also random"); Untitled Draft Document, *supra* note 318, at 1 (reporting that the Law School's "library consisted of broken sets of the U.S. Supreme Court Reports, Tennessee Reports, Bacon's Abridgement, and a few old text books").

409. 1 VU:BOTM, *supra* note 15, pt. 2, at 675 (Aug. 2, 1889).

410. Later the law library was allocated even larger space in the Law and Dental Building. *See* 3 *id.* at 143 (June 14, 1897) (noting that the law library was moved to "more ample accommodations" on a different floor).

411. *See* Untitled Draft Document, *supra* note 318, at 1.

412. 1 VU:BOTM, *supra* note 15, pt. 2, at 670 (June 17, 1889). A Board committee studying this matter issued a report favorable to the Law School's request. *See* 1 *id.* at 673–74 (concluding that (1) "[t]he presence of a good Law library in the building would add very greatly to the desirability of the offices which are for

rent," (2) "a large number of books will be given to the University by its friends, if a suitable library and competent librarian are provided," and (3) "[a] large number of books will also be loaned to the library by attorneys").

Those leasing space in the Law and Dental Building could use the law library free of charge, but nonoccupant users were required to pay an annual fee. REGISTER 1891–92, *supra* note 176, at 62.

413. 1 VU:BOTM, *supra* note 15, pt. 2, at 670 (June 17, 1889). The enrollment did not double. It did jump from thirty-seven in 1888–89 to fifty the following year, but then declined each of the next four years to thirty students in 1893–94. *See supra* note 362 and accompanying figure.

414. 1 VU:BOTM, *supra* note 15, pt. 2, at 675–76 (Aug. 2, 1889). *See generally* Fligeltaub, *supra* note 6, at 38–39 (discussing the law librarian's job).

415. 1 VU:BOTM, *supra* note 15, pt. 2, at 676 (Aug. 2, 1889) (specifying that, as Law School secretary, the law librarian was responsible for managing "the matriculation of law students, and shall receive and receipt for . . . all tuition and other fees due from them").

416. REGISTER 1888–89, *supra* note 157, at 5 (listing Barclay as a member of the Board of Trust); 1 VU:BOTM, *supra* note 15, pt. 2, at 617 (May 7, 1889) (identifying Barclay as a Board member present); 2 *id.* at 56 (June 17, 1890) (noting Barclay's resignation from the Board).

417. 1 VU:BOTM, *supra* note 15, pt. 2, at 677 (Aug. 5, 1889). In late 1892, Barclay stepped down as law librarian and was succeeded by Annie Warren. At that juncture, the Board placed "oversight" of the Law and Dental Building in the hands of outside managers, directed the University bursar to handle law student tuition payments, and decreased the law librarian's yearly salary to $300. The expectation was that Warren would be able to earn substantial supplemental income by providing stenographic services to lawyers and others who rented office space on the premises. *See* 2 *id.* at 205 (Sept. 21, 1892); 3 *id.* at 72 (June 15, 1896); 3 *id.* at 143 (June 14, 1897) (noting that the law librarian's annual salary had been raised to $400).

418. 2 *id.* at 55 (June 17, 1890) (Barclay's report as law librarian).

419. 2 *id.* (noting that "Godfrey M. Fogg, Esq., gave us the valuable library bequeathed him by his distinguished uncle, the late Francis B. Fogg"); REGISTER 1890–91, *supra* note 96, at 65; REGISTER 1891–92, *supra* note 176, at 61; CONKIN, *supra* note 8, at 120.

420. 2 VU:BOTM, *supra* note 15, at 55 (June 17, 1890) (Barclay's report as law librarian); REGISTER 1890–91, *supra* note 96, at 65–66; REGISTER 1891–92, *supra* note 176, at 61; CONKIN, *supra* note 8, at 120; Untitled Draft Document, *supra* note 318, at 1–2.

421. 2 VU:BOTM, *supra* note 15, at 121 (June 11, 1891) (reporting that Dean Malone estimated the value of the law library holdings at "perhaps $14,000"); REGISTER 1890–91, *supra* note 96, at 65; CONKIN, *supra* note 8, at 120; *see also* Untitled Draft Document, *supra* note 318, at 2–3 (describing the Cooper acquisition).

422. REGISTER 1899–1900, *supra* note 17, at 100; *see also* REGISTER 1900–01, *supra* note 334, at 103 (describing the contents of the law library).

423. *See* Fligeltaub, *supra* note 6, at 35–38 (discussing law library finances).

424. *Id.* at 35.

425. 2 VU:BOTM, *supra* note 15, at 49 (June 16, 1890) (Law School proposal); 2 *id.* at 55–56 (June 17, 1890) (Barclay report supporting the Law School proposal and emphasizing the importance of "a complete law library" to remain competitive for "first class tenants"); 2 *id.* at 56 (Board of Trust action).

426. *See supra* notes 418, 423 and accompanying text.

427. *See* 1 VU:BOTM, *supra* note 15, pt. 2, at 678 (Oct. 18, 1889).

428. *See* 2 *id.* at 150 (June 13, 1892) ("Statement of Vanderbilt Endowment Re-investment Fund Account"); 2 *id.* at 188–89 (containing the committee's expression of dissatisfaction with the arrangement and its opinion that "the Law Faculty will be slow to pay this debt and perhaps in the end all we will have to show for the $2000.00 will be the books themselves").

429. 2 *id.* at 270–71 (June 18, 1894) (Kirkland also discussed other pertinent factors, noting that Dean Malone was absent when the arrangement was made and that any agreement entered by the law faculty "must certainly have been limited to the term of their lease.").

430. *See* 4 *id.* at 50–51 (June 17, 1901) (including a comment by Chancellor Kirkland that "the entry as it is on our books is purely fictitious"); 4 *id.* at 59 (June 18, 1901) (directing that the listing be moved to the "equipment" category).

431. 2 *id.* at 121 (June 11, 1891) (noting that Cooper's library had an estimated value of $7,000).

432. 2 *id.* at 222 (June 19, 1893).

433. *See* 3 *id.* at 11 (June 17, 1895).

434. *See supra* notes 129–30 and accompanying text.

435. *See* CONKIN, *supra* note 8, at 122 (discussing objectives that Kirkland achieved by the 1900 Law School restructuring).

436. 3 VU:BOTM, *supra* note 15, at 201–02 (June 13, 1898). Kirkland added that in the event the Board should decide differently and choose to enter another law school lease arrangement, "it will be much easier to make a favorable contract for leasing a successful department than one which is comparatively weak." 3 *id.* at 202.

437. 3 *id.* at 249 (June 19, 1899).

438. *See* 1 *id.* pt. 1, at 61 (May 25, 1875); *supra* notes 137–36 and accompanying text (discussing lease provisions).

439. *See supra* notes 416–17 and accompanying text (discussing law librarian).

440. *See* discussion of lease provisions *supra* The "Lease" section; discussion of Law School financial situation *supra Finances* subsection in Infrastructure section.

441. *See supra* notes 362–78 and accompanying figure and text (analyzing enrollment data).

442. 3 VU:BOTM, *supra* note 15, at 71 (June 15, 1896).

443. 3 *id.* at 201 (June 13, 1898).

444. 3 *id.* at 249 (June 19, 1899). Kirkland opined that the size of Vanderbilt Law School's student body was adversely affected by the existence of the diploma privilege in Tennessee which, in his view, "puts a premium on cheap schools with short courses and lax requirements, and makes it hard for such departments as our own to secure the pre-eminence they deserve." 3 *id.* For discussion of the diploma privilege, see *supra* notes 44–48 and accompanying text.

445. *See supra* figure and text accompanying notes 362–78.

446. 3 VU:BOTM, *supra* note 15, at 293, 312 (June 18, 1900); *see also supra* figure accompanying note 362.

447. 3 VU:BOTM, *supra* note 15, at 313 (June 18, 1900).

448. *See* REED, *supra* note 26, at 184–87 (discussing the trend among universities to assert greater authority over their law schools). *See generally* Bartholomew, *supra* note 82.

449. *See* 3 VU:BOTM, *supra* note 15, at 202 (June 13, 1898); 3 *id.* at 249 (June 19, 1899).

450. *See* CONKIN, *supra* note 8, at 120, 122; *supra* notes 422, 430–33 and accompanying text.

451. *See* 3 VU:BOTM, *supra* note 15, at 312–15 (June 18, 1900); 3 *id.* at 350, 352 (June 19, 1900); 4 *id.* at 1 (June 26, 1900) (listing law faculty appointments and their compensation).

452. 3 *id.* at 313 (June 18, 1900).

453. 3 *id.*

454. CONKIN, *supra* note 8, at 122; *see also* Holladay, *supra* note 51, at 14.

455. *See* Kirkland, *supra* note 74, at 95; *supra* notes 184–85 and accompanying text (discussing Malone's and other lessees' accomplishments in legal education).

456. *See* 3 VU:BOTM, *supra* note 15, at 313–15 (June 18, 1900) (setting forth the reorganization scheme); 4 *id.* at 1 (June 26, 1900) (listing law faculty appointments and their compensation). For discussion of the "reorganization," see CONKIN, *supra* note 8, at 122; MIMS, *supra* note 7, at 214; Laska, supra note 19, at 519–22.

457. 3 VU:BOTM, *supra* note 15, at 313 (June 18, 1900); *see also* CONKIN, *supra* note 8, at 122.

458. 3 VU:BOTM, *supra* note 15, at 313 (June 18, 1900). John Bell Keeble was named to this position. 4 *id.* at 1 (June 26, 1900). For discussion of Keeble, see *supra* note 226 and accompanying text.

459. 3 VU:BOTM, *supra* note 15, at 313 (June 18, 1900) (observing "perhaps it would be better to provide 12 hours"); *see also* 4 *id.* at 1 (June 26, 1900) (listing class hours to be taught by each law faculty member); REGISTER 1900–01, *supra* note 334, at 100 (stating that "[e]ach class attends two lectures five days in the week").

460. *See* 3 VU:BOTM, *supra* note 15, at 315 (June 18, 1900); REGISTER 1900–01, *supra* note 334, at 100 (noting that "on Saturday both classes meet in the moot court").

461. *See* 3 VU:BOTM, *supra* note 15, at 313 (June 18, 1900).

462. 3 *id.*

463. 3 *id.*

464. 3 *id.* at 314–15; Conkin, *supra* note 8, at 122–23.

465. *See* 4 VU:BOTM, *supra* note 15, at 1 (June 26, 1900) (naming the law faculty, establishing a Law School faculty salary scale which was inapplicable to Lurton who had a "special arrangement" regarding salary, and setting the salary for each faculty member); Register 1900–01, *supra* note 334, at 101; *supra* notes 223–29 and accompanying text (discussing members of the expanded faculty and their salaries).

466. Conkin, *supra* note 8, at 122; Hood, *supra* note 137, at 8.

467. 3 VU:BOTM, *supra* note 15, at 315 (June 18, 1900).

468. 4 *id.* at 1 (June 26, 1900) (noting that Judge Lurton was not covered by either the Law School faculty salary scale or the salary bonus scheme given his "special arrangement"); *see also* 3 *id.* at 315 (June 18, 1900) (excluding Lurton from salary bonus scheme).

469. Kirkland, *supra* note 74, at 94–95.

470. Kirkland spoke of the law faculty's "twenty-five years of splendid achievement" rendered "with sublime indifference to their own personal advantage." *Id.* at 95; *see also* 3 VU:BOTM, *supra* note 15, at 313 (June 18, 1900) (Kirkland observing that "work done by the Law faculty has always been of a high and thorough character" and noting that the law professors "have seemed at all times indifferent to the question of their own remuneration" in developing "a very worthy department of instruction").

CHAPTER TWO

1. The nomenclature "Law School" will be used throughout this chapter. On June 15, 1915, the Board of Trust approved a change in terminology, so that the Law Department would thereafter be designated the "School of Law," and the academic or literary department was to be known as the College of Arts and Science. Vanderbilt Board of Trust Minutes, VII, June 15, 1915, p. 225 (hereafter BOT Minutes). On June 9, 1999, the Board approved a change in the official name from Vanderbilt University School of Law to Vanderbilt University Law School. BOT Minutes, CVII, June 9, 1999, p. 8.

2. Robert A. McGaw and Reba Wilcoxon, *A Brief History of Vanderbilt University* (Nashville: Vanderbilt University, 1983), p. 25. Phi Beta Kappa chartered its Vanderbilt chapter in 1901.

3. J.H. Kirkland, "Twenty-five Years of University Work," *Vanderbilt University Quarterly*, I, no. 1 (March 1901), p. 95. Address delivered at the Twenty-Fifth Anniversary Celebration of Vanderbilt University.

4. Paul Conkin, *Gone with the Ivy* (Knoxville: University of Tennessee Press, 1985), p. 122.

5.   Conkin, *Gone with the Ivy*, p. 122; BOT Minutes, V, June 16, 1902, p. 91.

6.   BOT Minutes, V, June 13, 1094, pp. 177–78.

7.   Thomas S. Weaver, "Thomas H. Malone, M.A.," *Vanderbilt University Quarterly*, 7 (April 1907), p. 104, (quoting an unnamed former student who responded to Weaver's request to give his impression of Malone).

8.   Horace Lurton to James Kirkland, September 23, 1904. Copies of all correspondence referenced are on file with the author and, unless otherwise noted, are in the Special Collections of the Jean and Alexander Heard Library, Vanderbilt University, Nashville, Tennessee.

9.   Horace Lurton to James Kirkland, October 7, 1904.

10.   John Bell Keeble, "The Law School and Some Men Who Have Helped Make It," *The Vanderbilt Alumnus,* 3, no. 7 (May 1918), p. 201.

11.   Minutes of the Law School Faculty Meetings, Dean's Office, Vanderbilt University Law School (Nashville, Tennessee) (hereafter Faculty Meeting Minutes).

12.   BOT Minutes, VI, June 17, 1907, p. 20.

13.   BOT Minutes, VI, June 13, 1910, p.156.

14.   BOT Minutes, V, June 15, 1903, p.138.

15.   BOT Minutes, V, June 19, 1903, p. 163; BOT Minutes, IV, April 4, 1904, p. 167.

16.   BOT Minutes, VI, June 17, 1907, p. 20.

17.   Bruce A. Kimball, "The Principle, Politics and Finances of Introducing Academic Merit as the Standard of Hiring for 'the teaching of law *as a career*,' 1870–1900," *Law & Social Inquiry*, 31, no. 3 (Summer 2006), p. 621.

18.   BOT Minutes, VI, June 13, 1910, pp. 156–57.

19.   James H. Kirkland, "Vanderbilt University School of Law: Its Accomplishments and Needs," undated. (On file with author, and in Special Collections, Jean and Alexander Heard Library, Vanderbilt University). The move to the main campus was not actually completed until two months after Hall's death.

20.   James H. Kirkland to Allen G. Hall, memorandum, June 21, 1907. At the time, Hall expressed his disappointment that he had not yet been able to establish an LL.M. degree program as he had hoped. Hall to Kirkland, June 4, 1907.

21.   Allen G. Hall to James H. Kirkland, March 8, 1909, and June 5, 1909.

22.   Allen G. Hall to James H. Kirkland, March 8, 1909.

23.   Examples are a March 3, 1910 letter to P. D. Maddin that chronicles his absenteeism, and a May 24, 1913, letter addressed individually to each faculty member. In the May 24th letter, he asked each faculty member to report on the number of cases covered, the assignments requiring work in the library, and the number of cases assigned that were not included in the casebook.

24.   Allen G. Hall letter addressed individually to each Law School faculty member, May 19, 1915.

25.   Allen G. Hall, Dean's Annual Report to the Chancellor, May 24, 1915.

26.   Resolutions Adopted by the Junior Law Class, March 11, 1904 (signed by Frank Kyle, W. Clark Williams, J. Hamilton Brown, and John Bell Tansil).

27. Allen G. Hall, Dean's Annual Report to the Chancellor, 1907/08.

28. Allen G. Hall, Dean's Annual Report to the Chancellor, May 30, 1914.

29. BOT Minutes, VII, September 19, 1914, p. 177.

30. "Dr. Allen G. Hall," *Vanderbilt University Quarterly*, 15 (1915), p. 256.

31. James M. Peden, "The History of Law School Administration," in *The History of Legal Education in the United States: Commentaries and Primary Sources*, II, Steve Sheppard (ed.) (Pasadena, CA: Salem Press, 1999), p. 1109.

32. BOT Minutes, VIII, June 9, 1919, p. 151.

33. Edwin Mims, *History of Vanderbilt University* (Nashville: Vanderbilt University Press, 1946) , pp. 126–27.

34. "Vanderbilt Law School Grows," *The Vanderbilt Alumnus*, VIII, no. 2 (November 1922), p. 44.

35. BOT Minutes, VIII, June 12, 1916, p. 19.

36. John Bell Keeble, Dean's Annual Report to the Chancellor, June 9, 1916.

37. BOT Minutes, VIII, June 9, 1919, p. 151. Vanderbilt historian Paul Conkin commented on Keeble's staying power as Dean: "Keeble was a busy, successful railroad lawyer and thus was unable to provide the supervision needed by the school. Yet he was an eminent, proud, long-term friend of the university; no one dared supplant him." Conkin, p. 261.

38. BOT Minutes, XII, June 7, 1926, p.135.

39. BOT Minutes, V, June 15, 1903, p. 138.

40. Mims, *History of Vanderbilt University*, p. 126.

41. Report of the Twenty-Third Annual Meeting of the American Bar Association, August 29–31, 1900, pp. 569–70. Schools were invited by a committee of the Section on Legal Education of the American Bar Association.

42. Arnold J. Harno, *Legal Education in the United States* (San Francisco: Bancroft-Whitney Co., 1953), p. 90.

43. Proceedings of the Tenth Annual Meeting of the Association of American Law Schools, August 29–30, 1910, p. 41. These initial requirements were: (1) "It shall require of candidates for its degree the completion of a high school course of study, or its equivalent . . . [or] shall be required to pass an examination in studies equivalent to those required of high school graduates . . ." and (2) "The course of study leading to its degree shall cover at least two years of thirty weeks per year . . . *provided*, that after the year 1905, members of this Association shall require a three years' course." Report of the Twenty-Third Annual Meeting of the American Bar Association, August 29–31, 1900, at 572.

44. Vanderbilt had actually been approved for admission by the Executive Committee in 1909, but then had withdrawn its application when it became clear that the School would not yet be in full compliance at the beginning of the 1909/10 academic year.

45. BOT Minutes, VI, June 15, 1908, p. 67.

46. Minutes of the John Marshall Law Club, March 27, 1914.

47. James H. Kirkland to E. E. Barthell, May 5, 1917.

48. James H. Kirkland to E. E. Barthell, May 5, 1927. Kirkland noted that Keeble's remarks were printed in full in the proceedings of the Association, and they "do not create a very good impression." Ibid.

49. Handbook of the Association of American Law Schools and Proceedings of the Twenty-Fourth Annual Meeting, Chicago, December 29–31, 1926, p. 77.

50. BOT Minutes, XIII, June 6, 1927, p. 85 (Kirkland reporting to the Board of Trust).

51. Albert J. Harno to James H. Kirkland, October 26, 1929.

52. Handbook of the Association of American Law Schools and Proceedings of the Twenty-Fourth Annual Meeting, Chicago, December 29–31, 1926, p. 7.

53. Ibid., pp. 79–80.

54. Mark Bartholomew, "Legal Separation: The Relationship Between the Law School and the Central University in the Late Nineteenth Century," *Journal of Legal Education*, 53, no. 3 (September 2003), pp. 388–89.

55. Robert Stevens, *Law School: Legal Education in America from the 1850s to the 1980s* (Chapel Hill: University of North Carolina Press, 1983), pp. 430–31.

56. Report of the President to the Fellows of Yale University, pp. 15, 29 (1902). [quoted in Bartholomew, pp. 390–91] The movement to create higher standards for admission to the bar created divisions in the wider profession. While some practitioners were motivated by a commitment to an ethical, educated bar, others were motivated by an interest in reducing competition, or by desires to exclude Jews, African-Americans, recent immigrants, and women. Stephen M. Feldman, "The Transformation of an Academic Discipline: Law Professors in the Past and Future (or Toy Story Two)," *Journal of Legal Education*, 54, no. 4 (December 2004), p. 481; Robert Boking Stevens, *Law School: Legal Education in America from the 1850s to the 1980s* (Chapel Hill: University of North Carolina Press, 1983), pp. 92–111.

57. Bartholomew, "Legal Separation," pp. 389, 391–2.

58. BOT Minutes, VI, July 23, 1907, p. 45. The 1908/09 Law School catalogue specified that the examination would be tied to the level of the Fogg High School in Nashville. (p. 15).

   The term Law School catalogue is used as shorthand for the annual publication which has existed throughout the School's history, but with periodic changes in title.

59. BOT Minutes, VII, June 15, 1914, pp. 149–50; BOT Minutes, VII, June 14, 1915, pp. 191–92.

60. AALS Proceedings, pp. 72–74.

61. "School of Law Plans Being Studied," *The Vanderbilt Alumnus*, 12, no. 3 (January 1927), p. 84.

62. Editorial, "School of Law Reinstated," *The Vanderbilt Alumnus*, 15, no. 2 (November–December 1929), p. 27.

63. Mims, *History of Vanderbilt University*, pp. 130–56, 143.

64. BOT Minutes, XIII, June 6, 1927, p. 81.

65. Ibid., p. 87.

66. James H. Kirkland to E. E. Barthell, May 5, 1927.

67. Annual report of the President of the Carnegie Foundation for the Advancement of Teaching, 1919, cited in Beatrice Doerschuk, *Women in the Law: An Analysis of Training, Practice and Salaried Positions,* Bulletin no. 3 (New York: The Bureau of Vocational Information, 1920) p.19. Doerschuk attributes the slow pace in raising standards to "the tradition that it is an inherent right of every citizen to practice law just as it is his right to follow any other calling." p.16.

68. Stevens, *Law School*, p. 173. In 1927, the ABA list of approved schools was "almost identical" with the membership of the AALS. Ibid., p. 174.

69. Stevens, *Law School*, p. 115. Alfred Z. Reed, "Recent Progress in Legal Education," *The American Law School Review*, V, no. 12 (1926), p. 702.

70. "Law Schools Meet Association Standards," *American Bar Association Journal*, 9, no. 11 (November 1923), p. 728.

71. "Additional Law Schools in Class B," *American Bar Association Journal,* 9, no. 12 (December 1923), p. 762.

72. Earl C. Arnold to James H. Kirkland, December 9, 1930.

73. Alfred Z. Reed, *Present-Day Law Schools in the United States and Canada,* Bulletin no. 21, (New York: Carnegie Foundation for the Advancement of Teaching, 1928), pp. 43, 405–513. The other four schools were University of Alabama, Southern Methodist University, University of Denver, and University of Utah.

74. BOT Minutes, XIII, June 6, 1927, p. 85.

75. BOT Minutes, XIII, June 6, 1927, p. 87.

76. Stevens, *Law School*, pp. 173, 182 n. 19.

77. BOT Minutes, XIII, June 6, 1927, p. 89.

78. BOT Minutes, XIII, June 7, 1927, p. 153; BOT Minutes, XIII, June 21, 1927, p. 179.

79. BOT Minutes, XIII, June 11, 1928, p. 267.

80. Ibid.

81. BOT Minutes, XIV, June 10, 1929, p. 223.

82. John Bell Keeble to Schermerhorn, September 21, 1929.

83. Albert J. Harno to James H. Kirkland, October 26, 1929. Harno sent the letter, despite receiving a telegram assuring the executive committee that Kirkland would authorize the required library funds. Schermerhorn to Harno, telegram, October 23, 1929.

84. James H. Kirkland to Albert J. Harno, November 6, 1929.

85. Handbook of the Association of American Law Schools and Proceedings of the Twenty-Seventh Annual Meeting (New Orleans, December 27, 28, 30, 1929), p. 7.

86. Allen G. Hall to W. R. Vance, March 8, 1909. Vance replied promptly, on March 11th: "I have gone over the catalogue and am glad to say that the Vanderbilt Law School now complies in every respect with the requirements of the Association

of Law Schools, and I may safely assure you that it will be recommended for
admission by the Executive Committee, and admitted at the next meeting of
the Association in Detroit. . . . congratulating you most heartily on the splendid
progress made by the Vanderbilt Law School. . . ."

87.   Proceedings of the Fifth Annual Meeting, Association of American Law Schools
      (August 22, 1905), pp. 33–37.
88.   Julia P. Hardin, "Polishing the Lamp of Justice: A History of Legal Education at
      the University of Tennessee, 1890–1990," *Tennessee Law Review*, 57 (1990), p. 154.
89.   Handbook of the Association of American Law Schools and Proceedings of the
      Twenty-Fourth Annual Meeting, (December, 29–31, 1916), p. 62.
90.   Ibid., p. 67.
91.   Ibid., pp. 68–69.
92.   See, generally, Howard N. Rabinowitz, *The First New South: 1865–1920*
      (Arlington Heights, IL: Harlan Davidson, Inc., 1992).
93.   BOT Minutes, VII, June 14, 1915, p. 197.
94.   BOT Minutes, XIII, June 11, 1928, p. 269.
95.   John Bell Keeble to Governor Joseph Sayers of Texas, August 5, 1924 (counting
      students from twenty states enrolled in the Law School).
96.   BOT Minutes, XIV, June 10, 1929, p. 233.
97.   BOT Minutes, XIII, June 6, 1927, pp. 83, 85.
98.   H.W. Arant, "A Survey of Legal Education in the South," in *The Inauguration
      of Oliver C. Carmichael as Chancellor of Vanderbilt University and Symposium on
      Higher Education in the South* (Nashville: Vanderbilt University, 1938), p. 176.
99.   E.W. Huffcut, "A Decade of Progress in Legal Education," *The American Lawyer*
      10, (1902), p. 405.
100. Lewis Laska, "Our Sordid Past: Anecdotes of Tennessee's Legal Folklore,"
      Tennessee Bar Journal, (May/June 1995), p. 30. Nashville College Law School's
      William Farr was convicted of mail fraud in 1905, but was allowed to leave
      Nashville and served no time in jail.
101. Acts of the State of Tennessee Passed by the Fifty-Third General Assembly, 1903
      (Nashville, 1903), Chapter 247, pp. 575–76.
102. Proceedings of the Twenty-Second Annual Meeting of the Bar Association of
      Tennessee, (July 1–3, 1903), pp. 12–19.
103. Clyde Conley Street, "A History of Legal Education in Tennessee," (Master's
      Thesis, University of Tennessee, 1941), p. 18. [citing TBA proceedings of 38th
      session, 1919, p. 71]
104. David J. Langum and Howard P. Walthall, *From Maverick to Mainstream:
      Cumberland School of Law, 1847–1997* (Athens: University of Georgia Press,
      1997), p. 104.
105. "Registrar" (MWH) to University of Missouri Registrar, June 22, 1920.
106. Feldman, "The Transformation of an Academic Discipline," (2004), pp. 475–87.
107. L.M. Friedman, *A History of American Law*, (New York: Simon and Schuster,
      1973), p. 616-17.

108. Mark Bartholomew, "Legal Separation: The Relationship Between the Law School and the University in the Late Nineteenth Century," *Journal of Legal Education* 53 (2003), p. 368.

109. Robert Stevens, "Two Cheers for 1870: The American Law School," *Law in American History,* Donald Fleming and Bernard Bailyn (eds.) (Boston: Little, Brown & Co., 1971), p. 440, n. 61.

110. Frederick C. Hicks, *Yale Law School: 1895–1915, Twenty Years of Hendrie Hall* (New Haven: Yale University Press, 1938), p. 44.

111. Langum and Walthal, *From Maverick to Mainstream*, p. 105.

112. David J. Mays, *The Pursuit of Excellence: A History of the University of Richmond Law School* (Richmond: University of Richmond Press, 1970), p. 19.

113. William H. Fligeltaub, "Vanderbilt Law Department 1875–1904: Survival Without Stagnation" (unpublished senior writing requirement paper), January 1976, p. 16.

114. Fligeltaub, p. 16, quoting address by Thomas H. Malone Jr., Malone Inn, Phi Delta Phi and Delegates of the Provincial Convention, December 8, 1922, in *Memoir of Thomas H. Malone: An Autobiography Written for His Children* (1928), p. 224.

115. Allen G. Hall, Dean's Annual Report to the Chancellor, 1907/08.

116. Allen G. Hall, Dean's Annual Report to the Chancellor, May 24, 1915. Kirkland himself needed no convincing on this subject, as he had reported to the Board of Trust that the growth in the use of the case method was "in accord with the better class of institutions elsewhere." BOT Minutes, VII, June 16, 1913, p. 84.

117. BOT Minutes, V, June 18, 1901, p. 69; Faculty Meeting Minutes, March 29, 1905, May 24, 1905, and January 9, 1923.

118. Allen G. Hall to J. E. Hart (Bursar of the University), September 28, 1910.

119. James H. Kirkland to Allen G. Hall, October 13, 1910.

120. *The Vanderbilt Hustler*, October 15, 1910, pp. 1,2; *The Vanderbilt Hustler*, October 22, 1910, pp. 1,4; *The Commodore* (The Year Book of Vanderbilt University), 3, (Nashville: Vanderbilt University, 1911) p. 390.

121. Fred Russell, *Fifty Years of Vanderbilt Football* (Nashville: F. Russell and M. E. Benson, 1938), p. 64. Allen G. Hall to Frederick Moore (Dean of the Academic Department), September 28, 1910.

122. "Vanderbilt University Literary Societies," (undated)., in Box 27, Student Activities, Literary Societies, Special Collections. See also, *The Observer*, May, 1909, pp. 337–43, and November, 1909, p. 5.

123. Minutes of the Tau Kappa Alpha Fraternity (on file with author).

124. Charles H. Wilber to John Bell Keeble, October 9, 1916.

125. James H. Kirkland to Allen G. Hall, October 20, 1910.

126. *Law School Catalogue*, 1916/17, p. 74.

127. John Bell Keeble to James H. Kirkland, November 13, 1915; James H. Kirkland to John Bell Keeble, November 21, 1915.

128. Dean H. C. Tolman to Charles H. Turck, October 5, 1922.

129. BOT Minutes, XI, June 8, 1925, p. 235. At the same meeting, the Board accepted the offer of the Alumnae Council to provide $3,000 per annum for three years to pay the salary of the first Dean of Women. Ibid., June 9, 1925, p. 287.
130. "Forty-Fifth Opening at Vanderbilt," *The Vanderbilt Alumnus*, 5, no. 1 (October 1919), p. 7.
131. BOT Minutes, X, June 11, 1923, p. 145.
132. BOT Minutes, XI, June 8, 1925, p. 249.
133. Lewis L. Laska, "A History of Legal Education in Tennessee, 1770–1970," (Ph.D. dissertation, George Peabody College for Teachers, 1978), p. 751. Other schools in the state had begun admitting women toward the end of the nineteenth century.
134. Nadine Helm to Allen G. Hall, November 27, 1907; Allen G. Hall to Nadine Helm, November 30, 1907.
135. Nadine Helm to Allen G. Hall, December 3, 1907; Allen G. Hall to Nadine Helm, January 18, 1908.
136. Allen G. Hall to Crane & McGlenen, May 21, 1908; Allen G. Hall to Crane & McGlenen, June 19, 1908.
137. Law School Catalogue, 1918/19.
138. Statement of Mrs. Marion Caldwell.
139. Charlotte E. Gauer, "National Association of Women Lawyers," *Women Lawyers Journal,* 35, no. 4 (Fall 1949), p. 15.
140. Virginia G. Drachman, *Sisters in Law: Women Lawyers in Modern American History* (Cambridge: Harvard University Press, 1988), p. 176.
141. *Ibid.*, pp. 174, 177, 254.
142. Faculty Meeting Minutes, March 11, 1949. The first woman inducted into the Vanderbilt Order of the Coif Chapter was Mrs. Virginia Cowan in 1951. Doug Fisher, "Vanderbilt Vigil," *The Nashville Banner*, April 5, 1951, p. 24.
143. Faculty Meeting Minutes, May 31, 1956.
144. "Report of the Chancellor," *Vanderbilt University Quarterly*, 3, (1903), p. 187.
145. McAlister apparently completed his study of law at the University of Nashville in 1871, without receiving his law degree. "State Pays Tribute to Judge McAlister," *The Vanderbilt Alumnus*, VIII, no. 6 (April, May, June 1923), p. 178. "Vanderbilt Law School Grows," *The Vanderbilt Alumnus*, VIII, no. 2 (November 1922), p. 44.
146. Allen G. Hall to James H. Kirkland, March 8, 1909; Allen G. Hall to James H. Kirkland, June 5, 1909.
147. BOT Minutes, VII, June 16, 1913, p. 84. Kirkland's comments suggest that there were pedagogical concerns, in addition to budgetary issues, that had supported the use of part-time faculty. The other faculty member who resigned that summer was Maddin, who had had a somewhat unusual relationship with the University. He served as President of the Board of Directors of the Galloway Memorial Hospital, an ill-fated venture to build a hospital for Vanderbilt's use that ended in bankruptcy. See Conkin, *Gone with the Ivy*, pp. 267–74. He

represented the Methodist Church in its lawsuit against Vanderbilt over control of the institution, and resigned from the faculty following a Chancery Court decision against the University, a decision that was overturned the following year by the Tennessee Supreme Court. *College of Bishops v. Vanderbilt University*, 164 S.W. 1151, (Tenn. 1914).

148. BOT Minutes, VII, June 15, 1914, p. 150.

149. BOT Minutes, VIII, June 9, 1919, p. 151.

150. BOT Minutes, XXX, February 3, 1947, p. 137.

151. Keeble, "The Law School and Some Men . . ." p. 201. David Burner, "James C. McReynolds," in Leon Friedman and Fred L. Israel, *The Justices of the United States Supreme Court: Their Lives and Major Opinions*, 3, ed. Leon Friedman and Fred L. Israel (New York: Chelsea House Publishers, 1997), 1009–10.

152. BOT Minutes, XXXI, June 4, 1948, pp. 47, 203.

153. Mims, *History of Vanderbilt University*, pp. 283, 290.

154. Fred Russell, *Fifty Years of Vanderbilt Football*, p. 63.

155. Lewis Laska, "A Review of David J. Langum & Howard P. Walthall, *From Maverick to Mainstream: Cumberland Law School: 1847–1997*," *Cumberland Law Review*, XXX (2000), p. 504.

156. Glen-Peter Ahlers, Sr., *The History of Law School Libraries in the United States: From Laboratory to Cyberspace* (Buffalo, NY: William S. Hein & Co., 2002), p. 17. The AALS used 5,000 volumes when it established its first minimum collection size for association membership in 1912. Ibid., p. 21.

157. BOT Minutes, V, June 15, 1903, p. 144; BOT Minutes, VII, June 16, 1913, p. 96.

158. BOT Minutes, XXV, February 1, 1943, p. 193.

159. "New Home for the Law School," *Vanderbilt University Quarterly*, 15 (1915), p. 276.

160. Beginning in 1905, the University had allowed students in the Academic and Engineering departments to take law classes, in an attempt to bind law students more closely to the student body on campus. "The Opening of a New Session," *Vanderbilt University Quarterly*, 5 (1905), p. 269.

161. BOT Minutes, VIII, June 11, 1917, p. 58.

162. BOT Minutes, IV, June 18, 1900, p. 313.

163. "Present Enrollment of the University," *Vanderbilt University Quarterly*, 11, (1911), p. 247.

164. BOT Minutes, VII, June 16, 1913, pp. 84–85.

165. BOT Minutes, VII, June 14, 1915, pp. 197, 199.

166. BOT Minutes, VIII, June 11, 1918, p. 121.

167. BOT Minutes, XI, June 9, 1924, p. 65.

168. BOT Minutes, X, June 11, 1923, pp. 63, 65. By way of comparison, the percent of cost covered by student tuition payments was 43% in the College, 16% in the Medical School, and 3% in the School of Religion.

169. BOT Minutes, XI, June 9, 1924, p. 63.

170. BOT Minutes, XIII June 6, 1927, p. 91.

171. BOT Minutes, XIV, June 19, 1929, p. 225. In almost the same breath, the Chancellor said, "We cannot for one moment consider the abandonment of the School of Law." It was perhaps this latter conviction of Kirkland's, which he regularly pronounced to the Board over three decades, that allowed the Law School to survive when other professional schools were being closed.

172. McGaw and Wilcoxon, *A Brief History of Vanderbilt University*, p. 27.

173. Conkin, *Gone with the* Ivy, p. 261.

CHAPTER THREE

1. BOT Minutes, XV, February 3, 1930, p. 35.
2. Conkin, *Gone with the Ivy*, p. 262.
3. Elliott E. Cheatham to Earl C. Arnold, December 23, 1942.
4. BOT Minutes, XV, October 16, 1929, p. 9.
5. Allen G. Hall, Annual Report to the Chancellor, 1907/08.
6. BOT Minutes, XV, March 28, 1930, p. 47.
7. Earl C. Arnold, "The School of Law Makes Progress," *The Vanderbilt Alumnus*, 16, no. 7 (May 1931), p. 193.
8. Earl C. Arnold to the faculty, January 7, 1931; Record of the Society of Lincoln's Inn of the Vanderbilt University School of Law (on file in the Dean's Office.)
9. When Kirkland became Chancellor Emeritus on July 1, 1937, College Hall, the University's main administration building and the Law School's home, was renamed Kirkland Hall.
10. BOT Minutes, XIX, June 8, 1936, p. 133.
11. Earl C. Arnold to H. W. Arant (AALS Secretary), February 4, 1937. Just two years earlier, in response to "recurring rumors" of Kirkland's retirement, the entire faculty submitted a letter to the Board of Trust expressing their confidence in Kirkland and stating that his leadership was "necessary" for the success of the Law School. Letter from the faculty of Vanderbilt Law School to W. T. Hale, Jr., Secretary of the Executive Committee of the Board of Trust, January 30, 1935.
12. BOT Minutes, XX, June 8, 1937, p. 25.
13. BOT Minutes, XXI, June 12, 1939, p. 241. Interestingly, after leaving Vanderbilt, Carmichael returned to campus in 1949 as the Commencement speaker and he returned the $200 honorarium to be donated to the recently-formed Law School endowment fund.
14. BOT Minutes, XV, June 9, 1931, p. 245.
15. Law School Catalogue, 1930/31, p. 12.
16. The Board of Trust Budget Committee commented: "We cannot refrain from commending the generous spirit of Dean Arnold in accepting a reduction which by contract he was not called on to do." BOT Minutes, XVII, June 13, 1933, p. 7.
17. BOT Minutes, Report of the Committee on the Budget, XVII, June 12, 1934, p. 231.
18. BOT Minutes, XVII, June 12, 1934, p. 271.

19. Earl C. Arnold to James H. Kirkland, January 31, 1935. During this time, a campaign for the School of Religion was soliciting all friends of the University (thus preempting any campaign for the Law School) and major gifts were being recorded for the Nursing School and the School of Religion, including gifts by Fred W. Vanderbilt and John D. Rockefeller, Jr.

20. James H. Kirkland to Earl C. Arnold, February 7, 1936.

21. BOT Minutes, XX, February 7, 1938, p. 175.

22. Indeed, one Board of Trust member who had donated $1,000 to the Law School building fund asked that his gift be transferred to the library fund.

23. Earl C. Arnold to Morton Hendrick, February 15, 1938. Chancellor Carmichael did tell the Board that he considered raising $1 million for the Law School to be "the most urgent need of the University, apart from the need for funds to match the conditional grant to the library." BOT Minutes, XX, February 7, 1938, p. 167.

24. Comments by Reber Boult, Meeting of the Executive Committee of the Law School Development Council, October 27, 1968.

25. Frazier Reams (alumnus) to Dean Ray Forrester, November 16, 1949. Even Chancellor Kirkland would remark in 1936, "My sincere conviction is that the University gets out of the School of Law all the return in the way of credible achievement that it is entitled to from the amount of money invested in it. If we could put more into the School of Law we should get more out of if." BOT Minutes, XIX, June 8, 1936, p. 133.

26. BOT Minutes, XVII, June 13, 1933, pp. 53, 55. In Arnold's view, legal education was a public service that could not pay its own way through tuition and fees.

27. BOT Minutes, XXI, June 12, 1939, p. 293. The following year Carmichael reported that "every effort" was being made to find funds for a new Law-Social Science building. BOT Minutes, XXIII, June 10, 1940, p. 49.

28. BOT Minutes, XX, June 7, 1938, p. 289.

29. Earl C. Arnold to Henry B. Witham, October 21, 1940.

30. Faculty Meeting Minutes, September 15, 1939.

31. BOT Minutes, XXI, December 28, 1938, p. 55. With the opening of the Joint University Library building, the Law Library expanded into the main reading room and stack space in Kirkland Hall that was vacated by the University's library.

32. Earl C. Arnold, Dean's Annual Report to the Chancellor, May 1, 1936.

33. Raymond E. Paty, E. W. McDiarmid, and John Dale Russell, "The Joint University Libraries: A Survey of the Equity and Adequacy of Their Financing and Operation," report, Vanderbilt University, November 19, 1951.

34. BOT Minutes, XXI, June 12, 1939, pp. 225, 227, 237; BOT Minutes, XXII, August 16, 1939, p. 15; BOT Minutes, XXII, June 10, 1940, pp. 229, 231.

35. BOT Minutes, XXIII, June 9, 1941, p. 285.

36. Bennett Douglas Bell was an 1878 Cumberland law graduate who served as a circuit court judge and on the Tennessee Supreme Court. James W. Ely, Jr. (ed.),

A History of the Tennessee Supreme Court (Knoxville, TN: University of Tennessee Press, 2002), pp. 157–58, 190–91.

37.   John W. Wade, "The Law School—Its Relationship to the University, Present Needs and Its Future," (unpublished report) circa 1960. Ten years after that conversation, Wade would write, "I dismissed it from my mind as the viewpoint of an embittered old gentleman, and I have never repeated the statement until now. But this spring it has come back to my mind, especially when I have heard members of the faculty using Dean Arnold's last phrase." Ibid.

38.   H.W. Arant, "A Survey of Legal Education in the South," in *The Inauguration of Oliver C. Carmichael as Chancellor of Vanderbilt University and Symposium on Higher Education in the South* (Nashville: Vanderbilt University, February 5, 1938), pp. 175–83.

39.   Ibid., p. 215.

40.   Shafroth would create the National Conference of Bar Examiners, which helped the ABA achieve its goal in most states of requiring graduation from an ABA-approved school to sit for the bar exam. When Shafroth took office, fifteen states required this minimum; when he stepped down, forty-two states were on that list. Langum and Walthall, *From Maverick to Mainstream*, p. 140.

41.   Earl C. Arnold to Robert L. Stearns, February 15, 1935.

42.   Henry B. Witham to Earl C. Arnold, March 30, 1934.

43.   Henry B. Witham to Earl C. Arnold, January 4, 1934; Henry B. Witham to Earl C. Arnold, January 16, 1934.

44.   Earl C. Arnold to Robert L. Stearns (Advisor to the ABA), June 22, 1935. Arnold's concern about competitor Cumberland Law School is evident in information he passed on to Stearns: "I noticed recently in a paper that the budget for that entire University next year had been passed at $85,000.00. You can imagine the type of instruction that could be given at $85,000.00."

        Arnold also sent the ABA the names of state Supreme Court justices, Courts of Appeals judges, and members of the Board of Bar Examiners so that the ABA would send the list of disapproved schools to these influential individuals. Earl C. Arnold to Robert L. Stearns, June 27, 1935.

45.   Earl C. Arnold to Robert L. Stearns, June 27, 1935. The "article" appeared without a by-line, was a short four paragraphs in length, and referred to no law schools other than Tennessee and Vanderbilt. "Tennessee Law School Standards Clarified," *The Nashville Banner*, June 26, 1935, p. 9.

46.   Earl C. Arnold to Will Shafroth, July 23, 1934.

47.   Earl C. Arnold to Will Shafroth, February 1, 1937.

48.   Clyde Conley Street, "A History of Legal Education in Tennessee," (M.A. Thesis: The University of Tennessee, June 1941), p. 21.

49.   Ibid., p. 22.

50.   Earl C. Arnold to Will Shafroth, June 16, 1937.

51.   H. Claude Horack and Will Shafroth, "The Law Schools of Tennessee: Report of the Survey Committee," *Tennessee Law Review*, 15 (1938), pp. 311–95.

52.   Noting that the study committee had found law schools that the Tennessee Board of Bar Examiners did not know existed, or had thought had been discontinued, the authors hesitated to state that there were no other law schools in operation in the state at that time. Horack and Shafroth, "The Law Schools of Tennessee," p. 313.

53.   Horack and Shafroth, "The Law Schools of Tennessee," pp. 314–31.

54.   "Proceedings of the Fifty-Sixth Annual Session of the Bar Association of Tennessee," *Tennessee Law Review*, 15 (December 1938), pp. 18, 80.

55.   Laska, *A History of Legal Education in Tennessee*, pp. 279.

56.   Earl C. Arnold to Professor Shepherd (Cincinnati School of Law), October 30, 1937; Henry B. Witham to Earl C. Arnold, April 26, 1938; Earl C. Arnold to Henry B. Witham, April 27, 1938; Earl C. Arnold to W. P. Armstrong, April 28, 1938; Henry B. Witham to Earl C. Arnold, May 11, 1938; Henry B. Witham to Earl C. Arnold, May 13, 1938.

57.   Earl C. Arnold to Will Shafroth, October 23, 1937.

58.   For example, he asked that a letter he wrote not be reproduced, or even quoted from, lest it antagonize the Tennessee Supreme Court and the Board of Examiners. Earl C. Arnold to Harold Shepherd, October 30, 1937.

59.   Other local schools, such as the Lebanon School of Law and the Andrew Jackson School of Law were judged by Arnold to be "worthless—much inferior to Cumberland." He saw the Y.M.C.A. Law School as doing "fair work for a night law school." Earl C. Arnold to Henry B. Witham, April 2, 1934.

60.   Will Shafroth to Earl C. Arnold, April 15, 1932.

61.   A. B. Neil, "Reply of Judge A. B. Neil, Dean of Cumberland University Law School to the Report of Will Shafroth and H. Claude Horack," *Tennessee Law Review*, XV (1938), pp. 490–93.

62.   A. B. Neil to Earl C. Arnold, June 9, 1938.

63.   Earl C. Arnold to A. B. Neil, June 12, 1938. Vanderbilt apparently succeeded in maintaining good relations with Neil. As the Chief Justice of the Tennessee Supreme Court, he was the principal speaker at Vanderbilt's installation ceremonies for its Order of the Coif chapter on March 25, 1949. Rollin M. Perkins (Acting Dean) to Cecil Sims, February 24, 1949 (inviting him to honorary membership in the Coif chapter).

64.   George H. Armistead, Jr., to Earl C. Arnold and Henry B. Witham, May 24, 1938 (which Armistead said he was not sending to any other law school deans).

65.   Dean Dale Coffman to Dean Emeritus Arnold, December 11, 1947; Dale Coffman to Cecil Sims, December 4, 1947.

66.   Hugh Allen Wilkerson, "Legal Education and Admission to the Bar," *Tennessee Law Review*, 22 (1951), p. 69. In 1951, the Tennessee Supreme Court adopted rules requiring three years of successful college work before admission to law school.

67.   Earl C. Arnold to E. E. Barthell, March 11, 1936, noting that Cumberland

"heretofore has drawn about two-thirds of its students from outside of Tennessee."

68. Arnold and Witham could not rest on their laurels. In November 1939, Arnold wrote Witham telling him of a "quiet movement" to have the next legislature repeal the action of the Supreme Court that increased the standards. Their plan, which had to be kept confidential, was to work on securing proper leadership in the state legislature, and in the Tennessee Bar Association. Earl C. Arnold to Henry B. Witham, November 13, 1939.

69. Carmichael reported to the Board that the enrollment picture should be definitely improved by the Supreme Court's action. BOT Minutes, XXI, February 6, 1939, p. 127. At least one unaccredited law school responded to the new standards by establishing its own college, a process that was virtually unregulated in Tennessee. Earl C. Arnold to M. R. Kirkwood, September 20, 1938.

70. BOT Minutes, XVII, June 12, 1934, p. 275.

71. Alfred Z. Reed, "Legal Education, 1925–1928," *The American Law School Review*, VI, no. 12 (1929), p. 769.

72. Publications of the faculty members of the College of Arts and Science, the School of Engineering, the School of Religion, the School of Law (December 1, 1930–December 20, 1935, through January 1, 1941–December 31, 1945: *Bulletin of Vanderbilt University*, Nashville, Tennessee).

73. H. W. Arant to Earl C. Arnold, January 25, 1937. Arant did observe that the quarters were still inadequate, another professor should be added as soon as possible because the teaching load was too heavy, and stricter grading standards should be adopted.

74. H. W. Arant to James H. Kirkland, January 25, 1937.

75. Faculty Meeting Minutes, September 22, 1930. As of 1933, no special students had been admitted under the new procedures. Association of American Law Schools Questionnaire (1933) (on file).

76. Faculty Meeting Minutes, October 29, 1930.

77. Will Shafroth to Earl C. Arnold, November 26, 1930. Shafroth sent to Arnold the academic rules at Yale, Cornell, Michigan, Colorado, and Harvard (which had excluded 745 students in the prior three years).

78. Earl C. Arnold to Will Shafroth, December 1, 1930.

79. Faculty Meeting Minutes, June 6, 1936.

80. Earl C. Arnold to Morton Hendrick, February 15, 1938, and July 20, 1938. Three students were excluded for academic reasons in 1935/36, and five were excluded in 1936/37. Earl C. Arnold, Report to the ABA, Fall 1937.

81. BOT Minutes, XXIII, February 3, 1941, p. 175.

82. Earl C. Arnold to E. E. Barthell, March 11, 1935.

83. H. W. Arant to Earl C. Arnold, March 7, 1936.

84. Earl C. Arnold to E. E. Barthell, March 11, 1936 (quoting Arant's letter).

85. E. E. Barthell to Earl C. Arnold, April 20, 1936. When responding to an ABA questionnaire in the Fall of 1937 which asked what teaching method was used, given the alternatives of case book, text book, lecture, or combination, Arnold wrote "Case book."

86. Earl C. Arnold and Oliver C. Carmichael, exchange of letters from July 7, 1930, through February 3, 1931.

87. Morton Hendrick to Earl C. Arnold, April 1, 1938.

88. Earl C. Arnold to Morton Hendrick, telegram, September 8, 1939; Morton Hendrick to Earl C. Arnold, telegram, September 8, 1939.

89. Earl C. Arnold to Morton Hendrick, September 9, 1939.

90. Faculty Meeting Minutes, September 15, 1939.

91. Earl C. Arnold to John Kirkland Clark, April 11, 1932.

92. Earl C. Arnold to Morton Hendrick, February 8, 1939.

93. Carmichael in particular was advocating increased work across disciplines, including his plan to construct a new building that would jointly serve the Law School and the Social Sciences division of the College. BOT Minutes, XXI, February 6, 1939, p. 129; BOT Minutes, XXI, June 12, 1939, p. 197; BOT Minutes, XXIII, February 3, 1941, p. 175.

94. Robert A. Leflar, "Survey of Curricula in Smaller Law Schools," *The American Law School Review*, IX, no. 3 (May 1939), pp. 255–67.

95. Vanderbilt's Tennessee Practice course was not, of course, available at other schools outside the state.

96. BOT Minutes, XXIII, June 10, 1940, p. 49.

97. Faculty Meeting Minutes, February 6, 1935.

98. BOT Minutes, XXIV, June 9, 1941, p. 17.

99. Lowe Watkins to Dean Coffman, July 25, 1947.

CHAPTER FOUR

1. By the early 1940s, "student discontent was widespread. Students believed Dean Arnold to be arbitrary in many of his decisions." Conkin, *Gone with the Ivy*, p. 387. In 1941, Carmichael had communicated to the Board reports that students at the school were not happy and were discontented with the "spirit of the administration." The dissatisfaction seemed to be related to a belief that the dean had not always dealt with them "openly and sympathetically." BOT Minutes, XXIV, June 9, 1941, p. 17.

2. BOT Minutes, XXV, June 5, 1942, p. 21. This decline of 16% compared favorably with the drop of 29% nationally and 39% in Tennessee.

3. BOT Minutes, XXV, February 1, 1943, p. 217. The draft age had been lowered to eighteen by that time.

4. Nationally, law school enrollment had decreased from 28,174 students in 1938 to 4,803 students in 1943—about half of whom were registered for evening

classes. At least seven of the 110 ABA-approved schools had already closed. BOT Minutes, XXVI, February 7, 1944, p. 243.

5. BOT Minutes, XXIV, February 2, 1942, p. 191.

6. BOT Minutes, XXV, February 1, 1943, p. 215.

7. David C. Rutherford, "A Brief History of the Nashville School of Law," *Bench and Bar II* (Nashville: Nashville Bar Foundation, 2003), p. 277. The school's founders were directors of the Nashville Y.M.C.A. and members of its education committee, but the school's only formal connection with the Y.M.C.A. organization was leasing space in the Downtown Y.M.C.A. building. In 1986 the name of the school was changed to the Nashville School of Law.

8. BOT Minutes, XXVI, June 4, 1943, pp. 55, 99, 101.

9. BOT Minutes, XXVI, February 7, 1944, p. 283. (Copy of resolution also on file.)

10. BOT Minutes, XXVI, February 7, 1944, p. 287.

11. Ibid.

12. Earl C. Arnold to Henry B. Witham, February 11, 1944.

13. Earl C. Arnold to Oliver C. Carmichael, March 29, 1943.

14. Earl C. Arnold to Dave Alexander, February 20, 1942.

15. Earl C. Arnold to Morton Hendrick, February 17, 1944.

16. BOT Minutes, XXV, September 28, 1942, p. 149.

17. Faculty Meeting Minutes, June 3, 1943.

18. The second faculty member who rejoined the School after the war was Harold Verrall, who began his teaching at Vanderbilt in 1931, after serving on the Cornell and LSU law faculties and the political science faculty at Minnesota. He returned from his leave in 1946, but left in 1949 to go to UCLA.

19. Faculty Meeting Minutes, January 9, 1945.

20. Trudy King to Earl C. Arnold, February 25, 1944.

21. Earl C. Arnold to Morton Hendrick, January 13, 1944.

22. Earl C. Arnold to Morton Hendrick, February 17, 1944.

23. Earl C. Arnold to Oliver C. Carmichael, March 1, 1944.

CHAPTER FIVE

1. BOT Executive Committee Minutes, XXIX, February 8, 1946, p. 103.

2. Conkin, *Gone with the Ivy*, pp. 437–38.

3. L. Dale Coffman, "A Lawyer's Education is Never Done," *Tennessee Law Review*, 19 (1946), p. 507.

4. L. Dale Coffman to Vice Chancellor C. M. Sarratt, May 1, 1946.

5. Mason Ladd, Iowa Dean, to L. Dale Coffman, June 7, 1946.

6. Conkin, *Gone with the Ivy*, p. 439.

7. "The University School of Law," *Vanderbilt Alumnus*, 31, no. 8 (September 1946), p. 9.

8. James Perry Foster, Diaries. Tennessee State Library and Archives. Box One,

Book Three (1947–1950), p. 72. The journal of first-year student J. P. Foster records that the first meeting of the class resulted in no action. Bobby Cook attempted to claim the chair of the meeting "among great uproar," prompting several students to complain about Parliamentary procedures and one student to threaten to poke him in the nose. The next day, third-year student and student body president Jack Ginnini reconvened the group and the decision to reschedule was reached "with little trouble."

9. Coffman, "A Lawyer's Education is Never Done," pp. 507–8.

10. Faculty Meeting Minutes, November 7, 1947.

11. Faculty Meeting Minutes, February 20, 1948.

12. BOT Minutes, XXXII, June 3, 1949, p. 185.

13. L. Dale Coffman to The Tennessee Alumni of Vanderbilt Law School, May 14, 1948; L. Dale Coffman to Louis Farrell, Jr. (representing the TBA legal education and admissions to the bar committee), April 7, 1948.

14. "New Standards in Law Schools Sought by Bar," *Chattanooga Daily Times*, June 6, 1948, p. 1; "Changes Asked in Bar Laws," *Nashville Tennessean*, June 8, 1948, p. 1.

15. Phil Sullivan, "Fight Develops on Law Schools," *Nashville Tennessean*, June 9, 1948, p. 1; "Preserve this Asset," [editorial] *Nashville Tennessean*, June 10, 1948, p. 12; Albert Cason, "Legion Opposes Bar Amendment," *Nashville Tennessean*, June 10, 1948, p. 17.

16. "Bar Group Fails to Act; Night Law Schools Safe," *Nashville Tennessean*, June 21, 1948.

17. Laska, *History of Legal Education in Tennessee*, pp. 330–31.

18. Rollin M. Perkins to Harvie Branscomb, May 10, 1949.

19. Harvie Branscomb to N. Baxter Jackson, February 1, 1949.

20. John W. Wade to Dean M. Leigh Harrison, University of Alabama School of Law, who had written to Wade asking for information in connection with Coffman's candidacy for the presidency of the University of Alabama, February 7, 1957.

21. "Dean Wade Interview," (videotape), October 13, 1989 (on file in Massey Law Library, Vanderbilt Law School).

22. Ray Allen to Harvie Branscomb, February 7, 1956.

23. Harvie Branscomb to Ray Allen, February 13, 1956. Professor Eddie Morgan was quite blunt in his response to a similar letter from Allen, writing that while he personally liked Coffman, discussions with Vanderbilt faculty had led him to conclude that Coffman had been "extremely dictatorial" during his Vanderbilt deanship, making arbitrary decisions and refusing to listen to positions with which he disagreed. Eddie Morgan to Ray Allen, March 23, 1956.

24. L. Dale Coffman to James G. Stahlman, June 26, 1956.

25. James G. Stahlman to L. Dale Coffman, June 29, 1956.

26. L. Dale Coffman to James G. Stahlman, January 23, 1959. James G. Stahlman to L. Dale Coffman, January 26, 1959.

27. William Ray Forrester to "Alumni and Friends," December 27, 1949.
28. AALS "Questionnaire on Student Attrition—Class of 1952."
29. Harold Verrall to William Ray Forrester, October 18, 1950.
30. Paul Hartman to Wendell G. Holladay, October 15, 1964; John W. Wade to Wendell G. Holladay, July 2, 1965.
31. BOT Minutes, XXVII, June 2, 1944, p. 85.
32. BOT Minutes, XXVII, June 2, 1944, p. 131.
33. BOT Minutes, XXVIII, June 8, 1945, p. 75. Kirkland observed that the national law schools with large endowments had secured them through large gifts or bequests—"The reason is that little enthusiasm can be generated for the development of a school in which relatively few people are directly interested."
34. BOT Minutes, XXIX, February 4, 1946, pp. 83, 85, 87, 91.
35. BOT Minutes, XXIX, June 7, 1946, p. 259.
36. BOTE Minutes XXIX, April 23, 1946, p. 143.
37. BOT Minutes, XXX, June 6, 1947, p. 199.
38. L. Dale Coffman to Harvie Branscomb (memorandum), April 3, 1948.
39. BOT Minutes, XXXVII, October 23, 1953.

CHAPTER SIX

1. Statement of Mary Moody Wade (on file with author).
2. Elliott Cheatham to John W. Wade, October 1, 1970. "As a dean," recalled Wade's successor Robert Knauss, "Wade was a giant." Interview with Robert L. Knauss, September 1, 2006.
3. Erwin Griswold, Harvard Law School Dean, wrote to Coffman of Wade's appointment, "I think the chances are very great that you might conclude that you had made a real find." Erwin Griswold to L. Dale Coffman, March 15, 1947.
4. Paul H. Sanders, "John W. Wade and the Development of the Vanderbilt Law School," *Vanderbilt Law Review* 25, (1972) p. 19. Sanders pointed out that the early volumes of the *Review* under Wade's leadership had been cited well in excess of any other journal in the region from Texas through Virginia, some of which had been publishing twenty-five years or more.
5. Harvie Branscomb, *Purely Academic: An Autobiography* (Nashville: Vanderbilt University, 1978), pp. 173–76.
6. John W. Boult, *Sheltered Places* (Nashville: Xlibris Corporation, 2001), p. 16. This assessment came from a former student who, a few months into his legal education, had his scholarship taken away by Wade because he discovered that the student was the nephew of Reber Boult (a 1929 graduate of the Law School who would later serve of Vanderbilt's Board of Trust), and Wade decided that the scholarship should be transferred to someone with greater need. Ibid., pp. 127–28. Boult—who married the only woman in his graduating class, Jimmie Lou Foster—also provided a glimpse of life in the Vanderbilt classroom during

this period: "We had all been forewarned that we were entering a mind-numbing Socratic thicket in which the finest undergraduate minds had quickly become hopelessly lost. We had been admonished that if we fell even one assignment or one day behind there would be no recovery, no way to catch up again. Because of these dire warnings, all of our waking moments during the early weeks of law school were spent either in the classroom or preparing for tomorrow. . . . Failure to respond correctly was a singularly humiliating experience." Ibid., p. 129.

7.   Mary Moody Wade's observation was, "He poured his life into this School." She would receive the School's Distinguished Service Award herself in 1993. She was credited with helping to create and foster the School's communal character through her care of faculty and student wives, tending the ill, entertaining visiting alumni and speakers, and standing in for the Dean when he was out of town. "She was legendary," said Jim Cheek. "Her influence went much farther than being the Dean's wife." "Dean's Council Dinner," *The Vanderbilt Lawyer*, 24, no. 1 (February 1993), p. 18.

8.   Faculty Meeting Minutes, September 25, 1967; Faculty Meeting Minutes, October 9, 1968; BOT Minutes, LIII, November 10, 1967, p. 217; BOT Minutes, LV, March 4, 1969, p. 163.

9.   Faculty Meeting Minutes, September 30, 1970.

10. John W. Wade to Members of the Law School Development Council, October 2, 1970.

11. "The Dean's Report to the Chancellor," *The Reporter*, IV, no. 1 (Winter 1973), p. 3.

12. The last faculty meeting that Wade presided over as Dean was January 26, 1972. Knauss was in the chair for the February 16, 1972, meeting.

13. BOT Minutes, XXII, February 4, 1940, p. 93.

14. See, for example, BOT Minutes, XX, February 7, 1938, p. 171; BOT Minutes, XX, June 7, 1938, p. 269; BOT Minutes, XXI, June 12, 1939, p. 239; BOT Minutes, XXII, June 10, 1940, pp. 231, 233.

15. BOT Minutes, XX, June 7, 1938, p. 287.

16. Albert Ewing, Jr., to Chancellor Carmichael, March 13, 1944.

17. BOT Minutes, XXXIII, December 15, 1949, p. 85.

18. Kathy Sawyer, "12-Year Chapter in Race Relations Reporting Ended," *The Nashville Tennessean*, July 7, 1968, p. 1-B.

19. Harvie Branscomb to John Wade (memorandum), March 15, 1957.

20. Branscomb, *Purely Academic*, p. 167. Branscomb met with the Law faculty in October 1957 to explain the ideas he had advanced with Heald and to outline plans for a visit the next day by a representative of the Ford Foundation. Faculty Meeting Minutes, October 2, 1957.

21. Comprehensive Report on Ford Foundation 7-Year Grant to Vanderbilt Law School (1965); Faculty Meeting Minutes, March 26, 1958.

22. BOT Minutes, XLIV, October 7, 1960, p. 137. The grant was part of a $46 million Ford Foundation contribution to universities in different regions. The

other schools were Johns Hopkins, Notre Dame, Denver, and Stanford, with Stanford receiving the lion's share at $25 million.

23. BOT Minutes, XLVI, July 6, 1962, p. 69. The School also received smaller grants from the Fund for the Advancement of Education, the Rockefeller Foundation, and the National Association of Legal Aid Clinics.

24. 1965 Comprehensive Report on Ford Foundation 7-Year Grant to Vanderbilt Law School, p. 1.

25. BOT Minutes, XLIX, May 15, 1965, p. 141.

26. BOT Minutes, XLVI, February 8, 1963, p. 257.

27. Holladay, "The Case History of Vanderbilt Law School," *Vanderbilt Lawyer*, (Spring/Summer 1999), p. 17.

28. Faculty Meeting Minutes, September 28, 1951; October 23, 1951.

29. William Ray Forrester to Harvie Branscomb, April 26, 1951.

30. "Summary—School Visitations 1959–1960," an undated report.

31. Gil Merritt to "Tom" (memorandum), October 21, 1961.

32. John Beasley to Members of the Faculty (memorandum), undated. In the fall's entering class, Yale was second only to Vanderbilt as a feeder school with nine of the 134 first-years coming from that university, a position Yale continued to occupy for a decade.

33. *Vanderbilt University Law School: A Future Even Greater than Its Past*, videotape (Arlington, VA: Paul Wagner Productions, 1988).

34. BOT Minutes, XLVII, May 3, 1963, p. 75.

35. BOT Minutes, L, February 18, 1966, p. 193.

36. BOT Minutes, XXVIII, June 8, 1945, p. 107.

37. Madison Sarratt to Board, BOT Minutes, XXIX June 7, 1946, p. 185.

38. BOT Minutes, XXX, June 6, 1947, p. 237; BOT Minutes, XXXI, June 4, 1948, p. 195.

39. BOT Minutes, XXXVI, May 2, 1953, p. 243.

40. An architect was drafting plans for a building as early as 1950. William Ray Forrester to Harvie Branscomb, September 23, 1950.

41. Statement of Mary Moody Wade. The president of Duke had approached Wade, telling him that he wanted to integrate the Duke Law School and that Wade had just had the experience of doing that successfully at Vanderbilt. After Wade informed the Duke president that he was not interested in leaving Vanderbilt, he traveled to Nashville to attempt to persuade Wade to change his mind. Eddie Morgan to John Lord, October 21, 1957.

42. BOT Minutes, XL, April 10, 1957, pp. 239, 241.

43. BOT Minutes, XL, May 3, 1957, p. 261. A building committee was appointed consisting of Cecil Sims, William Waller, and James A. Simpson. Simpson made the first gift to the building fund, 2,000 shares of the Exchange Security Bank valued at $12,500. BOT Minutes, XLI, September 21, 1957, p. 129.

44. BOT Minutes, XLIII, May 20, 1960, p. 235. Sims himself contributed $50,000 to the fund.

45. Faculty Meeting Minutes, October 2, 1957; Faculty Meeting Minutes, October 17, 1957.

46. Harvie Branscomb, "The Dedication," *Vanderbilt Law Review*, 17 (1963), p. 147.

47. John W. Wade to Harvie Branscomb, October 19, 1959.

48. The final cost was $1,575,000, the last $300,000 coming from the Ford Foundation grant. The other large gift to the building fund was a $221,000 bequest from alumnus Thomas E. Lipscomb.

49. John W. Wade to Vanderbilt, November 15, 1960.

50. Branscomb, "The Dedication," *Vanderbilt Law Review*, 17 (1963) p. 151.

51. "Cecil Sims Lectureship Begun," *The Reporter*, 3, no. 4 (April 1972), p. 8.

52. John W. Wade, "Legal Education and the Demands for Stability and Change Through Law," *Vanderbilt Law Review*, 17 (1963) p. 156.

    Only three years later, the Law School was attempting to raise funds to add an additional story to the office wing of the building. Paul H. Sanders to Chairman, Faculty Committee for $55 Million Campaign (memorandum), November 25, 1966.

53. Dean's report, BOT Minutes, XLVII, May 3, 1963, p. 73.

54. "These publications have done more than anything else to promote the national stature of the Law School." John Wade reporting to the Board of Trust, BOT Minutes, XLI, May 9, 1958, p. 289.

55. Faculty Meeting Minutes, October 9, 1965.

56. Curriculum Committee Report, November 18, 1963.

57. BOT Minutes, LIV, May 17, 1968, p. 91.

58. A story, perhaps apocryphal, is told that illustrates Harbison's intellect and modesty. He was well-known for quoting specific citations from a wide range of cases when responding to students' questions in class. He regularly referred to notes he had brought to class, apparently in anticipation of the direction the discussions would take. One day, after class, a student noticed that the "notes" on the podium were blank sheets of paper. Harbison was doing it all from memory, but did not want to appear to be "showing off" his extensive and intimate knowledge of case law.

59. Correspondence among Thomas W. Steele and deans Wade, William Wicker (University of Tennessee), and Grissim Walker (Cumberland), December 16, 1960, through January 27, 1961.

    In 1961, 47% of the students enrolled in Tennessee law schools were in the three schools in the state that were not approved by the ABA and would not have met this standard of three full-time faculty members. Nationwide, 92% of law students were enrolled in ABA schools. William Wicker, "Legal Education in Tennessee," *Tennessee Law Review*, 29, no. 3 (Spring 1962), pp. 326, 336.

60. Langum and Walthall, *From Maverick to Mainstream*, pp. 197–201.

61. Interview with Wilson Sims, October 26, 2006.

62. BOT Minutes, XLI, May 3, 1957, p. 13.

63. Sims Crownover to Harvie Branscomb, December 10, 1955. (copied to the *Nashville Tennessean* and the *Nashville Banner*).

64. James G. Stahlman to Sims Crownover, December 12, 1955. Over the years, Stahlman did not hesitate to criticize developments on the Vanderbilt campus from the editorial pages of the *Nashville Banner*. He was particularly strident in advocating the expulsion of Divinity School student James Lawson for his civil rights activities in 1960, and in condemning the appearance of Stokely Carmichael on campus in 1967. But Stahlman also supported his University, finally writing an editorial that commended Branscomb's handing of the first case, and acquiescing in the latter case in a Board conclusion that the invitation to invite Carmichael was an administrative matter best delegated to Chancellor Heard. Conkin, *Gone with the Ivy*, pp. 548–70, 617–23.

65. BOT Minutes, XLII, May 15, 1959, p. 287.

66. John W. Wade to Law School alumni, December, 1963.

67. "Information Compiled at the Request of Edwin O. Norris, a Member of the Executive Committee of the Development Council of the Vanderbilt Law School," (undated).

68. Kevin Grady to Ralph Kirkendall (Director of Alumni and Development Affairs) (memorandum), March 8, 1971.

69. Trabue, who also served as Secretary of the University's Board of Trust, was a 1933 graduate of the Law School. His son, Charles Trabue III, continued the family tradition as a member of the Vanderbilt law class of 1968.

70. Kevin E. Grady to Ralph Kirkendall (memorandum), March 8, 1971; "Information Compiled at the Request of Edwin O. Norris;" Edwin O. Norris to Kevin E. Grady, December 23, 1970.

71. Dean's annual report, BOT Minutes, XLVII, May 3, 1963, p. 73.

72. BOT Minutes, LVIII, April 30, 1971, p. 43.

73. John Beasley to John W. Wade (memorandum), September 4, 1969. Beasley reported on meetings he had had with students about the meager representation of African-American students, and of a $25,000 scholarship that had been created by Time, Inc., as a result of a visit by him and Richard Sinkfield, an "impressive" student. Sinkfield became a prominent Atlanta attorney and served on the School's Alumni Board and on the University's Board of Trust.

74. Harvie Branscomb to Professor E. M. Morgan, October 26, 1956. On that Saturday, Wade faced Law School alumni, and Branscomb and Board President Harold S. Vanderbilt faced University alumni in the aftermath of the School's integration.

75. Rodriguez graduated in 1935; Acevedo began in 1916 as a first-year student from Panama; Christ registered as a special student in 1922/23, and as a summer student the following summer.

76. BOT Minutes, XXXII, June 20, 1949, p. 291.

77. Harvie Branscomb, *Purely Academic*, p. 154.

78. Faculty Meeting Minutes, December 4, 1951.

79. Harvie Branscomb to William Ray Forrester (memorandum), December 6, 1951.

80. Branscomb, *Purely Academic*, p. 154.

81. BOT Minutes, XXXVI, October 10, 1952, p. 93.

82. John W. Wade to Harvie Branscomb, May 4, 1955.

83. Memorandum attached to John W. Wade letter to Harvie Branscomb, May 4, 1955.

84. BOT Minutes, XXXVIII, May 6, 1955, p. 227. Sims went on the road to speak in favor of desegregation at the Southeast Regional Conference of State Boards of Education, the Annual Convention of the Tennessee School Boards Association, and as the third speaker (along with novelist William Faulkner and Morehouse College President Benjamin E. Mayes) at the 1956 annual meeting of the Southern Historical Association. In May 1959, he testified against a proposed constitutional amendment to overturn *Brown v. Board of Education* before the U.S. Senate Subcommittee on Constitutional Amendments.

85. BOT Minutes, XL, September 26, 1956, p. 99. Z. Alexander Looby had operated the Kent College of Law out of his law office beginning in 1932. Kent was the only law school for African-American students in the Confederate South when Shafroth and Horack conducted their survey in 1937, and while its graduates sat for and passed the Tennessee bar exam, the school was never accredited by the ABA. Looby, who had earned his LL.B. from Columbia and his S.J.D. from NYU, tutored fewer than twenty students at a time. ABA records contain no enrollment figures for the school after 1939, and the school was dropped from the association's listings in 1947. Laska, *History of Legal Education in Tennessee*, p. 702.

   In February 1955, three months before the Vanderbilt Board action to integrate the Law School, the Tennessee Evening Law School was organized for African-American students in reaction to the Y.M.C.A. Night School's refusal to integrate. Enrolling about a dozen students a year, the school was apparently approved by the Tennessee Board of Law Examiners, but not accredited by the ABA, and closed after four years when the Y.M.C.A. school decided to admit African-Americans. Ibid., p. 709.

86. John W. Wade to Clayton E. Williams (Dean, Washington & Lee University School of Law), August 5, 1955.

87. David F. Cavers to John W. Wade, October 13, 1955; John W. Wade to David F. Cavers, October 18, 1955.

88. "Dean Wade Interview," (videotape) October 13, 1989 (on file in Massey Law Library, Vanderbilt Law School).

89. Robert McGaw, "A Policy the University Can Defend," *Vanderbilt Alumnus*, (Nov./Dec. 1956), p. 13.

90. Interviews with Frederick T. Work and E. Melvin Porter, December 6, 2006.

91. E. Melvin Porter to John W. Wade, March 23, 1960.

92. The resolution adopted by the Memphis Vanderbilt Commodore Club on September 25, 1956, was representative, expressing its alarm and disapproval. The

resolution addresses Vanderbilt's responsibility to the South, "to maintain the separation of the races and the kindred practices and principles traditional to the South." Unaware of the Board's action in allowing the admission of Work and Porter, the club expressed its hope that the Board "will regain its rightful control . . . will reprimand the administrative officials responsible . . . and will chart for the University a course consistent with its traditions and those of the South."

93. Letter to the Alumni Association, Vanderbilt University, October 7, 1956.

94. Theodore A. Smedley, "The Old Order Changeth," *Vanderbilt Law Review*, 31 (1978), p. 781.

95. Eddie Morgan to Harvie Branscomb, October 22, 1956.

96. Boult, *Sheltered Places*, pp. 135–36. He adds that they encountered no trouble whatsoever at the basketball game.

97. John W. Work to John W. Wade, June 9, 1959.

98. Underwood Auditorium, built as part of the 1962 construction of the Law School building, was named in memory of Peter Fondren Underwood, in recognition of contributions to the Law School and the University by the Fondren and Underwood families. The auditorium was razed in 2000 to make way for the expansion of the Law School building.

    The Underwood family's generosity extended to endowing the Milton R. Underwood Chair in Free Enterprise, named for the 1928 graduate of the School who served on Vanderbilt's Board of Trust, and student scholarships.

99. Plaque in the north lobby of the Law School Building.

100. Conkin, *Gone with the Ivy*, p. 575.

101. BOT Minutes, XLVI, January 5, 1963, p. 185. A committee of University administrators was established to handle "marginal cases" which required quick and routine approval, such as weddings in the University's Benton Chapel.

102. "Statement of Law Deans," *The Nashville Tennessean*, July 7, 1963, p. 2-A.

103. "Lawyer Group Blasts Wallace School Stand," *Birmingham News*, September 13, 1963, p. 1. The entry for the first signer was: "John Aade [sic], Dean, Vanderbilt University Law School."

104. Elliott E. Cheatham to John W. Wade, September 30, 1963.

105. John W. Wade to Lloyd N. Cutler, October 3, 1963.

106. Robert N. Rust, III, Vanderbilt Bar Association President, to J. G. Lackey, President, Nashville Bar Association, November 2, 1965. At that time, the 570-member Nashville bar excluded African-Americans, seventeen of whom were served by a separate organization, the J. C. Napier Bar Association. "VU Unit Votes Bar Censure," *The Nashville Tennessean*, November 3, 1965, p. 1.

107. Jim Squires, "Bar Votes Admittance of Negroes," *The Nashville Tennessean*, December 10, 1965, p. 1.

108. Undated resolution on file with author.

109. Andrew W. Bolt to Members of the House of Representatives, April 5, 1968.

110. L. Dale Coffman to Harvie Branscomb (memorandum), August 2, 1947.

111.   Eddie Morgan to Harvie Branscomb, June 5, 1958. One sign of the faculty's dedication to the School was its 100 percent participation rate in the University's $30 Million for Vanderbilt campaign, with the highest average gift for any college or school at Vanderbilt. Paul H. Sanders to The Faculty and Staff of the Law School (memorandum), December 19, 1966.

112.   Faculty Meeting Minutes, March 31, 1961; Faculty Meeting Minutes, May 10, 1961.

113.   Eddie Morgan to Harvie Branscomb, June 5, 1958.

114.   "Student Loan Fund Honors Hartman," *The Reporter*, 7, no. 1 (Fall 1976), p. 9.

115.   Sawyer, "12-Year Chapter in Race Relations Reporting Ended," *Nashville Tennessean*, July 7, 1968, p. 2-B.

116.   Wade, "Ted Smedley and the Law School," *Vanderbilt Law Review*, 31 (1978), p. 771.

117.   Wade, "Ted Smedley and the Law School," p. 772. Smedley's published teaching materials were used extensively at other schools.

118.   Paul Sanders, making Dean's Report to BOT due to the illness of John Wade, BOT Minutes, XLV, May 5, 1961, p. 27.

119.   Roberts, a future Board of Trust member, was an outstanding student. He was the winner of something like a triple crown in his senior year, earning the Founder's Medal, serving as Editor-in-Chief of the *Vanderbilt Law Review*, and being selected by the faculty for the Bennett Douglas Bell Award. Julia Bunting was the only other student to duplicate this feat, achieving all three honors in 1994, before going on to clerk for U.S. Supreme Court Justice Sandra Day O'Connor.

120.   Merritt later returned for a short stint as Associate Professor of Law and administrator in the Urban and Regional Development Center, and for many years as an adjunct faculty member. His career culminated in his judgeship on the U.S. Sixth Circuit Court of Appeals.

121.   Elliott Cheatham to Paul Sanders (memorandum), chair of the Dean Search Committee, January 20, 1971.

122.   The group's other members were law professors Hal Maier, Karl Warden, and Bruce Gagnon; students Tom Mountjoy, Jim Wildman, Jim Irvin, Charlie Chilton, Alan Glenn, and Frank Clemmer; and statistical biologist Homer Sprague.
        In 1989, Covington would organize The Headnotes, an a cappella singing group made up of a variety of students and faculty over the years.

123.   BOT Minutes, XXXVII, May 7, 1954, p. 273.

124.   BOT Minutes, XL, May 3, 1957, p. 287. When Wade came to Vanderbilt, he turned down two other offers that paid more. When he declined the deanship at Duke, it was ten years before his Vanderbilt salary reached the amount it would have been at Duke. Statement of Mary Moody Wade. One measure of the stature of the faculty is that four of the nine full-time faculty in 1958 had been law school deans. BOT Minutes, May 9, 1958, XLI, p. 289.

125. Dean's Report, BOT Minutes, LI, May 5, 1966, p. 81. Only one faculty member, Daniel Gifford, departed, going to the State University of New York at Buffalo.

126. Thomas Roady to Paul Hartman, May 3, 1966 (copied to Chancellor Heard and Dean Wade).

127. Roady himself was persuaded not to leave in 1966, but a year later he took a medical leave, and then returned to the University of Tennessee law faculty where he had started his law teaching career.

128. Mary Kay Messner and Joseph Sweat, "Sojourn on Skid Row," *Vanderbilt Alumnus*, 52, no. 6 (July–August 1967), pp. 14–17.

129. Wade, "Legal Education and the Demands for Stability and Change Through Law," *Vanderbilt Law Review*, 17 (1963), pp. 158–60. "Our goal," wrote Wade, "should be not merely to instruct in the principles of the law but to prepare the whole lawyer, the complete lawyer, the great lawyer—practicing law 'in the grand manner,' to paraphrase Justice Holmes' words." Ibid., p. 161.

130. *Vanderbilt Law Alumni Newsletter*, III, no. 1 (Fall 1957), (attached to Faculty Meeting Minutes, October 17, 1957); John W. Wade to George Neff Stevens, Dean at University of Washington School of Law, April 11, 1962; BOT Minutes, XLVI, May 4, 1962, p. 43

131. Bill Hopkins, "How Good Is Vanderbilt Law School? Nation's Educators Respond Favorably," *The Vanderbilt Dicta*, III, no. 3 (February 1966), p. 4.

132. Robert N. Covington, "The Development of the Vanderbilt Legal Writing Program," *Journal of Legal Education*, 16 (1064), pp. 342–47.

133. Sims had been appointed University Attorney in 1934. When he was appointed Lecturer in Law in 1949 to teach the Practice of Law course, he accepted the appointment only on the condition that he be paid no salary, setting a precedent followed later that year by William Waller and other part-time faculty in the years to come. Branscomb recommended, and the Board approved, setting aside an amount equivalent to what Sims would have been paid to be used for law student scholarships. BOT Minutes, XXXIII, September 28, 1949, p. 25. Sims was also uncompensated for much of his work as University Attorney. BOT Minutes, LIV, April 16, 1968, p. 17. Sims became a Life Trustee on the Vanderbilt Board of Trust.

134. Ray Forrester to Irving Ward-Steinman, April 11, 1952.

135. Sims' views received national attention. His article, "Lawyers and the Classics: The Spreading Technology Illiteracy," was published in the January 1957 issue of the *American Bar Association Journal*. The piece prompted an inquiry from Prentice-Hall about a book on the subject, which Sims declined, citing the press of duties.

136. John W. Wade, "Legal Education in Tennessee," *Tennessee Law Review*, 29, no. 3 (Spring 1962), p. 350.

137. "Modern Trends in Legal Education," *Columbia Law Review*, 64 (April 1964), p. 723.

138. Theodore A. Smedley, "The Pervasive Approach on a Large Scale—'The Vanderbilt Experiment,'" *Journal of Legal Education*, 15 (1963), pp. 435–43.

139. *Dicta*, II, no. 2 (new series) (November 27, 1964), p. 1; *Dicta*, II, no. 5 (March 31, 1965), p. 2; *Dicta*, II, no. 6 (May 1, 1965), p. 4. The *Dicta* evolved in later years, as the quarterly publication became a bi-weekly mimeographed piece that focused more on humor and intramural sports. The movement from factual reporting to satire and humor seemed to accelerate with the demise of an underground annual publication devoted to "harassing the faculty." This underground publication was known by many different names over the years, most often as the *Dandybilt Flaw Review*. It appears to have been published from about 1949 to 1973.

140. BOT Minutes, LXI, August 1, 1974, p. 79.

141. "This Entire Law Faculty Is Over 65 Years Old," *AMA News*, April 6, 1959, p. 9. The clipping of this newspaper story was found in John Wade's files.

142. Dean's Report to the Chancellor, May 20–21, 1960.

143. Erwin N. Griswold, Dean, Harvard Law School, "Edmund Morris Morgan," a memorial prepared on the occasion of his death.

144. Ray Forrester to Harvie Branscomb, August 30, 1949.

145. Branscomb reporting to Board of Trust, BOT Minutes, XXXIII, December 15, 1949, p. 95. Wade credited Cecil Sims with persuading Morgan to come to Vanderbilt. Untitled, unpublished notes found among Wade's papers.

146. While Morgan looked forward to his association with Vanderbilt, he called his departure from Harvard the "unhappy experience of being pushed out of the Harvard Law School because I was born too soon." Eddie Morgan to Frederick H. Stinchfield, December 2, 1949.

147. Griswold, "Edmund Morris Morgan."

148. "13 Members of Faculty Bid Farewell to Their Posts This June and August," *The Harvard Crimson*, May 31, 1950, p. 4.

149. Eddie Morgan to William Ray Forrester, May 3, 1950. Forrester replied that he thought the students would be willing.

150. Eddie Morgan to William Ray Forrester, January 31, 1952.

151. Eddie Morgan to William Ray Forrester, July 16, 1951.

152. Elliott Cheatham to John W. Wade, February 12, 1958.

153. Eddie Morgan to Elliott Cheatham, March 3, 1959. Morgan had turned down a similar offer from Hastings to come to Vanderbilt.

154. Eddie Morgan to Granville S. Ridley, November 15, 1960.

155. Editorial comment (Jean Bass Crawford, editor), *Vanderbilt Alumnus*, 52, no. 1 (July–August 1966), p. 1.

156. Erwin Griswold, "Elliott E. Cheatham," *Vanderbilt Law Review,* 22, no. 6 (1968), p. 7. At the time, Griswold was Solicitor General of the United States, following his deanship at Harvard Law School.

157. John W. Wade, "EEC," *Vanderbilt Law Review,* 22, no. 21 (1968), p. 22. An indication of Cheatham's devotion to his new academic home was his wife's

donation of their house on Hillside Drive in Nashville to Vanderbilt, after his death in 1972, with the proceeds treated as an unrestricted gift to the Law School.

158. "Elliott Evan Cheatham Dead at 83," *The Reporter*, III, no. 4 (April 1972), p. 14.

159. Ferson had resigned from the Chair as of July 1, 1951. BOT Minutes, XXXIV, June 5, 1951, pp. 153, 155; BOT Minutes, XXXIV, July 17, 1951, p. 291.

CHAPTER SEVEN

1. "School of Law: A self-study prepared for the Southern Association of Colleges and Schools," submitted by John J. Costonis, Dean, August, 1985, p. 11.

2. L. Dale Coffman, "A Lawyer's Education is Never Done," *Tennessee Law Review*, 19 (1946), pp. 499, 507.

3. Faculty Meeting Minutes, January 27, 1950. The faculty later supported periodic evening meetings to discuss generally legal education at the Law School. Faculty Meeting Minutes, September 21, 1960.

4. Elliott E. Cheatham, "The Law Schools of Tennessee," *Tennessee Law Review*, 21 (1950), p. 290.

5. Curriculum Committee Report, Elliott Cheatham, chair, November 18, 1963.

6. John W. Wade, "Legal Education and the Demands for Stability and Change through Law," *Vanderbilt Law Review*, 17 (1963) p. 165. Delivered on April 6, 1963.

7. John W. Wade, "The School of Law: Vanderbilt University," (unpublished), February 22, 1968.

8. During that five years, Foundation Press published *Cases and Materials for a Course on Legal Methods*, a collaborative project by Covington, Stason, Wade, Cheatham, and Smedley; as well as Wade's *Cases and Materials on Restitution* (2nd ed.) and *Cases and Materials on Torts* (5th ed.); Cheatham's *Cases on the Legal Profession*; and *The Profession of Law* by Patterson and Cheatham. Covington had published *Discrimination in Employment* and *Social Legislation* (both with BNA Books), and Bigham was publishing a text on Tennessee Commercial Law (with West) and supplements to *Pritchard Wills and Estates* (with Anderson). Patterson was also the author of *Copyright in Historical Perspective*, published by Vanderbilt University Press.

9. Faculty Meeting Minutes, December 14, 1971.

10. Faculty Meeting Minutes, December 7, 1973.

11. Conkin, *Gone with the Ivy*, p. 665.

12. Publications of the faculty/Vanderbilt University (Nashville: Office of Information & Publications, 1959–1976).

13. Faculty meeting minutes, January 16, 1979. His wife, Angela T. Knauss, had received her J.D. from the Law School in December, 1978.

14. Emmett B. Fields, "From the President," *Vanderbilt Alumnus*, 65, no. 2 (Winter 1979), p. 3.

15. BOT Minutes, LXXV, October 5, 1982, np). The next time Wyatt spoke to the Board, he did some damage control: "There is general concern in the society today about the number of lawyers. I say that there may be too many lawyers—there are not too many Vanderbilt lawyers." (BOT Minutes, LXXVI, April 29, 1983, Appendix C-2).

16. BOT Minutes, LXXVI, April 29, 1983, Appendix C-4, C-5. BOT Minutes, LXXVI, November 4, 1983, p. 15. The committee was also charged to address the process that encourages students into graduate programs and careers in teaching and research.

17. CART Report, January 27, 1984, Appendix I.

18. BOT Minutes, LXXVIII, October 26, 1984, np.

19. The ten, half of the tenured faculty at the Law School, were Bob Belton, Jon Bruce, Bob Covington, James Ely, Don Hall, Igor Kavass, Hal Maier, John Marshall, Tom McCoy, and Larry Soderquist. The three emeritus professors were Paul Hartman, Paul Sanders, and Herman Trautman. John Wade, as Distinguished Professor of Law, Emeritus, served on the committee in addition to Blumstein.

20. Memorandum from "The Undersigned Members of the Law School Faculty" to "Chancellor Wyatt and the University Community," (undated).

21. CART Report, p. 6

22. BOT Minutes, LXXX, September, 16, 1986, np.

23. Thomas Burish, "Making the University Stronger: The Faculty, 1998," an essay written by the Provost with advice from Vice-Chancellor Harry Jacobson, presented to the Board of Trust at a February 1998 retreat; BOT Minutes, CIII, February 27, 1998, p. 5.

24. BOT Minutes, LVII, April 7, 1970, p. 5.

25. Burish, "Making the University Stronger," p. 5.

26. The Dean's suite in the Law School building is now named for Dent Bostick and his wife Sue.

27. Other Law School faculty members who received this award, in addition to Paul Hartman, were Robert N. Covington in 1992, and Thomas R. McCoy in 2002.

28. Dean's Report, BOT Minutes, LII, June 6, 1967, p. 289.

29. BOT Minutes, LXXIX, November 1, 1985, p. 5.

30. Faculty Meeting Minutes, October 25, 1946.

31. BOT Minutes, XLVI, May 4, 1962, p. 19.

32. BOT Minutes, L, July 18, 1965, Appendix, p. 3.

33. Cecil Sims to Joe H. Foy, April 15, 1957.

34. Voices of Vanderbilt: An Oral History of Vanderbilt University, Interview on December 4, 1997 (Amy Sturgis, interviewer). *http://libll.library.vanderbilt.edu/diglib/voices-search.pll*.

35. BOT Minutes, CIII, February 27, 1998, pp. 20–22. Among the Southern values identified were civility, a respect for others, a service orientation, and a strong sense of community that recognizes the rights of individuals and accepts diversity.

36. C. Dent Bostick, "How Admissions Process Works," *The Reporter*, 8, no. 1, (Spring 1977), p. 34.

37. "A Talk with the Dean," *The Vanderbilt Lawyer*, 23, no. 2 (Spring 1993), p. 2.

38. John W. Wade to Mrs. Weldon B. White, March 28, 1968.

39. Alexander Heard, "From the Chancellor's Desk," *Vanderbilt Alumnus*, 61, no. 2 (Winter 1976), p. 5.

40. BOT Minutes, LX, May 3, 1974, p. 229.

41. Faculty Meeting Minutes, October 28, 1980. The policy stated, in part: "The Vanderbilt University School of Law admissions policy recognizes that certain groups in our society historically have been denied equal opportunities, particularly in the fields of education and employment. This holds true for legal education and employment in the legal profession. As a result, it is currently desirable to facilitate the entry of members of these groups into the legal profession. Moreover, the presence of members of such groups within the student body enhances diversity and improves the educational climate within the law school. Accordingly Vanderbilt University School of Law has an affirmative action policy applicable to the admissions process. Under this policy, membership in one of those groups is a factor that will enhance an applicant's admissibility."

42. "News and Views; Calculating the African-American Graduation Rate at the Nation's Highest-Ranked Law Schools: The Dropout Rate is Close to Zero," *The Journal of Blacks in Higher Education*, (Spring 2004), pp. 42–43.

43. Michael Cass, "Black Law Students Protest Unusual Exclusion," *The Tennessean*, March 27, 2004, 1B; Michael Cass, "VU to Pick 45 First-Year Students for Law Journals Based on Writing," *The Tennessean*, April 13, 2004, p. 3B.

44. Nancy A. Ransom, "A Comparative History of Faculty Women at George Peabody College for Teachers and Vanderbilt University, 1875 to 1970," Ph.D. dissertation, Vanderbilt University (1988), p. 166. The other woman was Mrs. Perle Hedges, Librarian of the Medical Department. The first woman listed at Vanderbilt with a professorial rank was Ada Bell Stapleton in 1926.

45. While she was not listed on the faculty register until 1914, Elliott actually assumed her position in 1910. These women functioned as something of a student affairs dean: "She was ever ready with counsel and sympathy to help any student over rough places, scholastic or financial, and her heart was the repository of the emotions and troubles of every budding lawyer who came under her influence." "Vanderbilt Law School Grows," *The Vanderbilt Alumnus*, 8, no. 2 (November 1922), p. 44.

46. Faculty meeting minutes, January 27, 1971. In 1970, women made up 2.8% of all

lawyers. The percentage nationally of law students who were women rose from 3.4% in 1965 to 10% in 1970. Ronald Chester, *Unequal Access: Women Lawyers in a Changing America* (South Hadley, Mass: Bergin & Gravey Pubs., 1985), p. 8.

47.   Mary Elizabeth Basile, "False Starts: Harvard Law School's Efforts Toward Integrating Women in the Faculty, 1928–1981," *The Harvard Journal of Law & Gender*, 28 (2005), pp. 158–59.

48.   Zibart, "Women at the Bar," *Vanderbilt Alumnus*, (Autumn 1973), p. 7. Kenneth Jost, "VU Law Faculty Adds First Woman," *The Nashville Tennessean*, August 29, 1972, p. 1.

49.   Daughtrey reflected on her years as a law student and faculty member in "Going Against the Grain: Personal Reflections on the Emergence of Women in the Legal Profession," *Montana Law Review*, 67 (Summer 2006), pp. 159–76.

50.   Faculty Meeting Minutes, April 15, 1977; BOT Minutes, LXXV, June 15, 1983, Appendix G-1.

51.   Faculty Meeting Minutes, March 13, 1984.

52.   BOT Minutes, LXXVIII, September 18, 1984, np.

53.   Ibid.

54.   BOT Minutes, LXXX, April 1, 1986, p. 6.

55.   Margaret Howard memo to The Student Body of Vanderbilt Law School, March 20, 2001.

56.   See Kent D. Syverud, "A School or an Olympics: Reflection on Competition and Altruism Among and Within Law Schools and Universities," presentation for Vanderbilt University Faculty Luncheon Group, September 22, 1997, draft.

57.   Ibid., p. 3.

58.   BOT Minutes, LXVII, July 25, 1978, p. 129.

59.   Jack Gourman, *The Gourman Report: A Rating of Graduate and Professional Programs in American and International Universities*. 2nd ed., revised (Los Angeles, National Educational Standards, 1983), p. 71.

60.   Brett S. Martin, "How to Really Rank the Best Law Schools." *The National Jurist*, (May/June 1997), p. 32.

61.   Professor Leiter's rankings are found online at *www.utexas.edu/law/faculty/bleiter/rankings/*.

62.   "A Message to Law School Applicants," a letter addressed to law school applicants, signed by deans of 181 of the 190 ABA-approved law schools, distributed by the Law School Admissions Council, April 2005.

63.   For examples, see Alex Wellen, "The $8.78 Million Maneuver," *The New York Times*, July 31, 2005, Section 4A, p. 18; Dale Whitman, "Doing the Right Thing," *The Newsletter: A quarterly publication of the Association of American Law Schools*, No. 2002–2, (April 2002), pp. 1–4. Whitman wrote, "The desire for high rankings seems increasingly to induce us to behave in ways that we would not otherwise choose, and to distort our educational judgments and priorities." A list of steps of dubious educational value that law schools could take to improve their *U.S. News* ratings can be found at Jeffrey E. Stake, "Interplay of Rankings

Criteria and Effects: Toward Responsible Rankings," *Indiana Law Journal*, 81, no. 1 (Winter 2006), p. 229.

U.S. News devised a strategy for securing the cooperation of law schools in its data gathering. In the inaugural ranking, *U.S. News* made its own estimates (noted with asterisks) for data the Schools did not provide. For example, the magazine "estimated" Harvard's placement success ranking as eighteenth in the country, contributing to an overall ranking of fifth. "Best Law Schools," *U.S. News & World Report*, March 19, 1990, p. 59. Few law schools were willing to take their chances with the magazine's estimates after that.

64. "*U.S. News* Corrects Law School Rankings," press release, March 5, 1997.

65. Anne Brandt is exemplary of the many administrative staff members who devoted much of their professional lives to the Law School. She appeared first as editor of the alumni magazine, then Placement Director, Director of Admissions, and eventually Assistant Dean for Admissions and Student Affairs, before leaving to become Associate Executive Director of the Law School Admissions Council.

66. Robert L. Knauss, "Law School Update," *The Reporter*, 9, no. 1 (Spring 1978), p. 12. (referring to Gourman)

67. C. Dent Bostick, "Acting Dean," *The Reporter*, 10, no. 2 (Fall 1979), p. 2.

68. The School ranked fifteenth or sixteenth through the first decade of the rankings, and then settled into four consecutive seventeenth place finishes in the years immediately after the turn of the century.

69. BOT Minutes, LIX, November 4, 1972, p. 165. At a Board of Trust retreat twenty-four years later, Provost Thomas Burish echoed these sentiments, stating that the factor most closely associated with the ranking of a university is the size of the endowment. BOT Minutes, CIII, February 27, 1998, p. 16.

70. BOT Minutes, LVIII, October 7, 1971, p. 135.

71. BOT Minutes, LVIII, November 5, 1971, p. 163.

72. "VU Law School Exceeds Campaign Goal," News release (VU Office of Public Information)(undated).

73. Minutes, Development Committee Meeting, November 12, 1976.

74. Robert L. Knauss, "Law School Update," *The Reporter*, 9, no. 1 (Spring 1978), p. 16.

75. As is true of any national law school, Vanderbilt's alumni have achieved personal success and attracted national acclaim in a number of areas. U.S. Senators James Sasser (Class of 1961) and Fred Thompson (Class of 1967, and a 2008 Presidential hopeful) are prominent examples.

Some observers have singled out the Class of 1957 for special mention, particularly as graduates of that class have contributed to the city of Nashville. Matt Pulle, "They Might Be Giants: How the Vanderbilt Law School Class of '57 Shaped a City," *Vanderbilt Lawyer*, 34, no. 1 (Spring 2004), pp. 12–19 (reprinted from *The Nashville Scene*, February 14, 2002. This group included Watergate prosecutor and defense attorney Jim Neal, labor lawyer and civil rights advocate George Barrett, federal judge Tom Higgins, district attorney and criminal court judge Tom Shriver, Federal Communications Commission chair William Henry, and others who have achieved prominence in federal and state government positions and in the practice of law.

76. BOT Minutes, LXVIII, December 5, 1978, p. 7.

77. A comparative measure of the size of the collection was the fact that Vanderbilt's library had fewer than half as many volumes as any law school library on a list of the twenty-four largest law school collections.

78. L. Dale Coffman to Harvie Branscomb, May 8, 1947.

79. Memorandum to Wade from "Law Library," dated March 24, 1966.

80. David Kaiser to Mary Polk Green, January 2, 1963.

81. Branscomb memorandum to Wade, February 1, 1962.

82. Wade memorandum to Branscomb, February 2, 1962.

83. ABA Inspection Report, submitted May 9, 1961, from visit of April 24–25, 1961.

84. "The Past is Prologue," *The Reporter*, 11, no. 1 (Summer 1980), pp. 16–17.

85. BOT Minutes, XCV, February 16, 1994, p. 4.

86. Faculty Meeting Minutes, September 7, 1995.

87. Faculty Meeting Minutes, May 27, 1987.

88. The faculty decided in September 1996 not to appeal further the ABA's findings. Faculty Meeting Minutes, September 5, 1996.

89. BOT Minutes, CIV, April 24, 1998, p. 12; BOT Minutes, CV, December 16, 1998, p. 3.

90. "Kent Syverud Accepts Deanship," *The Vanderbilt Lawyer*, 27, no. 1, (1997), p. 4.

91. Kent D. Syverud, "A 'Student-Centered School' Emerges from Strategic Planning Process," *The Vanderbilt Lawyer*, 30, no. 2 (Fall/Winter 2000), p. 2.

92. *The Princeton Review Student Access Guide to The Best Law Schools*, 1994 ed., pp. 94, 96. The faculty's teaching was ranked tenth nationally.

93. Wilson Sims to Don Welch, November 14, 2006.

94. *Vanderbilt Law Review*, 27, no. 4, (May 1974), pp. 681–813.

95. BOT Minutes, LIX, November 4, 1972, p. 167.

96. BOT Minutes, XCVI, October 28, 1994, p. 6.

97. Burish, "Making the University Stronger." p. 1.

98. "Law School Aims to Be the Best," *Vanderbilt Alumnus* 56, no. 5, (May–June 1971), p. 11.

99. Another nine students were enrolled from Tulane and Loyola of New Orleans law schools in the wake of Hurricane Katrina, but they paid their tuition that semester to the devastated schools in New Orleans, and were required to return to those schools in the spring semester. Even with an enrollment of 641 Vanderbilt was a relatively modest-sized school, falling in the bottom half of all ABA-approved schools.

100. "A Survey of Law School Curricula, 1992–2002," prepared by the Curriculum

Committee of the American Bar Association Section on Legal Education and Admissions to the Bar, p. 8.

101.   Two committees in the 1940s examined the possibility of coordinating the resources of the Law School and the Division of Social Sciences in the College of Arts and Science.

102.   Faculty Meeting Minutes, March 31, 1966. The faculty's enthusiasm for interdisciplinary work had been renewed by a visit from Justice White who saw a weakness in legal education in the "relative lack of reliance upon fields touching but lying in some sense outside the law." Ibid.

103.   Clifford S. Russell and Claudia A. McCauley, *VIPPS History: 1976–1991* (Nashville: Vanderbilt Institute for Public Policy Studies, 1991).

104.   Faculty Meeting Minutes, April 5, 1976.

105.   BOT Minutes, CXI, September 20, 2000, p. 3.

106.   The fund was created by the Board of Trust from a tax stabilization reserve, quasi-endowment funds, an additional tax on income producing units of the University, philanthropy, and income from technology transfer activities. BOT Minutes, CXII, February 28, 2001, p. 4.

107.   Faculty Meeting Minutes, November 29, 2000. Almost continuous planning for a graduate program during the Wade deanship never came to fruition. BOT Minutes, XLII, May 15, 1959, p. 287; BOT Minutes, XLVII, May 3, 1963, p. 77; Faculty Meeting Minutes, September 15, 1963; Faculty Meeting Minutes, March 31, 1966.

108.   Faculty Meeting Minutes, March 28, 2002.

109.   Earl Arnold to John S. Bradway, Director, Legal Aid Clinic, Duke University, February 27, 1940. Arnold blamed lethargy and jealousy among other difficulties for the delay in getting the program off the ground.

110.   Law School Catalogue, 1957/58, p. 20.

111.   "Vanderbilt Law Students Participate in Nashville Legal Aid Groups," *The Reporter of Vanderbilt Law School*, 1, no. 3 (March 1969), p. 6.

112.   "Law Students Aid the Poor," *Vanderbilt Today*, 10, no. 5 (November 1970), p. 3.

113.   "Clinical Legal Education Program Expanded," *The Reporter*, III, no. 4 (April 1972), p. 5.

114.   Faculty Meeting Minutes, April 12, 1977.

115.   Reassessment Report to the Board of Trust of Vanderbilt University, April 25, 1980 (attached as Appendix B to BOT Minutes, LXX, April 25–26, 1980). Law professor Hal Maier chaired the University-wide panel of ten faculty and four students; third-year law student Michael McCrossin was one of four student members.

116.   Faculty Meeting Minutes, March 21, 1981.

117.   *Legal Education and Professional Development—An Educational Continuum, Report of the Task Force on Law Schools and the Profession: Narrowing the Gap.* (Chicago, 1992), p. 332.

118.   John J. Costonis, "The MacCrate Report: Of Loaves, Fishes, and the Future of

American Legal Education," *Journal of Legal Education*, 43, no. 2 (June 1993), pp. 157–97.

119.   BOT Minutes, XLIX, May 14, 1965, p. 143.

120.   Faculty Meeting Minutes, May 15, 1973.

EPILOGUE

1.   "Vanderbilt University Law School: A Future Even Greater than Its Past," videotape (Arlington, Virginia: Paul Wagner Productions), 1998. This quote, and the titles of that video and this epilogue, are an echo of Wayne Hyatt's assessment of the students recruited by John Beasley in the 1960s.

2.   Edward Rubin, "What's Wrong with Langdell's Method, and What to Do About It," *Vanderbilt Law Review*, 60(2007), pp. 609–65.

3.   "Gee outlines challenges facing faculty, University," *Vanderbilt Register*, at *www.vanderbilt.edu/News/register/Sep5_00/story10.html*.

4.   "Chancellor Gordon Gee's Spring Faculty Assembly Address," *Vanderbilt Register*, at *www.vanderbilt.edu/register/articles?id=18983*.

5.   The center's $2.9 million endowment was provided through a *cy pres* settlement of a class action law suit, Lankford v. Dow Chemical, brought by the firm of Branstetter, Stranch & Jennings. The center is named for Cecil Branstetter, a member of the first class to enter and graduate from Vanderbilt after its reopening in 1946.

6.   "Premier Scholars Tapped to Lead Law and Economics Ph.D. Program," *Vanderbilt Register*, XXVI, no. 11 (January 30-February 12, 2006), p. 1.

Index

Costonis, John J., 166, 167, 171, 172, 174, 175, 180, 188–89, 190, 198
Covington, Robert N., 149–50, 151, 204
Culbreth, Elizabeth, 199
Cresswell, Isaiah, 144
Crossley, Mary A., 192
Crouch, Charles, 194
Crownover, Sims, 135–36
Cumberland University School of Law, 4, 7, 10, 24, 56, 62, 88–91, 115, 134–35, 212n44
Cutler, Lloyd N., 146

Dandybilt Flaw Review, 272n139
Daughtrey, Martha Craig, xi, 178, 179
Davidson, Donald, 63
Davidson, Theresa Scherer, 43, 50, 63, 83
Dental School, 30, 33, 35, 68, 73
depression, the great, 79, 81–82
DeWitt, John H., 59
Dialectic Literary Society, 59
Dickinson, Edmund C., 66–67
Dickinson, Jacob M., 6, 17, 18, 226n212
Dicta, The, 154, 272n139
diploma privilege, 6, 25–26, 55, 210n31, 211–12n41
Divinity School (School of Religion), 8, 73, 82, 114, 139, 140, 144, 194, 195
Douglas, Lee, 99
Douglas, William O., 154
Dudney, Doris Ann, 64, 177
Dwyer, Frank X., 114
Dwyer, Walter W., 114, 117

Eames, Patricia, 179, 181
East, Edward H., 9
East Tennessee Law School, 89
Eberle, Kathryn V., 3
Edelman, Paul H., 196
Elliott, Annie Mary, 178, 275n45
Ely, James W., Jr., xii, 3
endowment, 69, 71–73, 80–81, 120, 136–37, 185, 188–89

enrollment, 11, 24, 27–29, 34, 66, 70–72, 80–81, 93, 98, 120–21, 122, 193
Ewing, Albert, Jr., 126

faculty research, 92, 168, 172–73; and teaching 165–73
faculty recruitment, development and retention, 64–67; 94–95, 96–97, 113–15, 117–18, 122, 147–49, 150–52, 154–58, 166–68, 178–82, 192–94; "recycled faculty," 113, 118, 154–58
faculty salaries, 11, 13, 18, 27–28, 66, 77, 81, 132, 150–51, 227n219
faculty size, 9–11, 12, 17–18, 35, 66–67, 101, 137, 173, 193, 199
Fellowship of Southern Churchmen, 144–45
Fels, Charles, 192
Ferson, Morton, 113, 118, 155
Fields, Emmett B. 168, 198
finances of School, 9, 12–13, 27–29, 33–34, 35, 66, 69–73, 77, 80–85, 98–100, 119–21, 127–29, 132, 136–37, 147, 150–51, 185–89, 193, 202–03
Fisk University, 138, 141
Fogg, Francis B., 31
Follin, G. W., 60
Folts, Aubrey, 116
Ford Foundation grants, 126–29, 130, 135–36, 142, 152, 156, 195
Fordham, Jefferson Barnes, 114
Forrester, William Ray, 118–19, 123, 129, 139, 148, 155, 156, 194
Frank C. Rand Professorship, 114, 118, 156–58
Frierson, J. Nelson, 53
fund raising, 69, 71–73, 80, 81–82, 84–85, 100, 102, 119–20, 127, 132–33, 136–37, 185–86, 188–89

Galvin, Charles O., 171
Garland, Landon C., 7, 12, 21–23
Garman, Doris Blossom, 64